Undergraduate Topics in Computer Science

Undergraduate Topics in Computer Science (UTiCS) delivers high-quality instructional content for undergraduates studying in all areas of computing and information science. From core foundational and theoretical material to final-year topics and applications, UTiCS books take a fresh, concise, and modern approach and are ideal for self-study or for a one- or two-semester course. The texts are all authored by established experts in their fields, reviewed by an international advisory board, and contain numerous examples and problems. Many include fully worked solutions.

More information about this series at http://www.springer.com/series/7592

Peter Sestoft

Programming Language Concepts

Second Edition

With a chapter by Niels Hallenberg

 Springer

BP53

Peter Sestoft
IT University of Copenhagen, Computer
   Science Department
Copenhagen
Denmark

-

ISSN 1863-7310   ISSN 2197-1781   (electronic)
Undergraduate Topics in Computer Science
ISBN 978-3-319-60788-7   ISBN 978-3-319-60789-4   (eBook)
DOI 10.1007/978-3-319-60789-4

Library of Congress Control Number: 2017949164

Printed on acid-free paper

This Springer imprint is published by Springer Nature
The registered company is Springer International Publishing AG
The registered company address is: Gewerbestrasse 11, 6330 Cham, Switzerland

3/07/18

Preface

This book takes an operational approach to programming language concepts, studying those concepts in interpreters and compilers for some toy languages, and pointing out their relations to real-world programming languages.

What is Covered

Topics covered include abstract and concrete syntax; functional and imperative programming languages; interpretation, type checking, and compilation; peep-hole optimizations; abstract machines, automatic memory management and garbage collection; the Java Virtual Machine and Microsoft's .NET Common Language Runtime; and real machine code for the x86 architecture.

Some effort is made throughout to put programming language concepts into their historical context, and to show how the concepts surface in languages that the students are assumed to know already; primarily Java or C#.

We do not cover regular expressions and parser construction in much detail. For this purpose, we refer to Torben Mogensen's textbook; see Chap. 3 and its references.

Apart from various updates, this second edition adds a synthesis chapter, contributed by Niels Hallenberg, that presents a compiler from a small functional language called micro-SML to an abstract machine; and a chapter that presents a compiler from a C subset called micro-C to real x86 machine code.

Why Virtual Machines?

The book's emphasis is on virtual stack machines and their intermediate languages, often known as bytecode. Virtual machines are machine-like enough to make the central purpose and concepts of compilation and code generation clear, yet they are much simpler than present-day microprocessors such as Intel i7 and similar.

Full understanding of performance issues in real microprocessors, with deep pipelines, register renaming, out-of-order execution, branch prediction, translation lookaside buffers and so on, requires a very detailed study of their architecture, usually not conveyed by compiler textbooks anyway. Certainly, a mere understanding of the instruction set, such as x86, conveys little information about whether code will be fast or not.

The widely used object-oriented languages Java and C# are rather far removed from the real hardware, and are most conveniently explained in terms of their virtual machines: the Java Virtual Machine and Microsoft's Common Language Infrastructure. Understanding the workings and implementation of these virtual machines sheds light on efficiency issues, design decisions, and inherent limitations in Java and C#. To understand memory organization of classic imperative languages, we also study a small subset of C with arrays, pointer arithmetics, and recursive functions. We present a compiler from micro-C to an abstract machine, and this smoothly leads to a simple compiler for real x86 hardware.

Why F#?

We use the functional language F# as presentation language throughout, to illustrate programming language concepts, by implementing interpreters and compilers for toy languages. The idea behind this is twofold.

First, F# belongs to the ML family of languages and is ideal for implementing interpreters and compilers because it has datatypes and pattern matching and is strongly typed. This leads to a brevity and clarity of examples that cannot be matched by languages without these features.

Secondly, the active use of a functional language is an attempt to add a new dimension to students' world view, to broaden their imagination. The prevalent single-inheritance class-based object-oriented programming languages (namely, Java and C#) are very useful and versatile languages. But they have come to dominate computer science education to a degree where students may become unable to imagine other programming tools, especially to use a completely different paradigm. Knowledge of a functional language will make the student a better designer and programmer, whether in Java, C# or C, and will prepare him or her to adapt to the programming languages of the future.

For instance, the so-called generic types and methods appeared in Java and C# in 2004, but have been part of other languages, most notably ML, since 1978. Similarly, garbage collection has been used in functional languages since Lisp in 1960, but entered mainstream use more than 30 years later, with Java. Finally, functional programming features were added to C# in 2010 and to Java in 2014.

Appendix A gives a brief introduction to those parts of F# used in this book. Students who do not know F# should learn those parts during the first-third of this course, using the appendix or a textbook such as Hansen and Rischel or a reference such as Syme et al.; see Appendix A and its references.

Supporting Material

There are practical exercises at the end of each chapter. Moreover, the book is accompanied by complete implementations in F# of lexer and parser specifications, abstract syntaxes, interpreters, compilers, and runtime systems (abstract machines, in Java and C) for a range of toy languages. This material, and lecture slides in PDF, are available separately from the book's homepage: http://www.itu.dk/people/sestoft/plc/.

Acknowledgements

This book originated as lecture notes for courses held at the IT University of Copenhagen, Denmark. I would like to thank Andrzej Wasowski, Ken Friis Larsen, Hannes Mehnert, David Raymond Christiansen and past students, in particular Niels Kokholm, Mikkel Bundgaard, and Ahmad Salim Al-Sibahi, who pointed out mistakes and made suggestions on examples and presentation in earlier drafts. Niels Kokholm wrote an early version of the machine code generating micro-C compiler presented in Chap. 14. Thanks to Luca Boasso, Mikkel Riise Lund, and Paul Jurczak for pointing out misprints and unclarities in the first edition. I owe a lasting debt to Neil D. Jones and Mads Tofte who influenced my own view of programming languages and the presentation of programming language concepts.

Niels Hallenberg deserves a special thanks for contributing all of Chap. 13 to this second edition.

Copenhagen, Denmark   Peter Sestoft

Contents

Chapter 1
Introduction

This chapter introduces the approach taken and the plan followed in this book. We show how to represent arithmetic expressions and other program fragments as data structures in F# as well as Java, and how to compute with such program fragments. We also introduce various basic concepts of programming languages.

1.1 Files for This Chapter

File	Contents
Intro/Intro1.fs	simple expressions without variables, in F#
Intro/Intro2.fs	simple expressions with variables, in F#
Intro/SimpleExpr.java	simple expressions with variables, in Java

1.2 Meta Language and Object Language

In linguistics and mathematics, an *object language* is a language we study (such as C++ or Latin) and the *meta language* is the language in which we conduct our discussions (such as Danish or English). Throughout this book we shall use the F# language as the meta language. We could use Java or C#, but that would be more cumbersome because of the lack of pattern matching.

F# is a strict, strongly typed functional programming language in the ML family. Appendix A presents the basic concepts of F#: value, variable, binding, type, tuple,

© Springer International Publishing AG 2017
P. Sestoft, *Programming Language Concepts*, Undergraduate Topics
in Computer Science, DOI 10.1007/978-3-319-60789-4_1

function, recursion, list, pattern matching, and datatype. Several books give a more detailed introduction, including Hansen and Rischel [1] and Syme et al. [6].

It is convenient to run F# interactive sessions inside Microsoft Visual Studio (under MS Windows), or executing `fsharpi` interactive sessions using Mono (under Linux and MacOS X); see Appendix A.

1.3   A Simple Language of Expressions

As an example object language we start by studying a simple language of expressions, with constants, variables (of integer type), let-bindings, nested scope, and operators; see files `Intro1.fs` and `Intro2.fs`.

1.3.1   Expressions Without Variables

First, let us consider expressions consisting only of integer constants and two-argument (dyadic) operators such as (+) and (*). We represent an expression as a term of an F# datatype `expr`, where integer constants are represented by constructor `CstI`, and operator applications are represented by constructor `Prim`:

```
type expr =
  | CstI of int
  | Prim of string * expr * expr
```

A value of type `expr` is an *abstract syntax tree* that represents an expression. Here are some example expressions and their representations as `expr` values:

Expression	Representation in type `expr`
17	CstI 17
$3 - 4$	Prim("-", CstI 3, CstI 4)
$7 \cdot 9 + 10$	Prim("+", Prim("*", CstI 7, CstI 9), CstI 10)

An expression in this representation can be evaluated to an integer by a function `eval : expr -> int` that uses pattern matching to distinguish the various forms of expression. Note that to evaluate $e_1 + e_2$, it must first evaluate e_1 and e_2 to obtain two integers and then add those integers, so the evaluation function must call itself recursively:

```
let rec eval (e : expr) : int =
    match e with
    | CstI i -> i
    | Prim("+", e1, e2) -> eval e1 + eval e2
    | Prim("*", e1, e2) -> eval e1 * eval e2
    | Prim("-", e1, e2) -> eval e1 - eval e2
    | Prim _             -> failwith "unknown primitive";;
```

The eval function is an *interpreter* for "programs" in the expression language. It looks rather boring, as it implements the expression language constructs directly by similar F# constructs. However, we might change it to interpret the operator (-) as cut-off subtraction, whose result is never negative. Then we get a "language" with the same expressions but a very different meaning. For instance, $3 - 4$ now evaluates to zero:

```
let rec evalm (e : expr) : int =
    match e with
    | CstI i -> i
    | Prim("+", e1, e2) -> evalm e1 + evalm e2
    | Prim("*", e1, e2) -> evalm e1 * evalm e2
    | Prim("-", e1, e2) ->
      let res = evalm e1 - evalm e2
      if res < 0 then 0 else res
    | Prim _             -> failwith "unknown primitive";;
```

1.3.2 Expressions with Variables

Now, let us extend our expression language with variables such as x and y. First, we add a new constructor Var to the syntax:

```
type expr =
    | CstI of int
    | Var of string
    | Prim of string * expr * expr
```

Here are some expressions and their representation in this syntax:

Expression	Representation in type expr
17	CstI 17
x	Var "x"
$3 + a$	Prim("+", CstI 3, Var "a")
$b \cdot 9 + a$	Prim("+", Prim("*", Var "b", CstI 9), Var "a")

Next we need to extend the `eval` interpreter to give a meaning to such variables.
To do this, we give `eval` an extra argument env, a so-called *environment*. The role
of the environment is to associate a value (here, an integer) with a variable; that is,
the environment is a map or dictionary, mapping a variable name to the variable's
current value. A simple classical representation of such a map is an *association list*:
a list of pairs of a variable name and the associated value:

```
let env = [("a", 3); ("c", 78); ("baf", 666); ("b", 111)];;
```

This environment maps `"a"` to 3, `"c"` to 78, and so on. The environment has
type `(string * int) list`. An empty environment, which does not map any
variable to anything, is represented by the empty association list

```
let emptyenv = [];;
```

To look up a variable in an environment, we define a function `lookup` of type
`(string * int) list -> string -> int`. An attempt to look up variable x in an empty environment fails; otherwise, if the environment associates y with
v, and x equals y, the result is v; else the result is obtained by looking for x in the
rest r of the environment:

```
let rec lookup env x =
    match env with
    | []        -> failwith (x + "not found")
    | (y, v)::r -> if x=y then v else lookup r x;;
```

As promised, our new `eval` function takes both an expression and an environment,
and uses the environment and the `lookup` function to determine the value of a
variable Var x. Otherwise the function is as before, except that env must be passed
on in recursive calls:

```
let rec eval e (env : (string * int) list) : int =
    match e with
    | CstI i            -> i
    | Var x             -> lookup env x
    | Prim("+", e1, e2) -> eval e1 env + eval e2 env
    | Prim("*", e1, e2) -> eval e1 env * eval e2 env
    | Prim("-", e1, e2) -> eval e1 env - eval e2 env
    | Prim _            -> failwith "unknown primitive";;
```

Note that our `lookup` function returns the *first* value associated with a variable, so
if env is `[("x", 11); ("x", 22)]`, then `lookup env "x"` is 11, not 22.
This is useful when we consider nested scopes in Chap. 2.

1.4 Syntax and Semantics

We have already mentioned syntax and semantics. *Syntax* deals with form: is this program text well-formed? *Semantics* deals with meaning: what does this (well-formed) program mean, how does it behave – what happens when we execute it?

- One may distinguish two kinds of syntax:

  - By *concrete syntax* we mean the representation of a program as a text, with whitespace, parentheses, curly braces, and so on, as in "3+ (a)".
  - By *abstract syntax* we mean the representation of a programs as a tree, either an F# datatype term `Prim("+", CstI 3, Var "a")` as in Sect. 1.3 above, or by an object structure as in Sect. 1.5. In such a representation, whitespace, parentheses and so on have been abstracted away; this simplifies the processing, interpretation and compilation of program fragments. Chapter 3 shows how to systematically create abstract syntax from concrete syntax.

- One may distinguish two kinds of semantics:

  - *Dynamic semantics* concerns the meaning or effect of a program at run-time; what happens when it is executed? Dynamic semantics may be expressed by `eval` functions such as those shown in Sect. 1.3 and later chapters.
  - *Static semantics* roughly concerns the compile-time correctness of the program: are variables declared, is the program well-typed, and so on; that is, those properties that can be checked without executing the program. Static semantics may be enforced by closedness checks (is every variable defined, Sect. 2.3.2), type checks (are all operators used with operands of the correct type, Sect. 4.8), type inference (Sect. 6.4), and more.

The distinction between syntax and static semantics is not clear-cut. Syntax can tell us that `x12` is a legal variable name (in Java), but it is impractical to use syntax to check that we do not declare `x12` twice in the same scope (in Java). Hence this restriction is usually enforced by static semantics checks.

  In the rest of the book we shall study a small expression language, two small functional languages (a first-order and a higher-order one), a subset of the imperative language C, and a subset of the backtracking language Icon. In each case we take the following approach:

- We describe abstract syntax using F# datatypes.
- We describe concrete syntax using lexer and parser specifications (see Chap. 3), and implement lexers and parsers using the tools `fslex` and `fsyacc`.
- We describe semantics using F# functions, both static semantics (checks) and dynamic semantics (execution). The dynamic semantics can be described in two ways: by direct interpretation, using functions typically called `eval`, or by compilation to another language, such as stack machine code, using functions typically called `comp`.

In addition we study some abstract stack machines, both homegrown ones and two widely used so-called managed execution platforms: The Java Virtual Machine (JVM) and Microsoft's Common Language Infrastructure (CLI, also known as .Net).

1.5 Representing Expressions by Objects

In most of the book we use a functional language to represent expressions and other program fragments. In particular, we use the F# algebraic datatype `expr` to represent expressions in the form of *abstract syntax*. We use the `eval` function to define their *dynamic semantics*, using pattern matching to distinguish the different forms of expressions: constants, variables, operators applications.

In this section we briefly consider an alternative object-oriented modeling (in Java, say) of expression syntax and expression evaluation. In general, this would require an abstract base class `Expr` of expressions (instead of the `expr` datatype), and a concrete subclass for each expression form (instead of a datatype constructor for each expression form):

```
abstract class Expr { }
class CstI extends Expr {
  protected final int i;
  public CstI(int i) { this.i = i; }
}
class Var extends Expr {
  protected final String name;
  public Var(String name) { this.name = name; }
}
class Prim extends Expr {
  protected final String oper;
  protected final Expr e1, e2;
  public Prim(String oper, Expr e1, Expr e2) {
    this.oper = oper; this.e1 = e1; this.e2 = e2;
  }
}
```

Note that each `Expr` subclass has fields of exactly the same types as the arguments of the corresponding constructor in the `expr` datatype from Sect. 1.3.2. For instance, class `CstI` has a field of type `int` just as constructor `CstI` has an argument of type `int`. In object-oriented terms `Prim` is a *composite* because it has fields whose type is its base type `Expr`; in functional programming terms one would say that type `expr` is a recursively defined datatype.

How can we define an evaluation method for expressions similar to the F# `eval` function in Sect. 1.3.2? That `eval` function uses pattern matching, which is not available in Java or C#. A poor solution would be to use an `if-else` sequence that tests on the class of the expression, as in `if (e instanceof CstI)` and so on.

The proper object-oriented solution is to declare an abstract method `eval` on class
`Expr`, override the `eval` method in each subclass, and rely on virtual method calls
to invoke the correct override in the composite case. Below we use a Java map from
variable name (String) to value (Integer) to represent the environment:

```
abstract class Expr {
  abstract public int eval(Map<String,Integer> env);
}
class CstI extends Expr {
  protected final int i;
  ...
  public int eval(Map<String,Integer> env) {
    return i;
  }
}
class Var extends Expr {
  protected final String name;
  ...
  public int eval(Map<String,Integer> env) {
    return env.get(name);
  }
}
class Prim extends Expr {
  protected final String oper;
  protected final Expr e1, e2;
  ...
  public int eval(Map<String,Integer> env) {
    if (oper.equals("+"))
      return e1.eval(env) + e2.eval(env);
    else if (oper.equals("*"))
      return e1.eval(env) * e2.eval(env);
    else if (oper.equals("-"))
      return e1.eval(env) - e2.eval(env);
    else
      throw new RuntimeException("unknown primitive");
  }
}
```

An object built by `new Prim("-", new CstI(3), new CstI(4))` will
then represent the expression "3 − 4", much as Sect. 1.3.1. In fact, most of the development in this book could have been carried out in an object-oriented language, but
the extra verbosity (of Java or C#) and the lack of pattern matching would often make
the presentation considerably more verbose.

1.6   The History of Programming Languages

Since 1956, thousands of programming languages have been proposed and implemented, several hundred of which have been widely used. Most new programming languages arise as a reaction to some language that the designer knows (and likes or dislikes) already, so one can propose a family tree or genealogy for programming languages, just as for living organisms. Figure 1.1 presents one such attempt. Of course there are many many more languages than those shown, in particular if one counts also more domain-specific languages such as Matlab, SAS and R, and strange "languages" such as spreadsheets [5].

In general, languages lower in the diagram (near the time axis) are closer to the real hardware than those higher in the diagram, which are more "high-level" in some sense. In Fortran77 or C, it is fairly easy to predict *what* instructions and *how many* instructions will be executed at run-time for a given line of program. The mental machine model that the C or Fortran77 programmer must use to write efficient programs is close to the real machine.

Conversely, the top-most languages (SASL, Haskell, Standard ML, F#, Scala) are functional languages, possibly with lazy evaluation, with dynamic or advanced static type systems and with automatic memory management, and it is in general difficult to predict how many machine instructions are required to evaluate any given expression. The mental machine model that the Haskell or Standard ML or F# or Scala programmer must use to write efficient programs is far from the details of a real machine, so he can think on a rather higher level. On the other hand, he loses control over detailed efficiency.

It is remarkable that the recent mainstream languages Java and C#, especially their post-2004 incarnations, have much more in common with the academic languages of the 1980's than with those languages that were used in the "real world" during those years (C, Pascal, C++).

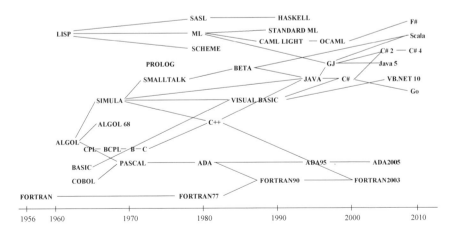

Fig. 1.1 The genealogy of programming languages

Some interesting early papers on programming language design principles are due to Landin [3], Hoare [2] and Wirth [9]. Building on Landin's work, Tennent [7, 8] proposed the language design principles of *correspondence* and *abstraction*.

The principle of correspondence requires that the mechanisms of name binding (the declaration and initialization of a variable `let x = e`, or the declaration of a type `type T = int`, and so on) must behave the same as parametrization (the passing of an argument `e` to a function with parameter `x`, or using a type `int` to instantiate a generic type parameter T).

The principle of abstraction requires that any construct (an expression, a statement, a type definition, and so on) can be named and parametrized over the identifiers that appear in the construct (giving rise to function declarations, procedure declarations, generic types, and so on).

Tennent also investigated how the programming language Pascal would have looked if those principles had been systematically applied. It is striking how well modern languages, such as Scala and C#, adhere to Tennent's design principles, but also that Standard ML [4] did so already in 1986.

1.7 Exercises

Exercise 1.1 (i) File `Intro2.fs` contains a definition of the `expr` expression language and an evaluation function `eval`. Extend the `eval` function to handle three additional operators: `"max"`, `"min"`, and `"=="`. Like the existing operators, they take two argument expressions. The equals operator should return 1 when true and 0 when false.

(ii) Write some example expressions in this extended expression language, using abstract syntax, and evaluate them using your new `eval` function.

(iii) Rewrite one of the `eval` functions to evaluate the arguments of a primitive before branching out on the operator, in this style:

```
let rec eval e (env : (string * int) list) : int =
    match e with
    | ...
    | Prim(ope, e1, e2) ->
      let i1 = ...
      let i2 = ...
      match ope with
        | "+" -> i1 + i2
        | ...
```

(iv) Extend the expression language with conditional expressions `If(e1, e2, e3)` corresponding to Java's expression `e1 ? e2 : e3` or F#'s conditional expression `if e1 then e2 else e3`.

You need to extend the `expr` datatype with a new constructor `If` that takes three `expr` arguments.

(v) Extend the interpreter function `eval` correspondingly. It should evaluate `e1`, and if `e1` is non-zero, then evaluate `e2`, else evaluate `e3`. You should be able to evaluate the expression `If(Var "a", CstI 11, CstI 22)` in an environment that binds variable `a`.

Note that various strange and non-standard interpretations of the conditional expression are possible. For instance, the interpreter might start by testing whether expressions `e2` and `e3` are syntactically identical, in which case there is no need to evaluate `e1`, only `e2` (or `e3`). Although possible, this shortcut is rarely useful.

Exercise 1.2 (i) Declare an alternative datatype `aexpr` for a representation of arithmetic expressions without let-bindings. The datatype should have constructors `CstI`, `Var`, `Add`, `Mul`, `Sub`, for constants, variables, addition, multiplication, and subtraction.

Then $x * (y + 3)$ is represented as `Mul(Var "x", Add(Var "y", CstI 3))`, not as `Prim("*", Var "x", Prim("+", Var "y", CstI 3))`.

(ii) Write the representation of the expressions $v - (w + z)$ and $2 * (v - (w + z))$ and $x + y + z + v$.

(iii) Write an F# function `fmt : aexpr -> string` to format expressions as strings. For instance, it may format `Sub(Var "x", CstI 34)` as the string `"(x - 34)"`. It has very much the same structure as an `eval` function, but takes no environment argument (because the *name* of a variable is independent of its *value*).

(iv) Write an F# function `simplify : aexpr -> aexpr` to perform expression simplification. For instance, it should simplify $(x + 0)$ to x, and simplify $(1 + 0)$ to 1. The more ambitious student may want to simplify $(1 + 0) * (x + 0)$ to x. Hint: Pattern matching is your friend. Hint: Don't forget the case where you cannot simplify anything.

You might consider the following simplifications, plus any others you find useful and correct:

$$0 + e \longrightarrow e$$
$$e + 0 \longrightarrow e$$
$$e - 0 \longrightarrow e$$
$$1 * e \longrightarrow e$$
$$e * 1 \longrightarrow e$$
$$0 * e \longrightarrow 0$$
$$e * 0 \longrightarrow 0$$
$$e - e \longrightarrow 0$$

(v) Write an F# function to perform symbolic differentiation of simple arithmetic expressions (such as `aexpr`) with respect to a single variable.

Exercise 1.3 Write a version of the formatting function fmt from the preceding exercise that avoids producing excess parentheses. For instance,

```
Mul(Sub(Var "a", Var "b"), Var "c")
```

should be formatted as "(a-b)*c" instead of "((a-b)*c)", and

```
Sub(Mul(Var "a", Var "b"), Var "c")
```

should be formatted as "a*b-c" instead of "((a*b)-c)". Also, it should be taken into account that operators associate to the left, so that

```
Sub(Sub(Var "a", Var "b"), Var "c")
```

is formatted as "a-b-c", and

```
Sub(Var "a", Sub(Var "b", Var "c"))
```

is formatted as "a-(b-c)".

Hint: This can be achieved by declaring the formatting function to take an extra parameter pre that indicates the precedence or binding strength of the context. The new formatting function then has type fmt : int -> expr -> string.

Higher precedence means stronger binding. When the top-most operator of an expression to be formatted has higher precedence than the context, there is no need for parentheses around the expression. A left associative operator of precedence 6, such as minus (-), provides context precedence 5 to its left argument, and context precedence 6 to its right argument.

As a consequence, Sub(Var "a", Sub(Var "b", Var "c")) will be parenthesized a-(b-c) but Sub(Sub(Var "a", Var "b"), Var "c") will be parenthesized a-b-c.

Exercise 1.4 This chapter has shown how to represent abstract syntax in functional languages such as F# (using algebraic datatypes) and in object-oriented languages such as Java or C# (using a class hierarchy and composites).

(i) Use Java or C# classes and methods to do what we have done using the F# datatype aexpr in the preceding exercises. Design a class hierarchy to represent arithmetic expressions: it could have an abstract class Expr with subclasses CstI, Var, and Binop, where the latter is itself abstract and has concrete subclasses Add, Mul and Sub. All classes should implement the toString() method to format an expression as a String.

The classes may be used to build an expression in abstract syntax, and then print it, as follows:

```
Expr e = new Add(new CstI(17), new Var("z"));
System.out.println(e.toString());
```

(ii) Create three more expressions in abstract syntax and print them.
(iii) Extend your classes with facilities to evaluate the arithmetic expressions, that is, add a method int eval(env).
(iv) Add a method Expr simplify() that returns a new expression where algebraic simplifications have been performed, as in part (iv) of Exercise 1.2.

References

1. Hansen, M.R., Rischel, H.: Functional Programming Using F#. Cambridge University Press (2013)
2. Hoare, C.: Hints on programming language design. In: ACM SIGACT/SIGPLAN Symposium on Principles of Programming Languages 1973, Boston, Massachusetts. ACM Press (1973)
3. Landin, P.: The next 700 programming languages. Commun. ACM **9**(3), 157–166 (1966)
4. Milner, R., Tofte, M., Harper, R.: The Definition of Standard ML. The MIT Press (1990)
5. Sestoft, P.: Spreadsheet Implementation Technology. Basics and Extensions. MIT Press (2014). ISBN 978-0-262-52664-7, 325 pages
6. Syme, D., Granicz, A., Cisternino, A.: Expert F#. Apress (2007)
7. Tennent, R.: Language design methods based on semantic principles. Acta Inform. **8**, 97–112 (1977)
8. Tennent, R.: Principles of Programming Languages. Prentice-Hall (1981)
9. Wirth, N.: On the design of programming languages. In: Rosenfeldt, J. (ed.) IFIP Information Processing 74, Stockholm, Sweden, pp. 386–393. North-Holland (1974)

Chapter 2
Interpreters and Compilers

This chapter introduces the distinction between interpreters and compilers, and demonstrates some concepts of compilation, using the simple expression language as an example. Some concepts of interpretation are illustrated also, using a stack machine as an example.

2.1 Files for This Chapter

File	Contents
Intcomp/Intcomp1.fs	very simple expression interpreter and compilers
Intcomp/Machine.java	abstract machine in Java (see Sect. 2.8)
Intcomp/prog.ps	a simple Postscript program (see Sect. 2.6)
Intcomp/sierpinski.eps	an intricate Postscript program (see Sect. 2.6)

2.2 Interpreters and Compilers

An *interpreter* executes a program on some input, producing an output or result; see Fig. 2.1. An interpreter is usually itself a program, but one might also say that an Intel or AMD x86 processor (used in many portable, desktop and server computers) or an ARM processor (used in many mobile phones and tablet computers) is an interpreter, implemented in silicon. For an interpreter program we must distinguish the interpreted language L (the language of the programs being executed, for instance our expression language expr) from the implementation language I (the language in

© Springer International Publishing AG 2017
P. Sestoft, *Programming Language Concepts*, Undergraduate Topics
in Computer Science, DOI 10.1007/978-3-319-60789-4_2

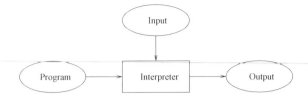

Fig. 2.1 Interpretation in one stage

Fig. 2.2 Compilation and execution in two stages

which the interpreter is written, for instance F#). When the program in the interpreted language *L* is a sequence of simple instructions, and thus looks like machine code, the interpreter is often called an abstract machine or virtual machine.

A *compiler* takes as input a source program and generates as output another program, called a target program, which can then be executed; see Fig. 2.2. We must distinguish three languages: the source language *S* (e.g. expr) of the input programs, the target language *T* (e.g. texpr) of the output programs, and the implementation language *I* (for instance, F#) of the compiler itself.

The compiler does not execute the program; after the target program has been generated it must be executed by a machine or interpreter which can execute programs written in language *T*. Hence we can distinguish between compile-time (at which time the source program is compiled into a target program) and run-time (at which time the target program is executed on actual inputs to produce a result). At compile-time one usually also performs various so-called well-formedness checks of the source program: are all variables bound, do operands have the correct type in expressions, and so on.

2.3 Scope and Bound and Free Variables

The *scope* of a variable binding is that part of a program in which it is visible. For instance, the scope of x in this F# function definition is just the function body x+3:

```
let f x = x + 3
```

A language has *static scope* if the scopes of bindings follow the syntactic structure of the program. Most modern languages, such as C, C++, Pascal, Algol, Scheme, Java, C# and F# have static scope; but see Sect. 4.7 for some that do not.

A language has *nested scope* if an inner scope may create a "hole" in an outer scope by declaring a new variable with the same name, as shown by this F# function definition, where the second binding of x hides the first one in x*2 but not in x+3, so f 1 evaluates to $(8 \cdot 2) + (1 + 3) = 20$:

```
let f x = (let x = 8 in x * 2) + (x + 3)
```

Nested scope is known also from Algol, Pascal, C, C++, and Standard ML; and from Java and C#, for instance when a parameter or local variable in a method hides a field from an enclosing class, or when a declaration in a Java anonymous inner class or a C# anonymous method hides a local variable already in scope.

It is useful to distinguish bound and free occurrences of a variable. A variable occurrence is *bound* if it occurs within the scope of a binding for that variable, and *free* otherwise. That is, x occurs bound in the body of this let-binding:

```
let x = 6 in x + 3
```

but x occurs free in this one:

```
let y = 6 in x + 3
```

and in this one

```
let y = x in y + 3
```

and it occurs free (the first time) as well as bound (the second time) in this expression

```
let x = x + 6 in x + 3
```

2.3.1 Expressions with Let-Bindings and Static Scope

Now let us extend the expression language from Sect. 1.3 with let-bindings of the form let x = e1 in e2 end, here represented by the Let constructor:

```
type expr =
  | CstI of int
  | Var of string
  | Let of string * expr * expr
  | Prim of string * expr * expr
```

Using the same environment representation and lookup function as in Sect. 1.3.2, we can evaluate let x = erhs in ebody end as follows. We evaluate the right-hand side erhs in the same environment as the entire let-expression, obtaining

a value `xval` for `x`; then we create a new environment `env1` by adding the association (`x`, `xval`) and interpret the let-body `ebody` in that environment; finally we
return the result as the result of the let-binding:

```
let rec eval e (env : (string * int) list) : int =
    match e with
    | CstI i              -> i
    | Var x               -> lookup env x
    | Let(x, erhs, ebody) ->
      let xval = eval erhs env
      let env1 = (x, xval) :: env
      eval ebody env1
    | ...
```

The new binding of `x` will hide any existing binding of `x`, thanks to the definition of
`lookup`. Also, since the old environment `env` is not destructively modified — the
new environment `env1` is just a temporary extension of it — further evaluation will
continue in the old environment. Hence we obtain nested static scopes.

2.3.2 Closed Expressions

An expression is *closed* if no variable occurs free in the expression. In most programming languages, a program must be closed: it cannot have unbound (undeclared)
names. To efficiently test whether an expression is closed, we define a slightly more
general concept, `closedin e vs`, of an expression `e` being closed in a list `vs` of
bound variables:

```
let rec closedin (e : expr) (vs : string list) : bool =
    match e with
    | CstI i -> true
    | Var x  -> List.exists (fun y -> x=y) vs
    | Let(x, erhs, ebody) ->
      let vs1 = x :: vs
      closedin erhs vs && closedin ebody vs1
    | Prim(ope, e1, e2) -> closedin e1 vs && closedin e2 vs
```

A constant is always closed. A variable occurrence `x` is closed in `vs` if `x` appears
in `vs`. The expression `let x=erhs in ebody end` is closed in `vs` if `erhs` is
closed in `vs` and `ebody` is closed in `x :: vs`. An operator application is closed
in `vs` if both its operands are.

Now, an expression is closed if it is closed in the empty environment `[]`:

```
let closed1 e = closedin e []
```

2.3.3 The Set of Free Variables

Now let us compute the set of variables that occur free in an expression. First, we represent a set of variables as a list without duplicates, so `[ ]` represents the empty set, and `[x]` represents the singleton set containing just x, and one can compute set union and set difference like this, where `mem x ys` is true if x is in the list `ys`, and false if not:

```
let mem x ys = List.exists (fun y -> x=y) ys
let rec union (xs, ys) =
    match xs with
    | []     -> ys
    | x::xr -> if mem x ys then union(xr, ys)
               else x :: union(xr, ys)
let rec minus (xs, ys) =
    match xs with
    | []     -> []
    | x::xr -> if mem x ys then minus(xr, ys)
               else x :: minus (xr, ys)
```

Now the set of free variables can be computed easily:

```
let rec freevars e : string list =
    match e with
    | CstI i -> []
    | Var x   -> [x]
    | Let(x, erhs, ebody) ->
      union (freevars erhs, minus (freevars ebody, [x]))
    | Prim(ope, e1, e2) -> union (freevars e1, freevars e2)
```

The set of free variables in a constant is the empty set `[ ]`. The set of free variables in a variable occurrence x is the singleton set `[x]`. The set of free variables in `let x=erhs in ebody end` is the union of the free variables in `erhs`, with the free variables of `ebody` minus x. The set of free variables in an operator application is the union of the sets of free variables in its operands.

This gives another way to compute whether an expression is closed; simply check that the set of its free variables is empty:

```
let closed2 e = (freevars e = [])
```

2.3.4 Substitution: Replacing Variables by Expressions

In the preceding sections we have seen how to compute the free variables of an expression. In this section we show how to perform *substitution*, replacing free variables by expressions. The basic idea is to have an environment env that maps some variable names to expressions. For instance, this environment says that variable z should be replaced by the expression $5-4$ and all other variables should be left as is:

```
[("z", Prim("-", CstI 5, CstI 4))]
```

Applying this substitution to y*z should produce y*(5-4) in which y is left as is. The above substitution environment may be written $[(5-4)/z]$, and the application of that substitution to y*z is written $[(5-4)/z](y*z)$.

To implement a substitution function in F#, we need a version of lookup that maps each variable present in the environment to the associated expression, and maps absent variables to themselves. We call this function lookOrSelf:

```
let rec lookOrSelf env x =
    match env with
    | []         -> Var x
    | (y, e)::r -> if x=y then e else lookOrSelf r x
```

Moreover, a substitution should only replace *free* variables. Applying the substitution $[(5-4)/z]$ to let z=22 in y*z end should *not* produce let z=22 in y*(5-4) end because the occurrence of z is bound, and should always evaluate to 22, not to -1. When we "go below" a let-binding of a variable z, then z should be removed from the substitution environment; hence this auxiliary function:

```
let rec remove env x =
    match env with
    | []         -> []
    | (y, e)::r -> if x=y then r else (y, e) :: remove r x
```

Finally we can present a substitution function (which, alas, turns out to be somewhat naive):

```
let rec nsubst (e : expr) (env : (string * expr) list) : expr =
    match e with
    | CstI i -> e
    | Var x  -> lookOrSelf env x
    | Let(x, erhs, ebody) ->
      let newenv = remove env x
      Let(x, nsubst erhs env, nsubst ebody newenv)
    | Prim(ope, e1, e2) ->
      Prim(ope, nsubst e1 env, nsubst e2 env)
```

Explanation: Substitution does not affect constants CstI so the given expression e is returned. Substitution replaces a variable x with whatever the substitution environment env says, or with itself if it is not bound in the environment. Substitution replaces a primitive operation with the same operation, after applying the substitution to both operand expressions e1 and e2. Substitution replaces a let-binding let x = erhs in ebody end by another let-binding, after applying the substitution to erhs, and applying a slightly different substitution to ebody where the variable x has been removed from the substitution environment.

Apparently, this works fine, correctly replacing z but not y in e6, and correctly replacing none of them in e9:

```
> let e6 = Prim("+", Var "y", Var "z");;
> let e6s2 = nsubst e6 [("z", Prim("-", CstI 5, CstI 4))];;
val e6s2 : expr = Prim ("+",Var "y",Prim ("-",CstI 5,CstI 4))

> let e9 = Let("z",CstI 22,Prim("*",Var "y",Var "z"));;
> let e9s2 = nsubst e9 [("z", Prim("-", CstI 5, CstI 4))];;
val e9s2 : expr = Let ("z",CstI 22,Prim ("*",Var "y",Var "z"))
```

However, if we try a slightly fancier substitution [z/y], where we want to replace y by z, then we discover a problem, namely, *variable capture*:

```
> let e9s1 = nsubst e9 [("y", Var "z")];;
val e9s1 = Let ("z",CstI 22,Prim ("*",Var "z",Var "z"))
```

In an attempt to replace a free variable y by another free variable z, the free z got "captured" under the let-binding and thereby turned into a bound variable z. There is a simple way around this problem, which is to systematically rename all the let-bound variables with fresh names that are used nowhere else. This can be implemented elegantly by the substitution process itself, to obtain capture-avoiding substitution:

```
let rec subst (e : expr) (env : (string * expr) list) : expr =
    match e with
    | CstI i -> e
    | Var x  -> lookOrSelf env x
    | Let(x, erhs, ebody) ->
      let newx = newVar x
      let newenv = (x, Var newx) :: remove env x
      Let(newx, subst erhs env, subst ebody newenv)
    | Prim(ope, e1, e2) ->
      Prim(ope, subst e1 env, subst e2 env)
```

where a simple newVar auxiliary may be defined like this (provided no "normal" variable name ends with a number):

```
let newVar : string -> string =
    let n = ref 0
    let varMaker x = (n := 1 + !n; x + string (!n))
    varMaker
```

Now the problematic example above is handled correctly because the let-bound variable z gets renamed to z4 (or similar), so the free variable z does not get captured:

```
> let e9s1a = subst e9 [("y", Var "z")];;
val e9s1a = Let ("z4",CstI 22,Prim ("*",Var "z",Var "z4"))
```

Note that we systematically rename *bound* variables to avoid capture of *free* variables. Capture-avoiding substitution plays an important role in program transformation and in programming language theory.

2.4   Integer Addresses Instead of Names

For efficiency, symbolic variable names are replaced by variable addresses (integers) in real machine code and in most interpreters. To show how this may be done, we define an abstract syntax `texpr` for target expressions that uses (integer) variable indexes instead of symbolic variable names:

```
type texpr =
  | TCstI of int
  | TVar of int                        (* run-time index *)
  | TLet of texpr * texpr              (* erhs and ebody *)
  | TPrim of string * texpr * texpr
```

Then we can define `tcomp : expr -> string list -> texpr`, a compiler from `expr` to `texpr`, like this:

```
let rec tcomp (e : expr) (cenv : string list) : texpr =
    match e with
    | CstI i -> TCstI i
    | Var x  -> TVar (getindex cenv x)
    | Let(x, erhs, ebody) ->
      let cenv1 = x :: cenv
      TLet(tcomp erhs cenv, tcomp ebody cenv1)
    | Prim(ope, e1, e2) ->
      TPrim(ope, tcomp e1 cenv, tcomp e2 cenv);;
```

This compiler simply replaces symbolic variable names by numeric variable indexes; it therefore also drops the name of the bound variable from each `let`-binding.

Note that the compile-time environment `cenv` in `tcomp` is just a `string list`, a list of the bound variables. The position of a variable in the list is its binding depth (the number of other let-bindings between the variable occurrence and the binding of the variable). Function `getindex` (not shown) uses `cenv` to map a symbolic name `x` to its integer variable index, simply by looking for the first occurrence of `x` in the `cenv` list.

Correspondingly, the run-time environment `renv` in the `teval` interpreter shown below is an `int list` storing the values of the variables in the same order as their

names in the compile-time environment cenv. Therefore we can simply use the
binding depth of a variable to access the variable at run-time. The integer giving the
position is called an *offset* by compiler writers, and a *deBruijn index* by theoreticians
(in the lambda calculus, Sect. 5.6): the number of binders between an occurrence of
a variable and its binding.

The teval: texpr -> int list -> int evaluator for texpr can be
defined like this:

```
let rec teval (e : texpr) (renv : int list) : int =
    match e with
    | TCstI i -> i
    | TVar n   -> List.nth renv n
    | TLet(erhs, ebody) ->
      let xval = teval erhs renv
      let renv1 = xval :: renv
      teval ebody renv1
    | TPrim("+", e1, e2) -> teval e1 renv + teval e2 renv
    | TPrim("*", e1, e2) -> teval e1 renv * teval e2 renv
    | TPrim("-", e1, e2) -> teval e1 renv - teval e2 renv
    | TPrim _             -> failwith "unknown primitive";;
```

Note that in one-stage interpretive execution (eval) the environment had type
(string * int) list and contained both variable names and variable values. In the two-stage compiled execution, the compile-time environment (in tcomp)
had type string list and contained variable names only, whereas the run-time
environment (in teval) had type int list and contained variable values only.

Thus effectively the joint environment from interpretive execution has been split
into a compile-time environment and a run-time environment. This is no accident:
the purpose of compiled execution is to perform some computations (such as variable
lookup) early, at compile-time, and perform other computations (such as multiplications of variables' values) only later, at run-time.

The correctness requirement on a compiler can be stated using equivalences such
as this one:

$$teval \ (tcomp \ e \ []) \ [] \quad equals \quad eval \ e \ []$$

which says that

- if te = tcomp e [] is the result of compiling the closed expression e in the
  empty compile-time environment [],
- then evaluation of the target expression te using the teval interpreter and empty
  run-time environment [] produces the same result as evaluation of the source
  expression e using the eval interpreter and an empty environment [].

2.5   Stack Machines for Expression Evaluation

Expressions, and more generally, functional programs, are often evaluated by a *stack machine*. We shall study a simple stack machine (an interpreter that implements an abstract machine) for evaluation of expressions in *postfix* or *reverse Polish* form.

Stack machine instructions for an example language without variables (and hence without let-bindings) may be described using this F# type:

```
type rinstr =
  | RCstI of int
  | RAdd
  | RSub
  | RMul
  | RDup
  | RSwap
```

The state of the stack machine is a pair (c, s) of the control and the stack. The control c is the sequence of instructions yet to be evaluated. The stack s is a list of values (here integers), namely, intermediate results.

The stack machine can be understood as a transition system, described by the rules shown in Fig. 2.3. Each rule says how the execution of one instruction causes the machine to go from one state to another. The stack top is to the right.

For instance, the second rule says that if the two top-most stack elements are 5 and 7, so the stack has form $s, 7, 5$ for some s, then executing the RAdd instruction will cause the stack to change to $s, 12$.

The rules of the abstract machine are quite easily translated into an F# function reval:

```
let rec reval (inss : rinstr list) (stack : int list) : int =
    match (inss, stack) with
    | ([], v :: _) -> v
    | ([], [])        -> failwith "reval: no result on stack!"
    | (RCstI i :: insr,              stk) ->
      reval insr (i::stk)
    | (RAdd    :: insr, i2 :: i1 :: stkr) ->
      reval insr ((i1+i2)::stkr)
    | (RSub    :: insr, i2 :: i1 :: stkr) ->
      reval insr ((i1-i2)::stkr)
    | (RMul    :: insr, i2 :: i1 :: stkr) ->
      reval insr ((i1*i2)::stkr)
    | (RDup    :: insr,       i1 :: stkr) ->
      reval insr (i1 :: i1 :: stkr)
    | (RSwap   :: insr, i2 :: i1 :: stkr) ->
      reval insr (i1 :: i2 :: stkr)
    | _ -> failwith "reval: too few operands on stack";;
```

Fig. 2.3 Stack machine instructions for expression evaluation. The stack top is to the right

Instruction	Stack before	Stack after	Effect
RCst i	s	$\Rightarrow s, i$	Push constant
RAdd	s, i_1, i_2	$\Rightarrow s, (i_1 + i_2)$	Addition
RSub	s, i_1, i_2	$\Rightarrow s, (i_1 - i_2)$	Subtraction
RMul	s, i_1, i_2	$\Rightarrow s, (i_1 * i_2)$	Multiplication
RDup	s, i	$\Rightarrow s, i, i$	Duplicate stack top
RSwap	s, i_1, i_2	$\Rightarrow s, i_2, i_1$	Swap top elements

The machine terminates when there are no more instructions to execute. The result of a computation is the value v on top of the stack when the machine stops.

The *net effect principle* for stack-based evaluation says: regardless what is on the stack already, the net effect of the execution of an instruction sequence generated from an expression e is to push the value of e onto the evaluation stack, leaving the given contents of the stack unchanged.

Expressions in postfix or reverse Polish notation are used by scientific pocket calculators made by Hewlett-Packard, primarily popular with engineers and scientists. A significant advantage of postfix notation is that one can avoid the parentheses found on other calculators. The disadvantage is that the user must "compile" expressions from their usual infix algebraic notation to stack machine notation, but that is surprisingly easy to learn.

2.6 Postscript, a Stack-Based Language

Stack-based interpreted languages are widely used. The most notable among them is Postscript (ca. 1984), which is implemented in almost all high-end printers. By contrast, Portable Document Format (PDF), also from Adobe Systems, is not a full-fledged programming language.

In Postscript one can write

```
4 5 add 8 mul =
```

to compute $(4 + 5) * 8$ and print the result, and

```
/x 7 def
x x mul 9 add =
```

to bind x to 7 and then compute x*x+9 and print the result. The "=" function in Postscript pops a value from the stack and prints it. A name, such as x, that appears by itself causes its value to be pushed onto the stack. When defining the name (as opposed to using its value), it must be escaped with a slash as in /x.

The following defines the factorial function under the name fac:

```
/fac { dup 0 eq { pop 1 } { dup 1 sub fac mul } ifelse} def
```

This is equivalent to the F# function declaration

```
let rec fac n = if n=0 then 1 else n * fac (n-1)
```

Note that Postscript's `ifelse` conditional expression is postfix also, and expects to find three values on the stack: a boolean, a then-branch, and an else-branch. The then-and else-branches are written as code fragments, which in Postscript are enclosed in curly braces { ... }.

Similarly, a Postscript for-loop expects four values on the stack: a start value, a step value, an end value (for the loop index), and a loop body. It repeatedly pushes the loop index and executes the loop body. Thus one can compute and print factorial of $0, 1, \ldots, 12$ this way:

```
0 1 12 { fac = } for
```

One can use the `gs` (Ghostscript) interpreter to experiment with Postscript programs. Under Linux or MacOS, use

```
gs -dNODISPLAY
```

and under Windows, use something like

```
gswin32 -dNODISPLAY
```

For more convenient interaction, run Ghostscript inside an Emacs shell (under Linux or MS Windows).

If `prog.ps` is a file containing Postscript definitions, `gs` will execute them on start-up if invoked with

```
gs -dNODISPLAY prog.ps
```

A function definition entered interactively in Ghostscript must fit on one line, but a function definition included from a file need not.

The example Postscript program below (file `prog.ps`) prints some text in Times Roman and draws a rectangle. If you send this program to a Postscript printer, it will be executed by the printer's Postscript interpreter, and a sheet of printed paper will be produced:

```
/Times-Roman findfont 25 scalefont setfont
100 500 moveto
(Hello, Postscript!!) show
newpath
100 100 moveto
300 100 lineto 300 250 lineto
100 250 lineto 100 100 lineto stroke
showpage
```

Another much fancier Postscript example is found in file `sierpinski.eps`. It defines a recursive function that draws a *Sierpinski curve*, in which every part is similar to the whole. The core of the program is function `sierp`, which either draws a triangle (first branch of the `ifelse`) or calls itself recursively three times (second branch). The percent sign (%) starts an end-of-line comment in Postscript.

2.7   Compiling Expressions to Stack Machine Code

The datatype `sinstr` is the type of instructions for a stack machine with variables, where the variables are stored on the evaluation stack:

```
type sinstr =
   | SCstI of int          (* push integer           *)
   | SVar of int           (* push variable from env *)
   | SAdd                  (* pop args, push sum     *)
   | SSub                  (* pop args, push diff.   *)
   | SMul                  (* pop args, push product *)
   | SPop                  (* pop value/unbind var   *)
   | SSwap                 (* exchange top and next  *)
```

Since both the run-time enviroments `renv` in `teval` (Sect. 2.4) and `stack` in `reval` (Sect. 2.5) behave as stacks, and because of lexical scoping, they could be replaced by a single stack, holding both variable bindings and intermediate results. The important property is that the binding of a let-bound variable can be removed once the entire let-expression has been evaluated.

Thus we define a stack machine `seval` that uses a unified stack both for storing intermediate results and bound variables. We write a new version `scomp` of `tcomp` to compile every use of a variable into an offset from the stack top. The offset depends not only on the variable declarations, but also the number of intermediate results currently on the stack. Hence the same variable may be referred to by different indexes at different occurrences. In the expression

```
Let("z", CstI 17, Prim("+", Var "z", Var "z"))
```

the two uses of `z` in the addition get compiled to two different offsets, like this:

```
[SCstI 17, SVar 0, SVar 1, SAdd, SSwap, SPop]
```

The expression $20 + (\text{let } z = 17 \text{ in } z + 2 \text{ end}) + 30$ is compiled to

```
[SCstI 20, SCstI 17, SVar 0, SCst 2, SAdd, SSwap, SPop, SAdd,
 SCstI 30, SAdd]
```

Note that the let-binding $z = 17$ is on the stack above the intermediate result 20, but once the evaluation of the let-expression is over, only the intermediate results 20 and 19 are on the stack, and can be added. The purpose of the `SSwap`, `SPop` instruction sequence is to discard the let-bound value stored below the stack top.

The correctness of the `scomp` compiler and the stack machine `seval` relative to the expression interpreter `eval` can be asserted as follows. For an expression `e` with no free variables,

```
seval (scomp e []) []  equals  eval e []
```

More general functional languages are often compiled to stack machine code with stack offsets for variables, using a single stack for temporary results, function parameter bindings, and let-bindings.

2.8   Implementing an Abstract Machine in Java

An abstract machine implemented in F# may not seem very machine-like. One can get a little closer to real hardware by implementing the abstract machine in Java. One technical problem is that the `sinstr` instructions must be represented as numbers, so that the Java program can read the instructions from a file. We can adopt a representation such as this one:

Instruction	Bytecode
`SCst i`	0 i
`SVar x`	1 x
`SAdd`	2
`SSub`	3
`SMul`	4
`SPop`	5
`SSwap`	6

Note that most `sinstr` instructions are represented by a single number ("byte") but that those that take an argument (`SCst i` and `SVar x`) are represented by two numbers: the instruction code and the argument. For example, the [`SCstI 17, SVar 0, SVar 1, SAdd, SSwap, SPop`] instruction sequence will be represented by the number sequence 0 17 1 0 1 1 2 6 5.

This form of numeric program code can be executed by the Java method `seval` shown in Fig. 2.4.

2.9   History and Literature

Reverse Polish form (Sect. 2.5) is named after the Polish philosopher and mathematician Łukasiewicz (1878–1956). The first description of compilation of arithmetic expressions to stack operations was given in 1960 by Bauer and Samelson [3].

The stack-based language Forth (ca. 1968) is an ancestor of Postscript. It is used in embedded systems to control scientific equipment, satellites etc. The Postscript Language Reference [1] can be downloaded from Adobe Corporation.

Kamin's 1990 textbook [2] presents a range of programming languages through interpreters.

2.10   Exercises

The goal of these exercises is to understand the compilation and evaluation of simple arithmetic expressions with variables and let-bindings.

```
class Machine {
  final static int
    CST = 0, VAR = 1, ADD = 2, SUB = 3,
    MUL = 4, POP = 5, SWAP = 6;
  static int seval(int[] code) {
    int[] stack = new int[1000];          // eval and env stack
    int sp = -1;                          // stack top pointer
    int pc = 0;                           // program counter
    int instr;                            // current instruction
    while (pc < code.length)
      switch (instr = code[pc++]) {
      case CST:
        stack[sp+1] = code[pc++]; sp++; break;
      case VAR:
        stack[sp+1] = stack[sp-code[pc++]]; sp++; break;
      case ADD:
        stack[sp-1] = stack[sp-1] + stack[sp]; sp--; break;
      case SUB:
        stack[sp-1] = stack[sp-1] - stack[sp]; sp--; break;
      case MUL:
        stack[sp-1] = stack[sp-1] * stack[sp]; sp--; break;
      case POP:
        sp--; break;
      case SWAP:
        { int tmp      = stack[sp];
          stack[sp]    = stack[sp-1];
          stack[sp-1]  = tmp;
          break;
        }
      default: ... error: unknown instruction ...
    return stack[sp];
  }
}
```

Fig. 2.4 Stack machine in Java for expression evaluation (file `Machine.java`)

Exercise 2.1 Extend the expression language `expr` from `Intcomp1.fs` with multiple *sequential* let-bindings, such as this (in concrete syntax):

```
let x1 = 5+7    x2 = x1*2 in x1+x2 end
```

To evaluate this, the right-hand side expression 5+7 must be evaluated and bound to x1, and then x1*2 must be evaluated and bound to x2, after which the let-body x1+x2 is evaluated.

The new abstract syntax for `expr` might be

```
type expr =
  | CstI of int
  | Var of string
  | Let of (string * expr) list * expr    (* CHANGED *)
  | Prim of string * expr * expr
```

so that the `Let` constructor takes a list of bindings, where a binding is a pair of a variable name and an expression. The example above would be represented as:

```
Let ([("x1", ...); ("x2", ...)], Prim("+", Var "x1", Var "x2"))
```

Revise the `eval` interpreter from `Intcomp1.fs` to work for the `expr` language extended with multiple sequential let-bindings.

Exercise 2.2 Revise the function `freevars : expr -> string list` to work for the language as extended in Exercise 2.1. Note that the example expression in the beginning of Exercise 2.1 has no free variables, but `let x1 = x1+7 in x1+8 end` has the free variable `x1`, because the variable `x1` is bound only in the body (`x1+8`), not in the right-hand side (`x1+7`), of its own binding. There *are* programming languages where a variable can be used in the right-hand side of its own binding, but ours is not such a language.

Exercise 2.3 Revise the `expr`-to-`texpr` compiler `tcomp : expr -> texpr` from `Intcomp1.fs` to work for the extended `expr` language. There is no need to modify the `texpr` language or the `teval` interpreter to accommodate multiple sequential let-bindings.

Exercise 2.4 Write a bytecode assembler (in F#) that translates a list of bytecode instructions for the simple stack machine in `Intcomp1.fs` into a list of integers. The integers should be the corresponding bytecodes for the interpreter in `Machine.java`. Thus you should write a function `assemble : sinstr list -> int list`.

Use this function together with `scomp` from `Intcomp1.fs` to make a compiler from the original expressions language `expr` to a list of bytecodes `int list`.

You may test the output of your compiler by typing in the numbers as an `int` array in the `Machine.java` interpreter. (Or you may solve Exercise 2.5 below to avoid this manual work).

Exercise 2.5 Modify the compiler from Exercise 2.4 to write the lists of integers to a file. An F# list `inss` of integers may be output to the file called `fname` using this function (found in `Intcomp1.fs`):

```
let intsToFile (inss : int list) (fname : string) =
    let text = String.concat " " (List.map string inss)
    System.IO.File.WriteAllText(fname, text)
```

Then modify the stack machine interpreter in `Machine.java` to read the sequence of integers from a text file, and execute it as a stack machine program. The name of the text file may be given as a command-line parameter to the Java program. Reading numbers from the text file may be done using the StringTokenizer class or StreamTokenizer class; see e.g. *Java Precisely* [4, Example 194].

It is essential that the compiler (in F#) and the interpreter (in Java) agree on the intermediate language: what integer represents what instruction.

Exercise 2.6 Now modify the interpretation of the language from Exercise 2.1 so that multiple let-bindings are *simultaneous* rather than sequential. For instance,

```
let x1 = 5+7   x2 = x1*2 in x1+x2 end
```

should still have the abstract syntax

```
Let ([("x1", ...); ("x2", ...)], Prim("+", Var "x1", Var "x2"))
```

but now the interpretation is that all right-hand sides must be evaluated before any left-hand side variable gets bound to its right-hand side value. That is, in the above expression, the occurrence of x1 in the right-hand side of x2 has nothing to do with the x1 of the first binding; it is a free variable.

Revise the `eval` interpreter to work for this version of the `expr` language. The idea is that all the right-hand side expressions should be evaluated, after which all the variables are bound to those values simultaneously. Hence

```
let x = 11 in let x = 22   y = x+1 in x+y end end
```

should compute 12 + 22 because x in x+1 is the outer x (and hence is 11), and x in x+y is the inner x (and hence is 22). In other words, in the let-binding

```
let x1 = e1   ...   xn = en in e end
```

the scope of the variables x1 ... xn should be e, not e1 ... en.

Exercise 2.7 Define a version of the (naive, exponential-time) Fibonacci function

```
let rec fib n = if n<2 then n else fib(n-1) + fib(n-2)
```

in Postscript. Compute Fibonacci of 0, 1, ..., 25.

Exercise 2.8 Write a Postscript program to compute the sum $1 + 2 + \cdots + 1000$. It must really do the summation, not use the closed-form expression $\frac{n(n+1)}{2}$ with $n = 1000$. (Trickier: do this using only a for-loop, no function definition).

References

1. Adobe Systems: Postscript Language Reference, Third edn. Addison-Wesley (1999). http://www.adobe.com/products/postscript/pdfs/PLRM.pdf
2. Kamin, S.: Programming Languages: An Interpreter-Based Approach. Addison-Wesley (1990)
3. Samelson, K., Bauer, F.: Sequential formula translation. Commun. ACM **3**(2), 76–83 (1960)
4. Sestoft, P.: Java Precisely, 3rd edn. The MIT Press, Cambridge (2016)

Chapter 3
From Concrete Syntax to Abstract Syntax

Until now, we have written programs in abstract syntax, which is convenient when handling programs as data. However, programs are usually written in concrete syntax, as sequences of characters in a text file. So how do we get from concrete syntax to abstract syntax?

First of all, we must give a concrete syntax describing the structure of well-formed programs.

We use regular expressions to describe local structure, that is, small things such as names, constants, and operators.

We use context free grammars to describe global structure, that is, statements, the proper nesting of parentheses within parentheses, and (in Java) of methods within classes, etc.

Local structure is often called *lexical* structure, and global structure is called *syntactic* or *grammatical* structure.

3.1   Preparatory Reading

As background reading for this chapter, we recommend these parts of Torben Mogensen's *Introduction to Compiler Design* [12]:

- Sections 1.1–1.8 about regular expressions, non-deterministic finite automata, and lexer generators. A lexer generator such as `fslex` turns a regular expression into a non-deterministic finite automaton, then creates a deterministic finite automaton from that.
- Sections 2.1–2.5 about context-free grammars and syntax analysis.
- Sections 2.11 and 2.12 about LL-parsing, also called recursive descent parsing.

© Springer International Publishing AG 2017
P. Sestoft, *Programming Language Concepts*, Undergraduate Topics
in Computer Science, DOI 10.1007/978-3-319-60789-4_3

- Section 2.16 about using LR parser generators. An LR parser generator such as fsyacc turns a context-free grammar into an LR parser. This probably makes more sense once we have discussed a concrete example application of an LR parser in Sect. 3.6 below.

3.2 Lexers, Parsers, and Generators

A *lexer* or *scanner* is a program that reads characters from a text file and assembles them into a stream of *lexical tokens* or *lexemes*. A lexer usually ignores the amount of whitespace (blanks " ", newlines "\n", carriage returns "\r", tabulation characters "\t", and page breaks "\f") between non-blank symbols.

A *parser* is a program that accepts a stream of lexical tokens from a lexer, and builds an *abstract syntax tree* (AST) representing that stream of tokens.

Lexers and parser work together as shown in Fig. 3.1.

A *lexer generator* is a program that converts a lexer specification (a collection of regular expressions) into a lexer (which recognizes tokens described by the regular expressions).

A *parser generator* is a program that converts a parser specification (a decorated context free grammar) into a parser. The parser, together with a suitable lexer, recognizes program texts derivable from the grammar. The decorations on the grammar say how a text derivable from a given production should be represented as an abstract syntax tree.

We shall use the lexer generator fslex and the parser generator fsyacc, which generate F# code.

The classical lexer and parser generators for C are called lex [11] and yacc [9] (Bell Labs, early 1970s). The modern powerful GNU versions are called flex and bison; they are part of all Linux distributions. There are also free lexer and parser generators for Java, for instance JLex and JavaCup (available from Princeton University), or JavaCC (lexer and parser generator in one, see Sect. 3.9). For C#, there is a combined lexer and parser generator called CoCo/R from the University of Linz.

The parsers we are considering here are called *bottom-up parsers*, or *LR parsers*, and they are characterized by reading characters from the Left and making derivations

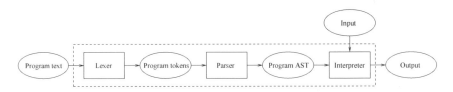

Fig. 3.1 From program text to abstract syntax tree (AST)

from the Right-most nonterminal. The `fsyacc` parser generator is quite representative of modern LR parsers.

Hand-written parsers (including those built using so-called parser combinators in functional languages), are usually *top-down parsers*, or *LL parsers*, which read characters from the Left and make derivations from the Left-most nonterminal. The JavaCC and Coco/R parser generators generate LL-parsers, which make them in some ways weaker than `bison` and `fsyacc`. Section 3.8 presents a simple hand-written LL-parser. For an introductory presentation of hand-written top-down parsers in Java, see *Grammars and Parsing with Java* [16].

3.3 Regular Expressions in Lexer Specifications

The regular expression syntax used in `fslex` lexer specifications is shown in Fig. 3.2. Regular expressions for the tokens of our example expression language may look like this. There are three keywords:

```
LET        "let"
IN         "in"
END        "end"
```

Fslex Token	Meaning
`'char'`	A character constant, with a syntax similar to that of F# character constants. Match the denoted character.
`_`	Match any character.
`eof`	Match the end of the lexer input.
`"string"`	A string constant, with a syntax similar to that of F# string constants. Match the denoted string.
`[character-set]`	Match any single character belonging to the given character set. Valid character sets are: single character constants $'c'$; ranges of characters $'c_1'$ – $'c_2'$ (all characters between c_1 and c_2, inclusive); and the union of two or more character sets, denoted by concatenation.
`[^character-set]`	Match any single character not belonging to the given character set.
`regexp *`	Match the concatenation of zero or more strings that match regexp. (Repetition).
`regexp +`	Match the concatenation of one or more strings that match regexp. (Positive repetition).
`regexp ?`	Match the empty string, or a string matching regexp. (Option).
$regexp_1$ | $regexp_2$	Match any string that matches $regexp_1$ or $regexp_2$. (Alternative).
$regexp_1$ $regexp_2$	Match the concatenation of two strings, the first matching $regexp_1$, the second matching $regexp_2$. (Concatenation).
`abbrev`	Match the same strings as the regexp in the `let`-binding of abbrev.
`( regexp )`	Match the same strings as regexp.

Fig. 3.2 Notation for token specifications in `fslex`

There are six special symbols:

```
PLUS            '+'
TIMES           '*'
MINUS           '-'
EQ              '='
LPAR            '('
RPAR            ')'
```

An integer constant `INT` is a non-empty sequence of the digits 0 to 9:

```
['0'-'9']+
```

A variable `NAME` begins with a lowercase (a–z) or uppercase (A–Z) letter, ends with zero or more letters or digits (and is not a keyword):

```
['a'-'z''A'-'Z']['a'-'z''A'-'Z''0'-'9']*
```

The actual `fslex` lexer specification for expressions is in Sect. 3.6.3.

3.4 Grammars in Parser Specifications

A *context free grammar* has four components:

- *terminal symbols* such as identifiers x, integer constants 12, string constants "foo", special symbols (+ and *) etc, keywords let, in, ...
- *nonterminal symbols* A, denoting abstract syntax classes
- a *start symbol S*
- *grammar rules* or *productions* of the form

$$A:: = tnseq$$

where *tnseq* is a sequence of terminal or nonterminal symbols.

An informal grammar for our expression language may be given as follows:

```
Expr  ::= NAME
      |   INT
      |   - INT
      |   ( Expr )
      |   let NAME = Expr in Expr end
      |   Expr * Expr
      |   Expr + Expr
      |   Expr - Expr
```

Usually one specifies that there must be no input left over after parsing, by requiring that a well-formed expression is followed by end-of-file:

```
Main  ::= Expr EOF
```

Hence we have two nonterminals (`Main` and `Expr`), of which `Main` is the start symbol. There are eight productions (seven for `Expr` and one for `Main`), and the terminal symbols are the tokens of the lexer specification.

The grammar given above is *ambiguous*: a string such as 1 + 2 * 3 can be derived in two ways:

```
Expr
-> Expr * Expr
-> Expr + Expr * Expr
-> 1 + 2 * 3
```

and

```
Expr
-> Expr + Expr
-> Expr + Expr * Expr
-> 1 + 2 * 3
```

where the former derivation corresponds to (1 + 2) * 3 and the latter corresponds to 1 + (2 * 3). The latter is the one we want: multiplication (*) should bind more strongly than addition (+) and subtraction (-). With most parser generators, one can specify that some operators should bind more strongly than others.

Also, the string 1 - 2 + 3 could be derived in two ways:

```
Expr
-> Expr - Expr
-> Expr - Expr + Expr
```

and

```
Expr
-> Expr + Expr
-> Expr - Expr + Expr
```

where the former derivation corresponds to 1 - (2 + 3) and the latter corresponds to (1 - 2) + 3. Again, the latter is the one we want: these particular arithmetic operators of the same precedence (binding strength) should be grouped from left to right. This is indicated in the parser specification in file `ExprPar.fsy` by the `%left` declaration of the symbols `PLUS` and `MINUS` (and `TIMES`); see Sect. 3.6.2.

3.5 Working with F# Modules

So far we have been working inside the F# Interactive windows of Visual Studio, or equivalently, the `fsharpi` interactive system, entering type and function declarations and evaluating expressions. Now we need more modularity and encapsulation in our programs, so we shall declare the expression language abstract syntax inside a separate file called `Absyn.fs`:

```
module Absyn

type expr =
  | CstI of int
  | Var of string
  | Let of string * expr * expr
  | Prim of string * expr * expr
```

Such a file defines an F# module `Absyn`, where the module name is specified by the `module` declaration.

It makes sense to let the file name `Absyn.fs` correspond to the module name. Other modules may refer to type `expr` in module `Absyn` by `Absyn.expr`, or may use the declaration `open Absyn` and then refer simply to `expr`. Any modules referring to `Absyn` must come after it in the Solution Explorer's file list in Visual Studio, and in command line arguments to `fsharpi` or `fsharpc`.

We shall primarily use `fsharpi` from a command prompt for F# interactive sessions; this works the same way under Windows, Linux and MacOS. If one starts `fsharpi` with command line argument `Absyn.fs`, then `fsharpi` will compile and load the module but not open it. In the interactive session we can then open it or not as we like; executing `#q;;` terminates the session:

```
fsharpi Absyn.fs
> Absyn.CstI 17;;
> open Absyn;;
> CstI 17;;
> #q;;
```

The same approach works for compiling and loading multiple modules, as we shall see below.

3.6   Using `fslex` and `fsyacc`

The following subsections present an example of complete lexer and parser specifications for `fslex` and `fsyacc`. These lexer and parser specifications, as well as an F# program to combine them, can be found in the `Expr` subdirectory:

File	Contents
Expr/Absyn.fs	abstract syntax
Expr/ExprLex.fsl	lexer specification, input to `fslex`
Expr/ExprPar.fsy	parser specification, input to `fsyacc`
Expr/Parse.fs	declaration of an expression parser

3.6.1 Installing and Using **fslex** and **fsyacc**

The fslex and fsyacc tools are not included with standard F# distributions, but are part of the FsLexYacc package at http://fsprojects.github.io/FsLexYacc/. For up-to-date information about getting and installing them, see the book's homepage http://www.itu.dk/people/sestoft/plc/.

The F# code generated by fslex and fsyacc uses the modules Lexing and Parsing. These will be installed automatically along with fslex and fsyacc, but you may need to copy file FsLexYacc.Runtime.dll to the directory where you run programs that include components generated by fslex and fsyacc, or to create a symlink to the file.

Use command line option fslex --unicode to generate a lexer that processes Unicode files, defining a LexBuffer<char>.

The simplest way to use fslex and fsyacc is to run them from the command line, whether in Linux, MacOS or Windows.

It is also possible to integrate fslex and fsyacc in the build process of Visual Studio, so that fslex --unicode ExprLex.fsl is automatically re-run every time the lexer specification ExprLex.fsl has been edited, and so on, but this tends to be somewhat non-trivial. See the FsLexYacc project homepage for guidance.

3.6.2 Parser Specification for Expressions

A complete parser specification for the simple expression language is found in file Exprpar.fsy. It begins with declarations of the tokens, or terminal symbols, CSTINT, NAME, and so on, followed by declarations of operator associativity and precedence:

```
%token <int> CSTINT
%token <string> NAME
%token PLUS MINUS TIMES EQ
%token END IN LET
%token LPAR RPAR
%token EOF


%left MINUS PLUS        /* lowest precedence  */
%left TIMES             /* highest precedence */
```

After the token declarations, the parser specification declares that nonterminal Main is the start symbol, and then gives the grammar rules for both nonterminals Main and Expr:

```
%start Main
%type <Absyn.expr> Main
%%
```

```
Main:
      Expr EOF                              { $1                       }
Expr:
      NAME                                  { Var $1                   }
    | CSTINT                                { CstI $1                  }
    | MINUS CSTINT                          { CstI (- $2)              }
    | LPAR Expr RPAR                        { $2                       }
    | LET NAME EQ Expr IN Expr END          { Let($2, $4, $6)          }
    | Expr TIMES Expr                       { Prim("*", $1, $3)  }
    | Expr PLUS  Expr                       { Prim("+", $1, $3)  }
    | Expr MINUS Expr                       { Prim("-", $1, $3)  }
```

For instance, the first rule says that to parse a Main, one must parse an Expr followed by an EOF, that is, end of file. The rules for Expr say that we can parse an Expr by parsing a NAME token, or a CSTINT token, or a minus sign (−) followed by a CSTINT token, or a left parenthesis followed by an Expr followed by a right parenthesis, and so on.

The expressions in curly braces on the right describe what result will be produced by a successful parse — remember that the purpose of parsing is to produce an abstract syntax representation by reading a text file (concrete syntax). For instance, the result of parsing an Expr as NAME is Var($1), that is, a variable represented as abstract syntax. The name of that variable is taken from the string carried by the previously declared NAME token; the $1 means "the value associated with symbol number 1 on the right-hand side of the grammar rule", here NAME. Similarly, the result of parsing an Expr as Expr MINUS Expr is Prim("-", $1, $3), that is, abstract syntax for an subtraction operator whose operands are the two expressions on the rule right-hand side, namely $1 and $3.

To summarize, the curly braces contain F# expressions that produce the result of a successful parse. They are sometimes called *semantic actions*.

The %type declaration says that a successful parse of a Main nonterminal produces a value of type Absyn.expr, that is, an expression in abstract syntax.

To turn the above parser specification file ExprPar.fsy into a parser program, we must run the fsyacc tool like this:

```
fsyacc --module ExprPar ExprPar.fsy
```

This produces a parser as an F# source program in file ExprPar.fs, with module name ExprPar, and a corresponding signature file ExprPar.fsi (similar to a Java or C# interface).

3.6.3 Lexer Specification for Expressions

A complete lexer specification for the simple expression language is found in file ExprLex.fsl. The first part of the lexer specification contains declarations of

auxiliary functions and so on. This is ordinary F# code, but note that all of it is
enclosed in a pair of curly braces ({) and (}):

```
{
  module ExprLex

  open Microsoft.FSharp.Text.Lexing
  open ExprPar

  let lexemeAsString lexbuf =
      LexBuffer<char>.LexemeString lexbuf
  let keyword s =
      match s with
      | "let" -> LET
      | "in"  -> IN
      | "end" -> END
      | _     -> NAME s
}
```

The open declarations make some F# modules accessible, including the ExprPar
module generated from the parser specification, because we need the tokens NAME,
CSTINT, and so on, declared there; see Sect. 3.6.2.

The function declarations are useful in most lexer specifications. The keyword
function is used by the actual lexer (see below) to distinguish keywords or reserved
names (here let, in, end) of the expression language from variable names (such
as x, square, and so on). Although one could use regular expressions to distinguish
reserved names from variable names, this may make the resulting automaton very
large. So in practice, it is better to let the lexer recognize everything that looks like
a variable name or reserved word by a single regular expression, and then use an
auxiliary function such as keyword to distinguish reserved names.

The real core of the lexer specification, however, is the second part which defines
the tokenizer Token. It specifies the possible forms of a token by regular expressions,
and for each regular expression, it gives the resulting token:

```
rule Token = parse
  | [' ' '\t' '\r'] { Token lexbuf }
  | '\n'            { lexbuf.EndPos <- lexbuf.EndPos.NextLine;
                      Token lexbuf }
  | ['0'-'9']+      { CSTINT (System.Int32.Parse
                                    (lexemeAsString lexbuf)) }
  | ['a'-'z''A'-'Z']['a'-'z''A'-'Z''0'-'9']*
                    { keyword (lexemeAsString lexbuf) }
  | '+'             { PLUS  }
  | '-'             { MINUS }
  | '*'             { TIMES }
  | '='             { EQ    }
```

```
| '('                    { LPAR  }
| ')'                    { RPAR  }
| '['                    { LPAR  }
| ']'                    { RPAR  }
| eof                    { EOF   }
| _                      { failwith "Lexer error: illegal symbol" }
```

For instance, the third rule says that the regular expression `['0'-'9']+` corresponds to a `CSTINT` token. The fourth rule gives a more complicated regular expression that covers both reserved words and names; the auxiliary function `keyword`, defined above, is called to decide whether to produce a LET, IN, END or NAME token.

The first rule deals with whitespace (blank, tab, and carriage return) by calling the tokenizer recursively instead of returning a token, thus simply discarding the whitespace. The second rule deals with a newline by updating the lexer's line counter and then discarding the newline character.

Comments can be dealt with in much the same way as whitespace, see the lexer example mentioned in Sect. 3.7.1.

The call `lexemeAsString lexbuf` returns the F# string matched by the regular expression on the left-hand side, such as the integer matched by `['0'-'9']+`.

To turn the above lexer specification file `ExprLex.fsl` into a lexer program, we must run the `fslex` tool like this:

```
fslex --unicode ExprLex.fsl
```

This generates a lexer as an F# program in file `ExprLex.fs`.

Since the parser specification defines the `token` datatype, which is used by the generated lexer, the parser must be generated and compiled before the resulting lexer is compiled.

In summary, to generate the lexer and parser, and compile them together with the abstract syntax module, do the following (in the directory `Expr/` which contains file `ExprPar.fsy` and so on):

```
fslex --unicode ExprLex.fsl
fsyacc --module ExprPar ExprPar.fsy
fsharpi -r FSharp.PowerPack.dll Absyn.fs ExprPar.fs ExprLex.fs ^
    Parse.fs
```

The hat symbol (^) above is the Windows command line continuation symbol; in Linux and MacOS use backslash (\). The example file `Parse.fs` defines a function `fromString : string -> expr` that combines the generated lexer function `Exprlex.Token` and the generated parser function `ExprPar.Main` like this:

```
let fromString (str : string) : expr =
    let lexbuf = Lexing.LexBuffer<char>.FromString(str)
    try
      ExprPar.Main ExprLex.Token lexbuf
    with
      | exn -> let pos = lexbuf.EndPos
```

```
failwithf "%s near line %d, column %d\n"
(exn.Message) (pos.Line+1) pos.Column
```

The function creates a lexer buffer lexbuf from the string, and then calls the parser's entry function ExprPar.Main (Sect. 3.6.2) to produce an expr by parsing, using the lexer's tokenizer Exprlex.Token (Sect. 3.6.3) to read from lexbuf. If the parsing succeeds, the function returns the expr as abstract syntax. If lexing or parsing fails, an exception is raised, which will be reported on the console in this style:

```
Lexer error: illegal symbol near line 17, column 12
```

3.6.4   The ExprPar.fsyacc.output File Generated by fsyacc

The generated parser in file ExprPar.fs is just an F# program, so one may try to read and understand it, but that is an unpleasant experience: it consists of many tables represented as arrays of unsigned integers, plus various strange program fragments.

Luckily, one can get a high-level description of the generated parser by calling fsyacc with option -v, as in

```
fsyacc -v --module ExprPar ExprPar.fsy
```

This produces a log file ExprPar.fsyacc.output containing a description of the parser as a stack (or pushdown) automaton: a finite automaton equipped with a stack of the nonterminals parsed so far.

The file contains a description of the states of the finite stack automaton; in the case of ExprPar.fsy the states are numbered from 0 to 23. For each numbered automaton state, three pieces of information are given: the corresponding parsing state (as a set of so-called LR(0)-items), the state's action table, and its goto table.

For an example, consider state 11. In state 11 we are trying to parse an Expr, we have seen the keyword LET, and we now expect to parse the remainder of the let-expression. This is shown by the dot (.) in the LR-item, which describes the current position of the parser inside a phrase. The transition relation says that if the remaining input does begin with a NAME, we should read it and go to state 12; all other inputs lead to a parse error:

```
state 11:
  items:
    Expr -> 'LET' . 'NAME' 'EQ' Expr 'IN' Expr 'END'
  actions:
    action 'EOF' (noprec):   error
    action 'LPAR' (noprec):   error
    action 'RPAR' (noprec):   error
    action 'END' (noprec):   error
    action 'IN' (noprec):   error
```

```
      action 'LET' (noprec):     error
      action 'PLUS' (noprec):    error
      action 'MINUS' (noprec):    error
      action 'TIMES' (noprec):    error
      action 'EQ' (noprec):    error
      action 'NAME' (noprec):    shift 12
      action 'CSTINT' (noprec):    error
      action 'error' (noprec):    error
      action '#' (noprec):    error
      action '$$' (noprec):    error
    immediate action: <none>
  gotos:
```

The read operation is called a *shift* action: the symbol is shifted from the input to the parse stack; see Sect. 3.6.5 below.

For another example, consider state 8. According to the parsing state, we are trying to parse an Expr, we have seen a left parenthesis LPAR, and we now expect to parse an Expr and then a right parenthesis RPAR. According to the transition relation, the remaining input must begin with a left parenthesis, or the keyword LET, or a minus sign, or a name, or an integer constant; all other input leads to a parse error. If we see an acceptable input symbol, we shift (read) it and go to state 8, 11, 6, 4, or 5, respectively. When later we have completed parsing the Expr, we go to state 9, as shown at the end of the state description:

```
state 8:
  items:
    Expr -> 'LPAR' . Expr 'RPAR'
  actions:
    action 'EOF' (noprec):     error
    action 'LPAR' (noprec):     shift 8
    action 'RPAR' (noprec):     error
    action 'END' (noprec):     error
    action 'IN' (noprec):    error
    action 'LET' (noprec):     shift 11
    action 'PLUS' (noprec):    error
    action 'MINUS' (explicit left 9999):    shift 6
    action 'TIMES' (noprec):    error
    action 'EQ' (noprec):    error
    action 'NAME' (noprec):     shift 4
    action 'CSTINT' (noprec):     shift 5
    action 'error' (noprec):     error
    action '#' (noprec):    error
    action '$$' (noprec):    error
  immediate action: <none>
  gotos:
    goto Expr: 9
```

For yet another example, consider state 19 below. According to the state's LR items, we have seen Expr PLUS Expr. According to the state's actions (the transition relation) the remaining input must begin with one of the operators TIMES, PLUS or MINUS, or one of the the keywords IN or END, or a right parenthesis, or end of file.

In all cases except the TIMES symbol, we will *reduce* using the grammar rule Expr -> Expr PLUS Expr backwards. Namely, we have seen Expr PLUS Expr, and from the grammar rule we know that this sequence may be derived from the nonterminal Expr.

In case we see the TIMES symbol, we shift (read) the symbol and go to state 21. Further investigation of parser states (not shown here) reveals that state 21 expects to find an Expr, and after that goes to state 18, where we have:

```
Expr PLUS Expr TIMES Expr
```

which will then be reduced, using the grammar rule Expr -> Expr TIMES Expr backwards, to

```
Expr PLUS Expr
```

at which point we're back at state 19 again. The effect is that TIMES binds more strongly than PLUS, as we are used to in arithmetics. If we see any other input symbol, we reduce Expr PLUS Expr on the parse stack by using the grammar rule Expr -> Expr PLUS Expr backwards, thus getting an Expr.

```
state 19:
  items:
     Expr -> Expr . 'TIMES' Expr
     Expr -> Expr . 'PLUS' Expr
     Expr -> Expr 'PLUS' Expr .
     Expr -> Expr . 'MINUS' Expr
  actions:
     action 'EOF' (...): reduce Expr --> Expr 'PLUS' Expr
     action 'LPAR' (...): reduce Expr --> Expr 'PLUS' Expr
     action 'RPAR' (...): reduce Expr --> Expr 'PLUS' Expr
     action 'END' (...): reduce Expr --> Expr 'PLUS' Expr
     action 'IN' (...): reduce Expr --> Expr 'PLUS' Expr
     action 'LET' (...): reduce Expr --> Expr 'PLUS' Expr
     action 'PLUS' (...): reduce Expr --> Expr 'PLUS' Expr
     action 'MINUS' (...): reduce Expr --> Expr 'PLUS' Expr
     action 'TIMES' (...): shift 21
     action 'EQ' (...): reduce Expr --> Expr 'PLUS' Expr
     action 'NAME' (...): reduce Expr --> Expr 'PLUS' Expr
     action 'CSTINT' (...): reduce Expr --> Expr 'PLUS' Expr
     action 'error' (...): reduce Expr --> Expr 'PLUS' Expr
     action '#' (...): reduce Expr --> Expr 'PLUS' Expr
     action '$$' (...): reduce Expr --> Expr 'PLUS' Expr
  immediate action: <none>
  gotos:
```

The terminal symbols ' # ' and ' $$ ' used in a few of the states are auxiliary symbols introduced by the fsyacc parser generator to properly handle the start and end of the parsing process; we shall ignore them here.

3.6.5 Exercising the Parser Automaton

The parser generated by e.g. fsyacc looks like a finite automaton, but instead of just a single current state, it has a stack containing states and grammar symbols.

If there is an automaton state such as #20 on top of the stack, then that state's action table and the next input symbol determines the action. As explained above, the action may be "shift" or "reduce".

For example, if state 19 is on the stack top and the next input symbol is *, then according to the action table of state 19 (shown above) the action is shift 21 which means that * is removed from the input and pushed on the stack together with state #21.

If again state 19 is on the stack top but the next input symbol is EOF, then the action is to reduce by this grammar rule from the parser specification:

```
Expr ::= Expr PLUS Expr
```

The reduce action uses the grammar rule "in reverse", to remove the grammar symbols Expr PLUS Expr from the stack, and push Expr instead. After a reduce action, the state below the new stack top symbol Expr (for instance, state 0) is inspected for a suitable goto rule (for instance, goto Expr: 2), and the new state 2 is pushed on the stack.

For a complete parsing example, consider the parser states traversed during parsing of the string x + 52 * wk EOF:

```
Input       Parse stack (top on right)                             Action
------------------------------------------------------------------------------
x+52*wk&    #0                                                     shift #4
+52*wk&     #0 x #4                                                reduce by B
+52*wk&     #0 Expr                                                goto #2
+52*wk&     #0 Expr #2                                             shift #22
52*wk&      #0 Expr #2 + #22                                       shift #5
*wk&        #0 Expr #2 + #22 52 #5                                 reduce by C
*wk&        #0 Expr #2 + #22 Expr                                  goto #19
*wk&        #0 Expr #2 + #22 Expr #19                              shift #21
wk&         #0 Expr #2 + #22 Expr #19 * #21                        shift #4
&           #0 Expr #2 + #22 Expr #19 * #21 wk #4                  reduce by B
&           #0 Expr #2 + #22 Expr #19 * #21 Expr                   goto #18
&           #0 Expr #2 + #22 Expr #19 * #21 Expr #18               reduce by G
&           #0 Expr #2 + #22 Expr                                  goto #19
&           #0 Expr #2 + #22 Expr #19                              reduce by H
```

```
&            #0  Expr                                    goto #2
&            #0  Expr #2                                 shift 3
             #0  Expr #2 & #3                            reduce by A
             #0  Main                                    goto #1
             #0  Main #1                                 accept
```

The numbers #0, #1, ...are parser state numbers from the ExprPar.fsyacc.output file, the symbol & is here used to represent end-of-file (EOF), and the letters A, B, and so on, indicate which grammar rule is used (backwards) in a reduce step:

```
Main ::= Expr EOF                                        rule A
Expr ::= NAME                                            rule B
     |   CSTINT                                          rule C
     |   MINUS CSTINT                                    rule D
     |   LPAR Expr RPAR                                  rule E
     |   LET NAME EQ Expr IN Expr END                    rule F
     |   Expr TIMES Expr                                 rule G
     |   Expr PLUS  Expr                                 rule H
     |   Expr MINUS Expr                                 rule I
```

When the parser performs a reduction using a given rule, it evaluates the semantic action associated with that rule. It also pushes the result of the semantic action on the stack, but this is not shown above. Hence the $1, $2, and so on in a semantic action refers to the value, on the stack, associated with a given terminal or nonterminal symbol.

3.6.6   Shift/Reduce Conflicts

Studying the ExprPar.fsyacc.output file is useful if there are *shift/reduce conflicts* or *reduce/reduce conflicts* in the generated parser. Such conflicts arise because the grammar is ambiguous: some string may be derived in more than one way.

For instance, if we remove the precedence and associativity declarations (%left) from the tokens PLUS, MINUS and TIMES in the ExprPar.fsy parser specification, then there will be shift/reduce conflicts in the parser.

Then fsyacc will produce a conflict message like this on the console:

```
state 19: shift/reduce error on PLUS
state 19: shift/reduce error on TIMES
state 19: shift/reduce error on MINUS
```

and now state 19 looks like this:

```
state 19:
  items:
    Expr -> Expr . 'TIMES' Expr
    Expr -> Expr . 'PLUS' Expr
```

```
    Expr -> Expr 'PLUS' Expr .
    Expr -> Expr . 'MINUS' Expr
  actions:
    action 'EOF' :    reduce Expr --> Expr 'PLUS' Expr
    action 'LPAR' :    reduce Expr --> Expr 'PLUS' Expr
    action 'RPAR' :    reduce Expr --> Expr 'PLUS' Expr
    action 'END' :    reduce Expr --> Expr 'PLUS' Expr
    action 'IN' :    reduce Expr --> Expr 'PLUS' Expr
    action 'LET' :    reduce Expr --> Expr 'PLUS' Expr
    action 'PLUS' :    shift 22
    action 'MINUS' :    shift 23
    action 'TIMES' :    shift 21
    action 'EQ' :    reduce Expr --> Expr 'PLUS' Expr
    action 'NAME' :    reduce Expr --> Expr 'PLUS' Expr
    action 'CSTINT' :    reduce Expr --> Expr 'PLUS' Expr
    action 'error' :    reduce Expr --> Expr 'PLUS' Expr
    action '#' :    reduce Expr --> Expr 'PLUS' Expr
    action '$$' :    reduce Expr --> Expr 'PLUS' Expr
  immediate action: <none>
  gotos:
```

The LR-items describe a parser state in which the parser has recognized Expr PLUS Expr (which can be reduced to Expr), or is about to read a TIMES or PLUS or MINUS token while recognizing Expr <operator> Expr.

The third line of the conflict message says that when the next token is MINUS, for instance the second MINUS found while parsing this input:

```
11 + 22 - 33
```

then the parser generator does not know whether it should read (shift) the minus operator, or reduce Expr PLUS Expr to Expr before proceeding. The former choice would make PLUS right associative, as in 11 + (22 - 33), and the latter would make it left associative, as in (11 + 22) - 33.

We see from this line in the action table of state 19:

```
action 'MINUS' :    shift 23
```

that the parser generator decided, in the absence of other information, to shift (and go to state 23) when the next symbol is MINUS, which would make PLUS right associative. This not what we want.

By declaring

```
%left MINUS PLUS
```

in the parser specification we tell the parser generator to reduce instead, making PLUS and MINUS left associative, and this one problem goes away. This also solves the problem reported for PLUS in the second line of the message.

The problem with TIMES is similar, but the desired solution is different. The second line of the conflict message says that when the next token is TIMES, for instance the TIMES found while parsing this input:

```
11 + 22 * 33
```

then it is unclear whether we should shift that token, or reduce Expr PLUS Expr to Expr before proceeding. The former choice would make TIMES bind more strongly than PLUS, as in 11 + (22 * 33), and the latter would make TIMES and PLUS bind equally strongly and left associative, as in (11 + 22) * 33.

The former choice is the one we want, so in ExprPar.fsy we should declare

```
%left MINUS PLUS       /* lowest precedence  */
%left TIMES            /* highest precedence */
```

Doing so makes all conflicts go away.

3.7   Lexer and Parser Specification Examples

The following subsections show three more examples of lexer and parser specifications for fslex and fsyacc.

3.7.1   A Small Functional Language

Chapter 4 presents a simple functional language micro-ML, similar to a small subset of F#, in which one can write programs such as these:

```
let f x = x + 7 in f 2 end
```

```
let f x = let g y = x + y in g (2 * x) end
in f 7 end
```

The abstract syntax and grammar for that functional language are described in the following files:

File	Contents
Fun/grammar.txt	an informal description of the grammar
Fun/Absyn.sml	abstract syntax
Fun/FunLex.lex	lexer specification
Fun/FunPar.fsy	parser specification
Fun/Parse.fs	declaration of a parser

Follow the instructions in file Fun/README.TXT to build the lexer and parser using fslex and fsyacc, then start

```
fsharpi -r FSharp.PowerPack Absyn.fs FunPar.fs FunLex.fs Parse.fs
```

and evaluate

```
open Parse;;
fromString "let f x = x + 7 in f 2 end";;
```

What is missing, of course, is an interpreter (a semantics) for the abstract syntax of this language. We shall return to that in Chap. 4.

3.7.2 Lexer and Parser Specifications for Micro-SQL

The language micro-SQL is a small subset of SQL SELECT statements without WHERE, GROUP BY, ORDER BY etc. It permits SELECTs on (qualified) column names, and the use of aggregate functions. For instance:

```
SELECT name, zip FROM Person
SELECT COUNT(*) FROM Person
SELECT * FROM Person, Zip
SELECT Person.name, Zip.code FROM Person, Zip
```

The micro-SQL language abstract syntax and grammar are described in the following files:

File	Contents
Usql/grammar.txt	an informal description of the grammar
Usql/Absyn.fs	abstract syntax for micro-SQL
Usql/UsqlLex.fsl	lexer specification
Usql/UsqlPar.fsy	parser specification
Usql/Parse.fs	declaration of a micro-SQL parser

Follow the instructions in file `Usql/README.TXT` to build the lexer and parser using `fslex` and `fsyacc`, then start

```
fsharpi -r FSharp.PowerPack Absyn.fs UsqlPar.fs UsqlLex.fs Parse.fs
```

and evaluate, for instance:

```
open Parse;;
fromString "SELECT name, zip FROM Person";;
```

3.8 A Handwritten Recursive Descent Parser

The syntax of the Lisp and Scheme languages is particularly simple: An expression is a number, or a symbol (a variable name or an operator), or a parenthesis enclosing zero or more expressions, as in these five examples:

```
42
x
(define x 42)
(+ x (* x 1))
(define (fac n) (if (= n 0) 1 (* n (fac (- n 1)))))
```

We call this the S-expressions language, because it is similar to the basic syntax of
the Lisp or Scheme languages. This version of the S-expression language can be
described by this context-free grammar:

```
sexpr ::= number
      |   symbol
      |   ( sexpr* )
```

There are no infix operators and no operator precedence rules, so it is easy to parse
using recursive descent in a hand-written top-down parser. This can be done in any
language that supports recursive function calls; here we use C#.

The S-expression language has only four kinds of tokens: number, symbol, left
parenthesis, and right parenthesis. We can model this using an interface and four
classes:

```
interface IToken { }                  // Inherits Object.ToString()
class NumberCst : IToken { ... }
class Symbol : IToken { ... }
class Lpar : IToken { ... }
class Rpar : IToken { ... }
```

We can write a lexer as a static method that takes a character source in the form of a
System.IO.TextReader and produces a stream of tokens in the form of an IEnumer-
ator<IToken>:

```
public static IEnumerator<IToken> Tokenize(TextReader rd) {
  for (;;) {
    int raw = rd.Read();
    char ch = (char)raw;
    if (raw == -1)                    // End of input
      yield break;
    else if (Char.IsWhiteSpace(ch))   // Whitespace; skip
      {}
    else if (Char.IsDigit(ch))        // Nonneg number
      yield return new NumberCst(ScanNumber(ch, rd));
    else switch (ch) {
      case '(':                       // Separators
        yield return Lpar.LPAR; break;
      case ')':
        yield return Rpar.RPAR; break;
      case '-':                       // Neg num, or Symbol
        ...
```

```
        default:                                    // Symbol
          yield return ScanSymbol(ch, rd);
          break;
      }
    }
  }
```

Now a parser can be written as a static method that takes a token stream `ts` and looks at the first token to decide which form the S-expression being parsed must have. If the first token is a right parenthesis ")" then the S-expression is ill-formed; otherwise if it is a left parenthesis "(" then the parser keeps reading complete (balanced) S-expressions until it encounters the corresponding right parenthesis; otherwise if the first token is a symbol then the S-expression is a symbol; otherwise if it is a number, then the S-expression is a number:

```
public static void ParseSexp(IEnumerator<IToken> ts) {
  if (ts.Current is Symbol) {
    Console.WriteLine("Parsed symbol " + ts.Current);
  } else if (ts.Current is NumberCst) {
    Console.WriteLine("Parsed number " + ts.Current);
  } else if (ts.Current is Lpar) {
    Console.WriteLine("Started parsing list");
    Advance(ts);
    while (!(ts.Current is Rpar)) {
      ParseSexp(ts);
      Advance(ts);
    }
    Console.WriteLine("Ended parsing list");
  } else
    throw new ArgumentException("Parse err at " + ts.Current);
}
```

The auxiliary function `Advance(ts)` discards the current token and reads the next one, or throws an exception if there is no next token:

```
private static void Advance(IEnumerator<IToken> ts) {
  if (!ts.MoveNext())
    throw new ArgumentException("Expected sexp, found eof");
}
```

3.9 JavaCC: Lexer-, Parser-, and Tree Generator

JavaCC [8] can generate a lexer, a parser, and Java class representation of syntax trees from a single specification file. The generated parsers are of the LL or recursive descent type. They do not support operator precedence and associativity declarations, so often the grammar must be (re)written slightly to be accepted by JavaCC.

A JavaCC lexer and parser specification is written in a single file, see for instance
`Expr/javacc/Exprparlex.jj`. This file must be processed by the `javacc`
program to generate several Java source files, which are subsequently compiled:

```
javacc Exprparlex.jj
javac *.java
```

The lexer specification part of a JavaCC file `Expr/javacc/Exprparlex.jj`
describing the simple expression language discussed above may look like this:

```
SKIP :
{ " "
| "\r"
| "\n"
| "\t"
}


TOKEN :
{ < PLUS  : "+" >
| < MINUS : "-" >
| < TIMES : "*" >
}


TOKEN :
{ < LET    : "let" >
| < IN     : "in" >
| < END    : "end" >
}


TOKEN : /* constants and variables */
{ < CSTINT  : ( <DIGIT> )+ >
| < #DIGIT  : ["0" - "9"] >
| < NAME    : <LETTER> ( <DIGIT> | <LETTER> )* >
| < #LETTER : ["a"-"z", "A"-"Z"] >
}
```

The `SKIP` declaration says that blanks, newlines, and tabulator characters should be
ignored. The first `TOKEN` declaration defines the operators, the second one defines
the keywords, and the third one defines integer constants (`CSTINT`) and variables
(`NAME`). There is no requirement to divide the declarations like this, but it may
improve clarity. Note that `TOKEN` declarations may introduce and use auxiliary
symbols such as `#DIGIT` and `#LETTER`. The format of this lexer specification
is different from the `fslex` specification (Sect. 3.6.3), but it should be easy to relate
one to the other.

The parser specification part of the JavaCC file for the expression language is
quite different from the `fsyacc` specification (Sect. 3.6.2), on the other hand:

```
void Main() :
{}
{
   Expr() <EOF>
}

void Expr() :
{}
{
   Term() ( ( <PLUS> | <MINUS> ) Term() )*
}

void Term() :
{ }
{
   Factor() ( <TIMES> Factor() )*
}

void Factor() :
{ }
{
     <NAME>
   | <CSTINT>
   | <MINUS> <CSTINT>
   | "(" Expr() ")"
   | <LET> <NAME> "=" Expr() <IN> Expr() <END>
}
```

There are two reasons for this. First, JavaCC generates top-down or LL parsers, and these cannot handle grammar rules N ::= N ... in which the left-hand nonterminal appears as the first symbol in the right-hand side. Such rules are called *left-recursive* grammar rules; see for example the last three rules of the original Expr grammar:

```
Expr ::= NAME
       |   INT
       |   - INT
       |   ( Expr )
       |   let NAME = Expr in Expr end
       |   Expr * Expr
       |   Expr + Expr
       |   Expr - Expr
```

Secondly, in JavaCC one cannot specify the precedence of operators, so the grammar above is highly ambiguous. For these reasons, one must transform the grammar to avoid the left-recursion and to express the precedence. The resulting grammar will typically look like this:

```
Expr    ::= Term
          | Term + Expr
          | Term - Expr
Term    ::= Factor
          | Factor * Term
Factor  ::= NAME
          | INT
          | - INT
          | ( Expr )
          | let NAME = Expr in Expr end
```

Moreover, JavaCC has several extensions of the grammar notation, such as (. . .) *
for zero or more occurrences, and (. . . | . . .) for choice. Using such abbrevi-
ations we arrive at this shorter grammar which corresponds closely to the JavaCC
parser specification on p. 55:

```
Expr    ::= Term ((+ | -) Term)*
Term    ::= Factor (* Factor)*
Factor  ::= NAME
          | INT
          | - INT
          | ( Expr )
          | let NAME = Expr in Expr end
```

To use JavaCC, download it [8], unzip it, and run the enclosed Java program which
will unpack and install it. See JavaCC's example files for a careful walkthrough of
several other introductory examples.

3.10   History and Literature

Regular expressions were introduced by Stephen C. Kleene, a mathematician, in
1956. Michael O. Rabin and Dana Scott in 1959 gave the first algorithms for
constructing a deterministic finite automaton (DFA) from a nondeterministic finite
automaton (NFA), and for minimization of DFAs [14].

   Formal grammars were developed within linguistics by Noam Chomsky around
1956. They were first used in computer science by John Backus and Peter Naur
in 1960 to describe the Algol 60 programming language. This variant of grammar
notation was subsequently called Backus-Naur Form or BNF.

   Chomsky originally devised four grammar classes, each class more general than
those below it:

Chomsky hierarchy	Example rules	Characteristics
0: Unrestricted	a B b → c	General rewrite system
1: Context-sensitive	a B b → a c b	Non-abbreviating rewr. sys.
2: Context-free	B → a B b	
	Some subclasses of context-free grammars:	
	$LR(1)$	general bottom-up parsing, Earley
	$LALR(1)$	bottom-up, Yacc, fsyacc
	$LL(1)$	top-down, recursive descent
3: Regular	B → a | a B	parsing by finite automata

The unrestricted grammars cannot be parsed by machine in general; they are of theoretical interest but of little practical use in parsing. All context-sensitive grammars can be parsed, but may take an excessive amount of time and space, and so are also of little practical use. The context-free grammars are very useful in computing, in particular the subclasses LL(1), LALR(1), and LR(1) mentioned above. Earley gave an $O(n^3)$ algorithm for parsing general context-free grammars in 1969. The regular grammars are just regular expressions; parsing according to a regular grammar can be done in linear time using a constant amount of memory.

Donald E. Knuth described the LR subclass of context-free grammars and how to parse them in 1965 [10]. The first widely used implementation of an LR parser generator tool was the influential Yacc LALR parser generator for Unix created by S.C. Johnson at Bell Labs in 1975.

There is a huge literature about regular expressions, automata, grammar classes, formal languages, the associated computation models, practical lexing and parsing, and so on. Two classical textbooks are Aho, Hopcroft, Ullman 1974 [1], and Hopcroft, Ullman 1979 [6].

A classical compiler textbook with good coverage of lexing and parsing (and many other topics) is Aho, Lam, Sethi and Ullman [2].

Parser combinators for recursive descent (LL) parsing with backtracking are popular in the functional programming community. They were introduced by Burge in his — remarkably early — 1975 book on functional programming techniques [3]. A presentation using lazy languages is given by Hutton [7], and one using Standard ML is given by Paulson [13]. There is also a parser combinator library for F# called fparsec [18].

A recent development is Generalized LL (or GLL) parsers by Scott and Johnstone [15], which, like recursive descent parsers, are easy to construct, yet handle left recursion and other challenges well.

Other parsing techniques popular especially within the functional programming community are Brian Ford's parsing expression grammars (PEG) [5] and packrat parsers [4], where the latter essentially combine PEGs with memoization for efficiency. They describe language classes that fall outside the Chomsky hierarchy described above, avoid the split between lexing (based on regular expressions) and parsing (based on context-free grammars), and have many of the strengths of LR parsing techniques but without the implementation complications. Although these techniques have become popular only in the last decade, they are basically variants of "top-down parsing languages" described in the early 1970.

3.11 Exercises

The main goal of these exercises is to familiarize yourself with regular expressions, automata, grammars, the `fslex` lexer generator and the `fsyacc` parser generator.

Exercise 3.1 Do exercises 1.2 and 1.3 in Mogensen's book [12].

Exercise 3.2 Write a regular expression that recognizes all sequences consisting of *a* and *b* where two *a*'s are always separated by at least one *b*. For instance, these four strings are legal: *b*, *a*, *ba*, *abababbaba*; but these two strings are illegal: *aa*, *babaa*.

Construct the corresponding NFA. Try to find a DFA corresponding to the NFA.

Exercise 3.3 Write out the rightmost derivation of the string below from the expression grammar at the end of Sect. 3.6.5, corresponding to `ExprPar.fsy`. Take note of the sequence of grammar rules (A–I) used.

```
let z = (17) in z + 2 * 3 end EOF
```

Exercise 3.4 Draw the above derivation as a tree.

Exercise 3.5 Get `expr.zip` from the book homepage and unpack it. Using a command prompt, generate (1) the lexer and (2) the parser for expressions by running `fslex` and `fsyacc`; then (3) load the expression abstract syntax, the lexer and parser modules, and the expression interpreter and compilers, into an interactive F# session (`fsharpi`):

```
fslex --unicode ExprLex.fsl
fsyacc --module ExprPar ExprPar.fsy
fsharpi -r FSharp.PowerPack.dll Absyn.fs ExprPar.fs ExprLex.fs ^
     Parse.fs
```

Now try the parser on several example expressions, both well-formed and ill-formed ones, such as these, and some of your own invention:

```
open Parse;;
fromString "1 + 2 * 3";;
fromString "1 - 2 - 3";;
fromString "1 + -2";;
fromString "x++";;
fromString "1 + 1.2";;
fromString "1 + ";;
fromString "let z = (17) in z + 2 * 3 end";;
fromString "let z = 17) in z + 2 * 3 end";;
fromString "let in = (17) in z + 2 * 3 end";;
fromString "1 + let x=5 in let y=7+x in y+y end + x end";;
```

Exercise 3.6 Use the expression parser from `Parse.fs` and the compiler `scomp` (from expressions to stack machine instructions) and the associated datatypes from `Expr.fs`, to define a function `compString : string -> sinstr list` that parses a string as an expression and compiles it to stack machine code.

Exercise 3.7 Extend the expression language abstract syntax and the lexer and parser specifications with conditional expressions. The abstract syntax should be `If(e1, e2, e3)`, so modify file `Absyn.fs` as well as `ExprLex.fsl` and file `ExprPar.fsy`. The concrete syntax may be the keyword-laden F#/ML-style:

```
if e1 then e2 else e3
```

or the more light-weight C/C++/Java/C#-style:

```
e1 ? e2 : e3
```

Some documentation for `fslex` and `fsyacc` is found in this chapter and in *Expert F#* [17].

Exercise 3.8 Consider the parser generated from `ExprPar.fsy`, and determine what steps are taken during the parsing of this string:

```
let z = (17) in z + 2 * 3 end EOF
```

For each step, show the remaining input, the parse stack, and the action (shift, reduce, or goto) performed. You will need a printout of the parser states and their transitions in `ExprPar.fsyacc.output` to do this exercise. Sanity check: the sequence of reduce action rule numbers in the parse should be the exact reverse of that found in the derivation in Exercise 3.3.

Exercise 3.9 Files in the subdirectory `Usql/` contain abstract syntax abstract syntax (file `Absyn.fs`), an informal grammar (file `grammar.txt`), a lexer specification (`UsqlLex.fsl`) and a parser specification (`UsqlPar.fsy`) for micro-SQL, a small subset of the SQL database query language.

Extend micro-SQL to cover a larger class of SQL SELECT statements. Look at the examples below and decide your level of ambition. You should not need to modify file `Parse.fs`. Don't forget to write some examples in concrete syntax to show that your parser can parse them.

For instance, to permit an optional WHERE clause, you may add one more components to the `Select` constructor:

```
type stmt =
| Select of expr list          (* fields are expressions *)
           * string list        (* FROM ...               *)
           * expr option        (* optional WHERE clause   *)
```

so that SELECT...FROM...WHERE... gives `Select(..., ..., SOME ...)`, and SELECT...FROM... gives `Select(..., ..., NONE)`.

The argument to WHERE is just an expression (which is likely to involve a comparison), as in these examples:

```
SELECT name, zip FROM Person WHERE income > 200000
```

```
SELECT name, income FROM Person WHERE zip = 2300
```

```
SELECT name, town FROM Person, Zip WHERE Person.zip = Zip.zip
```

More ambitiously, you may add optional GROUP BY and ORDER BY clauses in a similar way. The arguments to these are lists of column names, as in this example:

```
SELECT town, profession, AVG(income) FROM Person, Zip
WHERE Person.zip = Zip.zip
GROUP BY town, profession
ORDER BY town, profession
```

References

1. Aho, A.V., Hopcroft, J.E., Ullman, J.D.: The Design and Analysis of Computer Algorithms. Addison-Wesley (1974)
2. Aho, A., Lam, M., Sethi, R., Ullman, J.: Compilers: Principles, Techniques and Tools, second edn. Addison-Wesley (2006)
3. Burge, W.: Recursive Programming Techniques. Addison-Wesley (1975)
4. Ford, B.: Packrat parsing: Simple, powerful, lazy, linear time. In: International Conference on Functional Programming, Pittsburgh, Pennsylvania, pp. 36–47. ACM Press (2002)
5. Ford, B.: Parsing expression grammars: A recognition-based syntactic foundation. In: Principles of Programming Languages, Venice, Italy, pp. 111–122. ACM Press (2004)
6. Hopcroft, J.E., Ullman, J.D.: Introduction to Automata Theory, Languages, and Computation. Addison-Wesley (1979)
7. Hutton, G.: Higher-order functions for parsing. J. Funct. Program. 2, 323–343 (1992). At http://www.cs.nott.ac.uk/~gmh/parsing.pdf
8. Java compiler compiler (JavaCC). At https://javacc.org/
9. Johnson, S.C.: Yacc — yet another compiler-compiler. Computing Science Technical Report 32, Bell Laboratories (1975)
10. Knuth, D.E.: On the translation of languages from left to right. Inf. Control 8, 607–639 (1965)
11. Lesk, M.E.: Lex — a lexical analyzer generator. Computing Science Technical Report 39, Bell Laboratories (1975)
12. Mogensen, T.: Introduction to Compiler Design. Springer (2011)
13. Paulson, L.: ML for the Working Programmer, second edn. Cambridge University Press (1996)
14. Rabin, M.O., Scott, D.: Finite automata and their decision problems. IBM J. Res. Dev. 3, 114–125 (1959)
15. Scott, E., Johnstone, A.: GLL parsing. Electron. Notes Theor. Comput. Sci. 253, 177–189 (2010)
16. Sestoft, P.: Grammars and parsing with Java. Tech. rep., KVL (1999). At http://www.itu.dk/people/sestoft/programmering/parsernotes.pdf
17. Syme, D., Granicz, A., Cisternino, A.: Expert F#. Apress (2007)
18. Tolksdorf, S.: Fparsec. a parser combinator library for F#. Homepage. At http://www.quanttec.com/fparsec/

Chapter 4
A First-Order Functional Language

This chapter presents a functional language micro-ML, a small subset of ML or F#. A *functional programming language* is one in which the evaluation of expressions and function calls is the primary means of computation. A *pure* functional language is one in which expressions cannot have side effects, such as changing the value of variables, or printing to the console. The micro-ML language is *first-order*, which means that functions cannot be used as values. Chapter 5 presents a higher-order functional language, in which functions *can* be used as values as in ML and F#.

4.1 Files for This Chapter

File	Contents
Fun/Absyn.sml	the abstract syntax (see Fig. 4.1)
Fun/grammar.txt	an informal grammar
Fun/FunLex.fsl	lexer specification
Fun/FunPar.fsy	parser specification
Fun/Parse.fs	combining lexer and parser
Fun/Fun.fs	interpreter `eval` for first-order `expr`
Fun/ParseAndRun.fs	load both parser and interpreter
TypedFun/TypedFun.fs	an explicitly typed `expr`, and its type checker

© Springer International Publishing AG 2017
P. Sestoft, *Programming Language Concepts*, Undergraduate Topics
in Computer Science, DOI 10.1007/978-3-319-60789-4_4

4.2   Examples and Abstract Syntax

Our first-order functional language extends the simple expression language of
Chapter 1 with if-then-else expressions, function bindings, and function calls. A
program is just an expression, but let-bindings may define functions as well as ordinary variables. Here are some example programs:

```
z + 8

let f x = x + 7 in f 2 end

let f x = let g y = x + y in g (2 * x) end
in f 7 end

let f x = if x=0 then 1 else 2 * f(x-1) in f y end
```

The first program is simply an expression. The program's input is provided through
its free variable z (see Sect. 2.3.3), and its output is the result of the expression. The
second program declares a function and calls it; the third one declares a function
f that declares another function g; and the last one declares a recursive function
that computes 2^y where y is a free variable. Note that in the third example, the first
occurrence of variable x is free relative to g, but bound in f.

For simplicity, functions can take only one argument. The abstract syntax for the
language is shown in Fig. 4.1.

The first two example programs would look like this in abstract syntax:

```
Prim("+", Var "z", CstI 8)

Letfun("f", "x", Prim("+", Var "x", CstI 7),
               Call(Var "f", CstI 2))
```

The components of a function binding Letfun (f, x, fBody, letBody) in
Fig. 4.1 have the following meaning, as in the concrete syntax let f x = fBody
in letBody end:

f	is the function name
x	is the parameter name
fBody	is the function body, or function right-hand side
letBody	is the let-body

The language is supposed to be first-order, but actually the abstract syntax in Fig. 4.1
allows the function f in a function call f(e) to be an arbitrary expression. In
this chapter we restrict the language to be first-order by requiring f in f(e) to be
a function name. In abstract syntax, this means that in a function call Call(e,
earg), the function expression e must be a name. So for now, all function calls
must have the form Call(Var f, earg), where f is a function name, as in the
example above.

```
type expr =
   | CstI of int
   | CstB of bool
   | Var of string
   | Let of string * expr * expr
   | Prim of string * expr * expr
   | If of expr * expr * expr
   | Letfun of string * string * expr * expr
               (* (f,        x,        fBody, letBody) *)
   | Call of expr * expr
```

Fig. 4.1 Abstract syntax of a small functional language

In Sect. 4.5 we shall show how to interpret this language (without an explicit evaluation stack) using an environment `env` that maps variable names to integers and function names to function closures.

4.3   Run-Time Values: Integers and Closures

A function closure is a tuple (`f`, `x`, `fbody`, `fDeclEnv`) consisting of the name of the function, the name of the function's parameter, the function's body expression, and the function's declaration environment. The latter is needed because a function declaration may have free variables. For instance, `x` is free in the declaration of function `g` above (but `y` is not free, because it is bound as a parameter to `g`). Thus the closures created for `f` and `g` above would be

```
("f", "x", "let g y = x + y in g (2 * x) end", [])
```

and

```
("g", "y", "x + y", [("x", 7)])
```

The name of the function is included in the closure to allow the function to call itself recursively.

In the `eval` interpreter in file `Fun.fs`, a recursive closure is a value

```
Closure(f, x, fBody, fDeclEnv)
```

where `f` is the function name, `x` is the parameter name, `fBody` is the function body, and `fDeclEnv` is the environment in which the function was declared: this is the environment in which `fBody` should be evaluated when `f` is called.

Since we do not really distinguish variable names from function names, the interpreter will use the same environment for both variables and functions. The environment maps a name (a string) to a value, which may be either an integer or a function closure, which in turn contains an environment. So we get a recursive definition of the `value` type:

```
type 'v env = (string * 'v) list;;

let rec lookup env x =
    match env with
    | []              -> failwith (x + " not found")
    | (y, v)::r -> if x=y then v else lookup r x;;

let emptyEnv = [];;
```

Fig. 4.2 A simple implementation of environments

```
type value =
  | Int of int
  | Closure of string * string * expr * value env
```

A value env is an environment that maps a name (a string) to a corresponding value; see Sect. 4.4.

4.4   A Simple Environment Implementation

When implementing interpreters and type checkers, we shall use a simple environment representation: a list of pairs, where each pair (k, d) contains a key k which is a name, in the form of a string, and some data d. The pair says that name k maps to data d. We make the environment type 'v env polymorphic in the type 'v of the data, as shown in Fig. 4.2.

For example, a run-time environment mapping variable names to values will have type value env (where type value was defined in Sect. 4.3 above), whereas a type checking environment mapping variable names to types will have type typ env (where type typ will be defined later in Sect. 4.8).

The value [] represents the empty environment.

The call lookup env x looks up name x in environment env and returns the data associated with x. The function has type 'a env -> string -> 'a.

The expression (x, v) :: env creates a new environment which is env extended with a binding of x to v.

4.5   Evaluating the Functional Language

Evaluation of programs (expressions) in the first-order functional language is a simple extension of evaluation the expression language from Chap. 2.

The interpreter (file Fun.fs) uses integers to represent numbers as well as logical values, where 0 represents false and 1 represents true. A variable x is looked up in the run-time environment, and its value must be an integer (not a function closure). Primitives are evaluated by evaluating the arguments, and then evaluating the primitive operation. Let-bindings are evaluated by evaluating the right-hand side in the old environment, extending the environment, and then evaluating the body of the let:

```
let rec eval (e : expr) (env : value env) : int =
    match e with
    | CstI i -> i
    | CstB b -> if b then 1 else 0
    | Var x   ->
      match lookup env x with
      | Int i -> i
      | _        -> failwith "eval Var"
    | Prim(ope, e1, e2) ->
      let i1 = eval e1 env
      let i2 = eval e2 env
      match ope with
      | "*" -> i1 * i2
      | "+" -> i1 + i2
      | "-" -> i1 - i2
      | "=" -> if i1 = i2 then 1 else 0
      | "<" -> if i1 < i2 then 1 else 0
      | _   -> failwith ("unknown primitive " + ope)
    | Let(x, eRhs, letBody) ->
      let xVal = Int(eval eRhs env)
      let bodyEnv = (x, xVal) :: env
      eval letBody bodyEnv
    | ...
```

All of this is as in the expression language. Now let us consider the cases that differ from the expression language, namely conditionals, function bindings, and function application:

```
let rec eval (e : expr) (env : value env) : int =
    match e with
    | ...
    | If(e1, e2, e3) ->
      let b = eval e1 env
      if b<>0 then eval e2 env
      else eval e3 env
    | Letfun(f, x, fBody, letBody) ->
      let bodyEnv = (f, Closure(f, x, fBody, env)) :: env
      eval letBody bodyEnv
    | Call(Var f, eArg) ->
      let fClosure = lookup env f
      match fClosure with
      | Closure (f, x, fBody, fDeclEnv) ->
        let xVal = Int(eval eArg env)
```

```
    let fBodyEnv = (x, xVal) :: (f, fClosure) :: fDeclEnv
    eval fBody fBodyEnv
  | _ -> failwith "eval Call: not a function"
| Call _ -> failwith "eval Call: not first-order function"
```

A conditional expression If(e1, e2, e3) is evaluated by first evaluating e1. If the result is true (not zero), then evaluate e2, otherwise evaluate e3.

A function binding Letfun(f, x, fBody, letBody) is evaluated by creating a function closure Closure(f, x, fBody, env) and binding that to f. Then letBody is evaluated in the extended environment.

A function call Call(Var f, eArg) is evaluated by first checking that f is bound to a function closure Closure (f, x, fBody, fDeclEnv). Then the argument expression eArg is evaluated to obtain an argument value xVal. A new environment fBodyEnv is created by extending the function's declaration environment fDeclEnv with a binding of f to the function closure and a binding of x to xVal. Finally, the function's body fBody is evaluated in this new environment.

4.6   Evaluation Rules for Micro-ML

Instead of presenting the evaluation of micro-ML using F# functions, one may use so-called *structural operational semantics* [17] or *natural semantics* [6].

Such a presentation uses evaluation rules as shown in Fig. 4.3. A rule, such as (e4), consists of zero or more premises (above the line), a horizontal line, and one conclusion (below the line). The rule says that if all premises hold, then the conclusion holds too.

Each conclusion, and most of the premises, consists of a *judgement* $\rho \vdash e \Rightarrow v$ that says: within environment ρ, evaluation of expression e terminates and produces value v. The Greek letter ρ (pronounced "rho") represents a value environment, where $\rho = [x_1 \mapsto v_1, \ldots, x_n \mapsto v_n]$ means that variable name x_1 has value v_1, and so on. The notation $\rho[x \mapsto v]$ means the environment ρ extended with a binding of x to value v.

In the figure, i is an integer, b a boolean, x a variable, and $e, e_1, \ldots$ are expressions. Let us explain the meaning of each rule in Fig. 4.3:

- Rule (e1) says that an integer constant i evaluates to the integer i.
- Rule (e2) says that a boolean constant b evaluates to the boolean value b.
- Rule (e3) says that a variable x evaluates to the value $\rho(x)$ that it has in the current environment ρ.
- Rule (e4) says that the expression $(e_1 + e_2)$ is evaluated by evaluating e_1 and e_2 separately, then adding the results. The same holds for other arithmetic expressions.
- Rule (e5) is similar, but describes comparison operations such as $(e_1 < e_2)$.
- Rule (e6) says that to evaluate a let-binding, one must evaluate the right-hand side e_r in the given environment ρ to a value v_r, then extend the environment

$$\frac{}{\rho \vdash i \Rightarrow i}\ (e1)$$

$$\frac{}{\rho \vdash b \Rightarrow b}\ (e2)$$

$$\frac{\rho(x) = v}{\rho \vdash x \Rightarrow v}\ (e3)$$

$$\frac{\rho \vdash e_1 \Rightarrow v_1 \qquad \rho \vdash e_2 \Rightarrow v_2 \qquad v = v_1 + v_2}{\rho \vdash e_1 + e_2 \Rightarrow v}\ (e4)$$

$$\frac{\rho \vdash e_1 \Rightarrow v_1 \qquad \rho \vdash e_2 \Rightarrow v_2 \qquad b = (v_1 < v_2)}{\rho \vdash e_1 < e_2 \Rightarrow b}\ (e5)$$

$$\frac{\rho \vdash e_r \Rightarrow v_r \qquad \rho[x \mapsto v_r] \vdash e_b \Rightarrow v}{\rho \vdash \texttt{let } x = e_r \texttt{ in } e_b \texttt{ end} \Rightarrow v}\ (e6)$$

$$\frac{\rho \vdash e_1 \Rightarrow \texttt{true} \qquad \rho \vdash e_2 \Rightarrow v}{\rho \vdash \texttt{if } e_1 \texttt{ then } e_2 \texttt{ else } e_3 \Rightarrow v}\ (e7t)$$

$$\frac{\rho \vdash e_1 \Rightarrow \texttt{false} \qquad \rho \vdash e_3 \Rightarrow v}{\rho \vdash \texttt{if } e_1 \texttt{ then } e_2 \texttt{ else } e_3 \Rightarrow v}\ (e7f)$$

$$\frac{\rho[f \mapsto (f,x,e_r,\rho)] \vdash e_b \Rightarrow v}{\rho \vdash \texttt{let } f\ (x) = e_r \texttt{ in } e_b \texttt{ end} \Rightarrow v}\ (e8)$$

$$\frac{\rho(f) = (f,x,e_r,\rho_{fdecl}) \qquad \rho \vdash e \Rightarrow v_x \qquad \rho_{fdecl}[x \mapsto v_x, f \mapsto (f,x,e_r,\rho_{fdecl})] \vdash e_r \Rightarrow v}{\rho \vdash f\ e \Rightarrow v}\ (e9)$$

Fig. 4.3 Evaluation rules for a first-order functional language

so that it binds variable x to value v_r, then evaluate the body e_b in that extended environment.

- Rules (e7t) and (e7f) describe the evaluation of a conditional expression, and describe that exactly one of the branches e_2 and e_3 need to be evaluated; which one depends on the value of the condition e_1.
- Rule (e8) says that a definition of function f will extend the given environment with a binding of the name f to a closure (f, x, e_r, ρ), then evaluate the let-binding's body e_b in that extended environment. Note that the environment ρ in which f is declared is part of the closure.
- Rule (e9) says that to evaluate a function call $f(e)$, first of all the given environment must contain a binding of the function name f to a closure $(f, x, e_r, \rho_{fdecl})$, where ρ_{fdecl} is the declaration environment of f. The argument expression e is evaluated in the given environment ρ to an argument value v_x. Then the declaration environment ρ_{fdecl} is extended with a binding of the parameter x to the argument value v_x, and a binding of f to its closure, and then the body e_b of f is evaluated in this extended environment.

These rules correspond precisely to the interpreter `eval` in Sect. 4.5. The conclusion of a rule is an evaluation judgement $\rho \vdash e \Rightarrow v$, where the environment ρ corresponds to the `env` parameter and the expression e corresponds to the `e` parameter of the

$$\cfrac{\cfrac{}{\rho \vdash 1 \Rightarrow 1}\ (e1) \qquad \cfrac{\cfrac{\rho[\mathtt{x} \mapsto 1](\mathtt{x}) = 1}{\rho[\mathtt{x} \mapsto 1] \vdash \mathtt{x} \Rightarrow 1}\ (e3) \qquad \cfrac{}{\rho[\mathtt{x} \mapsto 1] \vdash 2 \Rightarrow 2}\ (e1)}{\cfrac{\rho[\mathtt{x} \mapsto 1] \vdash \mathtt{x} < 2 \Rightarrow \mathtt{true}}{}}\ (e5)}{\rho \vdash \mathtt{let\ x} = 1\ \mathtt{in\ x} < 2\ \mathtt{end} \Rightarrow \mathtt{true}}\ (e6)$$

Fig. 4.4 Evaluation of `let x = 1 in x < 2 end` to true

$$\cfrac{\cfrac{\cfrac{}{\rho \vdash 1 \Rightarrow 1} \quad \cfrac{}{\rho \vdash 2 \Rightarrow 2}}{\rho \vdash 1 < 2 \Rightarrow \mathtt{true}}\ (e5) \qquad \cfrac{\cfrac{\rho'(\mathtt{z}) = \mathtt{true}}{\rho' \vdash \mathtt{z} \Rightarrow \mathtt{true}}\ (t3) \qquad \cfrac{}{\rho' \vdash 3 \Rightarrow 3}}{\rho[\mathtt{z} \mapsto \mathtt{true}] \vdash \mathtt{if\ z\ then\ 3\ else\ 4\ end} \Rightarrow 3}\ (e7t)}{\rho \vdash \mathtt{let\ z} = (1 < 2)\ \mathtt{in\ if\ z\ then\ 3\ else\ 4\ end} \Rightarrow 3}\ (e6)$$

Fig. 4.5 Evaluation of `let z = (1 < 2) in if z then 3 else 4 end` to 3. For brevity we write ρ' for the environment $\rho[\mathtt{z} \mapsto \mathtt{true}]$

`eval` function, and v is the value returned by the `eval` function. Each premise that involves an evaluation judgement such as $\rho \vdash e_1 \Rightarrow v_1$ corresponds exactly to a recursive function call in `eval`.

More precisely, rule (e1) corresponds to the `CstI` case in `eval`, rule (e2) to the `CstB` case, rule (e3) to the `Var` case, rules (e4) and (e5) to the `Prim` case, and rule (e6) to the `Let` case. Rules (e7t) and (e7f) correspond to the `If` case, rule (e8) to the `Letfun` case, and rule (e9) to the `Call` case.

Evaluation rules such as those in Fig. 4.3 may be used to build an evaluation tree. At the root (bottom) of the tree we find the conclusion, a judgement about the value v of some expression e. At the leaves (top) we find instances of rules that do not have premises. Internally in the tree we find nodes (branching points) that are instances of rules that do have premises.

As an illustration of this idea, consider the evaluation tree in Fig. 4.4. It shows that the expression `let x = 1 in x<2 end` evaluates to `false`. It uses rule (e1) for constants twice, rule (e3) for variables once, rule (e5) for comparisons once, and rule (e6) for let-binding once.

As another illustration, the tree in Fig. 4.5 shows that expression `let z = (1<2) in if z then 3 else 4 end` evaluates to 3. The evaluation tree is actually the call tree of the `eval` function when evaluating the expression in the conclusion of the tree.

4.7 Static Scope and Dynamic Scope

The language implemented by the interpreter (`eval` function) in Sect. 4.5 and by the evaluation rules in Sect. 4.6 has *static scope*, also called *lexical scope*. Static scope means that a variable occurrence refers to the (statically) *innermost enclosing* binding of a variable of that name. Thus one can decide, given just the program text, which binding a given variable occurrence refers to.

With static scope, the occurrence of y inside f refers to the binding y = 11 in this example, which must therefore evaluate to $3 + 11 = 14$:

```
let y = 11
in let f x = x + y
   in let y = 22
      in f 3
      end
   end
end
```

An alternative is *dynamic scope*. With dynamic scope, a variable occurrence refers to the (dynamically) *most recent* binding of a variable of that name. In the above example, when f is called, the occurrence of y inside f would refer to the second let-binding of y, which encloses the call to f, and the example would evaluate to $3 + 22 = 25$.

It is easy to modify the interpreter eval from Sect. 4.5 to implement dynamic scope. In a function call, the called function's body should simply be evaluated in an environment fBodyEnv that is built not from the environment fDeclEnv in the function's closure, but from the environment env in force when the function is called. Hence the only change is in the definition of fBodyEnv below:

```
let rec eval (e : expr) (env : value env) : int =
    match e with
    | ...
    | Call(Var f, eArg) ->
      let fClosure = lookup env f
      match fClosure with
      | Closure (f, x, fBody, fDeclEnv) ->
        let xVal = Int(eval eArg env)
        let fBodyEnv = (x, xVal) :: env          // CHANGE!
        eval fBody fBodyEnv
      | _ -> failwith "eval Call: not a function"
    | ...
```

There are two noteworthy points here. First, since env already contains the binding of f to its closure (unlike fDeclEnv), there is no need to re-bind f when creating fBodyEnv. Secondly, the fDeclEnv is not used any longer, and could be left out of the closure.

For these reasons, dynamic scope is easier to implement, and that may be the reason that the original version of the Lisp programming language (1960), as well as most scripting languages, use dynamic scope. But dynamic scope makes type checking and high-performance implementation difficult, and allows for very obscure programming mistakes and poor encapsulation, so almost all modern programming languages use static scope. The Perl language has both statically and dynamically scoped variables, declared using the somewhat misleading keywords my and `local`, respectively.

4.8 Type-Checking an Explicitly Typed Language

In this section we extend our first-order functional language with explicit types on function declarations, describing the types of function parameters and function results (as we are used to in Java, C#, ANSI C, C++, Ada, Pascal and so on).

We need a (meta-language) type `typ` of object-language types. The types are `int` and `bool` (and function types, for use in Chap. 5 when type checking a higher-order functional language):

```
type typ =
  | TypI                     (* int                          *)
  | TypB                     (* bool                         *)
  | TypF of typ * typ        (* (argumenttype, resulttype) *)
```

The abstract syntax of the explicitly typed functional language is shown in Fig. 4.6. The only difference from the untyped syntax in Fig. 4.1 is that types have been added to Letfun bindings (file `TypedFun.fs`).

A type checker for this language maintains a type environment of type `typ env` that maps bound variables and function names to their types. The type checker function `typ` analyses the given expression and returns its type. For constants it simply returns the type of the constant. For variables, it uses the type environment:

```
let rec typ (e : tyexpr) (env : typ env) : typ =
    match e with
    | CstI i -> TypI
    | CstB b -> TypB
    | Var x  -> lookup env x
    | ...
```

```
type tyexpr =
  | CstI of int
  | CstB of bool
  | Var of string
  | Let of string * tyexpr * tyexpr
  | Prim of string * tyexpr * tyexpr
  | If of tyexpr * tyexpr * tyexpr
  | Letfun of string * string * typ * tyexpr * typ * tyexpr
          (* (f,        x,       xTyp, fBody,  rTyp, letBody *)
  | Call of tyexpr * tyexpr
```

Fig. 4.6 Abstract syntax for explicitly typed function language

For a primitive operator such as addition (+) or less than (<) or logical and (&), and so on, the type checker recursively finds the types of the arguments, checks that they are as expected and then returns the type of the expression — or throws an exception if they are not:

```
let rec typ (e : tyexpr) (env : typ env) : typ =
    match e with
    | ...
    | Prim(ope, e1, e2) ->
      let t1 = typ e1 env
      let t2 = typ e2 env
      match (ope, t1, t2) with
      | ("*", TypI, TypI) -> TypI
      | ("+", TypI, TypI) -> TypI
      | ("-", TypI, TypI) -> TypI
      | ("=", TypI, TypI) -> TypB
      | ("<", TypI, TypI) -> TypB
      | ("&", TypB, TypB) -> TypB
      | _     -> failwith "unknown op, or type error"
    | ...
```

For a let-binding

```
let x = eRhs in letBody end
```

the type checker recursively finds the type xTyp of the right-hand side eRhs, binds x to xTyp in the type environment, and then finds the type of the letBody; the result is the type of the entire let-expression:

```
let rec typ (e : tyexpr) (env : typ env) : typ =
    match e with
    | ...
    | Let(x, eRhs, letBody) ->
      let xTyp = typ eRhs env
      let letBodyEnv = (x, xTyp) :: env
      typ letBody letBodyEnv
    | ...
```

For an explicitly typed function declaration

```
let f (x : xTyp) = fBody : rTyp in letBody end
```

the type checker recursively finds the type of the function body fBody under the assumption that x has type xTyp and f has type xTyp -> rTyp, and checks that the type it found for f's body is actually rTyp. Then it finds the type of letBody under the assumption that f has type xTyp -> rTyp:

```
let rec typ (e : tyexpr) (env : typ env) : typ =
    match e with
    | ...
```

```
| Letfun(f, x, xTyp, fBody, rTyp, letBody) ->
  let fTyp = TypF(xTyp, rTyp)
  let fBodyEnv = (x, xTyp) :: (f, fTyp) :: env
  let letBodyEnv = (f, fTyp) :: env
  if typ fBody fBodyEnv = rTyp
  then typ letBody letBodyEnv
  else failwith ("Letfun: return type in " + f)
| ...
```

For a function call

```
f eArg
```

the type checker first looks up the declared type of f, which must be a function type of form xTyp -> rTyp. Then it recursively finds the type of eArg and checks that it equals f's parameter type xTyp. If so, the type of the function call is f's result type rTyp:

```
let rec typ (e : tyexpr) (env : typ env) : typ =
    match e with
    | ...
    | Call(Var f, eArg) ->
      match lookup env f with
      | TypF(xTyp, rTyp) ->
        if typ eArg env = xTyp then rTyp
        else failwith "Call: wrong argument type"
      | _ -> failwith "Call: unknown function"
    | ...
```

This approach suffices because function declarations are explicitly typed: there is no need to guess the type of function parameters or function results. We shall see later in Chap. 6 that one can in fact systematically "guess" and then verify types, thus doing *type inference* as in ML, F# and recent versions of C#, rather than *type checking*.

4.9   Type Rules for Monomorphic Types

Just as expression evaluation can be described using rules (Sect. 4.6), expression type checking can be described using rules instead of the F# functions presented in Sect. 4.8. The rules use a type environment $\rho = [x_1 \mapsto t_1, \ldots, x_n \mapsto t_n]$ that maps variable names x to types t. By $\rho[x \mapsto t]$ we mean ρ extended with a binding of x to t. A *type judgement* $\rho \vdash e : t$ asserts that in type environment ρ, the expression e has type t. The type rules in Fig. 4.7 determine when one may conclude that expression e has type t in environment ρ. In the figure, i is an integer, b a boolean, x a variable, and $e, e_1, \ldots$ are expressions.

$$\frac{}{\rho \vdash i : \mathtt{int}} \ (t1)$$

$$\frac{}{\rho \vdash b : \mathtt{bool}} \ (t2)$$

$$\frac{\rho(x) = t}{\rho \vdash x : t} \ (t3)$$

$$\frac{\rho \vdash e_1 : \mathtt{int} \qquad \rho \vdash e_2 : \mathtt{int}}{\rho \vdash e_1 + e_2 : \mathtt{int}} \ (t4)$$

$$\frac{\rho \vdash e_1 : \mathtt{int} \qquad \rho \vdash e_2 : \mathtt{int}}{\rho \vdash e_1 < e_2 : \mathtt{bool}} \ (t5)$$

$$\frac{\rho \vdash e_r : t_r \qquad \rho[x \mapsto t_r] \vdash e_b : t}{\rho \vdash \mathtt{let}\ x = e_r\ \mathtt{in}\ e_b\ \mathtt{end}\ : t} \ (t6)$$

$$\frac{\rho \vdash e_1 : \mathtt{bool} \qquad \rho \vdash e_2 : t \qquad \rho \vdash e_3 : t}{\rho \vdash \mathtt{if}\ e_1\ \mathtt{then}\ e_2\ \mathtt{else}\ e_3 : t} \ (t7)$$

$$\frac{\rho[x \mapsto t_x, f \mapsto t_x \to t_r] \vdash e_r : t_r \qquad \rho[f \mapsto t_x \to t_r] \vdash e_b : t}{\rho \vdash \mathtt{let}\ f\ (x : t_x) = e_r : t_r\ \mathtt{in}\ e_b\ \mathtt{end}\ : t} \ (t8)$$

$$\frac{\rho(f) = t_x \to t_r \qquad \rho \vdash e : t_x}{\rho \vdash f\ e : t_r} \ (t9)$$

Fig. 4.7 Type rules for a first-order functional language

Just like the evaluation rules in Sect. 4.6, a type rule has a conclusion which is a judgement $\rho \vdash e : t$ about the type t of expression e. The rules may be explained and justified as follows:

- Rule (t1): An integer constant i, such as 0, 1, -1, ..., has type int.
- Rule (t2): A boolean constant b, such as true or false, has type bool.
- Rule (t3): A variable occurrence x has the type t of its binding. This type is given by the type environment ρ.
- Rule (t4): An addition expression $e_1 + e_2$ has type int provided e_1 has type int and e_2 has type int.
- Rule (t5): A comparison expression $e_1 < e_2$ has type bool provided e_1 has type int and e_2 has type int.
- Rule (t6): A let-binding let x = e_r in e_b end has the same type t as the body e_b. First find the type t_r of e_r, and then find the type t of e_b under the assumption that x has type t_r.
- Rule (t7): A conditional expression if e_1 then e_2 else e_3 has type t provided e_1 has type bool and e_2 has type t and e_3 has type t.
- Rule (t8): A function declaration let f $(x : t_x) = e_r : t_r$ in e_b end has the same type t as e_b. First check that e_r has type t_r under the assumption that x has type t_x and f has type $t_x \to t_r$. Then find the type t of e_b under the assumption that f has type $t_x \to t_r$.

$$\cfrac{\rho \vdash 1 : \text{int}}{} (t1) \quad \cfrac{\cfrac{\rho[x \mapsto \text{int}](x) = \text{int}}{\rho[x \mapsto \text{int}] \vdash x : \text{int}} (t3) \quad \cfrac{}{\rho[x \mapsto \text{int}] \vdash 2 : \text{int}} (t1)}{\rho[x \mapsto \text{int}] \vdash x < 2 : \text{bool}} (t5)$$
$$\cfrac{}{\rho \vdash \texttt{let x = 1 in x < 2 end} : \text{bool}} (t6)$$

Fig. 4.8 Type check for `let x = 1 in x < 2 end`

$$\cfrac{\cfrac{}{\rho \vdash 1 : \text{int}} \quad \cfrac{}{\rho \vdash 2 : \text{int}}}{\rho \vdash 1 < 2 : \text{bool}} (t5) \quad \cfrac{\cfrac{\rho'(z) = \text{bool}}{\rho' \vdash z : \text{bool}} (t3) \quad \cfrac{}{\rho' \vdash 3 : \text{int}} \quad \cfrac{}{\rho' \vdash 4 : \text{int}}}{\rho[z \mapsto \text{bool}] \vdash \texttt{if z then 3 else 4 end} : \text{int}} (t7)$$
$$\cfrac{}{\rho \vdash \texttt{let z = (1 < 2) in if z then 3 else 4 end} : \text{int}} (t6)$$

Fig. 4.9 Type check for `let z = (1 < 2) in if z then 3 else 4 end`. For brevity we write ρ' for the type environment $\rho[z \mapsto \text{bool}]$. In contrast to the evaluation tree in Fig. 4.5, which evaluates only one branch of the if-expression, here we type check both branches because we know only the type, not the value, of the condition z

- Rule (t9): A function application $f\ e$ has type t_r provided f has type $t_x \to t_r$ and e has type t_x.

Type rules such as those in Fig. 4.7 may be used to build a derivation tree; exactly as for the evaluation rules and evaluation trees in Sect. 4.6. At the root (bottom) of the tree we find the conclusion, a judgement about the type t of some expression e. At the leaves (top) we find instances of rules that do not have premises. Internally in the tree we find nodes (branching points) that are instances of rules that do have premises.

As an illustration of this idea, consider the tree in Fig. 4.8. It shows that the expression `let x = 1 in x<2 end` is well-typed and has type `bool`. It uses rule (t1) for constants twice, rule (t3) for variables once, rule (t5) for comparisons once, and rule (t6) for let-binding once.

As another illustration, the tree in Fig. 4.9 shows that expression `let z = (1<2) in if z then 3 else 4 end` is well-typed and has type `int`.

4.10   Static Typing and Dynamic Typing

Our original untyped functional language is not completely untyped. More precisely it is dynamically typed: it forbids certain monstrosities, such as adding a function and an integer. Hence this program is illegal, and its execution fails at run-time:

```
let f x = x+1 in f + 4 end
```

whereas this slightly odd program is perfectly valid in the original interpreter `Fun.eval`:

```
let f x = x+1 in if 1=1 then 3 else f + 4 end
```

It evaluates to 3 without any problems, because no attempt is made to evaluate the else-branch of the if-then-else expression.

By contrast, our typed functional language (abstract syntax type `tyexpr` in file `TypedFun.fs`) is statically typed: a program such as

```
if 1=1 then 3 else false+4
```

or, in `tyexpr` abstract syntax,

```
If(Prim("=", CstI 1, CstI 1),
   CstI 3,
   Prim("+", CstB false, CstI 4))
```

is ill-typed even though we never attempt to evaluate the addition `false+4`. Thus the type checker in a statically typed language may be overly pessimistic.

Even so, many languages are statically typed, for several reasons. First, type errors often reflect logic errors, so static (compile-time) type checking helps finding real bugs early. It is better and cheaper to detect and fix bugs at compile-time than at run-time, which may be after the program has been shipped to customers. Secondly, types provide reliable machine-checked documentation, to the human reader, about the intended and legal ways to use a variable or function. Finally, the more the compiler knows about the program, the better code can it generate. Types provide such information to the compiler, and advanced compilers use type information to generate target programs that are faster and use less memory.

Languages such as Lisp, Scheme, ECMAScript/Javascript [3], Perl, Postscript, Python and Ruby are dynamically typed. Although most parts of the Java and C# languages are statically typed, some are not. In particular, array element assignment and operations on pre-2004 non-generic collection classes require run-time checks.

4.10.1 Dynamic Typing in Java and C# Array Assignment

In Java and C#, assignment to an array element is dynamically typed when the array element type is a reference type. For instance, recall that the Java "wrapper" classes Integer and Double are subclasses of Number, where Integer, Double, and Number are built-in classes in Java. If we create an array whose element type is Integer, we can bind that to a variable `arrn` of type Number[]:

```
Integer[] arr = new Integer[16];
Number[] arrn = arr;
```

Note that `arr` and `arrn` refer to the same array, whose element type is Integer. Now one might believe (mistakenly), that when `arrn` has type Number[], one can store a value of any subtype of Number in `arrn`. But that would be wrong: if we could store a Double in `arrn`, then an access `arr[0]` to `arr` could return a Double object, which would be rather surprising, given that `arr` has type Integer[]. However, in general a variable `arrn` of type Number[] *might* refer to an array whose element type is Double, in which case we *can* store a Double object in the array. So the Java compiler should not refuse to compile such an assignment.

The end result is that the Java compiler will actually compile this assignment

```
arrn[0] = new Double(3.14);
```

without any complaints, but when it is executed, the run-time system checks that the element type of `arrn` is Double or a superclass of Double. In the above case it is not, and an ArrayStoreException is thrown.

Hence Java reference type array assignments are not statically typed, but dynamically typed. Array element assignment in C# works exactly as in Java.

4.10.2 *Dynamic Typing in Non-generic Collection Classes*

When we use pre-2004 non-generic collection classes, Java and C# provide no compile-time type safety:

```
LinkedList names = new LinkedList();
names.add(new Person("Kristen"));
names.add(new Person("Bjarne"));
names.add(new Integer(1998));        // Wrong; compiler accepts
names.add(new Person("Anders"));
...
Person p = (Person)names.get(2);     // Cast may fail at run-time
```

The elements of the LinkedList `names` are supposed to have class Person, but the Java compiler has no way of knowing that; it must assume that all elements are of class Person. This has two consequences: when storing something into the list, the compiler cannot detect mistakes (line 1); and when retrieving an element from the list, it must be checked *at run-time* that the element has the desired type (line 2).

Since Java version 5.0 and C# version 2.0, these languages support generic types and therefore can catch this kind of type errors at compile-time; see Sect. 6.5.

4.11 History and Literature

Functional, mostly expression-based, programming languages go back to Lisp [9, 10], invented by John McCarthy in 1960. Lisp is dynamically typed and has dynamic variable scope, but its main successor, Scheme [18] created by Gerald Sussman and Guy L. Steele in 1975, has static scope, which is much easier to implement efficiently, and more sensible. Guy Steele took part in the design of Java.

Like Lisp, Scheme is dynamically typed, but there are many subsequent statically typed functional languages, notably the languages in the ML family: ML [4] and Standard ML [11, 12] by Michael Gordon, Robin Milner, Christopher Wadsworth,

Mads Tofte, Bob Harper, and David MacQueen, and OCaml [8, 15] by Xavier Leroy and Damien Doligez.

Whereas these languages have so-called *strict* or *eager* evaluation – function arguments are evaluated before the function is called – another subfamily is made up of the so-called *non-strict* or *lazy* functional languages, including SASL and its successor Miranda [19] both developed by David Turner, Lazy ML [1, 5] developed by Lennart Augustsson and Thomas Johnsson, and Haskell [16] where driving forces are Simon Peyton Jones, John Hughes, Paul Hudak, and Phil Wadler. All the statically typed languages are statically scoped as well.

Probably the first publication about type checking in a compiler is Peter Naur's description [13] of the Algol 60 compilers developed at Regnecentralen in Copenhagen.

More general forms of static analysis or static checking have been studied under the name of data flow analysis [7], or control flow analysis, or abstract interpretation [2], and in much subsequent work. See Nielson, Nielson and Hankin [14] for much more information.

4.12 Exercises

The goal of these exercises is to understand the evaluation of a simple first-order functional language, and how explicit types can be stated and checked.

Exercise 4.1 Get archive `fun.zip` from the homepage and unpack to directory Fun. It contains lexer and parser specifications and interpreter for a small first-order functional language. Generate and compile the lexer and parser as described in `README.TXT`; parse and run some example programs with `ParseAndRun.fs`.

Exercise 4.2 Write more example programs in the functional language, and test them in the same way as in Exercise 4.1:

- Compute the sum of the numbers from 1000 down to 1. Do this by defining a function `sum n` that computes the sum $n + (n-1) + \cdots + 2 + 1$. (Use straightforward summation, no clever tricks).
- Compute the number 3^8, that is, 3 raised to the power 8. Again, use a recursive function.
- Compute $3^0 + 3^1 + \cdots + 3^{10} + 3^{11}$, using a recursive function (or two, if you prefer).
- Compute $1^8 + 2^8 + \cdots + 10^8$, again using a recursive function (or two).

Exercise 4.3 For simplicity, the current implementation of the functional language requires all functions to take exactly one argument. This seriously limits the programs that can be written in the language (at least it limits what that can be written without excessive cleverness and complications).

Modify the language to allow functions to take one or more arguments. Start by modifying the abstract syntax in `Absyn.fs` to permit a list of parameter names in `Letfun` and a list of argument expressions in `Call`.

Then modify the `eval` interpreter in file `Fun.fs` to work for the new abstract syntax. You must modify the closure representation to accommodate a list of parameters. Also, modify the `Letfun` and `Call` clauses of the interpreter. You will need a way to zip together a list of variable names and a list of variable values, to get an environment in the form of an association list; so function `List.zip` might be useful.

Exercise 4.4 In continuation of Exercise 4.3, modify the parser specification to accept a language where functions may take any (non-zero) number of arguments. The resulting parser should permit function declarations such as these:

```
let pow x n = if n=0 then 1 else x * pow x (n-1) in pow 3 8 end

let max2 a b = if a<b then b else a
in let max3 a b c = max2 a (max2 b c)
   in max3 25 6 62 end
end
```

You may want to define non-empty parameter lists and argument lists in analogy with the `Names1` nonterminal from `Usql/UsqlPar.fsy`, except that the parameters should not be separated by commas. Note that multi-argument applications such as `f a b` are already permitted by the existing grammar, but they would produce abstract syntax of the form `Call(Call(Var "f", Var "a"), Var "b")` which the `Fun.eval` function does not understand. You need to modify the AppExpr nonterminal and its semantic action to produce `Call(Var "f", [Var "a"; Var "b"])` instead.

Exercise 4.5 Extend the (untyped) functional language with infix operator "`&&`" meaning sequential logical "and" and infix operator "`||`" meaning sequential logical "or", as in C, C++, Java, C#, or F#. Note that `e1 && e2` can be encoded as `if e1 then e2 else false` and that `e1 || e2` can be encoded as `if e1 then true else e2`. Hence you need only change the lexer and parser specifications, and make the new rules in the parser specification generate the appropriate abstract syntax. You need not change `Absyn.fs` or `Fun.fs`.

Exercise 4.6 Extend the abstract syntax, the concrete syntax, and the interpreter for the untyped functional language to handle tuple constructors (. . .) and component selectors `#i` (where the first component is `#1`):

```
type expr =
  | ...
  | Tup of expr list
  | Sel of int * expr
  | ...
```

If we use the concrete syntax #2 (e) for Sel (2, e) and the concrete syntax (e1, e2) for Tup [e1; e2] then you should be able to write programs such as these:

```
let t = (1+2, false, 5>8)
in if #3(t) then #1(t) else 14 end
```

and

```
let max xy = if #1(xy) > #2(xy) then #1(xy) else #2(xy)
in max (3, 88) end
```

This permits functions to take multiple arguments and return multiple results.

To extend the interpreter correspondingly, you need to introduce a new kind of value, namely a tuple value TupV (vs), and to allow eval to return a result of type value (not just an integer):

```
type value =
  | Int of int
  | TupV of value list
  | Closure of string * string list * expr * value env

let rec eval (e : expr) (env : value env) : value = ...
```

Note that this requires some changes elsewhere in the eval interpreter. For instance, the primitive operations currently work because eval always returns an int, but with the suggested change, they will have to check (by pattern matching) that eval returns an Int i.

Exercise 4.7 Modify the abstract syntax tyexpr and the type checker functions typ and typeCheck in TypedFun/TypedFun.fs to allow functions to take any number of typed parameters.

This exercise is similar to Exercise 4.3, but concerns the typed language. The changes to the interpreter function eval are very similar to those in Exercise 4.3 and can be omitted; just delete the eval function.

Exercise 4.8 Add lists (CstN is the empty list [], ConC(e1,e2) is e1::e2), and list pattern matching expressions to the untyped functional language, where Match(e0, e1, (h,t, e2)) is match e0 with [] -> e1 | h::t -> e2.

```
type expr =
  | ...
  | CstN
  | ConC of expr * expr
  | Match of expr * expr * (string * string * expr)
  | ..
```

Exercise 4.9 Add type checking for lists. All elements of a list must have the same type. You'll need a new kind of type TypL of typ to represent the type TypL (t) of lists with elements of a given type t.

Exercise 4.10 Extend the functional language abstract syntax `expr` with mutually recursive function declarations, where a `fundef` tuple $(f, [x_1; \ldots; x_n], body)$ represents a function declaration $f(x_1, \ldots, x_n) = body$:

```
type expr =
    | ...
    | Letfun of fundef list * expr
    | ...
and fundef = string * string list * expr
```

Also, modify the `eval` function to correctly interpret such mutually recursive functions. This requires a change to the `vfenv` datatype because you need mutually recursive function environments.

Exercise 4.11 Write a whitebox test suite for the monomorphic type checker.

Exercise 4.12 Write a type checker for mutually recursive function declarations.

Exercise 4.13 Design a concrete syntax for the explicitly typed functional language, write lexer and parser specifications, and write some example programs in concrete syntax (including some that have type errors).

References

1. Augustsson, L.: A compiler for Lazy ML. In: 1984 ACM Symposium on Lisp and Functional Programming, Austin, Texas, pp. 218–227. ACM (1984)
2. Cousot, P., Cousot, R.: Abstract interpretation: A unified lattice model for static analysis of programs by construction or approximation of fixpoints. In: Fourth ACM Symposium on Principles on Programming Languages, Los Angeles, California, January 1977, pp. 238–252. ACM (1977)
3. Ecma International: ECMAScript language specification. Standard ECMA-262, 3rd edition. Ecma International (1999). At http://www.ecma-international.org/publications/standards/Ecma-262.htm
4. Gordon, M.J., Milner, R., Wadsworth, C.P.: Edinburgh LCF. Lecture Notes in Computer Science. Springer-Verlag, Berlin (1979)
5. Johnsson, T.: Efficient compilation of lazy evaluation. ACM SIGPLAN 1984 Symposium on Compiler Construction SIGPLAN Notices. **19**(6), 58–69 (1984)
6. Kahn, G.: Natural semantics. In: F. Brandenburg, G. Vidal-Naquet, M. Wirsing (eds.) STACS 87. 4th Annual Symposium on Theoretical Aspects of Computer Science, Passau, Germany (Lecture Notes in Computer Science, vol. 247), pp. 22–39. Springer-Verlag (1987)
7. Kam, J.B., Ullman, J.D.: Monotone data flow analysis frameworks. Acta Inf. **7**, 305–317 (1977)
8. Leroy, X.: The Zinc experiment: An economical implementation of the ML language. Rapport Technique 117, INRIA Rocquencourt, France (1990)
9. McCarthy, J.: Recursive functions of symbolic expressions. Commun. ACM **3**(4), 184–195 (1960)
10. McCarthy, J., et al.: Lisp 1.5 Programmer's Manual. MIT Press (1962)
11. Milner, R., Tofte, M., Harper, R.: The Definition of Standard ML. The MIT Press (1990)
12. Milner, R., Tofte, M., Harper, R., MacQueen, D.: The Definition of Standard ML (Revised). MIT Press (1997)

13. Naur, P.: Checking of operand types in ALGOL compilers. BIT **5**, 151–163 (1965)
14. Nielson, F., Nielson, H.R., Hankin, C.: Principles of Program Analysis, second edn. Springer (2005)
15. OCaml: Home page. At http://ocaml.org/
16. Peyton-Jones, S.: Haskell 98 Language and Libraries. The Revised Report. Cambridge University Press (2003)
17. Plotkin, G.D.: A structural approach to operational semantics. Tech. Rep. FN-19, DAIMI, Aarhus University, Denmark (1981)
18. Sussman, G.J., Steele, G.L.: Scheme: an interpreter for the extended lambda calculus. MIT AI Memo 349, Massachusetts Institute of Technology (1975)
19. Turner, D.A.: Miranda — a non-strict functional language with polymorphic types. In: J.P. Jouannaud (ed.) Functional Programming Languages and Computer Architecture, Nancy, France, September 1985. Lecture Notes in Computer Science, vol. 201, pp. 1–16. Springer-Verlag. (1985)

Chapter 5
Higher-Order Functions

A higher-order functional language is one in which a function may be used as a value, just like an integer or a boolean. That is, the value of a variable may be a function, and a function may take a function as argument and may return a function as a result.

5.1 Files for This Chapter

The abstract syntax of the higher-order functional language is the same as that of the first-order functional language; see Fig. 4.1. Also the concrete syntax, and hence the lexer and parser specifications, are the same as in Sect. 4.1. What is new in this chapter is an interpreter that permits higher-order functions.

File	Contents
Fun/HigherFun.fs	a higher-order evaluator for expr
Fun/ParseAndRunHigher.fs	parser and higher-order evaluator

5.2 Higher-Order Functions in F#

A hallmark of functional programming languages is the ability to treat functions as first-class values, just like integers and strings. Among other things, this means that a frequently used control structure, such as uniform transformation of the elements of a list, can be implemented as a *higher-order function*: a function that takes as argument (or returns) another function.

In F#, uniform transformation of a list's elements is called List.map; filtering to get those elements that satisfy a given predicate is called List.filter; and more general processing of a list is called List.foldBack. Definitions of these functions are shown in Sect. A.11.2. That section also shows that many list processing

© Springer International Publishing AG 2017
P. Sestoft, *Programming Language Concepts*, Undergraduate Topics
in Computer Science, DOI 10.1007/978-3-319-60789-4_5

functions, such as computing the sum of a of list of numbers, can be defined in terms
of the general `List.foldBack`, which encapsulates list pattern matching and
recursive calls.

Another simple but very convenient higher-order function in F# is the infix "pipe"
operator (x |> f) which simply computes f(x), that is, applies function f to
argument x. To see why it is useful, consider a computation where we process an
integer list xs by filtering out small elements, then square the remaining ones, then
compute their sum. This is quite easily expressed:

```
sum (map (fun x -> x*x) (filter (fun x -> x>10) xs))
```

However, this must be read backwards, from right to left and inside out: first `filter`,
then `map`, then `sum`. Using the pipe (|>) performs exactly the same computation,
but makes the three-stage processing much clearer, allowing us to read it from left
to right:

```
xs  |>  filter (fun x -> x>10)  |>  map (fun x -> x*x)  |>  sum
```

5.3   Higher-Order Functions in the Mainstream

A function closure (as in Sect. 4.3) is similar to a Java or C# object containing a
method: the object's fields bind the free variables of the method (function).

5.3.1   Higher-Order Functions in Java 5

To work with functions as values in Java, one may introduce an interface that describes
the type of the function, and then create a function as an instance of a class that
implements that interface. For example, the type of functions from int to int can
be described by this Java interface:

```
interface Int2Int {
  int invoke(int x);
}
```

A function of this type can be represented as an object of a class (typically an anonymous class) that implements the interface. Here is a definition and an application of
the function f that multiplies its argument by two, just like fun x -> 2*x in F#:

```
Int2Int f = new Int2Int() {
  public int invoke(int x) {
    return 2*x;
  }
};
int res = f.invoke(7);
```

Since Java 5, one can define generic interfaces to represent function types with various numbers of parameters, like this:

```
interface Func0<R> {
  public R invoke();
}
interface Func1<A1, R> {
  public R invoke(A1 x1);
}
interface Func2<A1, A2, R> {
  public R invoke(A1 x1, A2 x2);
}
```

A function from `int` to `boolean` can now be created as an anonymous inner class implementing `Func1<Integer,Boolean>`. This relies on Java 5's automatic boxing and unboxing to convert between primitive types and their boxed representations:

```
Func1<Integer,Boolean> p = new Func1<Integer,Boolean>() {
  public Boolean invoke(Integer x) { return x>10; }
};
```

Higher-order functions corresponding to F#'s `List.map` and `List.filter` and so on can be defined as generic Java methods. Note that to call a function, we must use its `invoke` method:

```
static <A,R> List<R> map(Func1<A,R> f, List<A> xs) {
  List<R> res = new ArrayList<R>();
  for (A x : xs)
    res.add(f.invoke(x));
  return res;
}
static <T> List<T> filter(Func1<T,Boolean> p, List<T> xs) {
  List<T> res = new ArrayList<T>();
  for (T x : xs)
    if (p.invoke(x))
      res.add(x);
  return res;
}
static <A,R> R fold(Func2<A,R,R> f, List<A> xs, R res) {
  for (A x : xs)
    res = f.invoke(x, res);
  return res;
}
```

With these definitions, the F# example from Sect. 5.2:

```
xs |> filter (fun x -> x>10) |> map (fun x -> x*x) |> sum
```

can be written in as a Java expression as follows:

```
fold(new Func2<Integer,Integer,Integer>()
    { public Integer invoke(Integer x,Integer r) {return x+r;} },
    map(new Func1<Integer,Integer>()                          ,
        { public Integer invoke(Integer x) {return x*x;} },
        filter(new Func1<Integer,Boolean>()
            { public Boolean invoke(Integer x) {return x>10;}},
            xs)),
    0);
```

This shows that it is rather cumbersome to use anonymous inner classes and generic interfaces to write anonymous functions and their types in Java. Also, some expected functional programming benefits, such as brevity and clarity are sorely absent.

5.3.2   Higher-Order Functions in Java 8

Since 2014 Java 8 and later versions support a considerably neater syntax for functional programming. For instance, the Java equivalents of the F# functions `fun x -> x*x` and `fun x -> x>10` look much the same, just without the `fun` keyword:

```
x -> x*x
x -> x>10
```

However, Java 8 function types are based on so-called functional interfaces and are still rather cumbersome to write. For instance, the types of the two anonymous functions above may be written Function<Integer,Integer> and Function<Integer, Boolean>. Moreover, the limitations of Java's run-time implementation of generics (Sect. 9.5) mean that just using the generic function interfaces such as Function<Integer,Integer> could lead to costly boxing of 32-bit `int` arguments to Integer objects. Since this would severely impact performance, the Java 8 libraries provide many primitive-type specialized versions of the generic functional interfaces [9, Sect. 23.3]. Hence the first function may also have type IntUnaryOperator, and the second one may have type Predicate<Integer> and IntFunction<Boolean> and Int-Predicate, where the latter is the preferred one: it avoids boxing of both argument and result values. The confusing proliferation of function interfaces may be avoided if some future version of the Java run-time system can specialize generic interfaces also to value type arguments.

Despite these complications with the type system, Java 8 successfully supports functional stream programming, using Java library classes such as Stream<T> and IntStream. For instance, the F# list processing pipeline shown at the end of Sect. 5.2 can be written like this in Java 8 when xs is an IntStream:

```
int result = xs.filter(x -> x>10).map(x -> x*x).sum();
```

Here `filter`, `map` and `sum` are methods on the IntStream interface. Note how well the object-oriented "dot notation" for method calls works when writing such pipelines. Experiments show that the implementation of such pipelines is extremely efficient. Moreover it parallelizes well on modern multicore hardware, and presumably that is the reason for introducing functional programming and higher-order functions in Java 8. High performance on modern computers require parallel programming, but imperative parallel programming is difficult and error-prone. On the other hand, stream processing for bulk data is easily parallelizable, provided all operations are functional and side effect free.

5.3.3 Higher-Order Functions in C#

In C#, a *delegate* created from an instance method is really a function closure: it encloses a reference to an object instance and hence to the object's fields, which may be free in the method. Recent versions of C# provide two different ways to write anonymous method expressions, corresponding to F#'s `fun x -> 2*x`, namely "delegate notation" and "lambda notation":

```
delegate(int x) { return 2*x; }    // Since C# 2.0, delegate
(int x) => 2*x                     // Since C# 3.0, lambda
x => 2*x                           // Same, implicitly typed
```

Higher-order functions are heavily used in C# since version 3.0, because the Linq (Language Integrated Query) syntax simply is "syntactic sugar" for calls to methods that take delegates as arguments. For instance, consider again the filter-square-sum processing of an integer list from Sect. 5.2. It can be expressed in C# by the following Linq query that filters the numbers in `xs`, squares them, and sums them:

```
(from x in xs where x>10 select x*x).Sum()
```

Although it looks very different from the F# version, it is simply a neater way to write a C# expression that passes lambda expressions to extension methods on the `IEnumerable<T>` interface:

```
xs.Where(x => x>10).Select(x => x*x).Sum()
```

Note in particular that the object-oriented "dot" operator `o.m()` here is very similar to the F# "pipe" operator (`x |> f`) presented in Sect. 5.2. In general, the "dot" operator performs virtual method calls, but precisely for extension methods (which are non-virtual) there is little difference between "dot" and "pipe".

Also, the Task Parallel Library in .NET 4.0 relies on expressing computations as anonymous functions. For instance, the `Parallel.For` method in the System.Threading namespace takes as argument a `from` value, a `to` value, and an `action` function, and applies the action to all the values of `from`, `from+1`, ..., `to-1` in some order, exploiting multiple processors if available:

```
For(100, 1000, i => { Console.Write(i + " "); });
```

5.3.4   Google MapReduce

The purpose of Google's MapReduce framework, developed by Dean and Ghemawat [3], is to efficiently and robustly perform "embarrassingly parallel" computations on very large (terabyte) datasets, using thousands of networked and possibly unreliable computers. MapReduce is yet another example of a higher-order framework, in which users write functions to specify the computations that the framework must carry out; the framework takes care of scheduling the execution of these computations. The name is inspired by Lisp's map and reduce functions, which correspond to F#'s List.map and List.fold functions. However, the Google MapReduce functions are somewhat more specialized than those general functions.

5.4   A Higher-Order Functional Language

It is straightforward to extend our first-order functional language from Chap. 4 to a higher-order one. The concrete and abstract syntaxes already allow the function part eFun in a call

```
Call(eFun, eArg)
```

to be an arbitrary expression; it need not be a function name.

In the interpreter eval in file HigherFun.fs one needs to accommodate the possibility that an expression evaluates to a function, and that a variable may be bound to a function, not just to an integer. A value of function type is a closure, as in the first-order language. Hence the possible values, and the variable environments, are described by these mutually recursive type declarations:

```
type value =
  | Int of int
  | Closure of string * string * expr * value env
```

where the four components of a closure are the function name, the function's parameter name, the function's body, and an environment binding the function's free variables at the point of declaration.

The only difference between the higher-order interpreter and the first-order one presented in Sect. 4.5 is in the handling of function calls. A call

```
Call(eFun, eArg)
```

is evaluated by evaluating eFun to Closure(f,x,fBody,fDeclEnv), that is, a closure; evaluating eArg to a value xVal; and then evaluating fBody in the environment obtained by extending fDeclEnv with a binding of x to xVal and of f to the closure. Here is the corresponding fragment of the eval function for the higher-order language:

```
let rec eval (e : expr) (env : value env) : value =
```

```
match e with
| ...
| Call(eFun, eArg) ->
  let fClosure = eval eFun env
  match fClosure with
  | Closure (f, x, fBody, fDeclEnv) ->
    let xVal = eval eArg env
    let fBodyEnv = (x, xVal) :: (f, fClosure) :: fDeclEnv
    in eval fBody fBodyEnv
  | _ -> failwith "eval Call: not a function";;
```

5.5   Eager and Lazy Evaluation

In a function call such as f (e), one may evaluate the argument expression e eagerly, to obtain a value v before evaluating the function body. That is what we are used to in Java, C#, F# and languages in the ML family.

Alternatively, one might evaluate e lazily, that is, postpone evaluation of e until we have seen that the value of e is really needed. If it is not needed, we never evaluate e. If it is, then we evaluate e and remember (cache) the result in case it will be needed again.

The distinction between eager and lazy evaluation makes a big difference in function such as this one:

```
let loop n = loop n
in let f x = 1
   in f (loop(2)) end
end
```

where the evaluation of loop(2) would never terminate. For this reason, the entire program would never terminate if we use eager evaluation as in F#. With lazy evaluation, however, we do not evaluate the expression loop(2) until we have found that f needs its value. And in fact f does not need it at all — because x does not appear in the body of f — so with lazy evaluation the above program would terminate with the result 1.

For a less artificial example, note that in an eager language a user cannot *define* a function that works like F#'s if-then-else expression. One might attempt to define it like this:

```
let myif b v1 v2 = if b then v1 else v2
```

but that is useless for defining recursive functions such as factorial:

```
let myif b v1 v2 = if b then v1 else v2
in let fac n = myif (n=0) 1 (n * fac(n-1))
   in fac 3 end
end
```

Eager evaluation of the third argument to `myif` would go into an infinite loop. Thus it is important that the built-in if-then-else construct is not eager.

Our small functional language is eager. That is because the interpreter (function `eval` in `Fun.fs`) evaluates the argument expressions of a function before evaluating the function body, and because the meta-language F# is strict. Most widely used programming languages (C, C++, Java, C#, Pascal, Ada, Lisp, Scheme, APL, ...) use eager evaluation. An exception is Algol 60, whose call-by-name parameter passing mechanism evaluates an argument only when needed (and reevaluates it every time it is needed).

Some modern functional languages, such as Haskell [4], have lazy evaluation. This provides for concise programs, extreme modularization, and very powerful and general functions, especially when working with lazy data structures. For instance, one may define an infinite list of the prime numbers, or an infinite tree of the possible moves in a two-player game (such as chess), and if properly done, this is quite efficient. Lazy languages require a rather different programming style than eager ones. They are studied primarily at Chalmers University (Gothenburg, Sweden), Yale University, University of Nottingham, and Microsoft Research Cambridge (where the main developers of GHC, the Glasgow Haskell Compiler, reside). All lazy languages are purely functional (no updatable variables, no direct input and output functions) because it is nearly impossible to understand side effects in combination with the hard-to-predict evaluation order of a lazy language.

One can implement lazy evaluation in a strict language by a combination of anonymous functions (to postpone evaluation of an expression) and side effects (to keep the value of the expression after it has been evaluated). Doing this manually is unwieldy, so some strict functional languages, including F#, provide more convenient syntax for lazy evaluation of particular expressions.

5.6   The Lambda Calculus

The lambda calculus is the simplest possible functional language, with only three syntactic constructs: variable, functions, and function applications. Yet every computable function can be encoded in the untyped lambda calculus. This is an interesting topic about which much can be said; here we give only the briefest introduction.

Anonymous functions such as F#'s

```
fun x -> 2 * x
```

are called lambda abstractions by theoreticians, and are written

$$\lambda x.2 * x$$

where the symbol λ is the Greek lowercase letter lambda. The lambda calculus is the prototypical functional language, invented by the logician Alonzo Church in the

1930s to analyse fundamental concepts of computability. The pure untyped lambda calculus allows just three kinds of expressions e:

Variables	x
Lambda abstractions	$\lambda x.e$
Applications	$e_1\,e_2$

The three kinds of expression are evaluated as follows:

- A variable x may be bound by an enclosing lambda abstraction, or may be free (unbound).
- A lambda abstraction ($\lambda x.e$) represents a function.
- A function application ($e_1\,e_2$) denotes the application of function e_1 to argument e_2. To evaluate the application (($\lambda x.e$) e_2) of a lambda abstraction ($\lambda x.e$) to an argument expression e_2, substitute the argument e_2 for x in e, and then evaluate the resulting expression. Substitution must be capture-avoiding as in Sect. 2.3.4.

Thus an abstract syntax for the pure untyped lambda calculus could look like this:

```
type lam =
  | Var of string
  | Lam of string * lam
  | App of lam * lam
```

This may seem to be a very restricted and rather useless language, but Church showed that the lambda calculus can compute precisely the same functions as Turing Machines (invented by the mathematician Alan Turing in the 1930s), and both formalism can compute precisely the same functions as an idealized computer with unbounded storage. Indeed, "computable" formally means "computable by the lambda calculus (or by a Turing Machine)". Everything that can be expressed in Java, F#, C#, ML, C++ or any other programming language can be expressed in the pure untyped lambda calculus as well.

In fact, it is fairly easy to encode numbers, lists, trees, arrays, objects, iteration, and recursion in the pure untyped lambda calculus. Recursion can be encoded using one of the so-called Y combinators. This is the recursion combinator for call-by-name evaluation:

$$Y = \lambda h.(\lambda x.h(x\ x))\ (\lambda x.h(x\ x))$$

This is a recursion operator for a call-by-value evaluation,

$$Y_v = \lambda h.(\lambda x.(\lambda a.h(x\ x)\ a))(\lambda x.(\lambda a.h(x\ x)\ a))$$

One can define a non-recursive variant of, say, the factorial function, and then make it recursive using the Y combinator:

$$fac' = \lambda fac.\lambda n.if\ n = 0\ then\ 1\ else\ n * fac(n-1)$$

then $fac = Y\ fac'$ since

$$
\begin{aligned}
& fac\ 2 \\
&= Y fac'\ 2 \\
&= (\lambda h.(\lambda x.h(x\ x))\ (\lambda x.h(x\ x)))\ fac'\ 2 \\
&= (\lambda x.fac'(x\ x))\ (\lambda x.fac'(x\ x))\ 2 \\
&= fac'((\lambda x.fac'(x\ x))\ (\lambda x.fac'(x\ x)))\ 2 \\
&= if\ 2 = 0\ then\ 1\ else\ 2 * (((\lambda x.fac'(x\ x))\ (\lambda x.fac'(x\ x)))\ (2-1)) \\
&= 2 * (((\lambda x.fac'(x\ x))\ (\lambda x.fac'(x\ x)))\ (2-1)) \\
&= 2 * (((\lambda x.fac'(x\ x))\ (\lambda x.fac'(x\ x)))1) \\
&= 2 * fac'\ ((\lambda x.fac'(x\ x))\ (\lambda x.fac'(x\ x)))\ 1 \\
&= 2 * (if\ 1 = 0\ then\ 1\ else\ 1 * ((\lambda x.fac'(x\ x))\ (\lambda x.fac'(x\ x)))\ (1-1)) \\
&= 2 * (1 * ((\lambda x.fac'(x\ x))\ (\lambda x.fac'(x\ x)))\ (1-1)) \\
&= 2 * (1 * ((\lambda x.fac'(x\ x))\ (\lambda x.fac'(x\ x)))\ 0) \\
&= 2 * (1 * fac'((\lambda x.fac'(x\ x))\ (\lambda x.fac'(x\ x)))\ 0) \\
&= 2 * (1 * (if\ 0 = 0\ then\ 1\ else\ 0 * ((\lambda x.fac'(x\ x))\ (\lambda x.fac'(x\ x)))\ (0-1))) \\
&= 2 * (1 * 1) \\
&= 2
\end{aligned}
$$

For the sake of illustration we here assumed that we can use arithmetic on integers in the lambda calculus, although this was not included in the syntax above.

But in fact, the natural numbers, or non-negative integers with addition, subtraction, multiplication, and test for zero, can be encoded as so-called Church numerals as follows, and also in a number of other ways:

zero	is	$\lambda f.\lambda x.x$
one	is	$\lambda f.\lambda x.fx$
two	is	$\lambda f.\lambda x.f(fx)$
three	is	$\lambda f.\lambda x.f(f(fx))$

and so on. Then successor (+1), addition and multiplication may be defined as follows:

succ	is	$\lambda m.\lambda f.\lambda x.f(mfx)$
add	is	$\lambda m.\lambda n.\lambda f.\lambda x.mf(nfx)$
mul	is	$\lambda m.\lambda n.\lambda f.\lambda x.m(nf)x$

Some of these encodings are possible only in the untyped lambda calculus, so the absence of (simple) type restrictions is important. In particular, the pure *simply typed* lambda calculus cannot encode unbounded iteration or recursion.

Several different evaluation strategies are possible for the untyped lambda calculus. To experiment with some encodings and evaluation strategies, you may try an online lambda calculus reducer [7].

5.7 History and Literature

Some references on the history of functional languages have been given already in Sect. 4.11, including a discussion of eager and lazy languages.

The lambda calculus was proposed the logician Alonzo Church in 1936 [2], long before there were programming languages that could be used to program electronic computers. The lambda calculus is routinely used in theoretical studies of programming languages, and there is a rich literature about it, not least Henk Barendregt's comprehensive monograph [1].

5.8 Exercises

The main goal of these exercises is to understand programming with higher-order functions in F# as well as Java/C#.

Exercises 5.1 and 5.3 are intended to illustrate the difference between F# and Java or C# programming style; the latter exercise uses higher-order functions. The exercises may look overwhelming, but that's mostly because of the amount of explanation. Do those exercises if you feel that you need to strengthen your functional programming skills.

Exercises 5.4 and 5.5 illustrate typical higher-order functions in F# and other ML-like languages.

Exercise 5.1 The purpose of this exercise is to contrast the F# and Java programming styles, especially as concerns the handling of lists of elements. The exercise asks you to write functions that merge two sorted lists of integers, creating a new sorted list that contains all the elements of the given lists.

(A) Implement an F# function

```
merge : int list * int list -> int list
```

that takes two sorted lists of integers and merges them into a sorted list of integers. For instance, merge ([3;5;12], [2;3;4;7]) should give [2;3;3;4;5;7;12].

(B) Implement a similar Java (or C#) method

```
static int[] merge(int[] xs, int[] ys)
```

that takes two sorted arrays of ints and merges them into a sorted array of ints. The
method should build a new array, and should not modify the given arrays. Two arrays
xs and ys of integers may be built like this:

```
int[] xs = { 3, 5, 12 };
int[] ys = { 2, 3, 4, 7 };
```

Exercise 5.2 This exercise is similar to Exercise 5.1 part (B), but here you must
merge two LinkedLists of Integers instead of arrays of ints. This turns out to be
rather cumbersome, at least if you try to use iterators to traverse the lists. Implement
a Java method

```
static LinkedList<Integer> merge(List<Integer> xs,
                                 List<Integer> ys) { ... }
```

that takes two sorted lists of Integer objects and merges them into a sorted List of
Integer objects. The method should build a new LinkedList, and should not modify
the given lists, only iterate over them. The interface List and the class LinkedList are
from the java.util package.

Two List<Integer> objects xs and ys may be built like this:

```
LinkedList<Integer> xs = new LinkedList<Integer>();
xs.addLast(3);
xs.addLast(5);
xs.addLast(12);
LinkedList<Integer> ys = new LinkedList<Integer>();
ys.addLast(2);
ys.addLast(3);
ys.addLast(4);
ys.addLast(7);
```

Exercise 5.3 This exercise is similar to Exercise 5.1, but now you should handle
sorted lists of arbitrary element type.

(A) Write an F# function

```
mergep : 'a list * 'a list * ('a * 'a -> int) -> 'a list
```

so that mergep(xs, ys, cmp) merges the two sorted lists xs and ys. The
third argument is a comparison function cmp : 'a * 'a -> int so that
cmp(x, y) returns a negative number if x is less than y, zero if they are equal,
and a positive number if x is greater than y.

For instance, with the integer comparison function

```
let icmp (x, y) = if x<y then -1 else if x>y then 1 else 0
```

the call mergep([3;5;12],[2;3;4;7],icmp) should return
[2;3;3;4;5;7;12].

Define a string comparison function `scmp` that compares two strings lexicograph-
ically as usual, and write a call to the `mergep` function that merges these lists of
strings:

```
ss1 = ["abc"; "apricot"; "ballad"; "zebra"]
ss2 = ["abelian"; "ape"; "carbon"; "yosemite"]
```

Using this function for lexicographical comparison of integer pairs

```
let pcmp ((x1, x2), (y1, y2)) =
    if x1<y1 then -1 else if x1=y1 then icmp(x2,y2) else 1
```

write a call to the `mergep` function that merges these lists of integer pairs:

```
ps1 = [(10, 4); (10, 7); (12, 0); (12, 1)]
ps2 = [(9, 100); (10, 5); (12, 2); (13, 0)]
```

(B) Write a similar generic Java method

```
static <T extends Comparable<T>> ArrayList<T>
        mergep(T[] xs, T[] ys) { ... }
```

that merges two sorted arrays `xs` and `ys` of T objects, where T must implement
Comparable<T>. That is, a T object has a method `int compareTo(T y)` so that
`x.compareTo(y)` returns a negative number if x is less than y, zero if they are
equal, and a positive number if x is greater than y. Since class Integer implements
Comparable<Integer>, your `mergep` method will be able to merge sorted arrays of
Integer objects.

As in (A) above, show how to call the `mergep` method to merge two arrays of
Strings. Class String implements Comparable<String>.

As in (A) above, show how to call the `mergep` method to merge two arrays of
IntPair objects, representing pairs of ints. You will need to define a class IntPair so
that it implements Comparable<IntPair>.

(C) Write a Java method

```
static <T> ArrayList<T>
        mergec(T[] xs, T[] ys, Comparator<T> cmp) { ... }
```

that merges two sorted arrays `xs` and `ys`. The Comparator<T> interface describes a
method `int compare(T x, T y)` such that `cmp.compare(x, y)` returns
a negative number if x is less than y, zero if they are equal, and a positive number
if x is greater than y. The Comparator<T> interface is from package java.util.

Show how to call the `mergec` method to merge two arrays of Integers.

Exercise 5.4 Define the following polymorphic F# functions on lists using the
`foldr` function for lists:

- `filter : ('a -> bool) -> ('a list -> 'a list)`
  where `filter p xs` applies p to all elements x of xs and returns a list of those
  for which `p x` is true.

- `forall : ('a -> bool) -> ('a list -> bool)`
  where `forall p xs` applies p to each element x of xs and returns true if all the results are true.
- `exists : ('a -> bool) -> ('a list -> bool)`
  where `exists p xs` applies p to each element x of xs and returns true if any of the results is true.
- `mapPartial: ('a -> 'b option) -> ('a list -> 'b list)`
  where `mapPartial f xs` applies f to all elements x of xs and returns a list of the values y for which `f x` has form `Some y`. You can think of `mapPartial` as a mixture of `map` and `filter`, where `None` corresponds to `false` and `Some y` corresponds to `true`. Thus

```
mapPartial (fun i -> if i>7 then Some(i-7) else None)
           [4; 12; 3; 17; 10]
```

should give `[5; 10; 3]`.

Exercise 5.5   Consider the polymorphic tree data type used in the Appendix A exercises:

```
type 'a tree =
    | Lf
    | Br of 'a * 'a tree * 'a tree;;
```

Just like the `foldr` function for the list datatype, one can define a uniform iterator `treeFold` function for trees:

```
let rec treeFold f t e =
    match t with
    | Lf              -> e
    | Br(v, t1, t2) -> f(v, treeFold f t1 e, treeFold f t2 e);;
```

Use `treeFold` to define the following polymorphic F# functions on trees:

- Function `count : 'a tree -> int` which returns the number of Br nodes in the tree.
- Function `sum : int tree -> int` which returns the sum of the Br node values in the tree.
- Function `depth : 'a tree -> int` which returns the depth of the tree, where Lf has depth zero and Br(v,t1,t2) has depth one plus the maximum of the depths of t1 and t2.
- Function `preorder1 : 'a tree -> 'a list` which returns the Br node values in preorder.
- Function `inorder1 : 'a tree -> 'a list` which returns the Br node values in inorder.
- Function `postorder1 : 'a tree -> 'a list` which returns the Br node values in postorder.

- Function `mapTree : ('a -> 'b) -> ('a tree -> 'b tree)`
  which applies the function to each node of the tree, and returns a tree of the same shape with the new node values.

The preorder, inorder, and postorder traversals are defined in Exercise A.3.

Exercise 5.6 This exercise is about using higher-order functions for production of HTML code. This is handy when generating static webpages from database information and when writing Web scripts in a functional style:

(A) Write an F# function

```
htmlrow : int * (int -> string) -> string
```

that builds one row of a numeric HTML table (with right-aligned table data). For example,

```
htmlrow (2, fun j -> string(j * 8))
```

should produce this string:

```
"<td align=right>0</td><td align=right>8</td>"
```

Write an F# function

```
htmltable : int * (int -> string) -> string
```

that builds an HTML table. For example,

```
htmltable (3, fun i -> "<td>" + string(i) + "</td>" +
                       "<td>" + string(i*8) + "</td>");
```

should produce an F# string that will print like this, including line breaks:

```
<table>
<tr><td>0</td><td>0</td></tr>
<tr><td>1</td><td>8</td></tr>
<tr><td>2</td><td>16</td></tr>
</table>
```

Newlines are represented by \n characters as in C, Java and C#. Similarly,

```
htmltable (10,
           fun i -> htmlrow(10,
                    fun j -> string((i+1)*(j+1))))
```

should produce a 10-by-10 multiplication table in HTML.

(B) Implement methods similar to `htmlrow` and `htmltable` in Java. (This is cumbersome, but instructive).

Exercise 5.7 Extend the monomorphic type checker to deal with lists. Use the following extra kinds of types:

```
type typ =
  | ...
  | TypL of typ                (* list, element type is typ *)
  | ...
```

Exercise 5.8 Study a lazy functional language such as Haskell [4].

Exercise 5.9 Study the implementation of a lazy language by reading Peyton Jones and Lester's book *Implementing functional languages* [6], or Sestoft's paper *Deriving a lazy abstract machine* [8]. Implement an interpreter for a small lazy functional language in F#. Inspiration for lexer and parser specifications, as well as abstract syntax, may be found in directory `mosml/examples/lexyacc/` in the Moscow ML distribution [5].

References

1. Barendregt, H.: The lambda calculus: its syntax and semantics. In: Studies in Logic and the Foundations of Mathematics, vol. 103, revised edn. North-Holland (1984)
2. Church, A.: An unsolvable problem of elementary number theory. Am. J. Math. **58**(2), 345–363 (1936)
3. Dean, J., Ghemawat, S.: Mapreduce: simplified data processing on large clusters. In: OSDI 2004 (2004)
4. Haskell programming language. http://www.haskell.org/
5. Moscow ML: http://mosml.org/
6. Peyton Jones, S., Lester, D.: Implementing Functional Languages. Prentice-Hall (1992)
7. Sestoft, P.: Lambda calculus reduction workbench. Web page (1996). http://www.itu.dk/people/sestoft/lamreduce/
8. Sestoft, P.: Deriving a lazy abstract machine. J. Funct. Program. **7**(3), 231–264 (1997)
9. Sestoft, P.: Java Precisely, 3rd edn. The MIT Press, Cambridge (2016)

Chapter 6
Polymorphic Types

This chapter discusses polymorphic types and type inference in F# and other ML-family languages, as well parametric polymorphism in Java and C#, often called generic types and methods.

6.1 Files for This Chapter

The implementation files include a polymorphic type inference algorithm for the higher-order functional language micro-ML previously discussed in Sect. 5.4.

File	Contents
Fun/TypeInference.fs	type inference for micro-ML
Fun/ParseAndType.fs	parsing and type inference for micro-ML
Fun/LinkedList.java	generic linked list class (Java/C#)

6.2 ML-Style Polymorphic Types

Consider an F# program with higher-order functions, such as this one:

```
let tw (g : int -> int) (y : int) = g (g y) : int;;
let mul2 (y : int) = 2 * y : int;;
let res = tw mul2 3;;
```

The function `tw` takes as argument a function `g` of type `int -> int` and a value `y` of type `int`, and applies `g` to the result of applying `g` to `y`, as in `g (g y)`, thus producing an integer. The function `mul2` multiplies its argument by 2. Type checking of this program succeeds with the type `int` as result.

© Springer International Publishing AG 2017
P. Sestoft, *Programming Language Concepts*, Undergraduate Topics
in Computer Science, DOI 10.1007/978-3-319-60789-4_6

The type explicitly ascribed to `tw` above is

```
tw : (int -> int) -> (int -> int)
```

which says that `tw` can be applied to a function of type `int -> int` and will return a function of type `int -> int`, that is, one that can be applied to an `int` and will then return an `int`. With a modest extension of the abstract syntax, our micro-ML type checker (file `TypedFun/TypedFun.fs`) might even have come up with this result. This is fine so long as we consider only *monomorphic* type rules, where every variable, parameter, expression and function is assigned just one (simple) type.

Now assume we strip the type constraints off the declaration of `tw`, like this:

```
let tw g y = g (g y);;
```

Then type `(int -> int) -> (int -> int)` is just one of infinitely many possible types for `tw`. For instance, another valid type instance would be

```
tw : (bool -> bool) -> (bool -> bool)
```

as in this program:

```
let tw g y = g (g y);;
let neg b = if b then false else true;;
let res = tw neg false;;
```

We want a polymorphic type, say ∀'b. (('b -> 'b) -> ('b -> 'b)), for `tw` that reflects this potential. The polymorphic type says that `tw` can have any type of the form (('b -> 'b) -> ('b -> 'b)) where 'b is some type. Letting 'b equal `int` gives the particular type found previously.

6.2.1 Informal Explanation of ML Type Inference

Here we informally explain polymorphic types in ML-like languages, such as F#, OCaml and Standard ML, and how such types may be inferred. Later we give formal type rules (Sect. 6.3) and sketch a practical implementation of ML-style type inference for micro-ML (Sect. 6.4).

We want to find the most general (possibly polymorphic) type for functions such as `tw` above. We could proceed by "guessing" suitable types for `tw`, `g` and `y`, and then prove that we have guessed correctly, but that seems hard to implement in an algorithm. But if we use type variables, such as 'a, 'b and so on, that can stand for any so far unknown type, then we can proceed to discover equalities that must hold between the type variables and ordinary types such as `int` and `bool`, and thereby systematically *infer* types.

So consider this declaration of `tw`:

```
let tw g y = g (g y);;
```

First we "guess" that parameter `g` has type 'a and that parameter `y` has type 'b, where 'a and 'b are type variables. Then we look at the body `g (g y)` of function tw, and realize that because g is applied to y in subexpression g y, type ′a must actually be a function type ′b -> ′c, where ′c is a new type variable. From this we conclude that the result of (g y) must have type ′c. But because g is applied also to (g y), the argument type ′b of g must equal the result type ′c of g, so type ′b must be equal to type ′c. Moreover, the result type of g (g y) must be ′c and therefore equal to ′b, so the result of tw g y must have type ′b. Hence the type of tw must be

```
tw : (′b -> ′b) -> (′b -> ′b)
```

where ′b can be any type — remember that ′b was a type variable "guessed" at the beginning of this process. So regardless what type ′b stands for, a valid type for function tw is obtained.

Since the function may have many different types, the type is said to be *polymorphic* (Greek: "many forms"), and since the type variable may be considered a kind of parameter for enumerating the possible types, the type is said be parametrically polymorphic. Virtual method calls in object-oriented languages are sometimes said to be polymorphic, but that is not the same as parametric polymorphism.

A polymorphic type is represented by a *type scheme*, which is a list of type variables together with a type in which those type variables occurs. In the case of tw, the list of type variables contains just ′b, so the type scheme for tw is

```
([′b], (′b -> ′b) -> (′b -> ′b))
```

This type scheme may be read as follows: for all ways to instantiate type variable ′b, the type (′b -> ′b) -> (′b -> ′b) is possible for tw. Therefore a type scheme is often written like this:

$$\forall ′b. \; ((′b \; \text{->} \; ′b) \; \text{->} \; (′b \; \text{->} \; ′b))$$

where ∀ is the universal quantifier "for all", known from logic.

In general, a type scheme is a pair (tvs, t) where tvs is a list of type variables and t is a type. A monomorphic (non-polymorphic) type t is the same as a type scheme of the form $([\,], t)$, also written $\forall().t$, where the list of type variables is empty.

A type scheme may be *instantiated* (or specialized) by systematically replacing all occurrences in t of the type variables from tvs by other types or type variables.

When x is a program variable (such as tw) with a polymorphic type represented by a type scheme (tvs, t), then type inference will create a fresh type instance for every use of the program variable in the program. This means that function tw may be used as type (int -> int) -> (int -> int) in one part of the program, and be used as type (bool -> bool) -> (bool -> bool) in another part of the program, as well as any other type that is an instance of its type scheme.

6.2.2 Which Type Parameters May Be Generalized

There are several restrictions on the generalization of type variables in F# and other ML-style languages. The first restriction is that only type variables in the types of let-bound variables and functions (such as tw) are generalized. In particular, type variables in the type of a function parameter g will not be generalized. So the example below is ill-typed; g cannot be applied both to int and bool in the body of f:

```
let f g = g 7 + g false              // Ill-typed!
```

The second restriction is that type variables in the type of a recursive function h are not generalized in the body of the function itself. So the example below is ill-typed; h cannot be applied both to int and bool in its own right-hand side:

```
let rec h x =
    if true then 22
    else h 7 + h false               // Ill-typed!
```

The above two restrictions are necessary for type inference to be implementable. The next restriction is necessary for type inference to be sound — that is, not accept programs that would crash. The restriction is that we cannot generalize a type variable that has been equated with a yet unresolved type variable in a larger scope. To understand this, consider the following program. The type of x in f should be constrained to be the same as that of y in g, because the comparison (x=y) requires x and y to have the same type:

```
let g y =
    let f x = (x=y)
    in f 1 && f false                // Ill-typed!
in g 2
```

So it would be wrong to generalize the type of f when used in the let-body f 1 && f false. Therefore type inference should proceed as follows, to obey the third restriction: Guess a type 'a for y in g, guess a type 'b for x in f, and then realize that 'a must equal 'b because x and y are compared by (x=y). Thus a plausible type for f is 'b -> bool. Now, can we generalize 'b in this type, obtaining the type scheme ∀'b.('b -> bool) for f? No, because that would allow us to apply f to any type, such as boolean, in the let-body. That would be unsound, because we could apply g to an integer in the outer let-body (as we actually do), and that would require us to compare booleans and integers, something we do not want.

The essential observation is that we cannot generalize type variable 'b (or 'a, which is the same) in the type of f because type variable 'b was invented in an *enclosing scope*, where it may later be equated to another type, such as int.

There is an efficient way to decide whether a type variable can be generalized. With every type variable we associate a *binding level*, where the outermost binding level is zero, and the binding level increases whenever we enter the right-hand side of a let-binding. When equating two type variables during type inference, we reduce the binding level of both type variables to the lowest (outermost) of their binding levels.

When generalizing a type in a let-binding, we generalize only those type variables whose binding level is not lower than the binding level of the let-binding — exactly those that are not bound in an enclosing scope.

In the above example, type variable 'a for y has level 1, and type variable 'b for x has level 2. When equating the two we set the level of 'b to 1, and hence we do not generalize 'b (or 'a) in f's body, which is at binding level 2.

6.3 Type Rules for Polymorphic Types

Section 4.9 presented rules for monomorphic types in a first-order explicitly typed functional language. This section presents rules for polymorphic types in a higher-order implicitly typed version of micro-ML, quite similar to the rules used for F#. These type rules basically present a formalization of ML-style polymorphic type inference, informally explained in Sect. 6.2.

In type rules, the type variables 'a, 'b, 'c and 'd are often written as Greek letters α, β, γ and δ, pronounced alpha, beta, gamma and delta. Likewise, type schemes are called σ (sigma), and type environments are called ρ (rho). Types are sometimes called τ (tau), but here we call them t.

A type environment $\rho = [x_1 \mapsto \sigma_1, \ldots, x_m \mapsto \sigma_m]$ maps variable names x to type schemes σ. A judgement $\rho \vdash e : t$ asserts that in type environment ρ, the expression e has type t. The type rules in Fig. 6.1 determine when one may conclude that expression e has type t in environment ρ. In the figure, i is an integer constant, b a boolean constant, x a variable, and e, e_1, and so on are expressions.

The notation $[t_1/\alpha_1, \ldots, t_n/\alpha_n]t$ is the same as the substitution notation from Sect. 2.3.4, only here applied to types instead of expressions; it means that type variable α_i is replaced by type t_i in t for all i. For instance, $[int/\alpha](\alpha \rightarrow \alpha)$ is the type $int \rightarrow int$.

In the figure, the side condition $\alpha_1, \ldots, \alpha_n$ *not free in* ρ means that the type variables must not be bound in an enclosing scope. If they are, they cannot be generalized, as explained in Sect. 6.2.2.

The polymorphic type rules for integer constants (p1), boolean constants (p2), addition (p4), comparison (p5) and conditional (p7) are exactly as for the monomorphic types in Sect. 4.9.

The following rules for polymorphic types are very different from the monomorphic ones:

- Rule (p3): An occurrence of a variable f can have any type $[t_1/\alpha_1, \ldots, t_n/\alpha_n]t$ resulting from substituting some types t_i for the type variables α_i in f's type scheme, as given by the environment ρ.
  For instance, if f has type scheme $\rho(x) = \forall \alpha_1.\alpha_1 \rightarrow \alpha_1$ in the environment, then an occurrence of f can have type $int \rightarrow int$, but also type $bool \rightarrow bool$, and type $(\beta \rightarrow \beta) \rightarrow (\beta \rightarrow \beta)$, and infinitely many other types.

$$\frac{}{\rho \vdash i : \texttt{int}} \ (p1)$$

$$\frac{}{\rho \vdash b : \texttt{bool}} \ (p2)$$

$$\frac{\rho(f) = \forall \alpha_1,\dots,\alpha_n.t}{\rho \vdash f : [t_1/\alpha_1,\dots,t_n/\alpha_n]t} \ (p3)$$

$$\frac{\rho \vdash e_1 : \texttt{int} \qquad \rho \vdash e_2 : \texttt{int}}{\rho \vdash e_1 + e_2 : \texttt{int}} \ (p4)$$

$$\frac{\rho \vdash e_1 : \texttt{int} \qquad \rho \vdash e_2 : \texttt{int}}{\rho \vdash e_1 < e_2 : \texttt{bool}} \ (p5)$$

$$\frac{\rho \vdash e_r : t_r \qquad \rho[x \mapsto \forall \alpha_1 \dots \alpha_n.t_r] \vdash e_b : t \qquad \alpha_1 \dots \alpha_n \text{ not free in } \rho}{\rho \vdash \texttt{let } x = e_r \texttt{ in } e_b \texttt{ end} : t} \ (p6)$$

$$\frac{\rho \vdash e_1 : \texttt{bool} \qquad \rho \vdash e_2 : t \qquad \rho \vdash e_3 : t}{\rho \vdash \texttt{if } e_1 \texttt{ then } e_2 \texttt{ else } e_3 : t} \ (p7)$$

$$\frac{\rho[x \mapsto t_x, f \mapsto t_x \to t_r] \vdash e_r : t_r \qquad \rho[f \mapsto \forall \alpha_1 \dots \alpha_n.t_x \to t_r] \vdash e_b : t \qquad \alpha_1 \dots \alpha_n \text{ not free in } \rho}{\rho \vdash \texttt{let } f\ x = e_r \texttt{ in } e_b \texttt{ end} : t} \ (p8)$$

$$\frac{\rho \vdash e_1 : t_x \to t_r \qquad \rho \vdash e_2 : t_x}{\rho \vdash e_1\ e_2 : t_r} \ (p9)$$

Fig. 6.1 Type rules for a higher-order functional language

- Rule (p6): A let-binding `let x = e_r in e_b end` can have type t provided that (a) the right-hand side e_r can have type t_r; and (b) the let-body e_b can have type t in an environment where the type scheme for x is obtained by generalizing its type t_r with type variables that are not free in the given environment ρ.
  The "not free in the environment" side condition is the same as the "not bound in an outer scope" condition in Sect. 6.2.2.
- Rule (p8): A function binding `let f x = e_r in e_b end` can have type t provided that (a) the function body e_r can have type t_r in an environment where the function parameter x has type t_x and the function f has type $t_x \to t_r$; and (b) the let-body e_r can have type t in an environment where the type scheme for function f is obtained by generalizing its type $t_x \to t_r$ with type variables that are not free in the given environment ρ.
  Note that, as explained in Sect. 6.2.2, the type $t_x \to t_r$ of f is not generalized in its own body e_r, only in the let-body e_b. Also, f's parameter x has monomorphic type t_x in f's body.
- Rule (p9): A function application $e_1\ e_2$ can have type t_r provided the function expression e_1 can have function type $t_x \to t_r$ and provided the argument expression e_2 can have type t_x.

For an example use of rule (p8), expression `let g y = 1+2 in g false end` can have type `int` because (a) the function body `1+2` can have type `int` in an environment in which g has type $\alpha \to$ `int`, and (b) the let-body can have type `int` in an environment in which the type scheme for g is $\forall \alpha.\alpha \to$ `int`; in particular

the occurrence of g can have the type `bool` $\rightarrow$ `int` by rule (p3), which is required
for the application g `false` to be well-typed by rule (p9).

6.4 Implementing ML Type Inference

Type inference basically is an implementation of the procedure informally presented
in Sect. 6.2: "guess" types of functions and variables in the form of type variables
`'a`, `'b`, ...; collect equalities between type variables and simple types; solve the
equations; and generalize remaining type variables to obtain a type scheme when
permissible.

The type inference algorithm we present finds the *principal type scheme* of an
expression, that is, the most general type that that expression can be given. In other
words, if the expression can have type t according to the rules in Fig. 6.1, then t is
an instance (Sect. 6.2.1) of the principal type scheme. It is a non-trivial property of
(purely functional) ML programs that such a most general type scheme exists [3].

The implementation also reflects what goes on in rules such as those in Fig. 6.1,
with some differences:

- Do not guess the types $t_1, \ldots, t_n$ to instantiate with in rule (p3). Instead instantiate
  with new type variables $\beta_1, \ldots, \beta_n$. Later these new type variables may be equated
  with other types. This relies on unification (Sect. 6.4.1), which in turn relies on
  the union-find algorithm (Sect. 6.4.2).
- Do not look through the type environment ρ to find free type variables in the
  `let` rules. Instead, as explained at the end of Sect. 6.2.2, associate with each type
  variable the level (depth of let-bindings) at which it was introduced. When equating
  two type variables, adjust the binding level of both variables to the lowest, that is
  outermost, of the two.
  If the level of a type variable is lower than the current level, then it is free in the
  type environment. In that case, do not generalize it.

So to implement type inference we need to work with type variables as well as
primitive types such as `int`, `bool`, and function types such as `int -> bool`,
`'b -> 'b`, and so on. In our meta-language F# we can therefore model micro-ML
(that is, object language) types like this:

```
type typ =
    | TypI                  (* integers                    *)
    | TypB                  (* booleans                    *)
    | TypF of typ * typ     (* (argumenttype, resulttype)  *)
    | TypV of typevar       (* type variable               *)
```

where a `typevar` is an updatable pair of the type variable's link and its binding
level:

```
and typevar =
     (tyvarkind * int) ref     (* kind and binding level      *)

and tyvarkind =
     | NoLink of string        (* just a type variable        *)
     | LinkTo of typ           (* equated to type typ         *)
```

The link is used in the union-find algorithm (Sect. 6.4.2) to solve equations between type variables and types.

With this setup, type inference proceeds by discovering, recording and solving equations between type variables and types. The required equations are discovered by traversing the program's expressions, and the equations between types are recorded and solved simultaneously by performing unification of types, as explained in Sect. 6.4.1.

Function typ lvl env e computes and returns the type of expression e at binding level lvl in type environment env, by pattern matching on the form of e. The four cases covering constants, variables and primitive operations correspond to rules (p1)–(p5) in Fig. 6.1. In the case of a primitive operation such as e1+e2, we first find the types t1 and t2 of the operands e1 and e2, then use unification, such as unify TypI t1, to force the type of e1 to equal TypI, that is, integer. Similarly, the unification unify t1 t2 in the (e1=e2) case forces the types of the two operands e1 and e2 to be equal:

```
let rec typ (lvl : int) (env : tenv) (e : expr) : typ =
    match e with
    | CstI i -> TypI
    | CstB b -> TypB
    | Var x  -> specialize lvl (lookup env x)
    | Prim(ope, e1, e2) ->
      let t1 = typ lvl env e1
      let t2 = typ lvl env e2
      match ope with
      | "*" -> (unify TypI t1; unify TypI t2; TypI)
      | "+" -> (unify TypI t1; unify TypI t2; TypI)
      | "-" -> (unify TypI t1; unify TypI t2; TypI)
      | "=" -> (unify t1 t2; TypB)
      | "<" -> (unify TypI t1; unify TypI t2; TypB)
      | "&" -> (unify TypB t1; unify TypB t2; TypB)
      | _   -> failwith ("unknown primitive " + ope)
    | ...
```

The case for let corresponds to rule (p6). Note that the binding level of the right-hand side eRhs is lvl+1, one higher than that of the enclosing expression, and that type variables in the type of the let-bound variable x get generalized (by an auxiliary function) in the environment of the let-body. The case for `if` corresponds to rule (p7). It requires the condition `e1` to have type `TypB`, that is, `bool`, and requires the types of the two branches to be equal. Again this is expressed using unification:

```
let rec typ (lvl : int) (env : tenv) (e : expr) : typ =
    match e with
    | ...
    | Let(x, eRhs, letBody) ->
      let lvl1 = lvl + 1
      let resTy = typ lvl1 env eRhs
      let letEnv = (x, generalize lvl resTy) :: env
      typ lvl letEnv letBody
    | If(e1, e2, e3) ->
      let t2 = typ lvl env e2
      let t3 = typ lvl env e3
      unify TypB (typ lvl env e1);
      unify t2 t3;
      t2
    | ...
```

The case for function definition `let f x = fBody in letBody end` corresponds to rule (p8) in Fig. 6.1. It creates ("guesses") fresh type variables for the type of `f` and `x` and adds them to the environment as monomorphic types `fTyp` and `xTyp`, then infers the type `rTyp` of `f`'s body in that extended environment. Then it unifies `f`'s type `fTyp` with the type `xTyp -> rTyp`, as in the first premise of rule (p8). Finally it generalizes `f`'s type, adds it to the original environment, and infers the type of the let-body in that environment:

```
let rec typ (lvl : int) (env : tenv) (e : expr) : typ =
    match e with
    | ...
    | Letfun(f, x, fBody, letBody) ->
      let lvl1 = lvl + 1
      let fTyp = TypV(newTypeVar lvl1)
      let xTyp = TypV(newTypeVar lvl1)
      let fBodyEnv = (x, TypeScheme([], xTyp))
                       :: (f, TypeScheme([], fTyp)) :: env
      let rTyp = typ lvl1 fBodyEnv fBody
      let _    = unify fTyp (TypF(xTyp, rTyp))
      let bodyEnv = (f, generalize lvl fTyp) :: env
      typ lvl bodyEnv letBody
    | ...
```

Finally, the case for function call `f x` corresponds to rule (p9). It infers types `tf` and `tx` for the function and argument expressions, creates a fresh type variable `tr` for the result of the expression, and unifies `tf` with `tx -> tr`. The unification forces `f` to have a function type, checks that `f`'s argument type matches the given `tx`, and binds `tr` to `f`'s result type:

```
let rec typ (lvl : int) (env : tenv) (e : expr) : typ =
    match e with
    | ...
    | Call(eFun, eArg) ->
      let tf = typ lvl env eFun
      let tx = typ lvl env eArg
      let tr = TypV(newTypeVar lvl)
      unify tf (TypF(tx, tr));
      tr
```

6.4.1   Type Equation Solving by Unification

Unification is a process for automatically solving symbolic equations, such as equations between types. The unification $\texttt{unify}\ t_1\ t_2$ of types t_1 and t_2 is performed as follows, depending on the form of the types:

t_1	t_2	Action
int	int	No action needed
bool	bool	No action needed
$t_{11} \to t_{12}$	$t_{21} \to t_{22}$	Unify t_{11} with t_{21}, and unify t_{12} with t_{22}
α	α	No action needed
α	β	Make α equal to β
α	t_2	Make α equal to t_2, provided α does not occur in t_2
t_1	α	Make α equal to t_1, provided α does not occur in t_1
All other cases		Unification fails; the types do not match

The side condition in the third last case, that α does not occur in t_2, is needed to prevent the creation of circular or infinite types. For instance, when t_2 is $\alpha \to \alpha$, unification of α and t_2 must fail, because there are no finite types solving the equation $\alpha = (\alpha \to \alpha)$.

Type unification is implemented by function $\texttt{unify}\ \texttt{t1}\ \texttt{t2}$ and strictly follows the above outline. The operations above called "make α equal to β" and similar are implemented by the $\texttt{Union}(\alpha, \beta)$ operations on the union-find data structure; see Sect. 6.4.2.

6.4.2   The Union-Find Algorithm

The union-find data structure is a simple and fast way to keep track of which objects, such as types, are equal to each other. The data structure is an acyclic graph, each of whose nodes represents a type or type variable. The nodes are divided into dynamically changing *equivalence classes* or *partitions*; all nodes in an equivalence class are considered equal to each other. Each equivalence class contains a node that is the *canonical representative* of the class.

The union-find data structure supports the following three operations:

- New: Create a new node that is in its own one-element equivalence class.
- Find n: Given a node n, find the node that is the canonical representative of its equivalence class.
- Union(n1,n2): Given two nodes n1 and n2, join their equivalence classes into one equivalence class. In other words, force the two nodes to be equal.

The implementation of the union-find data structure is simple. Each node has an updatable link field (p. 110) which is either NoLink (meaning the node is the canonical representative of its equivalence class), or LinkTo n, where n is another node in the same equivalence class. By following LinkTo links from a node until one reaches NoLink, one can find the canonical representative of a class.

The New operation is implemented by creating a new node whose link field has value NoLink. The Find(n) operation is implemented by following link field references until we reach a node whose link is NoLink, that is, a canonical representative. The Union(n1,n2) operation is implemented by Find'ing the canonical representatives for n1 and n2, and then making one representative LinkTo the other one.

In file TypeInference.cs, the New operation is implemented by function newTypeVar, the Find operation is implemented by function normType, and the Union operation is implemented by function linkVarToType.

Two optimizations make this data structure extremely fast. The Find operation can do "path compression", that is, update the intermediate node links to point directly to the canonical representative it finds. The Union operation can do "union by rank", that is create the link from one canonical representative to another in that direction that causes the smallest increase in the distance from nodes to canonical representatives. With these improvements, the total cost of N operations on the data structure is almost linear in N, so each operation is takes amortized almost constant time. The "almost" part is very intriguing: it is the inverse of the Ackermann function, that is, for practical purposes, a constant; see [14].

6.4.3   The Complexity of ML-Style Type Inference

Thanks to clever techniques such as unification (Sect. 6.4.1), the union-find data structure (Sect. 6.4.2), and associating scope levels with type variables (Sect. 6.2.2), ML-style type inference is fast in practice. Nevertheless, it has very high worst-case run-time complexity. It is complete for DEXPTIME, deterministic exponential time [6, 9], which means that it can be hopelessly slow in extreme cases.

A symptom of the problem (but far from the whole story) is that the type scheme of a program may involve a number of type variables that is exponential in the size of the program. For instance, the inferred type of the following F# program involves $2^5 = 64$ different type variables, and each new declaration p6, p7, ...in the same style will further double the number of type variables (try it):

```
let id x = x;;
let pair x y p = p x y;;
let p1 p = pair id id p;;
let p2 p = pair p1 p1 p;;
let p3 p = pair p2 p2 p;;
let p4 p = pair p3 p3 p;;
let p5 p = pair p4 p4 p;;
```

However, the programs that programmers actually write apparently have relatively non-complex types, so ML-style type inference is fast in practice.

6.5 Generic Types in Java and C#

The original versions of the Java and C# programming languages did not have parametric polymorphism. Since 2004, Java version 5.0 and C# version 2.0 have parametric polymorphic types (classes, interfaces, struct types, and delegate types) and parametric polymorphic methods, often called generic types and generic methods. In the extended languages, classes and other types as well as methods can have type parameters. In contrast to F# and ML, type parameters must be explicit in most cases: the Java and C# compilers perform less type inference.

Generic Java was proposed in 1998 by Bracha and others [1]. Generic C# was proposed in 2001 by Kennedy and Syme [8]. Syme later designed and implemented the F# language, using many ideas from Xavier Leroy's OCaml language.

The implementation of generic types in C# is safer and more efficient than that of Java, but required a new run-time system and extensions to the .NET bytecode language, whereas Java 5.0 required very few changes to the Java Virtual Machine.

Using Java 5.0 or later (C# is very similar) one can declare a generic or type-parametrized linked list class with a type parameter T as shown in Fig. 6.2.

A type instance LinkedList<Person> is equivalent to the class obtained by replacing T by Person everywhere in the declaration of LinkedList<T>. In an object of class LinkedList<Person>, the add method will accept arguments only of type Person (or one of its subclasses), and the get method can return only objects of class Person (or one of its subclasses). Thus LinkedList<T> in Java is very similar to T list in F# and ML.

Using this implementation of LinkedList, the dynamically typed collections example from Sect. 4.10.2 can become statically typed. We simply declare the list names to be of type LinkedList<Person> so that names.add can be applied only to expressions of type Person. This means that the third call to add in Fig. 6.3 will be rejected at compile-time. On the other hand, no cast will be needed in the initial-

```
class LinkedList<T> {
  private Node<T> first, last;

  private static class Node<T> {
    public Node<T> prev, next;
    public T item;
    public Node(T item) { this.item = item; }
    public Node(T item, Node<T> prev, Node<T> next) {
      this.item = item; this.prev = prev; this.next = next;
    }
  }

  public LinkedList() { first = last = null; }

  public T get(int index) { return getNode(index).item; }

  private Node<T> getNode(int n) {
    Node<T> node = first;
    for (int i=0; i<n; i++)
      node = node.next;
    return node;
  }

  public boolean add(T item) {
    if (last == null) // and thus first = null
      first = last = new Node<T>(item);
    else {
      Node<T> tmp = new Node<T>(item, last, null);
      last.next = tmp;
      last = tmp;
    }
    return true;
  }
}
```

Fig. 6.2 Generic LinkedList class in Java 5. The type parameter T is the list's element type. It can be used almost as a type in the declaration of LinkedList

```
LinkedList<Person> names = new LinkedList<Person>();
names.add(new Person("Kristen"));
names.add(new Person("Bjarne"));
names.add(new Integer(1998));       // Wrong, compiler rejects
names.add(new Person("Anders"));
...
Person p = names.get(2);            // No cast, cannot fail
```

Fig. 6.3 Using generic LinkedList<T> to discover type errors early

ization of p in the last line, because the object returned by names.get must have class Person (or one of its subclasses).

Both Java 5.0 and C# 2.0 (and later) support generic methods as well. For instance, in Java one may declare a method f that takes an argument x of any type T and returns a LinkedList<T> containing that element. Note that in Java the type parameter <T> of the method declaration precedes the return type LinkedList<T> in the method header:

```
public static <T> LinkedList<T> f(T x) {
  LinkedList<T> res = new LinkedList<T>();
  res.add(x);
  return res;
}
```

This is similar to the F# or ML function

```
let f x = [x]
```

which has type 'a -> 'a list.

6.6   Co-Variance and Contra-Variance

In languages such as Java and C#, one type may be a subtype (for instance, subclass) of another, and the question arises how subtypes and generic types interact. If Student is a subtype of type Person, one may think that LinkedList<Student> should be a subtype of LinkedList<Person>.

In general it should not, because that would lead to an unsound type system. Consider this example:

```
LinkedList<Student> ss = new LinkedList<Student>();
LinkedList<Person> ps = ss;               // Ill-typed!
ps.add(new Person(...));
Student s0 = ss.get(0);
```

If the assignment ps = ss were allowed, then we could use method add on the LinkedList<Person> class to add a Person object to the ps list. But ps refers to the exact same data structure as ss, so the subsequent call to ss.get(0) would return a Person object, which would be catastrophic because method get on a LinkedList<Student> has return type Student.

So in general a generic type must be *invariant* in its type parameters, and therefore LinkedList<Student> is not a subtype of LinkedList<Person>, nor is it a super-type. Sometimes this is needlessly restrictive. For instance, if we have a method PrintPeople that can print a sequence of Person objects, then invariance prevents us from calling it with a sequence of Student objects:

```
void PrintPeople(LinkedList<Person> ps) {
  ...
}
```

```
. . .
LinkedList<Student> students = ...;
PrintPeople(students);                    // Ill-typed!
```

But this seems silly: surely if the method can print Person objects, then it can also print Student objects. So here we would wish that the type LinkedList<T> were co-variant in its type parameter T. Then LinkedList<Student> would be a subtype of LinkedList<Person> just because Student is a subtype of Person.

Conversely, if we have a method that can register a new Student in a data structure of type LinkedList<Student>, then invariance prevents us from calling that method to add the student to a data structure of type LinkedList<Person>, although that would be completely safe:

```
void AddStudentToList(LinkedList<Student> ss) {
  ss.add(new Student(...));
}
. . .
AddStudentToList(new LinkedList<Person>());    // Ill-typed!
```

So here we would wish that LinkedList<T> were contra-variant in its parameter T. Then LinkedList<Person> would be a subtype of LinkedList<Student> just because Student is a subtype of Person, so we can call AddStudentToList with a LinkedList<Person> as argument.

Java 5.0 (from 2004) and C# 4.0 (from 2010) relax this restriction in different ways, which we discuss below.

6.6.1 Java Wildcards

Using the type wildcard notation LinkedList<? extends Person> we can declare that method PrintPeople accepts any linked list, so long as its item type — which is what the question mark stands for — is Person or a subtype of Person. This has several consequences. First, any item extracted from the list can be assigned to a variable of type Person in the method body, and second, the method can be called on a LinkedList<Student>:

```
void PrintPeople(LinkedList<? extends Person> ps) {
  for (Person p : ps) { ... }
}
. . .
PrintPeople(new LinkedList<Student>());
```

The extends wildcard in the example provides use-site *co-variance*. It also restricts the way parameter ps can be used in the method. For instance, the call ps.add(x) would be ill-typed for all arguments x, because the only thing we know about the item type of ps is that *it is a subtype* of Person; the ps list may actually be a list of Teacher objects.

For the second invariance problem identified above, we can use a type wildcard in LinkedList<? super Student> to declare that AddStudentToList accepts any linked list, so long as its item type is Student or a supertype of Student. This has several consequences. First, we can definitely add Student objects to the list. Second, the method can be called on a LinkedList<Person>, or indeed any linked list whose item type is a supertype of Student:

```
void AddStudentToList(LinkedList<? super Student> ss) {
  ss.add(new Student());
}
...
AddStudentToList(new LinkedList<Person>());
```

The super wildcard in the example provides use-site *contra-variance*. It also restricts the way parameter ss can be used in the method. For instance, the result of a call ss.get(...) inside AddStudentToList could not be assigned to a variable of type Student or Person, because the only thing we know about the item type of ss is that *it is a supertype* of Student. In fact, the only type we can find for the get function is Object, the supertype of all types.

6.6.2 C# Variance Declarations

In C# 4.0, one can declare that a generic interface or delegate type is co-variant or contra-variant in a type parameter, using the modifiers "out" and "in" respectively. Thus whereas Java provides use-site variance for all generic types, C# 4.0 provides declaration-site variance, but only for interfaces and delegate types.

The typical example of a generic interface that is *co-variant* in its type parameter T is IEnumerator<T>, which can only output T values:

```
interface IEnumerator<out T> {
  T Current { get; }
}
```

The out modifier on type parameter T declares that the interface is co-variant in T, so IEnumerator<Student> will be a subtype of IEnumerator<Person>. Intuitively this makes sense, because whenever we expect a generator of Person objects, we can surely use a generator of Student objects, a special case of Person. Formally, co-variance in T is correct because T appears only in "output position" in the interface, namely as return type of the Current property.

Similarly, the IEnumerable<T> interface can be co-variant in T:

```
interface IEnumerable<out T> {
  IEnumerator<T> GetEnumerator();
}
```

Again T appears only in "output position": it appears co-variantly in the return type of the GetEnumerator method.

The typical example of a generic interface that is *contra-variant* in its type parameter T is IComparer<T>, which can only input T values:

```
interface IComparer<in T> {
  int Compare(T x, T y);
}
```

The in modifier on type parameter T declares that the interface is contra-variant in T, so IComparer<Person> will be a subtype of IComparer<Student>. Intuitively this makes sense, because whenever we expect a comparer of Student objects, we can surely use a comparer of Person objects, a more general case than Student. Formally, contra-variance in T is correct because T appears only in "input position" in the interface, namely as parameter type of the Compare method.

Co-variant and contra-variant interfaces and delegate types for C# were discussed and type rules proposed by Emir, Kennedy, Russo and Yu in 2006 [4]. This design was adopted for C# 4.0 in 2010, but the new lower-bound type parameter constraints also proposed in the same paper have apparently not been adopted.

6.6.3 The Variance Mechanisms of Java and C#

As shown above, Java wildcards offer use-site variance, whereas C# interfaces and delegate types offer declaration-site variance. It is not obvious whether Java's variance mechanism is easier or harder for programmers to use than C#'s variance mechanism. However, there is some evidence that C#'s mechanism is better understood from the perspective of theory and implementation. A paper by Kennedy and Pierce [7] shows that C# with variance can be type checked efficiently, but also presents several examples of small Java programs that crash or seriously slow down a Java compiler. For instance, Sun's Java compiler version 1.6.0 spends many seconds type checking this tiny program, then throws a stack overflow exception:

```
class T { }
class N<Z> { }
class C<X> extends N<N<? super C<C<X>>>> {
  N<? super C<T>> cast(C<T> c) { return c; }
}
```

Although this program is both contrived and rather incomprehensible, it is the compiler's job to tell us whether the program is well-typed or not, but here it fails to do so.

6.7 History and Literature

ML-style parametric polymorphism, or let-polymorphism, which generalizes types to type schemes only at let-bindings, is called Hindley–Milner polymorphism, after J.R. Hindley and Robin Milner, who discovered this idea independently in 1968 and 1977.

The first type inference algorithm for ML, called algorithm W, was presented in 1982 by Luis Damas and Robin Milner [3]. Good introductions to polymorphic type inference include Hancock's [10] and Schwartzbach's [13].

The binding level technique for efficient type variable generalization mentioned in Sect. 6.2.2 is due to Didier Rémy [12]. Unification was invented by Alan Robinson [11] in 1965, and is a central implementation technique also in the Prolog language. Type variables are equated efficiently by means of the union-find algorithm [14, Chap. 2], described also in most algorithms textbooks, such as Cormen et al. [2, Chap. 21] or Goodrich and Tamassia [5, Sect. 4.2].

6.8 Exercises

The goals of these exercises are (1) to investigate the interpreter `eval` for the higher-order version of the micro-ML language (in file `HigherFun.fs`), and (2) to understand type ML-style type inference, including the implementation in file `TypeInference.fs`.

Exercise 6.1 Download and unpack `fun1.zip` and `fun2.zip` and build the micro-ML higher-order evaluator as described in file `README.TXT` point E.

Then run the evaluator on the following four programs. Is the result of the third one as expected? Explain the result of the last one:

```
let add x = let f y = x+y in f end
in add 2 5 end

let add x = let f y = x+y in f end
in let addtwo = add 2
   in addtwo 5 end
end

let add x = let f y = x+y in f end
in let addtwo = add 2
   in let x = 77 in addtwo 5 end
   end
end

let add x = let f y = x+y in f end
in add 2 end
```

Exercise 6.2 Add anonymous functions, similar to F#'s `fun x -> ...`, to the micro-ML higher-order functional language abstract syntax:

```
type expr =
    ...
  | Fun of string * expr
  | ...
```

For instance, these two expressions in concrete syntax:

```
fun x -> 2*x
let y = 22 in fun z -> z+y end
```

should parse to these two expressions in abstract syntax:

```
Fun("x", Prim("*", CstI 2, Var "x"))
Let("y", CstI 22, Fun("z", Prim("+", Var "z", Var "y")))
```

Evaluation of a `Fun (...)` should produce a non-recursive closure of the form

```
type value =
  | ...
  | Clos of string * expr * value env    (* (x,body,declEnv) *)
```

In the empty environment the two expressions shown above should evaluate to these two closure values:

```
Clos("x", Prim("*", CstI 2, Var "x"), [])
Clos("z", Prim("+", Var "z", Var "y"), [(y,22)])
```

Extend the evaluator `eval` in file `HigherFun.fs` to interpret such anonymous functions.

Exercise 6.3 Extend the micro-ML lexer and parser specifications in `FunLex.fsl` and `FunPar.fsy` to permit anonymous functions. The concrete syntax may be as in F#: `fun x -> expr` or as in Standard ML: `fn x => expr`, where x is a variable. The micro-ML examples from Exercise 6.1 can now be written in these two alternative ways:

```
let add x = fun y -> x+y
in add 2 5 end

let add = fun x -> fun y -> x+y
in add 2 5 end
```

Exercise 6.4 This exercise concerns type rules for ML-polymorphism, as shown in Fig. 6.1.

(i) Build a type rule tree for this micro-ML program (in the let-body, the type of f should be polymorphic – why?):

```
let f x = 1
in f f end
```

(ii) Build a type rule tree for this micro-ML program (in the let-body, f should *not* be polymorphic – why?):

```
let f x = if x<10 then 42 else f(x+1)
in f 20 end
```

Exercise 6.5 Download fun2.zip and build the micro-ML higher-order type inference as described in file README.TXT point F.

(1) Use the type inference on the micro-ML programs shown below, and report what type the program has. Some of the type inferences will fail because the programs are not typable in micro-ML; in those cases, explain why the program is not typable:

```
let f x = 1
in f f end

let f g = g g
in f end

let f x =
    let g y = y
    in g false end
in f 42 end

let f x =
    let g y = if true then y else x
    in g false end
in f 42 end

let f x =
    let g y = if true then y else x
    in g false end
in f true end
```

(2) Write micro-ML programs for which the micro-ML type inference report the following types:

- bool -> bool
- int -> int
- int -> int -> int
- 'a -> 'b -> 'a
- 'a -> 'b -> 'b
- ('a -> 'b) -> ('b -> 'c) -> ('a -> 'c)
- 'a -> 'b
- 'a

Remember that the type arrow (->) is right associative, so `int -> int -> int` is the same as `int -> (int -> int)`, and that the choice of type variables does not matter, so the type scheme `'h -> 'g -> 'h` is the same as `a' -> 'b -> 'a`.

Exercise 6.6 Write an F# function `check : expr -> bool` that checks that all variables and function names are defined when they are used, and returns `true` if they are. This checker should accept the micro-ML higher-order language. That is, in the abstract syntax `Call (e1, e2)` for a function call, the expression `e1` can be an arbitrary expression and need not be a variable name.

The `check` function needs to carry around an environment to know which variables are bound. This environment may just be a list of the bound variables.

Exercise 6.7 Add mutually recursive function declarations in the micro-ML higher-order functional language abstract syntax:

```
type expr =
    ...
  | Letfuns of (string * string * expr) list * expr
  | ...
```

Then extend the evaluator `eval` in `HigherFun.fs` to correctly interpret such functions. This requires a non-trivial change to the representation of closures because two functions f and g, declared in the same must `Letfuns` expression, must be able to call each other. Therefore the declaration environment, which is part of the closure of each function, must include a mapping of the other function to its closure. This can be implemented using recursive closures and references.

References

1. Bracha, G., Odersky, M., Stoutamire, D., Wadler, P.: Making the future safe for the past: adding genericity to the java programming language. In: ACM Symposium on Object Oriented Programming: Systems, Languages, and Applications (OOPSLA), Vancouver, British Columbia, pp. 183–200. ACM (1998)
2. Cormen, T., Leiserson, C., Rivest, R., Stein, C.: Introduction to Algorithms, vol. 2. The MIT Press, Cambridge (2001)
3. Damas, L., Milner, R.: Principal type schemes for functional programs. In: 9th ACM Symposium on Principles of Programming Languages (1982)
4. Emir, B., Kennedy, A., Russo, C., Yu, D.: Variance and generalized constraints for C# generics. ECOOP. Springer, Berlin (2006)
5. Goodrich, M.T., Tamassia, R.: Algorithm Design. Wiley, New Delhi (2002)
6. Henglein, F., Mairson, H.: The complexity of type inference for higher-order lambda calculi. In: 18th ACM Symposium on Principles of Programming Languages, January 1991, Orlando, Florida, pp. 119–130. ACM Press (1991)
7. Kennedy, A., Pierce, B.: On decidability of nominal subtyping with variance. In: International Workshop on Foundations and Developments of Object-Oriented Languages (FOOL/WOOD'07), Nice, France (2007)

8. Kennedy, A., Syme, D.: The design and implementation of generics for the .Net Common Language Runtime. In: Programming Language Design and Implementation, Snowbird, Utah, June 2001. pp. 1–23. ACM Press (2001)

9. Kfoury, A.J., Tiuryn, J., Urzyczyn, P.: ML typability is DEXPTIME-complete. In: Proceedings of the Fifteenth Colloquium on CAAP'90, 1990. pp. 206–220. Copenhagen, Denmark (1990)

10. Peyton-Jones, S.L.: The Implementation of Functional Programming Languages, Chap. 8 and 9. Prentice-Hall International, New York (1987)

11. Robinson, J.A.: A machine-oriented logic based on the resolution principle. Commun. ACM **5**, 23–41 (1965)

12. Rémy, D.: Extension of ML type system with a sorted equational theory on types. INRIA Rapport de Recherche 1766, INRIA, France (1992)

13. Schwartzbach, M.: Polymorphic type inference. Technical report, DAIMI, Aarhus University (1995). At http://www.daimi.au.dk/~mis/

14. Tarjan, R.: Data Structures and Network Algorithms. CBMS, vol. 44. Society for Applied and Industrial Mathematics, Philadelphia (1983)

Chapter 7
Imperative Languages

This chapter discusses *imperative programming languages*, in which the value of a variable may be modified by assignment. We first present a naive imperative language where a variable denotes an updatable store cell, and then present the environment/store model used in real imperative programming languages. Then we show how to evaluate micro-C, a C-style imperative language, using an interpreter, and present the concepts of expression, variable declaration, assignment, loop, output, variable scope, lvalue and rvalue, parameter passing mechanisms, pointer, array, and pointer arithmetics.

7.1 Files for This Chapter

File	Contents
Imp/Naive.fs	naive imperative language interpreter
Imp/Parameters.cs	call-by-reference parameters in C#
Imp/array.c	array variables and array parameters in C
MicroC/Absyn.fs	micro-C abstract syntax (Fig. 7.6)
MicroC/grammar.txt	informal micro-C grammar and parser specification
MicroC/CLex.fsl	micro-C lexer specification
MicroC/CPar.fsy	micro-C parser specification
MicroC/Parse.fs	micro-C parser
MicroC/Interp.fs	micro-C interpreter (Sect. 7.6.1)
MicroC/ex1.c-ex21.c	micro-C example programs (Fig. 7.8)

© Springer International Publishing AG 2017
P. Sestoft, *Programming Language Concepts*, Undergraduate Topics
in Computer Science, DOI 10.1007/978-3-319-60789-4_7

Fig. 7.1 Abstract syntax for
expressions in naive
imperative language

```
type expr =
  | CstI of int
  | Var of string
  | Prim of string * expr * expr
```

Fig. 7.2 Abstract syntax for
statements in naive
imperative language

```
type stmt =
  | Asgn of string * expr
  | If of expr * stmt * stmt
  | Block of stmt list
  | For of string * expr * expr * stmt
  | While of expr * stmt
  | Print of expr
```

7.2 A Naive Imperative Language

We start by considering a naive imperative language (file Naive.fs). It has expressions as shown in Fig. 7.1, and statements as shown in Fig. 7.2: assignment, conditional statements, statement sequences, for-loops, while-loops and a print statement.

Variables are introduced as needed, as in sloppy Perl programming; there are no declarations. Unlike C/C++/Java/C#, the language has no blocks to delimit variable scope, only statement sequences.

For-loops are as in Pascal or Basic, not C/C++/Java/C#, so a for loop has the form

```
for i = startval to endval do
    stmt
```

where start and end values are given for the controlling variable i, and the controlling variable cannot be changed inside the loop.

The store naively maps variable names to values; see Fig. 7.3. This is similar to a functional language, but completely unrealistic for imperative languages.

The distinction between statement and expression has been used in imperative languages since the very first one, Fortran in 1956.

The purpose of executing a *statement* is to modify the state of the computation (by modifying the store, by producing some output, or similar). The purpose of

Fig. 7.3 Naive store, a
direct mapping of variables
to values

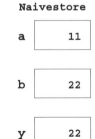

evaluating an *expression* is to compute a value. In most imperative languages, the evaluation of an expression can modify the store also, by a so-called *side effect*. For instance, the C/C++/Java/C# expression i++ has the value of i, and as a side effect increments i by one.

In F# and other ML-like languages, there are no statements; state changes are produced by expressions that have side effects and type unit, such as printf "Hello!". Expressions can be evaluated for their side effect only, by separating them by semicolons and enclosing them in parentheses. Executing the sequence (printf "Hello "; printf "world!"; 42) has the side effect of printing Hello world! on the console, and has the value 42.

In Postscript, there are no expressions, so values are computed by statements (instruction sequences) that leave a result of the stack top, such as 4 5 add 6 mul.

7.3 Environment and Store

Real imperative languages such as C, Pascal and Ada, and imperative object-oriented languages such as C++, Java, C# and Ada95, have a more complex state (or store) model than functional languages:

- An *environment* maps variable names (x) to store locations (0x34B2)
- An updatable *store* maps locations (0x34B2) to values (117).

The micro-C interpreter implementation shown in Sect. 7.6.1 uses a functional store implemented as an immutable F# map from addresses (integers) to values (also integers). The store type supports these operations:

- emptyStore returns a new empty store.
- setSto store addr value returns a new store that is like store except that address addr has the given value.
- getSto store addr returns the value at address addr in the store (or throws an exception).
- initSto loc n store returns a new store that is like store except that addresses loc, ..., loc+n-1 have a default value, such as −999. This is for allocation of arrays.

It is useful to distinguish two kinds of values in such languages. When a variable x or array element a[i] occurs as the target of an assignment statement:

```
x = e
```

or as the operand of an increment operator (in C/C++/Java/C#):

```
x++
```

or as the operand of an address operator (in C/C++/C#; see below):

```
&x
```

Fig. 7.4 Environment
(variable to location) and
store (location to value)

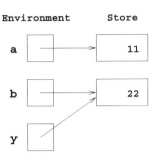

then we use the *lvalue* ("left hand side value") of the variable or array element. The lvalue is the location (or address) of the variable or array element in the store.

Otherwise, when the variable x or array element a[i] occurs in an expression such as this:

```
x + 7
```

then we use its *rvalue* ("right hand side value"). The rvalue is the value stored at the variable's location in the store. Only expressions that have a location in the store can have an lvalue. Thus in C/C++/Java/C# this expression makes no sense:

```
(8 + 2)++
```

because the expression (8 + 2) has an rvalue (10) but does not have an lvalue.

In other words, the environment maps names to lvalues; the store maps lvalues to rvalues; see Fig. 7.4.

When we later study the compilation of imperative programs to machine code (Chap. 8), we shall see that the environment exists only at compile-time, when the code is generated, and the store exists only at run-time, when the code is executed.

In all imperative languages the store is *single-threaded*: at most one copy of the store needs to exist at a time. That is because we never need to look back (for instance, by discarding all changes made to the store since a given point in time).

7.4   Parameter Passing Mechanisms

In a declaration of a procedure (or function or method)

```
void p(int x, double y) { ... }
```

the x and y are called *formal parameters* or just *parameters*. In a call to a procedure (or function or method)

```
p(e1, e2)
```

the expressions e1 and e2 are called *actual parameters*, or argument expressions.

When executing a procedure call p(e1, e2) in an imperative language, the values of the argument expressions must be bound to the formal parameters x and y somehow. This so-called parameter passing can be done in several different ways:

- Call-by-value: a copy of the argument expression's rvalue is made in a new location, and the new location is passed to the procedure. Thus updates to the corresponding formal parameter do not affect the actual parameter (argument expression).
- Call-by-reference: the lvalue (location) of the argument expression is passed to the procedure. Thus updates to the corresponding formal parameter do affect the actual parameter. Note that the actual parameter must have an lvalue, so it must be a variable or an array element (or a field of an object or structure).
  Call-by-reference is useful for returning multiple results from a procedure. It is also useful for writing recursive functions that modify trees, so some binary tree algorithms can be written more elegantly in languages that support call-by-reference (including Pascal, C++ and C#) than in Java (that does not).
- Call-by-value-return: a copy of the argument expression's rvalue is made in a new location, and the new location (lvalue) is passed to the procedure. When the procedure returns, the current value in that location is copied back to the argument expression (if it has an lvalue).

Pascal, C++, C#, and Ada permit both call-by-value and call-by-reference. Fortran (at least some versions) uses call-by-value-return.

Java, C, and most ML-like languages permit only call-by-value, but in C (and micro-C) one can pass variable x by reference just by passing the address &x of x and making the corresponding formal parameter xp be a pointer. Note that Java does not copy objects and arrays when passing them as parameters, because it passes (and copies) only references to objects and arrays [6]. When passing an object by value in C++, the object gets copied. This is usually *not* what is intended. For instance, if the object being passed is a file descriptor, the result is unpredictable.

Here are a few examples (in C#, see file Parameters.cs) to illustrate the difference between call-by-value and call-by-reference parameter passing.

The method swapV uses call-by-value:

```
static void swapV(int x, int y) {            // No effect!
  int tmp = x; x = y; y = tmp;
}
```

Putting a = 11 and b = 22, and calling swapV(a, b) has no effect at all on the values of a and b. In the call, the value 11 is copied to x, and 22 is copied to y, and they are swapped so that x is 22 and y is 11, but that does not affect a and b.

The method swapR uses call-by-reference:

```
static void swapR(ref int x, ref int y) {
  int tmp = x; x = y; y = tmp;
}
```

Putting a = 11 and b = 22, and calling swapR(ref a, ref b) will swap the values of a and b. In the call, parameter x is made to point to the same address as a, and y to the same as b. Then the contents of the locations pointed to by x and y are swapped, which swaps the values of a and b also.

The method square below uses call-by-value for its i parameter and call-by-reference for its r parameter. It computes i*i and assigns the result to r and hence to the actual argument passed for r:

```
static void square(int i, ref int r) {
  r = i * i;
}
```

After the call square(11, ref z), variable z has the value 121. Compare with the micro-C example in file MicroC/ex5.c: it passes an int pointer r by value instead of passing an integer variable by reference.

7.5   The C Programming Language

The C programming language [2], initially designed by Ritchie [5] in 1971–1973, is widely used in systems programming, and its syntax has inspired that of C++, Java, C#, and JavaScript although in essence these are very different languages. The C programming language descends from B (designed by Ken Thompson at MIT and Bell Labs 1969–1970), which descends from BCPL (designed by Martin Richards at Cambridge UK and MIT, 1967), which descends from CPL, a research language designed by Christopher Strachey and others (at Cambridge UK, early 1960s). The ideas behind CPL also influenced other languages, such as ML, Standard ML, OCaml, and F#.

The primary aspects of C modelled in this chapter are functions (procedures), parameter passing, arrays, pointers, and pointer arithmetics. The language presented here has no type checker (so far) and therefore is quite close to the B language, which was untyped: The types given in variable declarations are used only to allocate storage, not for compile-time type checking.

7.5.1 Integers, Pointers and Arrays in C

A variable i of type int may be declared as follows:

```
int i;
```

This reserves storage for an integer, and introduces the name i for that storage location. The integer is not initialized to any particular value.

A *pointer* p to an integer may be declared as follows:

```
int *p;
```

This reserves storage for a pointer, and introduces the name p for that storage location. It does not reserve storage for an integer. The pointer is not initialized to any particular value. A pointer is a store address, essentially. The integer pointed to by p (if any) may be obtained by dereferencing the pointer:

```
*p
```

A dereferenced pointer may be used as an ordinary value (an rvalue) as well as the destination of an assignment (an lvalue):

```
i = *p + 2;
*p = 117;
```

A pointer to an integer variable i may be obtained with the address operator (&):

```
p = &i;
```

This assignment makes *p an alias for the variable i. The dereferencing operator (*) and the address operator (&) are inverses, so *&i is the same as i, and &*p is the same as p.

An array ia of 10 integers can be declared as follows:

```
int ia[10];
```

This reserves a block of storage with room for 10 integers, and introduces the name ia for the storage location of the first of these integers. Thus ia is actually a pointer to an integer. The elements of the array may be accessed by the subscript operator ia[...], so

```
ia[0]
```

refers to the location of the first integer; thus ia[0] is the same as *ia. In general, since ia is a pointer, the subscript operator is just an abbreviation for dereferencing in combination with so-called *pointer arithmetics*. Thus

```
ia[k]
```

is the same as

```
*(ia+k)
```

where (ia+k) is simply a pointer to the k'th element of the array, obtained by adding k to the location of the first element, and clearly *(ia+k) is the contents of that location. A strange fact is that arr[5] may just as well be written 5[arr], since the former means *(arr+5) and the latter means *(5+arr), which is equivalent [2, Sect. A8.6.2]. But writing 5[arr] is very unusual and would confuse most people.

The existence of pointers, and the neat relation between array indexing and pointer arithmetics, means that C is an elegant language with few syntactic constructs and few but general concepts. However, the power of pointers and pointer arithmetics also carry great dangers. An attempt *p to dereference an uninitialized pointer p is likely to cause a Segmentation Fault (or Bus Error, or General Protection Fault), but it may also just return an arbitrary value, postponing the disaster in some unpredictable and irreproducible way. An assignment `*p = e` to a pointer can in principle modify any location in the memory of the running process, with equally horrible results if there is a mistake in the pointer expression p. In fact, Hoare wrote about pointers already in 1973: "Their introduction into high level languages has been a step backwards from which we may never recover" [1]. People implementing operating system kernels, device drivers or garbage collectors are likely to disagree, but for most other purposes, the risks of pointers and pointer arithmetics exceed their benefits. Nevertheless, the power and design coherence of pointers, structs, and arrays may be the reason C is still widely used whereas Pascal is not.

7.5.2   Type Declarations in C

In C, type declarations for pointer and array types have a tricky syntax, where the type of a variable x surrounds the variable name:

Declaration	Meaning
int x	x is an integer
int *x	x is a pointer to an integer
int x[10]	x is an array of 10 integers
int x[10][3]	x is an array of 10 arrays of 3 integers
int *x[10]	x is an array of 10 pointers to integers
int *(x[10])	x is an array of 10 pointers to integers
int (*x)[10]	x is a pointer to an array of 10 integers
int **x	x is a pointer to a pointer to an integer

The C type syntax is so obscure that a Unix program called `cdecl` was developed to help explain it. For instance,

```
cdecl explain "int *x[10]"
```

prints

```
declare x as array 10 of pointer to int
```

By contrast,

```
cdecl explain "int (*x)[10]"
```

prints

```
declare x as pointer to array 10 of int
```

The expression syntax for pointer dereferencing and array access is consistent with the declaration syntax, so if ipa is declared as

```
int *ipa[10]
```

then `*ipa[5]` means the integer contents of the location pointed to by element 5 of array ipa, that is, `*(ipa[5])`, or in pure pointer notation, `*(*(ipa+5))`.

Similarly, if `iap` is declared as

```
int (*iap)[10]
```

then `(*iap)[5]` is the integer contents of element 5 of the array pointed to by `iap`, or in pure pointer notation, `*((*iap)+5)`.

Beware that the C compiler will not complain about the expression

```
*iap[5]
```

which means something quite different, and most likely not what one intends. It means `*(*(iap+5))`, that is, add 5 to the address `iap`, take the contents of that location, use that contents as a location, and get its contents. This may cause a Segmentation Fault, or return arbitrary garbage bits.

This is one of the great risks of C: neither the type system (at compile-time) nor the run-time system provide much protection for the programmer.

7.6 The Micro-C Language

Micro-C is a small subset of the C programming language, but large enough to illustrate notions of evaluation stack, arrays, pointer arithmetics, and so on. Figure 7.5 shows a small program in micro-C (file `ex9.c`).

The recursive function `fac` computes the factorial of `n` and returns the result using a pointer `res` to the variable `r` in the `main` function.

The abstract syntax of micro-C is considerably more complex than that of the functional languages and the naive imperative language seen previously. The added complexity is caused by explicit types, the distinction between statements and expressions, the richness of access expressions, and the existence of global but not local

```
void main(int i) {
  int r;
  fac(i, &r);
  print r;
}

void fac(int n, int *res) {
  print &n;                 // Print n's address
  if (n == 0)
    *res = 1;
  else {
    int tmp;
    fac(n-1, &tmp);
    *res = tmp * n;
  }
}
```

Fig. 7.5 A micro-C program to compute and print factorial of `i`

```
type typ =
  | TypI                              (* Type int                *)
  | TypC                              (* Type char               *)
  | TypA of typ * int option         (* Array type              *)
  | TypP of typ                      (* Pointer type            *)
and expr =
  | Access of access                 (* x, *p, or  a[e]         *)
  | Assign of access * expr          (* x=e, *p=e, or a[e]=e    *)
  | Addr of access                   (* &x, &*p, or &a[e]       *)
  | CstI of int                      (* Constant                *)
  | Prim1 of string * expr           (* Unary primitive         *)
  | Prim2 of string * expr * expr    (* Binary primitive        *)
  | Andalso of expr * expr           (* Sequential and          *)
  | Orelse of expr * expr            (* Sequential or           *)
  | Call of string * expr list       (* Function call f(...)    *)
and access =
  | AccVar of string                 (* Variable access x       *)
  | AccDeref of expr                 (* Pointer deref    *p     *)
  | AccIndex of access * expr        (* Array indexing   a[e]   *)
and stmt =
  | If of expr * stmt * stmt         (* If statement            *)
  | While of expr * stmt             (* While loop              *)
  | Expr of expr                     (* Expr. statement    e;   *)
  | Return of expr option            (* Return from method      *)
  | Block of stmtordec list          (* Block                   *)
and stmtordec =
  | Dec of typ * string              (* Local variable dec      *)
  | Stmt of stmt                     (* A statement             *)
and topdec =
  | Fundec of typ option * string * (typ * string) list * stmt
  | Vardec of typ * string
and program =
  | Prog of topdec list
```

Fig. 7.6 Abstract syntax of micro-C

function declarations. The micro-C abstract syntax is shown in Fig. 7.6 and in file Absyn.fs.

As in real C, a micro-C program is a list of top-level declarations. A top-level declaration is either a function declaration or a variable declaration. A function declaration (Fundec) consists of an optional return type, a function name, a list of parameters (type and parameter name), and a function body which is a statement. A variable declaration (Vardec) consists of a type and a variable name.

A statement (stmt) is an if-, while-, expression-, return- or block-statement. An expression statement e; is an expression followed by a semicolon as in C, C++, Java and C#. A block statement is a list of statements or declarations.

All expressions have an rvalue, but only three kinds of expression have an lvalue: a variable x, a pointer dereferencing *p, and an array access a[e]. An expression of one of these forms may be called an *access expression*; such expressions are represented by the type access in the abstract syntax.

An expression (expr) may be a variable x, a pointer dereferencing *p, or an array element access a[e]. The value of such an expression is the rvalue of the access expression (x or *p or a[e]).

An expression may be an assignment x=e to a variable, or an assignment *p=e to a pointed-to cell, or an assignment a[e]=e to an array element. The assignment uses the lvalue of the access expression (x or *p or a[e]).

An expression may be an application &a of the address operator to an expression a, which must have an lvalue and so must be an access expression.

An expression may be a constant (an integer literal or the null pointer literal); or an application of a primitive; or a short-cut logical operator e1&&e2 or e1||e2; or a function call.

A micro-C type is either int or char or array t[] with element type t, or pointer t* to a value of type t.

7.6.1 Interpreting Micro-C

File Interp.fs and other files mentioned in Sect. 7.1 provide an interpretive implementation of micro-C. The interpreter's state is split into environment and store as described in Sect. 7.3. Variables must be explicitly declared (as in C), but there is no type checking (as in B). The scope of a variable extends to the end of the innermost block enclosing its declaration. In the interpreter, the environment is used to keep track of variable scope and the next available store location, and the store keeps track of the locations' current values.

We do not model the return statement in micro-C functions because it represents a way to abruptly terminate the execution of a sequence of statements. This is easily implemented by translation to a stack machine (Chap. 8), or by using a continuation-based interpreter (Chap. 11), but it is rather cumbersome to encode in the direct-style interpreter in Interp.fs.

The main functions of the direct-style micro-C interpreter are shown in Fig. 7.7. Later we shall compile micro-C to bytecode for a stack machine (Chap. 8).

7.6.2 Example Programs in Micro-C

Several micro-C example programs illustrate various aspects of the language, the interpreter (Sect. 7.6.1) and the compilers presented in later chapters. The example programs are summarized in Fig. 7.8.

`run : program -> int list -> store`
Execute an entire micro-C program by initializing global variables and then calling the program's `main` function with the given arguments.

`exec : stmt -> locEnv -> gloEnv -> store -> store`
Execute a micro-C statement `stmt` in the given local and global environments and store, producing an updated store.

`stmtordec: stmtordec->locEnv->gloEnv -> store -> locEnv * store`
Execute a micro-C statement (eg. `x = 2;`) or declaration (eg. `int x;`), producing an updated local environment and an updated store.

`eval : expr -> locEnv -> gloEnv -> store -> int * store`
Evaluate a micro-C expression `expr` in the given local and global environments and store, producing a result (an integer) and an updated store.

`access : access -> locEnv -> gloEnv -> store -> address * store`
Evaluate a micro-C access expression (variable x, pointer dereferencing *p, or array indexing a[e]), producing an address (index into the store), and an updated store.

`allocate : typ * string -> locEnv -> store -> locEnv * store`
Given a micro-C type and a variable name, bind the variable in the given environment and set aside space for it in the given store, producing an updated environment and an updated store.

Fig. 7.7 Main functions of the micro-C interpreter. A `locEnv` is a pair of a (local) environment and a counter indicating the next free store address. A `gloEnv` is a global environment: a pair of an environment for global variables and an environment for global functions

7.6.3 Lexer Specification for Micro-C

The micro-C lexer specification is rather similar to those we have seen already, for instance in Sect. 3.6.3. Tokens are collected from the input character stream by the `Token` lexer rule, names and keywords are recognized by a single regular expression, and an auxiliary F# function `keyword` is used to distinguish keywords from names.

The major new points are:

- The treatment of comments, where micro-C has both end-line comments (starting with / / . . .) and delimited comments (of the form / * . . . * /).
  An additional lexer rule `EndLineComment` is used to skip all input until the end of the current line. The `()` action says that the lexer must stop processing the comment and return to the `Token` lexer rule when meeting end of line or end of file, and the `EndLineComment lexbuf` action says that the lexer should continue processing the comment in all other cases:

  ```
  and EndLineComment = parse
    | ['\n' '\r']          { () }
    | (eof | '\026')       { () }
    | _                    { EndLineComment lexbuf }
  ```

Another lexer rule `Comment` reads to the end of a delimited comment, and correctly handles nested delimited comments (unlike real C). Namely, if it encounters

File	Contents, illustration	Use
ex1.c	while-loop that prints the numbers $n, n-1, n-2, \ldots, 1$	IC
ex2.c	declaring and using arrays and pointers	IC
ex3.c	while-loop that prints the numbers $0, 1, 2, \ldots, n-1$	IC
ex4.c	compute and print array of factorials $0!, 1!, 2!, \ldots, (n-1)!$	IC
ex5.c	compute square, return result via pointer; nested blocks	IC
ex6.c	recursive factorial function; returns result via pointer	IC
ex7.c	infinite while-loop, followed by dead code	IC
ex8.c	while-loop that performs 20 million iterations	IC
ex9.c	recursive factorial function; returns result via pointer	IC
ex10.c	recursive factorial function with ordinary return value	C
ex11.c	find and print all solutions to the n-queens problem	IC
ex11count.c	find and count all solutions to the n-queens problem	IC
ex12.c	perform n tail calls	C
ex13.c	decide whether n is a leap year; logical "and" and "or"	IC
ex14.c	compute integer square root; globally allocated integer	C
ex15.c	perform n tail calls and print $n, n-1, \ldots, 2, 1, 999999$	IC
ex16.c	conditional statement with empty then-branch	IC
ex17.c	call the Collatz function on arguments $0, 1, 2, \ldots$	C
ex18.c	nested conditional statements; backwards compilation	IC
ex19.c	conditional badly compiled by forwards compiler	IC
ex20.c	compilation of a logical expression depends on context	IC
ex21.c	the tail call optimization is unsound in micro-C	IC
ex22.c	leap year function	C
ex23.c	exponentially slow recursive Fibonacci function	C
ex24.c	Ackermann function	C

Fig. 7.8 Example programs in micro-C; n is a command line argument. Examples marked I can be executed by the micro-C interpreter (Sect. 7.6.1). Examples marked C can be compiled to the micro-C stack machine (Chaps. 8 and 12)

yet another comment start (/ *), then the lexer rule calls itself recursively. If it encounters an end of comment (* /) then it returns. If it encounters end of file, it throws an exception, complaining about an unclosed comment. If it encounters end of line or any other input character, it continues reading the comment:

```
and Comment = parse
  | "/*"              { Comment lexbuf; Comment lexbuf }
  | "*/"              { () }
  | ['\n' '\r']       { Comment lexbuf }
  | (eof | '\026')    { lexerError lexbuf "Unclosed comment" }
  | _                 { Comment lexbuf }
```

- The lexer also includes machinery for lexing of C string constants, including C-style string escapes such as `"abc\tdef\nghi"`. This is implemented by lexer rule `String` and auxiliary F# function `cEscape`. Lexer rule `String` takes a parameter `chars`, which is a list of the characters collected so far, in reverse order. When reaching the end of the string (that is, the terminating " character), the character list is reversed and turned into a string.

A complete lexer specification for micro-C is given in file `CLex.fsl`.

7.6.4   Parser Specification for Micro-C

The main challenges when writing a parser specification for micro-C or C are these:

(a) In variable declarations, such as `int *p` and `int *arr[10]`, the type of the variable, here `p` and `arr`, is scattered around the variable name itself. The type cannot be isolated syntactically from the variable name as in Standard ML, F#, Java and C#.
(b) When parsing expressions, we distinguish access expressions such as `x`, `*p` and `a[i]`, which have an lvalue, from other expressions.
(c) Micro-C and C allow balanced if-statements (`if (e) stmt else stmt`) as well as unbalanced ones (`if (e) stmt`), so there are two distinct ways to parse `if (e1) if (e2) stmt1 else stmt2`.
(d) Micro-C and C have a large number of prefix and infix operators, for which associativity and precedence must be declared to avoid grammar ambiguity.

To solve problem (a), the parsing of variable declarations, we invent the concept of a variable description `Vardesc` and parse a declaration `Type Vardesc`, that is, a type (such as `int`) followed by a variable description (such as `*p`).

```
Vardec:
    Type Vardesc                        { ((fst $2) $1, snd $2) }
```

A `Vardesc` is either a name `x`, or a pointer star `*p` on a `Vardesc`, or a `Vardesc` in parentheses, or a `Vardesc` with array brackets `arr[]`:

```
Vardesc:
    NAME
                    { ((fun t -> t), $1)                         }
  | TIMES Vardesc
                    { compose1 TypP $2                           }
  | LPAR Vardesc RPAR
                    { $2                                         }
  | Vardesc LBRACK RBRACK
                    { compose1 (fun t -> TypA(t, None)) $1       }
  | Vardesc LBRACK CSTINT RBRACK
                    { compose1 (fun t -> TypA(t, Some $3)) $1 }
```

The semantic actions build the `typ` abstract syntax for micro-C types (Fig. 7.6) using a bit of functional programming. More precisely, the result of parsing a `Vardesc` is a pair `(tyfun, x)` of a function and a variable name. The `tyfun` expresses how the variable declaration's type should be transformed into the declared variable's type. For instance, in the variable declaration `int *p`, the variable description `*p` will return the pair `((fun t -> TypP t), "p")`, and the `VarDec` rule will apply the function to `TypI`, obtaining the type `TypP(TypI)` for `p`. The `compose1` function composes a given function with the function part of a variable description; see the parser specification in `CPar.fsy` for details.

To solve problem (b), we introduce a new non-terminal `Access` which corresponds to lvalued-expressions such as x, (x), *p, * (p+2), and x[e]. The semantic actions simply build abstract syntax of type `access` from Fig. 7.6:

```
Access:
    NAME                        { AccVar $1           }
  | LPAR Access RPAR            { $2                  }
  | TIMES Access                { AccDeref (Access $2) }
  | TIMES AtExprNotAccess       { AccDeref $2         }
  | Access LBRACK Expr RBRACK   { AccIndex($1, $3)    }
```

To solve problem (c), we distinguish if-else-balanced from if-else-unbalanced statements by duplicating a small part of the grammar, using non-terminals `StmtM` and `StmtU`. An unbalanced statement is an `if-else` statement whose false-branch is an unbalanced statement, or an `if`-statement without `else`, or a `while`-statement whose body is an unbalanced statement:

```
StmtU:
    IF LPAR Expr RPAR StmtM ELSE StmtU { If($3, $5, $7)      }
  | IF LPAR Expr RPAR Stmt             { If($3, $5, Block[]) }
  | WHILE LPAR Expr RPAR StmtU         { While($3, $5)       }
```

By requiring that the true-branch always is balanced, we ensure that

```
if (expr1) if (expr2) stmt1 else stmt2
```

gets parsed as

```
if (expr1) { if (expr2) stmt1 else stmt2 }
```

and not as

```
if (expr1) { if (expr2) stmt1 } else stmt2
```

To solve problem (d) we use these associativity and precedence declarations:

```
%right ASSIGN              /* lowest precedence */
%nonassoc PRINT
%left SEQOR
%left SEQAND
%left EQ NE
%nonassoc GT LT GE LE
%left PLUS MINUS
%left TIMES DIV MOD
%nonassoc NOT AMP
%nonassoc LBRACK           /* highest precedence  */
```

Most of this can be taken straight from a C reference book [2], but the following should be noted. The high precedence given to the left bracket ([) is necessary to avoid ambiguity and parse conflicts in expressions and variable declarations. For expressions it implies that

- the parsing of &a[2] is &(a[2]), that is the address of a[2], not (&a)[2]
- the parsing of *a[2] is *(a[2]), that is the location pointed to by a[2], not (*a)[2]

For variable declarations, the precedence declaration implies that

- the parsing of int *a[10] is int *(a[10]), not int (*a)[10]

The low precedence given to the print keyword is necessary to avoid ambiguity and parse conflicts in expressions with two-argument operators. It implies that

- the parsing of print 2 + 5 is print (2 + 5), not (print 2) + 5

More details on the development of the micro-C parser specification are given in file grammar.txt. The complete parser specification itself is in file CPar.fsy.

7.7   Notes on Strachey's *Fundamental Concepts*

Christopher Strachey's lecture notes *Fundamental Concepts in Programming Languages* [7] from the Copenhagen Summer School on Programming in 1967 were circulated in manuscript and highly influential, although they were not formally published until 25 years after Strachey's death. They are especially noteworthy for introducing concepts such as lvalue, rvalue, ad hoc polymorphism, and parametric polymorphism, that shape our ideas of programming languages even today. Moreover, a number of the language constructs discussed in Strachey's notes made their way into CPL, and hence into BCPL, B, C, C++, Java, and C#.

Here we discuss some of the subtler points in Strachey's notes:

- The CPL assignment:

```
i  :=  (a > b -> j,k)
```

naturally corresponds to this assignment in C, C++, Java, C#:

```
i = (a > b ? j : k)                                    .
```

Symmetrically, the CPL assignment:

```
(a > b -> j, k)  :=  i
```

can be expressed in GNU C (the gcc compiler) like this:

```
(a > b ? j : k)  = i
```

and it can be encoded using pointers and the dereferencing and address operators in all versions of C and C++:

```
*(a > b ? &j : &k) = i
```

In Java, C#, and standard (ISO) C, conditional expressions cannot be used as lvalues. In fact the GNU C compiler (gcc -c -pedantic assign.c) says:

```
ISO C forbids use of conditional expressions as lvalues
```

- The CPL definition in Strachey's Sect. 2.3:

```
let q =~ p
```

defines the lvalue of q to be the lvalue of p, so they are aliases. This feature exists in C++ in the guise of an *initialized reference*:

```
int & q = p;
```

A "ref local" such as `ref int q = p` in C# version 7 (2017) has the same effect. So does call-by-reference parameter passing. For instance, in C#:

```
void m(ref int q) { ... }
... m(ref p) ...
```

When q is a formal parameter and p is the corresponding argument expression, then the lvalue of q is defined to be the lvalue of p.
- The semantic functions L and R in Strachey's Sect. 3.3 are applied only to an expression ϵ and a store σ, but should in fact be applied also to an environment, as in our `Interp.fs`, if the details are to work out properly.
- Note that the CPL block delimiters § and § in Strachey's Sect. 3.4.3 are the grand-parents (via BCPL and B) of C's block delimiters and . The latter are used also in C++, Java, Javascript, Perl, C#, and so on.
- The discussion in Strachey's Sect. 3.4.3 (of the binding mechanism for the free variables of a function) can appear rather academic until one realizes that in F# and other ML-like languages, a function closure always stores the rvalue of free variables, whereas in Java an object stores essentially the lvalue of fields that appear in a method. In Java an instance method (non-static method) m can have as "free variables" the fields of the enclosing object, and the methods refer to those fields via the object reference `this`. As a consequence, subsequent assignments to the fields affect the (r)value seen by the field references in m.

Moreover, when a Java method mInner is declared inside a local inner class CInner inside a method mOuter, then Java requires the variables and parameters of method mOuter referred to by mInner to be declared final (not updatable):

```
class COuter {
  void mOuter(final int p) {
    final int q = 20;

    class CInner {
      void mInner() {
        ... p ... q ...
      }
    }
  }
}
```

In reality the rvalue of these variables and parameters is passed, but when the variables are non-updatable, there is no observable difference between passing the lvalue and the rvalue. Thus the purpose of this "final" restriction on local variables and parameters in Java is to make free variables from the enclosing method *appear* to behave the same as free fields from the enclosing object!

C# does not have local classes, but C# 2.0 and later has anonymous methods, and in contrast to Java's inner classes and F#'s or ML's function closures, these anonymous methods capture the lvalue of the enclosing method's local variables. Therefore an anonymous method can assign to a captured local variable, such as sum in this method that computes the sum of the elements of an integer array:

```
static int ArraySum(int[] arr) {
    int sum = 0;
    Iterate(arr, delegate(int x) { sum += x; });
    return sum;
}
```

where the Iterate method applies delegate act to all items of an enumerable xs:

```
static void Iterate<T>(IEnumerable<T> xs, Action<T> act) {
    foreach (T x in xs)
        act(x);
}
```

Since an anonymous method may outlive the call to the method that created it, such captured local variables cannot in general be allocated in the stack, but must be allocated in an object on the heap.

• The type declaration in Strachey's Sect. 3.7.2 is quite cryptic, but roughly corresponds to this declaration in F#:

```
type LispList =
    | LAtom of atom
    | LCons of Cons
and atom = { PrintName : string; PropertyList : Cons }
and Cons =
    | CNil
    | Cons of cons
and cons = { Car : LispList; Cdr : Cons };;
```

or these declarations in Java (where the Nil pointer case is implicit):

```
abstract class LispList {}

class Cons extends LispList {
    LispList Car;
    Cons Cdr;
}
```

```
class Atom extends LispList {
  String PrintName;
  Cons PropertyList;
}
```

In addition, constructors and field selectors should be defined.

- Note that Strachey's Sect. 3.7.6 describes the C and C++ pointer dereferencing operator and address operator: `Follow[p]` is just `*p`, and `Pointer[x]` is `&x`.
- The "load-update-pairs" mentioned in Strachey's Sect. 4.1 are called *properties* in Common Lisp Object System, Visual Basic, and C#: get-methods and set-methods.

7.8 History and Literature

Many concepts in programming languages can be traced back to Strachey's 1967 Copenhagen summer school lecture notes [7], discussed in Sect. 7.7. Brian W. Kernighan and Dennis M. Ritchie wrote the authoritative book on the C programming language [2]. The development of C is recounted by Ritchie [5]. Various materials on the history of B (including a wonderfully short User Manual from 1972) and C may be found from Dennis Ritchie's home page [4]. A modern portable implementation of BCPL — which must otherwise be characterized as a dead language — is available from Martin Richards's homepage [3].

7.9 Exercises

The main goal of these exercises is to familiarize yourself with the interpretation of imperative languages, lexing and parsing of C, and the memory model (environment and store) used by imperative languages.

Exercise 7.1 Download `microc.zip` from the book homepage, unpack it to a folder `MicroC`, and build the micro-C interpreter as explained in `README.TXT` step (A).

Run the `fromFile` parser on the micro-C example in source file `ex1.c`. In your solution to the exercise, include the abstract syntax tree and indicate its parts: declarations, statements, types and expressions.

Run the interpreter on some of the micro-C examples provided, such as those in source files `ex1.c` and `ex11.c`. Note that both take an integer n as input. The former program prints the numbers from n down to 1; the latter finds all solutions to the n-queens problem.

Exercise 7.2 Write and run a few more micro-C programs to understand the use of arrays, pointer arithmetics, and parameter passing. Use the micro-C implementation in `Interp.fs` and the associated lexer and parser to run your programs, as in Exercise 7.1.

Be careful: there is no type checking in the micro-C interpreter and nothing prevents you from overwriting arbitrary store locations by mistake, causing your program to produce unexpected results. (The type system of real C would catch *some* of those mistakes at compile time).

(i) Write a micro-C program containing a function `void arrsum(int n, int arr[], int *sump)` that computes and returns the sum of the first n elements of the given array `arr`. The result must be returned through the `sump` pointer. The program's `main` function must create an array holding the four numbers 7, 13, 9, 8, call function `arrsum` on that array, and print the result using micro-C's non-standard `print` statement.

Remember that MicroC is very limited compared to actual C: You cannot use initializers in variable declarations like `"int i=0;"` but must use a declaration followed by a statement, as in `"int i; i=0;"` instead; there is no `for`-loop (unless you implement one, see Exercise 7.3); and so on.

Also remember to initialize all variables and array elements; this doesn't happen automatically in micro-C or C.

(ii) Write a micro-C program containing a function `void squares(int n, int arr[])` that, given n and an array `arr` of length n or more fills `arr[i]` with $i*i$ for $i = 0, \ldots, n-1$.

Your `main` function should allocate an array holding up to 20 integers, call function `squares` to fill the array with n square numbers (where $n \le 20$ is given as a parameter to the `main` function), then call function `arrsum` above to compute the sum of the n squares, and print the sum.

(iii) Write a micro-C program containing a function `void histogram(int n, int ns[], int max, int freq[])` which fills array `freq` the frequencies of the numbers in array `ns`. More precisely, when the function returns, element `freq[c]` must equal the number of times that value c appears among the first n elements of `arr`, for `0<=c<=max`. You can assume that all numbers in `ns` are between 0 and `max`, inclusive.

For example, if your `main` function creates an array `arr` holding the seven numbers 1 2 1 1 1 2 0 and calls `histogram(7, arr, 3, freq)`, then afterwards `freq[0]` is 1, `freq[1]` is 4, `freq[2]` is 2, and `freq[3]` is 0. Of course, `freq` must be an array with at least four elements. What happens if it is not? The array `freq` should be declared and allocated in the `main` function, and passed to histogram function. It does not work correctly (in micro-C or C) to stack-allocate the array in `histogram` and somehow return it to the `main` function. Your `main` function should print the contents of array `freq` after the call.

Exercise 7.3 Extend MicroC with a for-loop, permitting for instance

```
for (i=0; i<100; i=i+1)
  sum = sum+i;
```

To do this, you must modify the lexer and parser specifications in `CLex.fsl` and `CPar.fsy`. You may also extend the micro-C abstract syntax in `Absyn.fs` by defining a new statement constructor `Forloop` in the `stmt` type, and add a suitable case to the `exec` function in the interpreter.

But actually, with a modest amount of cleverness (highly recommended), you do not need to introduce special abstract syntax for for-loops, and need not modify the interpreter at all. Namely, a for-loop of the general form

```
for (e1; e2; e3)
  stmt
```

is equivalent to a block

```
{
  e1;
  while (e2) {
    stmt
    e3;
  }
}
```

Hence it suffices to let the semantic action . . . in the parser construct abstract syntax using the existing `Block`, `While`, and `Expr` constructors from the `stmt` type.

Rewrite your programs from Exercise 7.2 to use for-loops instead of while-loops.

Exercise 7.4 Extend the micro-C abstract syntax in `Absyn.fs` with the preincrement and predecrement operators known from C, C++, Java, and C#:

```
type expr =
    . . .
  | PreInc of access    (* C/C++/Java/C#  ++i   or   ++a[e]   *)
  | PreDec of access    (* C/C++/Java/C#  --i   or   --a[e]   *)
```

Note that the predecrement and preincrement operators work on lvalues, that is, variables and array elements, and more generally on any expression that evaluates to a location.

Modify the micro-C interpreter in `Interp.fs` to handle `PreInc` and `PreDec`. You will need to modify the `eval` function, and use the `getSto` and `setSto` store operations (Sect. 7.3).

Exercise 7.5 Extend the micro-C lexer and parser to accept ++e and −e also, and to build the corresponding abstract syntax.

Exercise 7.6 Add compound assignments += and *= and so on to micro-C, that is, lexer, parser, abstract syntax and interpreter (`eval` function). Just as for ordinary assignment, the left-hand side of a compound assignment must be an lvalue, but it is used also as an rvalue.

Exercise 7.7 Extend the micro-C lexer and parser to accept C/C++/Java/C# style conditional expressions

```
e1 ? e2 : e3
```

The abstract syntax for a conditional expression might be `Cond(e1, e2, e3)`, for which you need to change `Absyn.fs` as well.

Exercise 7.8 Most programming languages, including micro-C, prohibit range conditions such as `1 <= x < 365` that we are used to in mathematics. Modify the micro-C parser to accept such range conditions. You first need to decide what kinds of expressions you will accept; for instance, should one accept `z < x > y`, and what should it mean? Also, generate suitable abstract syntax for such expressions. What pitfalls are there in doing so?

Exercise 7.9 Using parts of the abstract syntax, lexer and parser for micro-C, write an F# program that can explain the meaning of C type declarations, in the style of the old Unix utility `cdecl`. For instance, it should be possible to use it as follows:

```
cdecl> explain int *arr[10]
declare arr as array 10 of pointer to int
cdecl> explain int (*arr)[10]
declare arr as pointer to array 10 of int
```

References

1. Hoare, C.: Hints on programming language design. In: ACM SIGACT/SIGPLAN Symposium on Principles of Programming Languages, Boston, Massachusetts 1973. ACM Press (1973)
2. Kernighan, B.W., Ritchie, D.M.: The C Programming Language, 2nd edn. Prentice-Hall, Englewood Cliffs (1988)
3. Richards, M.: Homepage. At http://www.cl.cam.ac.uk/~mr10/
4. Ritchie, D.M.: Homepage. At https://www.bell-labs.com/usr/dmr/www/
5. Ritchie, D.M.: The development of the C language. In: Second History of Programming Languages Conference, Cambridge, Massachusetts (1993)
6. Sestoft, P.: Java Precisely, 3rd edn. The MIT Press, Cambridge (2016)
7. Strachey, C.: Fundamental concepts in programming languages. High. Order Symb. Comput. **13**, 11–49 (2000). Written 1967 as lecture notes for a summer school

Chapter 8
Compiling Micro-C

In Chap. 2 we considered a simple stack-based abstract machine for the evaluation of expressions with variables and variable bindings. Here we continue that work, and extend the abstract machine so that it can execute programs compiled from an imperative language (micro-C). We also write a compiler from the imperative programming language micro-C to this abstract machine. Thus the phases of compilation and execution are:

lexing	from characters to tokens
parsing	from tokens to abstract syntax tree
static checks	check types, check that variables are declared, …
code generation	from abstract syntax to symbolic instructions
code emission	from symbolic instructions to numeric instructions
execution	of the numeric instructions by an abstract machine

8.1 Files for This Chapter

In addition to the micro-C files mentioned in Sect. 7.1, the following files are provided:

File	Contents
MicroC/Machine.fs	definition of micro-C stack machine instructions
MicroC/Machine.java	micro-C stack machine in Java (Sect. 8.2.4)
MicroC/machine.c	micro-C stack machine in C (Sect. 8.2.5)
MicroC/Comp.fs	compile micro-C to stack machine code (Sect. 8.4)
MicroC/prog0	example stack machine program: print numbers
MicroC/prog1	example stack machine program: loop 20m times

© Springer International Publishing AG 2017
P. Sestoft, *Programming Language Concepts*, Undergraduate Topics in Computer Science, DOI 10.1007/978-3-319-60789-4_8

Moreover, Sect. 12.2 and file `Contcomp.fs` show how to compile micro-C backwards, optimizing the generated code on the fly.

8.2   An Abstract Stack Machine

We define a stack-based abstract machine for execution of simple imperative programs, more precisely, micro-C programs.

8.2.1   The State of the Abstract Machine

The state of the abstract machine has the following components:

- a program p: an array of instructions. Each instruction is represented by a number 0, 1, ... possibly with an operand in the next program location. The array is indexed by the numbers (code addresses) 0, 1, ... as usual.
- a program counter pc indicating the next instruction in p to be executed
- a stack s of integers, indexed by the numbers 0, 1, ...
- a stack pointer sp, pointing at the stack top in s; the next available stack position is s[sp+1]
- a base pointer bp, pointing into the current stack frame (or activation record); it points at the first variable or parameter of the current function.

Similar state components may be found in contemporary processors, such as those based on Intel's x86 architecture, which has registers ESP for the stack pointer and EBP for the base pointer, see Sect. 14.2.2.

The abstract machine might be implemented directly in hardware (as digital electronics), in firmware (as field-programmable gate arrays), or in software (as interpreters written on some programming language). Here we do the latter: Sect. 8.2.4 and 8.2.5 present two software implementations of the machine, in Java and C.

The example abstract machine program (from file `prog0`) shown below prints the infinite sequence of numbers $n, n + 1, n + 2, \ldots$, where n is taken from the command line:

```
24 22 0 1 1 16 1
```

The corresponding symbolic bytecode is this:

```
LDARGS; PRINTI; 1; ADD; GOTO 1
```

because 24 = LDARGS; 22 = PRINTI; 0 1 = CSTI 1; 1 = ADD; and 16 1 = GOTO 1 as shown in Fig. 8.1. When executed, the above program loads the command line argument *n* onto the stack top, prints it, adds 1 to it, then goes back to instruction 1 (the `printi` instruction), forever.

Here is another program (in file `prog1`) that loops 20 million times:

```
0 20000000 16 7 0 1 2 9 18 4 25
```

or, in symbolic machine code:

```
20000000; GOTO 7; 1; SUB; DUP; IFNZRO 4; STOP
```

The instruction at address 7 is DUP, which duplicates the stack top element before the test; the instruction at address 4 pushes the constant 1 onto the stack. Loading and interpreting this takes less than 1.4 s with Sun JDK 1.6.0 HotSpot on a 1.6 GHz Intel Pentium M running Windows XP. The equivalent micro-C program (file `ex8.c`) compiled by the compiler presented in this chapter is four times slower than the above hand-written "machine code".

8.2.2 The Abstract Machine Instruction Set

The abstract machine has 26 different instructions, listed in Fig. 8.1. Most instructions are single-word instructions consisting of the instruction code only, but some instructions take one or two or three integer arguments, representing constants (denoted by *m*, *n*) or program addresses (denoted by *a*).

The execution of an instruction has an effect on the stack, on the program counter, and on the console if the program prints something. The stack effect of each instruction is also shown in Fig. 8.1, as a transition

$$s_1 \Rightarrow s_2$$

from the stack s_1 before instruction execution to the stack s_2 after the instruction execution. In both cases, the stack top is on the right, and comma (,) is used to separate stack elements.

Let us explain some of these instructions. The "push constant" instruction CSTI *i* pushes the integer *i* on the stack top. The addition instruction ADD takes two integers i_1 and i_2 off the stack top, computes their sum $i_1 + i_2$, and pushes that on the stack. The duplicate instruction DUP takes the *v* on the stack top, and pushes one more copy on the stack top. The "load indirect" instruction LDI takes an integer *i* off the stack top, uses it as an index into the stack (where the bottom item has index 0) and pushes the value *s*[*i*] onto the stack top. The "stack pointer increment" instruction INCSP *m* increases the stack pointer `sp` by *m*, thus decreasing it if *m* < 0. The

Instruction	Stack before	Stack after	Effect
0 CSTI i	s	$\Rightarrow s,i$	Push constant i
1 ADD	s,i_1,i_2	$\Rightarrow s,(i_1+i_2)$	Add
2 SUB	s,i_1,i_2	$\Rightarrow s,(i_1-i_2)$	Subtract
3 MUL	s,i_1,i_2	$\Rightarrow s,(i_1*i_2)$	Multiply
4 DIV	s,i_1,i_2	$\Rightarrow s,(i_1/i_2)$	Divide
5 MOD	s,i_1,i_2	$\Rightarrow s,(i_1\%i_2)$	Modulo
6 EQ	s,i_1,i_2	$\Rightarrow s,(i_1=i_2)$	Equality (0 or 1)
7 LT	s,i_1,i_2	$\Rightarrow s,(i_1<i_2)$	Less-than (0 or 1)
8 NOT	s,v	$\Rightarrow s,!v$	Negation (0 or 1)
9 DUP	s,v	$\Rightarrow s,v,v$	Duplicate
10 SWAP	s,v_1,v_2	$\Rightarrow s,v_2,v_1$	Swap
11 LDI	s,i	$\Rightarrow s,s[i]$	Load indirect
12 STI	s,i,v	$\Rightarrow s,v$	Store indirect $s[i]=v$
13 GETBP	s	$\Rightarrow s,bp$	Load base ptr bp
14 GETSP	s	$\Rightarrow s,sp$	Load stack ptr sp
15 INCSP m	s	$\Rightarrow s,v_1,..,v_m$	Grow stack ($m\geq 0$)
15 INCSP m	$s,v_1,..,v_{-m}$	$\Rightarrow s$	Shrink stack ($m<0$)
16 GOTO a	s	$\Rightarrow s$	Jump to a
17 IFZERO a	s,v	$\Rightarrow s$	Jump to a if $v=0$
18 IFNZRO a	s,v	$\Rightarrow s$	Jump to a if $v\neq 0$
19 CALL m a	$s,v_1,..,v_m$	$\Rightarrow s,r,bp,v_1,..,v_m$	Call function at a
20 TCALL m n a	$s,r,b,u_1,..,u_n,v_1,..,v_m$	$\Rightarrow s,r,b,v_1,..,v_m$	Tailcall function at a
21 RET m	$s,r,b,v_1,..,v_m,v$	$\Rightarrow s,v$	Return $bp=b$, $pc=r$
22 PRINTI	s,v	$\Rightarrow s,v$	Print integer v
23 PRINTC	s,v	$\Rightarrow s,v$	Print character v
24 LDARGS	s	$\Rightarrow s,i_1,..,i_n$	Command line args
25 STOP	s	$\Rightarrow \_$	Halt the machine

Fig. 8.1 The micro-C stack machine bytecode instructions and their effect. The instruction names (second column) are as defined in the compiler's `Machine.fs` and in the stack machine implementations `Machine.java` and `machine.c`. The first column gives the numeric instruction codes, and the second column gives the symbolic instruction names

GOTO a instruction has no effect on the stack but jumps to address a by changing the program counter pc to a. The "conditional jump" instruction IFZERO a takes a value v from the stack top, and jumps to a if v is zero; otherwise continues at the next instruction.

The CALL m a instruction is used to invoke a micro-C function at address a that takes m parameters. The instruction removes the m parameter values from the stack, pushes the return address r (which is the current program counter pc), pushes the current base pointer bp, and puts the m removed parameter values back — as a result, the stack now contains a new stack frame for the function being called; see Sect. 8.3. Then it jumps to address a, which holds the first instruction of the function.

The RET m instruction is used to return from a function that has m parameters; it ends a function invocation that was initiated by a CALL. The instruction expects the return value v computed by the function to be on the stack top, with a stack frame $r,b,v_1,\ldots,v_m$ below it. It discards this stack frame and pushes the return value v, sets the base pointer bp back to b, and jumps to the return address r.

The TCALL tail call instruction will be explained in Sect. 11.7.

Some instruction sequences are equivalent to others; this fact will be used to improve the compiler in Chap. 12. Alternatively, one could use the equivalences to reduce the instruction set of the abstract machine, which would simplify the machine but slow down the execution of programs. For instance, instruction NOT could be simulated by the sequence 0, EQ, and each of the instructions IFZERO and IFNZRO could be simulated by NOT and the other one.

8.2.3 The Symbolic Machine Code

To simplify code generation in our compilers, we define a symbolic machine code as an F# datatype (file Machine.fs), and also provide F# functions to emit a list of symbolic machine instructions to a file as numeric instruction codes. In addition, we permit the use of symbolic labels instead of absolute code addresses. The code emitter, implemented by function code2ints, transforms an instr list into an int list containing numeric instruction codes instead of symbolic ones, and absolute code addresses instead of labels.

Thus the above program prog0 could be written as follows, as an F# list of symbolic instructions:

```
[LDARGS;
 Label (Lab "L1"); PRINTI; CSTI 1; ADD;
 GOTO (Lab "L1")]
```

Note that Label is a pseudo-instruction; it serves only to indicate a position in the bytecode and gives rise to no instruction in the numeric code:

```
24 22 0 1 1 16 1
```

Abstract machines, or virtual machines, are very widely used for implementing or describing programming languages, including Postscript, Forth, Visual Basic, Java Virtual Machine, and Microsoft IL. More on that in Chap. 9.

8.2.4 The Abstract Machine Implemented in Java

File Machine.java contains an implementation of abstract machine as a Java program. It is invoked like this from a command prompt:

```
java Machine ex1.out 5
```

The abstract machine reads the program as numeric instruction codes from the given file, here ex1.out, and starts executing that file, passing any additional arguments, here the number 5, as integer arguments to the program.

The abstract machine may also be asked to trace the execution. In this case it will print the stack contents and the next instruction just before executing each instruction:

```
java Machinetrace ex1.out 5
```

The abstract machine implementation is based on precisely the five state components listed in Sect. 8.2.1 above: The program p, the program counter pc, the evaluation stack s, the stack pointer sp, and the base pointer bp. The core of the abstract machine is a loop that contains a switch on the next instruction code p[pc]. Here we show the cases for only a few instructions:

```
for (;;) {
  switch (p[pc++]) {
  case CSTI:
    s[sp+1] = p[pc++]; sp++; break;
  case ADD:
    s[sp-1] = s[sp-1] + s[sp]; sp--; break;
  case EQ:
    s[sp-1] = (s[sp-1] == s[sp] ? 1 : 0); sp--; break;
  case ...
  case DUP:
    s[sp+1] = s[sp]; sp++; break;
  case LDI:                   // load indirect
    s[sp] = s[s[sp]]; break;
  case STI:                   // store indirect, keep top value
    s[s[sp-1]] = s[sp]; s[sp-1] = s[sp]; sp--; break;
  case GOTO:
    pc = p[pc]; break;
  case IFZERO:
    pc = (s[sp--] == 0 ? p[pc] : pc+1); break;
  case ...
  case STOP:
    return sp;
  ...
  }
}
```

Basically this is an implementation of the transition rules shown in Fig. 8.1. The loop terminates when a STOP instruction is executed. The ADD and EQ instructions take two operands off the stack, perform an operation, and put the result back onto the stack. In the CSTI instruction, the actual constant follows the CSTI instruction code in the program. The LDI instruction takes the value s[sp] at the stack top and uses it as index into the stack s[s[sp]] and puts the result back on the stack top. A GOTO instruction is executed simply by storing the GOTO's target address p[pc] in the program counter register pc. A conditional jump IFZERO either continues at the jump's target address p[pc] or at the next instruction address pc+1.

8.2.5 The Abstract Machine Implemented in C

File machine.c contains an alternative implementation of the abstract machine as a C program. It is invoked like this from a command prompt:

```
./machine ex1.out 5
```

To trace the execution, invoked the abstract machine with option -trace:

```
./machine -trace ex1.out 5
```

The central loop in this implementation of the abstract machine is completely identical to that shown in Sect. 8.2.4 for the Java-based implementation. Only the auxiliary functions, such as reading the program from file and printing the execution trace, are different, due to the differences between C and Java libraries.

8.3 The Structure of the Stack at Run-Time

Function arguments and local variables (integers, pointers and arrays) are all allocated on the stack, and are accessed relative to the topmost stack frame, using the base pointer register bp (Sect. 8.2.1). Global variables are allocated at the bottom of the stack (low addresses) and are accessed using absolute addresses into the stack.

The stack contains

- a block of global variables, including global arrays:
- a sequence of stack frames for active function calls.

A *stack frame* or *activation record* for a function invocation has the following contents:

- return address;
- the old base pointer (that is, the calling function's base pointer);
- the values of the function's parameters;
- local variables and intermediate results of expressions (temporary values).

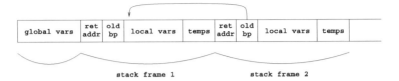

Fig. 8.2 Stack layout at run-time

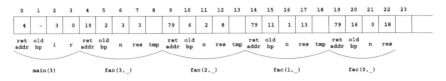

Fig. 8.3 The stack after four calls to the fac function

The stack of frames (above the global variables) is often called the *frame stack*. Figure 8.2 shows a schematic stack with global variables and two stack frames. The old bp field of stack frame 2 points to the base of the local variables in stack frame 1.

Figure 8.3 shows a snapshot of the stack during an actual execution of the micro-C program shown in Fig. 7.5, with the argument i to main being 3. There are no global variables, one activation record for main, and four activation records for fac, corresponding to the calls fac(3,_), fac(2,_), fac(1,_), and fac(0,_).

Note that the offset of a local variable relative to the base pointer is the same in every stack frame created for a given function. For instance, n, res and tmp are always at offset 0, 1 and 2 relative to the base pointer in a stack frame for fac.

Thus the offset of a local variable in a given function can be computed at compile-time. The micro-C compiler records such offsets in a compile-time environment. Note the relation between the run-time environment of the micro-C interpreter (Sect. 7.6.1) and the compile-time environment of the micro-C compiler. The interpreter's environment maps a variable name to an *absolute* address in memory, whereas the compiler's compile-time environment maps a variable name to an offset, or *relative* address. The code generated by the compiler will, at run-time, add that offset to the current base pointer bp to obtain an absolute address, just like that used in the interpreter.

8.4 Compiling Micro-C to Abstract Machine Code

The compiler (in file Comp.fs) compiles micro-C programs into sequences of instructions for this abstract machine. The generated instruction sequence consists of initialization code followed by code representing the bodies of compiled micro-C functions. The initialization code allocates global variables (those declared outside functions), loads the program's command line arguments (if any) onto the stack, and then calls the program's `main` function. The initialization code ends with the `STOP` instruction, so that when the `main` function returns, the bytecode interpreter stops.

The compiler works in three stages, where function `cProgram` performs stages 1 and 2, and function `compile2file` performs stage 3:

- Stage 1: Find all global variables and generate code to initialize them.
- Stage 2: Compile micro-C abstract syntax with symbolic variable and function names to symbolic abstract machine code with numeric addresses for variables, and symbolic labels for functions. One list of symbolic instructions is created for each function.
- Stage 3: Join the global initialization code lists of symbolic instructions with symbolic labels and emit the result to a text file as numeric machine instructions (using absolute code addresses instead of labels).

Expressions are compiled to reverse Polish notation as before, and are evaluated on the stack.

The main functions of the micro-C compiler are listed in Fig. 8.4.

8.5 Compilation Schemes for Micro-C

The compilation of micro-C constructs can be described schematically using compilation schemes:

- S⟦ `stmt` ⟧ is the result of compiling statement `stmt`. The S compilation scheme is shown in Fig. 8.5 and corresponds to compilation function `cStmt` in the micro-C compiler.
- E⟦ `e` ⟧ is the result of compiling expression `e`. The E compilation scheme is shown in Fig. 8.6 and corresponds to compilation function `cExpr` in the micro-C compiler.
- A⟦ `acc` ⟧ is the result of compiling access expression `acc`, such as a variable `x` or pointer dereferencing `*p` or array indexing `a[i]`. The A compilation scheme is shown in Fig. 8.7 and corresponds to compilation function `cAccess` in the micro-C compiler.
- D⟦ `stmtordec` ⟧ is the result of compiling a statement or declaration. When given a statement, the D compilation scheme will use the S scheme to compile it. When given a declaration, such as `int x` or `int arr[10]`, the D compilation scheme will generate code to extend the current stack frame to hold the declared variables. The D scheme (not shown) corresponds to compilation function `cStmtOrDec` in the micro-C compiler.

The lab1 and lab2 that appear in the compilation schemes are labels, assumed to be fresh in each of the compilation scheme cases.

```
cProgram : program -> instr list
```
Compile an entire micro-C program into an instruction sequence. The first part of the instruction sequence will initialize global variables, call the `main` function, and stop the bytecode interpreter when that function returns. The second part of the instruction sequence consists of code for all functions, including `main`.

```
cStmt : stmt -> varEnv -> funEnv -> instr list
```
Compile a micro-C statement into a sequence of instructions. The compilation takes place in a compile-time environment which maps global variables to absolute addresses in the stack (at the bottom of the stack), and maps local variables to offsets from the base pointer of the current stack frame. Also, a function environment maps function names to symbolic labels.

```
cStmtOrDec: stmtordec -> varEnv -> funEnv -> varEnv * instr list
```
Compile a statement or declaration (as found in a statement block { int x; ... }) to a sequence of instructions, either for the statement or for allocation of the declared variable (of type int or array or pointer). Return a possibly extended environment as well as the instruction sequence.

```
cExpr : expr -> varEnv -> funEnv -> instr list
```
Compile a micro-C expression into a sequence of instructions. The compilation takes place in a compile-time variable environment and a compile-time function environment. The code satisfies the *net effect principle* for compilation of expressions: If the compilation (cExpr e env fenv) of expression e returns the instruction sequence `instrs`, then the execution of `instrs` will leave the rvalue of expression e on the stack top (and thus will extend the current stack frame with one element).

```
cAccess : access -> varEnv -> funEnv -> instr list
```
Compile an access (variable x, pointer dereferencing *p, or array indexing a[e]) into a sequence of instructions, again relative to a compile-time environment. The net effect of executing the generated instructions is to leave a stack address, representing the lvalue of the access expression, on the stack top.

```
cExprs : expr list -> varEnv -> funEnv -> instr list
```
Compile a list of expressions into a sequence of instructions.

```
allocate: varkind-> typ*string ->varEnv -> varEnv * instr list
```
Given a micro-C type (int, pointer, or array) and a variable name, bind the variable in the compile-time environment. Return the extended environment together with code for allocating store for the variable at run-time. The `varkind` indicates whether the variable is local (to a function), or global (to the program).

Fig. 8.4 Main compilation functions of the micro-C compiler. A `varEnv` is a pair of a compile-time variable environment and the next available stack frame offset. A `funEnv` is a compile-time function environment

8.6 Compilation of Statements

To understand the compilation schemes, consider the compilation of the statement `if (e) stmt1 else stmt2` in Fig. 8.5. The generated machine code will first evaluate e and leave its value on the stack top. Then the instruction IFZERO will jump to label lab1 if that value is zero (which represents false). In that case, the compiled code for `stmt2` will be executed, as expected. In the opposite case, when the value of e is not zero, the compiled code for stmt1 will be executed, and then the instruction GOTO will jump to lab2, thus avoiding the execution of stmt2.

The compiled code for while (e) body begins with a jump to label lab2. The code at lab2 computes the condition e and leaves its value on the stack top. The instruction IFNZRO jumps to label lab1 if that value is non-zero (true). The code at label lab1 is the compiled body of the while-loop. After executing that code, the code compiled for expression e is executed again, and so on. This way of compiling while-loops means that one (conditional) jump is enough for each iteration of the loop. If we did not make the initial jump around the compiled code, then two jumps would be needed for each iteration of the loop. Since a loop body is usually executed many times, this initial jump is well worth its cost.

The compiled code for an expression statement e; consists of the compiled code for e, whose execution will leave the value of e on the stack top, followed by the instruction INCSP -1 which will drop that value from the stack (by moving the stack pointer down by one place).

The compilation of a return statement is shown in Fig. 8.5 also. When the return statement has an argument expression as in return e; the compilation is straightforward: we generate code to evaluate e and then the instruction RET *m* where *m* is the number of temporaries on the stack. If the corresponding function call is part of an expression in which the value is used, then the value will be on the stack top

Fig. 8.5 Compilation schemes for micro-C statements

S⟦if (e) stmt1 else stmt2⟧ =
  E⟦e⟧
  IFZERO lab1
  S⟦stmt1⟧
  GOTO lab2
  lab1: S⟦stmt2⟧
  lab2: ...

S⟦while (e) body⟧ =
  GOTO lab2
  lab1: S⟦body⟧
  lab2: E⟦e⟧
  IFNZRO lab1

S⟦e; ⟧ =
  E⟦e⟧
  INCSP -1

S⟦{stmtordecl, ..., stmtordecn}⟧ =
  D⟦stmtordecl⟧
  ...
  D⟦stmtordecn⟧
  INCSP locals

S⟦return; ⟧ =
  RET (locals-1)

S⟦return e; ⟧ =
  E⟦e⟧
  RET locals

$E[\![\,acc\,]\!] =$ where `acc` is an access expression
        $A[\![\,acc\,]\!]$
        LDI

$E[\![\,acc=e\,]\!] =$
        $A[\![\,acc\,]\!]$
        $E[\![\,e\,]\!]$
        STI

$E[\![\,i\,]\!] =$
        CSTI i

$E[\![\,null\,]\!] =$
        CSTI 0

$E[\![\,\&acc\,]\!] =$
        $A[\![\,acc\,]\!]$

$E[\![\,!e1\,]\!] =$
        $E[\![\,e1\,]\!]$
        NOT

$E[\![\,e1\ *\ e2\,]\!] =$
        $E[\![\,e1\,]\!]$
        $E[\![\,e2\,]\!]$
        MUL

$E[\![\,e1\ \&\&\ e2\,]\!] =$
        $E[\![\,e1\,]\!]$
        IFZERO lab1
        $E[\![\,e2\,]\!]$
        GOTO lab2
   lab1: CSTI 0
   lab2: ...

$E[\![\,e1\ ||\ e2\,]\!] =$
        $E[\![\,e1\,]\!]$
        IFNZRO lab1
        $E[\![\,e2\,]\!]$
        GOTO lab2
   lab1: CSTI 1
   lab2: ...

$E[\![\,f(e1,\ ...,\ en)\,]\!] =$
        $E[\![\,e1\,]\!]$
        ...
        $E[\![\,en\,]\!]$
        CALL(n, labf)

Fig. 8.6 Compilation schemes for micro-C expressions. The net effect of the code for an expression is to leave the expression's value (rvalue) on the stack top

$A[\![x]\!] =$ when x is global at address a
```
CSTI  a
```

$A[\![x]\!] =$ when x is local at offset a
```
GETBP
CSTI  a
ADD
```

$A[\![\ast e]\!] =$
$$[\![e]\!]$$

$A[\![a[i]]\!] =$
$A[\![a]\!]$
```
LDI
```
$E[\![i]\!]$
```
ADD
```

Fig. 8.7 Compilation schemes for micro-C access expressions: variable x, pointer dereferencing *p or array indexing a[i]. The net effect of the code for an access is to leave an address (lvalue) on the stack top

as expected. If the call is part of an expression statement f(...); then the value is discarded by an INCSP -1 instruction or similar, at the point of return.

In a void function, a return statement return; has no argument expression. Also, the function may return simply by reaching the end of the function body. This kind of return can be compiled to RET $(m - 1)$, where m is the number of temporary values on the stack. This has the effect of leaving a junk value on the stack top

$$\mathrm{RET}(m - 1) \quad s, r, b, v_1, .., v_m \Rightarrow s, v_1$$

Note that in the extreme case where $m = 0$, the junk value will be the old base pointer b, which at first seems completely wrong:

$$\mathrm{RET}(-1) \quad s, r, b \Rightarrow s, b$$

However, a void function f may be called only by an expression statement f(...);, so this junk value is ignored and cannot be used by the calling function.

8.7 Compilation of Expressions

The compilation of an expression e is an extension of the compilation of expressions to postfix form discussed in Chap. 2.

A variable access x or pointer dereferencing *p or array indexing a[i] is compiled by generating code to compute an address in the store (and leave it on the stack top), and then appending an LDI instruction to load the value at that address on the stack top.

An assignment x = e is compiled by generating code for the access expression x, generating code for the right-hand side e, and appending an STI instruction that stores e's value (on the stack top) at the store address computed from x.

Integer constants and the null pointer constant are compiled to code that pushes that constant onto the stack.

An address-of expression &acc is compiled to code that evaluates acc to an address and simply leaves that address on the stack top (instead of dereferencing it with LDI, as in a variable access).

A unary primitive operation such as negation ! e is compiled to code that first evaluates e and then executes instruction NOT to negate that value on the stack top.

A two-argument primitive operation such as times e1 * e2 is compiled to code that first evaluates e1, then e2, and then executes instruction MUL to multiply the two values of the stack top, leaving the product on the stack top.

The short-cut conditional e1 && e2 is compiled to code that first evaluates e1 and leaves its value on the stack top. Then if that value is zero (false), it jumps to label lab1 where the value zero (false) is pushed onto the stack again. Otherwise, if the value of e1 is non-zero (true), then e2 is evaluated and the value of e2 is the value of the entire expression. The jump to label lab2 ensures that the CST 0 expression is not executed in this case.

The short-cut conditional e1 || e2 is dual to e1 && e2 and is compiled in the same way, but zero has been replaced with non-zero and vice versa.

A function call f(e1, ..., en) is compiled to code that first evaluates e1, ..., en in order and then executes instruction CALL(n, labf) where labf is the label of the first instruction of the compiled code for f.

8.8   Compilation of Access Expressions

The compiled code A[[acc]] for an access expression acc must leave an address on the stack top. Thus if acc is a global variable x, the compiled code simply pushes the global store address of x on the stack. If acc is a local variable or parameter x, then the compiled code computes the sum of the base pointer register bp and the variable's offset in the stack frame.

If the access expression acc is a pointer dereferencing *e then the compiled code simply evaluates e and leaves that value on the stack as a store address.

If the access expression is an array indexing a[i], then the compiled code evaluates access expression a to obtain an address where the base address of the array is stored, executes instruction LDI to load that base address, then evaluates expression i to obtain an array index, and finally add the array base address and the index together.

8.9 Compilation to Real Machine Code

This chapter has described the compilation of micro-C to stack machine code, which is basically the task performed by a compiler for Java or Scala or C# or F#, all of which typically target an abstract machine as described in Chap. 9. Real C compilers, such as GNU gcc, generate code for register machines such as x86, ARM, MIPS or others, which adds many interesting complexities and challenges, but may achieve much faster execution of the compiled program.

We have chosen the stack machine approach because it displays the essence of the compilation process without those complications. Chapter 14 shows how the ideas from this chapter can be smoothly adapted to compile micro-C to real x86 machine code, albeit in a rather simple manner.

In particular, the Chap. 14 compiler can handle only relatively simple micro-C expressions because it performs very simple *register allocation*. More general register allocation is needed when compiling to a real machine because instead of an unbounded stack for local variables and intermediate results, there is a fixed (and small) number of registers. General register allocation is typically performed by solving a graph coloring problem, where a graph node represents a local variable or intermediate result and there is an edge between two nodes if the values they represent are live (need to be kept) at the same time. Each machine register is represented by a color; a coloring of the graph is a conflict-free way to assign values to registers. If there are too few registers (colors) to color the graph, then some values need to be "spilled", that is, temporarily stored on a stack anyway.

Also, *instruction selection* is needed to find the best (for instance, shortest or fastest) sequence of instructions that perform a given task, usually under the constraint that some operations may be performed only on particular registers.

Information about these and many more topics may be found in compiler texts [1, 2, 8].

8.10 History and Literature

The earliest compiler for a high-level language is that for Fortran developed by John Backus and others [3] in the years 1954–1957. Many other compilers soon followed. The compilers developed for Algol 60 contained many innovations because of the challenging features of Algol 60: nested variable scopes, call-by-name, procedures as parameters, and more. Notable contributions were made by, among many others, Bauer and Samelson [10] (who invented the compilation of arithmetic expressions to stack machine code); by Edsger Dijkstra (who invented the stack discipline for function calls) [4, 5]; and by Jørn Jensen and Peter Naur [7]. An early book-length treatment of Algol 60 implementation is given by Randell and Russell [9].

A beautiful and concise — less than 70 pages — textbook treatment of both (recursive descent) parsing and code generation for a small imperative language was given in 1976 by Niklaus Wirth [11, Chap. 5].

A widely used compiler text is the "dragon book", named for its cover picture, originally written in 1977 by Alfred Aho and Jeffrey Ullman. The most recent edition from 2006 is by Aho, Lam, Sethi and Ullman [1] and gives a very comprehensive treatment of compilation techniques.

Andrew Appel takes an approach more influenced by functional programming techniques in a series of textbooks [2] using Standard ML, C or Java as implementation language.

Grune has a comprehensive list [6] of compilation-related literature before 1980.

8.11 Exercises

The main goal of these exercises is to familiarize yourself with the compilation of micro-C to bytecode, and the abstract machine used to execute the bytecode.

Exercise 8.1 Download microc.zip from the book homepage, unpack it to a folder MicroC, and build the micro-C compiler as explained in README.TXT step (B).
(i) As a warm-up, compile one of the micro-C examples provided, such as that in source file ex11.c, then run it using the abstract machine implemented in Java, as described also in step (B) of the README file. When run with command line argument 8, the program prints the 92 solutions to the eight queens problem: how to place eight queens on a chessboard so that none of them can attack any of the others.
(ii) Now compile the example micro-C programs ex3.c and ex5.c using functions compileToFile and fromFile from ParseAndComp.fs as above.

Study the generated symbolic bytecode. Write up the bytecode in a more structured way with labels only at the beginning of the line (as in this chapter). Write the corresponding micro-C code to the right of the stack machine code. Note that ex5.c has a nested scope (a block ... inside a function body); how is that visible in the generated code?

Execute the compiled programs using java Machine ex3.out 10 and similar. Note that these micro-C programs require a command line argument (an integer) when they are executed.

Trace the execution using java Machinetrace ex3.out 4, and explain the stack contents and what goes on in each step of execution, and especially how the low-level bytecode instructions map to the higher-level features of MicroC. You can capture the standard output from a command prompt (in a file ex3trace.txt) using the Unix-style notation:

```
java Machinetrace ex3.out 4 > ex3trace.txt
```

Exercise 8.2 Compile and run the micro-C example programs you wrote in Exercise 7.2, and check that they produce the right result. It is rather cumbersome to fill an array with values by hand in micro-C, so the function `squares` from that exercise is very handy.

Exercise 8.3 This abstract syntax for preincrement ++e and predecrement --e was introduced in Exercise 7.4:

```
type expr =
    . . .
    | PreInc of access    (* C/C++/Java/C#  ++i  or  ++a[e]  *)
    | PreDec of access    (* C/C++/Java/C#  --i  or  --a[e]  *)
```

Modify the compiler (function `cExpr`) to generate code for `PreInc(acc)` and `PreDec(acc)`. To parse micro-C source programs containing these expressions, you also need to modify the lexer and parser.

It is tempting to expand ++e to the assignment expression e = e+1, but that would evaluate e twice, which is wrong. Namely, e may itself have a side effect, as in ++arr[++i].

Hence e should be computed only once. For instance, ++i should compile to something like this: `<code to compute address of i>`, DUP, LDI, CSTI 1, ADD, STI, where the address of i is computed once and then duplicated.

Write a program to check that this works. If you are brave, try it on expressions of the form ++arr[++i] and check that i and the elements of arr have the correct values afterwards.

Exercise 8.4 Compile ex8.c and study the symbolic bytecode to see why it is so much slower than the handwritten 20 million iterations loop in prog1.

Compile ex13.c and study the symbolic bytecode to see how loops and conditionals interact; describe what you see.

In a later chapter we shall see an improved micro-C compiler that generates fewer extraneous labels and jumps.

Exercise 8.5 Extend the micro-C language, the abstract syntax, the lexer, the parser, and the compiler to implement conditional expressions of the form (e1 ? e2 : e3).

The compilation of e1 ? e2 : e3 should produce code that evaluates e2 only if e1 is true and evaluates e3 only if e1 is false. The compilation scheme should be the same as for the conditional statement if (e) stmt1 else stmt2, but expression e2 or expression e3 must leave its value on the stack top if evaluated, so that the entire expression e1 ? e2 : e3 leaves its value on the stack top.

Exercise 8.6 Extend the lexer, parser, abstract syntax and compiler to implement `switch` statements such as this one:

```
switch (month) {
  case 1:
    { days = 31; }
  case 2:
    { days = 28; if (y%4==0) days = 29; }
  case 3:
    { days = 31; }
}
```

Unlike in C, there should be no fall-through from one `case` to the next: after the last statement of a `case`, the code should jump to the end of the `switch` statement. The parenthesis after `switch` must contain an expression. The value after a `case` must be an integer constant, and a case must be followed by a statement block. A `switch` with *n* cases can be compiled using *n* labels, the last of which is at the very end of the `switch`. For simplicity, do not implement the `break` statement or the `default` branch.

Exercise 8.7 (Would be convenient) Write a disassembler that can display a machine code program in a more readable way. You can write it in Java, using a variant of the method `insname` from `Machine.java`.

Exercise 8.8 Write more micro-C programs; compile and disassemble them. Write a program that contains the following definitions of `void` functions:

* A function `linsearch(int x, int len, int a[], int *res)` that searches for x in `a[0..len-1]`. It should use pointer `res` to return the least i for which `a[i] == x` if one exists, and return −1 if no `a[i]` equals x.
* A function `binsearch(int x, int n, int a[], int *res)` that searches for x in a sorted array `a[0..n-1]` using binary search. It should use pointer `res` to return the least i for which `a[i] == x` if one exists, and return −1 if no `a[i]` equals x.
* A function `swap(int *x, int *y)` that swaps the values of `*x` and `*y`.
* A function `sort(int n, int a[])` that sorts the array `a[0..n-1]` using insertion sort. (Or use selection sort and the auxiliary function `swap` developed above).

Exercise 8.9 Extend the language and compiler to accept initialized declarations such as

```
int i = j + 32;
```

Doing this for local variables (inside functions) should not be too hard. For global ones it requires more changes.

References

1. Aho, A., Lam, M., Sethi, R., Ullman, J.: Compilers: Principles, Techniques and Tools, 2nd edn. Addison-Wesley, Boston (2006)
2. Appel, A.W.: Modern Compiler Implementation in ML. Cambridge University Press, Cambridge (1997)
3. Backus, J., et al.: The Fortran automatic coding system. In: Western Joint Computer Conference, pp. 188–198. Los Angeles, California (1957)
4. Dijkstra, E.W.: Recursive programming. Numerische Mathematik **2**, 312–318 (1960). http://oai.cwi.nl/oai/asset/9253/9253A.pdf
5. Dijkstra, E.W.: Algol 60 translation. ALGOL Bull. **10** (1961). http://www.cs.utexas.edu/users/EWD/MCReps/MR35.PDF
6. Grune, D.: Compiler Construction Before 1980 (Literature List) (2010). https://dickgrune.com/CS/Summaries/CompilerConstruction-1979.html
7. Jensen, J., Naur, P.: An implementation of Algol 60 procedures. ALGOL Bull. **11**, 38–47 (1961)
8. Mogensen, T.: Introduction to Compiler Design. Springer, Berlin (2011)
9. Randell, B., Russell, L.: Algol 60 Implementation. Academic Press, Cambridge (1964)
10. Samelson, K., Bauer, F.: Sequential formula translation. Commun. ACM **3**(2), 76–83 (1960)
11. Wirth, N.: Algorithms + Data Structures = Programs. Prentice-Hall, Upper Saddle River (1976)

Chapter 9
Real-World Abstract Machines

This chapter discusses some widely used real-world *abstract machines*.

9.1 Files for This Chapter

File	Contents
virtual/ex6java.java	a linked list class in Java; see Fig. 9.4
virtual/ex13.java	a version of ex13.c in Java
virtual/ex13.cs	a version of ex13.c in C#; see Fig. 9.8
virtual/CircularQueue.cs	a generic circular queue in C#; see Fig. 9.10
virtual/Selsort.java	selection sort in Java
virtual/Selsort.cs	selection sort in C#

9.2 An Overview of Abstract Machines

An abstract machine is a device, which may be implemented in software or in hardware, for executing programs in an intermediate instruction-oriented language. The intermediate language is often called bytecode, because the instruction codes are short and simple compared to the instruction set of "real" machines such as the x86, PowerPC or ARM architectures. Abstract machines are also known as *virtual machines*. It is common to identify a machine with the source language it implements, although this is slightly misleading. Prime examples are Postscript (used in millions of printers and typesetters), P-code (widely used in the late 1970's in the UCSD implementation of Pascal for microcomputers), the Java Virtual Machine, and Microsoft's Common Language Infrastructure. Many projects exist whose goal

© Springer International Publishing AG 2017
P. Sestoft, *Programming Language Concepts*, Undergraduate Topics
in Computer Science, DOI 10.1007/978-3-319-60789-4_9

is to develop new abstract machines, either to be more general, or for some specific purpose.

The purpose of an abstract machine typically is to increase the portability and safety of programs in the source language, such as Java. By compiling Java to a single bytecode language (the JVM), one needs only a single Java compiler, yet the Java programs can be run with no changes on different "real" machine architectures and operating systems. Traditionally it is cumbersome to develop portable software in C, say, because an `int` value in C may have 16, 32, 36 or 64 bits depending on which machine the program was compiled for.

The Java Virtual Machine (JVM) is an abstract machine and a set of standard libraries developed by Sun Microsystems since 1994 [17]. Java programs are compiled to JVM bytecode to make Java programs portable across platforms. There are Java Virtual Machine implementations for a wide range of platforms, from large high-speed servers and desktop computers (Sun's Hotspot JVM, IBM's J9 JVM, Oracle/BEA JRockit and others) to very compact embedded systems (Sun's KVM, Myriad's Jbed, and others). There are even implementations in hardware, such as the AJ-80 and AJ-100 Java processors from aJile Systems [1].

The Common Language Infrastructure is an abstract machine and a set of standard libraries developed by Microsoft since 1999, with very much the same goals as Sun's JVM. The platform has been standardized by Ecma International [10] and ISO. Microsoft's implementation of CLI is known as the Common Language Runtime (CLR) and is part of .NET, a large set of languages, tools, libraries and technologies. The first version of CLI was released in January 2002, and version 2.0 with generics was released in 2005. The subsequent versions 3.5 (2008) and 4.0 (2010) mostly contain changes to the libraries and the source languages (chiefly C# and VB.NET), whereas the abstract machine bytecode remains the same as version 2.0.

The JVM was planned as an intermediate target language only for Java, but several other languages now target the JVM, for instance the dynamically typed Groovy, JRuby (a variant of Ruby), Jython (a variant of Python), Clojure, and the statically typed object/functional language Scala.

In contrast to the JVM, Microsoft's CLI was from the outset intended as a target language for a variety of high-level source languages, primarily C#, VB.NET (a successor of Visual Basic 6) and JScript (a version of Javascript), but also C++, COBOL, Standard ML, Eiffel, F#, IronPython (a version of Python) and IronRuby (a version of Ruby). In particular, programs written in any of these languages are supposed to be able to interoperate, using the common object model supported by the CLI. This has influenced the design of CLI, whose bytecode language is somewhat more general than that of the JVM, although it is still visibly slanted towards class-based, statically typed, single-inheritance object-oriented languages such as Java and C#. Also, CLI was designed with just-in-time compilation in mind. For this reason, CLI bytecode instructions are not explicitly typed; the just-in-time compilation phase must infer the types anyway, so there is no need to give them explicitly.

While the JVM has been implemented on a large number of platforms (Solaris, Linux, MS Windows, web browsers, mobile phones, personal digital assistants) from the beginning, CLI was primarily intended for modern versions of the Microsoft Windows operating system. However, the Mono project [19] has created an open source implementation of CLI for many platforms, including Linux, MacOS, Windows, Apple's iOS, Google's Android, and more.

The Parallel Virtual Machine (PVM) is a different kind of virtual machine: it is a library for C, C++ and Fortran programs that makes a network of computers look like a single (huge) computer [22]. Program tasks can easily communicate with each other, even between different processor architectures (x86, Sun Sparc, PowerPC) and different operating systems (Linux, MS Windows, Solaris, HP-UX, AIX, MacOS X). The purpose is to support distributed scientific computing.

Similarly, LLVM [11] is a compiler infrastructure that offers an abstract instruction set and hence a uniform view of different machine architectures. It is used as back-end in the C/C++/Objective-C compiler called Clang and as a platform for parallel programming. For instance, Apple uses it to target both the iPhone (using the ARM architecture) and MacOS (using the x86 architecture), the GHC Haskell compiler uses LLVM, the Mono implementation of CLI uses LLVM as a JIT backend, and Nvidia uses LLVM in some implementations of the CUDA C language [24] for programming general-purpose graphics processors (GPGPU).

9.3 The Java Virtual Machine (JVM)

9.3.1 The JVM Run-Time State

In general, a JVM runs one or more threads concurrently, but here we shall consider only a single thread of execution. The state of a JVM has the following components:

- classes that contain methods, where methods contain bytecode;
- a heap that stores objects and arrays;
- a frame stack for each executing thread;
- class loaders, security managers and other components that we do not care about here.

The *heap* is used for storing values that are created dynamically and whose lifetimes are hard to predict. In particular, all arrays and objects (including strings) are stored on the heap. The heap is managed by a *garbage collector*, which makes sure that unused values are thrown away so that the memory they occupy can be reused for new arrays and objects. Chapter 10 discusses the heap and garbage collection in more detail.

The JVM *frame stack* is a stack of frames (also called activation records), containing one frame for each method call that has not yet completed. For instance, when method `main` has called method `fac` on the argument 3, which has called itself recursively on the argument 2, and so on, the frame stack has the form shown in Fig. 9.1. Thus the stack has exactly the same shape as in the micro-C abstract machine, see Fig. 8.3.

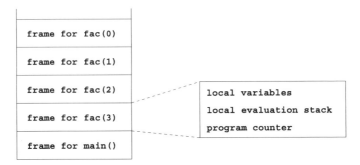

Fig. 9.1   JVM frame stack (*left*) and contents of a stack frame (*right*)

Each JVM stack frame has at least the following components:

- local variables for this method;
- the local evaluation stack for this method;
- the program counter (pc) for this method.

The local variables include the method's parameters, and also the current object reference (`this`) if the method is non-static. The `this` reference (if any) is the first local variable, followed by the method's parameters and the method's local variables. In the JVM bytecode, a local variable is named by its index; this is essentially the local variable's declaration number. For instance, in a non-static method, the current object reference (`this`) has local variable index 0, the first method parameter has index 1, and so on. In a static method, the first method parameter has index 0, and so on.

In the JVM the size of a value is one 32-bit word (for booleans, bytes, characters, shorts, integers, floats, references to array or object), or two words (longs and doubles). A local variable holding a value of the latter kind occupies two local variable indexes.

Only primitive type values (`int`, `char`, `boolean`, `double`, and so on) and references can be stored in a local variable or in the local evaluation stack. All objects and arrays are stored in the heap, but a local variable and the local evaluation stack can of course hold a reference to a heap-allocated object or array.

As shown in Fig. 9.1, and unlike the abstract machine of Chap. 8, the JVM keeps the expression evaluation stack separate from the local variables, and also keeps the frames of different method invocations separate from each other. All stack frames for a given method must have the same fixed size: the number of local variables and the maximal depth of the local evaluation stack must be determined in advance by the Java compiler.

The instructions of a method can operate on:

- the local variables (load variable, store variable) and the local evaluation stack (duplicate, swap);
- static fields of classes, given a class name and a field name;

Fig. 9.2 JVM instruction
type prefixes

Prefix	Type
i	int, short, char, byte
b	byte (in array instructions only)
c	char (in array instructions only)
s	short (in array instructions only)
f	float
d	double
a	reference to array or object

- non-static fields of objects, given an object reference and a field name;
- the elements of arrays, given an array reference and an index.

Classes (with their static fields), objects (with their non-static fields), strings, and arrays are stored in the heap.

9.3.2 The JVM Bytecode

As can be seen, the JVM is a stack-based machine quite similar to the micro-C abstract machine studied in Chap. 8. There is a large number of JVM bytecode instructions, many of which have variants for each argument type. An instruction name prefix indicates the argument type; see Fig. 9.2. For instance, addition of integers is done by instruction iadd, and addition of single-precision floating-point numbers is done by fadd.

The main categories of JVM instructions are shown in Fig. 9.3 along with the corresponding instructions in Microsoft's CLI.

The JVM bytecode instructions have symbolic names as indicated above, and they have fixed numeric codes that are used in JVM class files. A class file represents a Java class or interface, containing static and non-static field declarations, and static and non-static method declarations. A JVM reads one or more class files and executes the public static void main(String[]) method in a designated class.

9.3.3 The Contents of JVM Class Files

When a Java program is compiled with a Java compiler such as javac, one or more class files are produced. A class file MyClass.class describes a single class or interface MyClass. Nested classes within MyClass are stored in separate class files named MyClass$A, MyClass$1, and so on.

Java-based tools for working with JVM class files include ASM [2, 5], BCEL [6], Javassist [8, 14], gnu.bytecode and [29].

Category	JVM	CLI
push constant	bipush, sipush, iconst, ldc, aconst_null, ...	ldc.i4, ldc.i8, ldnull, ldstr, ldtoken
arithmetic	iadd, isub, imul, idiv, irem, ineg, iinc, fadd, fsub, ...	add, sub, mul, div, rem, neg
checked arithmetic		add.ovf, add.ovf.un, sub.ovf, ...
bit manipulation	iand, ior, ixor, ishl, ishr, ...	and, not, or, xor, shl, shr, shr.un
compare values		ceq, cgt, cgt.un, clt, clt.un
type conversion	i2b, i2c, i2s, i2f, f2i, ...	conv.i1, conv.i2, conv.r4, ...
load local var.	iload, aload, fload, ...	ldloc, ldarg
store local var.	istore, astore, fstore, ...	
load array element	iaload, baload, aaload, faload, ...	ldelem.i1, ldelem.i2, ldelem.r4, ...
store array element	iastore, bastore, aastore, fastore, ...	stelem.i1, stelem.i2, stelem.r4, ...
load indirect		ldind.i1, ldind.i2, ...
store indirect		stind.i1, stind.i2, ...
load address		ldloca, ldarga, ldelema, ldflda, ldsflda
stack	swap, pop, dup, dup_x1, ...	pop, dup
allocate array	newarray, anewarray, multianewarray, ...	newarr
load field	getfield, getstatic	ldfld, ldstfld
store field	putfield, putstatic	stfld, stsfld
method call	invokevirtual, invokestatic, invokespecial, ...	call, calli, callvirt
load method pointer		ldftn, ldvirtftn
method return	return, ireturn, areturn, ...	ret
jump	goto	br
compare to 0 and jump	ifeq, ifne, iflt, ifle, ifgt, ifge	brfalse, brtrue
compare values and jump	if_icmpeq, if_icmpne, ...	beq, bge, bge.un, bgt, bgt.un, ble, ble.un, blt, blt.un, bne.un
switch	lookupswitch, tableswitch	switch
object-related	new, instanceof, checkcast	newobj, isinst, castclass
exceptions	athrow	throw, rethrow
threads	monitorenter, monitorexit	
try-catch-finally	jsr, ret	endfilter, endfinally, leave
value types		box, unbox, cpobj, initobj, ldobj, stobj, sizeof

Fig. 9.3 Bytecode instructions in JVM and CLI

```
class LinkedList extends Object {
    Node first, last;

    void addLast(int item) {
        Node node = new Node();
        node.item = item;
        ...
    }

    void printForwards() { ... }
    void printBackwards() { ... }
}
```

Fig. 9.4 Java source code for class LinkedList (file ex6java.java)

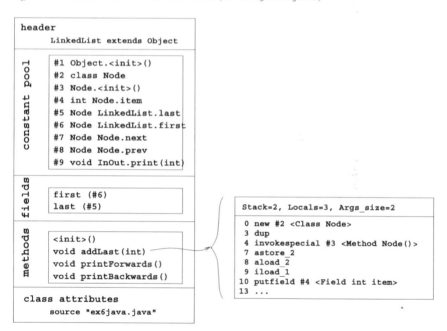

Fig. 9.5 JVM class file for class LinkedList in Fig. 9.4

Figure 9.4 outlines a Java class declaration LinkedList, and the corresponding class file is shown schematically in Fig. 9.5.

The main components of a JVM class file are:

- the name and package of the class;
- the superclass, superinterfaces, and access flags (`public` and so on) of the class;
- the constant pool, which contains field descriptions and method descriptions, string constants, large integer constants, and so on;
- the static and non-static field declarations of the class;

- the method declarations of the class, and possibly special methods <init> that correspond to the constructors of the class, and possibly a special method named <clinit> that corresponds to a static initializer block in the class;
- the attributes (such as source file name).

For each field declaration (type field_decl), the class file describes:

- the name of the field;
- the type of the field;
- the modifiers (static, public, final, ...);
- the attributes (such as source file line number).

For each method declaration (type method_decl), the class file describes:

- the name of the method;
- the signature of the method;
- the modifiers (static, public, final, ...);
- the attributes, including

  - the code for the method;
  - those checked exceptions that the method is allowed to throw (corresponding to the method's throws clause in Java).

The code for a method (attribute CODE) includes:

- the maximal depth of the local evaluation stack in the stack frame for the method; this helps the JVM allocate a stack frame of the right size for a method call;
- the number of local variables in the method;
- the bytecode itself, as a list of JVM instructions;
- the exception handlers, that is, try-catch blocks, of the method body; each handler describes the bytecode range covered by the handler, that is, the try block, the entry of the handler, that is, the catch block, and the exception class handled by this handler;
- code attributes, such as source file line numbers (for run-time error reports).

To study the contents of a class file MyClass.class you can disassemble it by executing:

```
javap -c MyClass
```

To display also the size of the local evaluation stack and the number of local variables, execute:

```
javap -c -verbose C
```

9.3.4 Bytecode Verification

Before a Java Virtual Machine (JVM) executes some bytecode, it will perform so-called *bytecode verification*, a kind of load-time check. The overall goal is to improve security: the bytecode program should not be allowed to crash the JVM or to perform illegal operations. This is especially important when executing "foreign" programs, such as applets within a browser, or other downloaded programs or plugins.

Bytecode verification checks the following things, among others, before the code is executed:

- that all bytecode instructions work on stack operands and local variables of the right type;
- that a method uses no more local variables than it claims to;
- that a method uses no more local stack positions than it claims to;
- that a method throws no other checked exceptions than it claims to;
- that for every point in the bytecode, the local stack has a fixed depth at that point (and thus the local stack does not grow without bounds);
- that the execution of a method ends with a return or throw instruction and does not "fall off the end of the bytecode";
- that execution does not try to use one half of a two-word value (a long or double) as a one-word value (integer or reference or ...).

This verification procedure has been patented [12]. This is a little strange, since (1) the patented procedure is a standard closure (fixed-point) algorithm, and (2) the published patent does not describe the really tricky point: verification of the JVM's so-called local subroutines.

9.4 The Common Language Infrastructure (CLI)

Documentation(l of Microsoft's Common Language Infrastructure (CLI) and its byte-code can be found at Microsoft's Docs site [18].

The CLI implements a stack-based abstract machine very similar to the JVM, with a heap, a frame stack, bytecode verification, and so on. A single CLI stack frame contains the same information as a JVM stack frame (Fig. 9.1), and in addition has space for local allocation of structs and arrays; see Fig. 9.6.

Fig. 9.6 A stack frame in common language infrastructure

```
incoming arguments

local variables

local evaluation stack

local allocation

program counter
```

The CLI's bytecode is called Common Intermediate Language (CIL), or some-times MSIL, and was intended as a target language for a range of different source languages, not just Java/C#, and therefore differs from the JVM in the following respects:

- CIL has a more advanced type system than that of JVM, to better support source languages that have parametric polymorphic types (generic types), such as F# and C# 2.0 and later (see Sect. 9.5);
- CIL's type system is also includes several kinds of pointer, native-size integers (that are 32 or 64 bit wide depending on the platform), and so on;
- CIL has support for tail calls (see Sect. 11.2), to better support functional source languages such as F#, but the run-time system may choose to implement them just like other calls;
- CIL permits the execution of unverified code (an escape from the "managed execution"), pointer arithmetics etc., to support more anarchic source languages such as C and C++;
- CIL has a canonical textual representation (an assembly language), and there is an assembler `ilasm` and a disassembler `ildasm` for this representation; the JVM has no official assembler format;
- CIL instructions are overloaded on type: there is only one `add` instruction, and load-time type inference determines whether it is an `int` add, `float` add, `double` add, and so on. This reflects a design decision in CIL, to support only just-in-time compilation rather than bytecode interpretation. A just-in-time compiler will need to traverse the bytecode anyway, and can thus infer the type of each instruction instead of just checking it.

When the argument type of a CIL instruction needs to be specified explicitly, a suffix is used; see Fig. 9.7. For instance, `ldc.i4` is an instruction for loading 4 byte integer constants.

The main CIL instruction kinds are shown in Fig. 9.3 along with the corresponding JVM instructions. In addition, there are some unverifiable (unmanaged) CIL instructions, useful when compiling C or C++ to CIL:

- jump to method (a kind of tail call): `jmp`, `jmpi`
- block memory operations: `cpblk`, `initblk`, `localloc`

The CLI machine does not have the JVM's infamous local subroutines. Instead so-called protected blocks (those covered by `catch` clauses or `finally` clauses) are subject to certain restrictions. One cannot jump out of or return from a protected block; instead a special instruction called `leave` must be executed, causing associated `finally` blocks to be executed.

A program in C#, F#, VB.Net, and so on, such as `ex13.cs` shown in Fig. 9.8, is compiled to a CLI file `ex13.exe`.

Despite the ".exe" suffix, the resulting file is not a classic MS Windows .exe file, but consists of a small stub that starts the .NET CLI virtual machine, followed by the bytecode generated by the C# compiler. Such a file can be disassembled to symbolic CIL code using

Suffix	Type or variant
i1	signed byte
u1	unsigned byte
i2	signed short (2 bytes)
u2	unsigned short or character (2 bytes)
i4	signed integer (4 bytes)
u4	unsigned integer (4 bytes)
i8	signed long (8 bytes)
u8	unsigned long (8 bytes)
r4	float (32 bit IEEE754 floating-point number)
r8	double (64 bit IEEE754 floating-point number)
i	native size signed integer
u	native size unsigned integer, or unmanaged pointer
r4result	native size result for 32-bit floating-point computation
r8result	native size result for 64-bit floating-point computation
o	native size object reference
&	native size managed pointer
s	short variant of instruction (small immediate argument)
un	unsigned variant of instruction
ovf	overflow-detecting variant of instruction

Fig. 9.7 CLI instruction types and variants (suffixes)

```
int n = int.Parse(args[0]);
int y;
y = 1889;
while (y < n) {
  y = y + 1;
  if (y % 4 == 0 && (y % 100 != 0 || y % 400 == 0))
    InOut.PrintI(y);
}
InOut.PrintC(10);
```

Fig. 9.8 A source program in C#. The corresponding bytecode is shown in Fig. 9.9

```
ildasm /text ex13.exe
```

This reveals the CIL code shown in the right-hand column of Fig. 9.9. It is very similar to the JVM code generated by `javac` for `ex13.java`, shown in the left-hand column. The only difference that `javac` puts the `while` loop condition before the loop body, and Microsoft `csc` puts it after the loop body.

```
JVM (javac 1.6.0_29)              CIL (csc /o 4.0.30319.1)
-------------------------------------------------------------
00 aload_0                       0000 ldarg.0
01 iconst_0                      0001 ldc.i4.0
02 aaload                        0002 ldelem.ref
03 invokestatic parseInt         0003 call Parse
06 istore_1                      0008 stloc.0
07 sipush 1889                   0009 ldc.i4 0x761
10 istore_2                      000e stloc.1
11 iload_2                       000f br 003b
12 iload_1                       0014 ldloc.1
13 if_icmpge 48                  0015 ldc.i4.1
16 iload_2                       0016 add
17 iconst_1                      0017 stloc.1
18 iadd                          0018 ldloc.1
19 istore_2                      0019 ldc.i4.4
20 iload_2                       001a rem
21 iconst_4                      001b brtrue 003b
22 irem                          0020 ldloc.1
23 ifne 11                       0021 ldc.i4.s 100
26 iload_2                       0023 rem
27 bipush 100                    0024 brtrue 0035
29 irem                          0029 ldloc.1
30 ifne 41                       002a ldc.i4 0x190
33 iload_2                       002f rem
34 sipush 400                    0030 brtrue 003b
37 irem                          0035 ldloc.1
38 ifne 11                       0036 call PrintI
41 iload_2                       003b ldloc.1
42 invokestatic printi          003c ldloc.0
45 goto 11                       003d blt 0014
48 bipush 10                     0042 ldc.i4.s 10
50 invokestatic printc          0044 call PrintC
53 return                        0049 ret
```

Fig. 9.9 Bytecode generated from Java source and the C# source in Fig. 9.8

9.5 Generic Types in CLI and JVM

As can be seen, in many respects the CLI and JVM abstract machines are similar, but their treatment of generic types and generic methods differs considerably. Whereas the CLI supports generic types and generic methods also at the bytecode level (since version 2 from 2005), the JVM bytecode has no notion of generic types or methods. This means that generic types and methods in Java are compiled to JVM bytecode by *erasure*, basically replacing each unconstrained type parameter T as in C<T> by type Object in the bytecode, and replacing each constrained type parameter as in C<T extends Sometype> by its bound Sometype. The consequences of this are explored in Sect. 9.5.2 below.

9.5.1 A Generic Class in Bytecode

To illustrate the difference between the CLI's and JVM's implementation of generics, consider the generic circular queue class shown in Fig. 9.10.

An excerpt of the CLI bytecode for the circular queue class is shown in Fig. 9.11. One can see that class CircularQueue is generic also at the CLI bytecode level, taking type parameter T which is used in the types of the class's fields and its methods.

Contrast this with Fig. 9.12, which shows the JVM bytecode obtained from a Java version of the same circular queue class. There is no type parameter on the class, and the methods have return type and parameter type Object, so the class is not generic at the JVM level.

```
class CircularQueue<T> {
  private readonly T[] items;
  private int count = 0, deqAt = 0;
  ...
  public CircularQueue(int capacity) {
    this.items = new T[capacity];
  }
  public T Dequeue() {
    if (count > 0) {
      count--;
      T result = items[deqAt];
      items[deqAt] = default(T);
      deqAt = (deqAt+1) % items.Length;
      return result;
    } else
      throw new ApplicationException("Queue empty");
  }
  public void Enqueue(T x) { ... }
}
```

Fig. 9.10 A generic class implementing a circular queue, in C#

```
.class private auto ansi beforefieldinit CircularQueue`1<T>
       extends [mscorlib]System.Object
{
  .field private initonly !T[] items
  ...
  .method [...] !T  Dequeue() cil managed { ... }
  .method [...] void Enqueue(!T x) cil managed { ... }
}
```

Fig. 9.11 CLI bytecode, with generic types, for generic class CircularQueue in Fig. 9.10. The class takes one type parameter, hence the `1 suffix on the name; the type parameter is called T; and the methods have return type and parameter type T — in the bytecode, this is written !T

```
class CircularQueue extends java.lang.Object {
    ...
    public java.lang.Object dequeue(); ...
    public void enqueue(java.lang.Object); ...
}
```

Fig. 9.12 JVM bytecode, having no generic types, for a Java version of CircularQueue<T> in Fig. 9.10. The class takes no type parameters, and the methods have return type and parameter type object

9.5.2 Consequences for Java

The absence of generic types in the JVM bytecode has some interesting consequences for the Java source language, not just for the JVM bytecode:

- Since type parameters are replaced by type Object in the bytecode, a type argument in Java must be a reference type such as Double; it cannot be a primitive type such as `double`. This incurs run-time wrapping and unwrapping costs in Java.
- Since type parameters do not exist in the bytecode, in Java one cannot reliably perform a cast `(T)e` to a type parameter, one cannot use a type parameter in an instance test `(e instanceof T)`, and one cannot perform reflection `T.class` on a type parameter.
- Since a type parameter is replaced by Object or another type bound, in Java one cannot overload method parameters on different type instances of a generic type. For instance, one cannot overload a method `put` on different type instances of CircularQueue<T>, like this:

```
void put(CircularQueue<Double> cqd) { ... }
void put(CircularQueue<Integer> cqd) { ... }
```

In the bytecode the parameter type would be just the raw type CircularQueue in both cases, so the two methods cannot be distinguished by the JVM.
- Since type parameters do not exist in the bytecode, in Java one cannot create an array whose element type involves a type parameter, as in `new T[n]`. The reason is that when the element type of an array is a reference type, then every assignment `arr[i]=o` to an array element must check that the run-time type of o is a subtype of the actual element type with which the array was created at run-time; see Sect. 4.10.1. Since the type parameter does not exist in the bytecode, it cannot be used as actual element type, so this array element assignment check cannot be performed. Therefore it is necessary to forbid the creation of an array instance whose element type involves a generic type parameter. (However, it is harmless to declare a variable of generic array type, as in `T[] arr;` — this does not produce an array instance).

It follows that the array creation in the constructor in Fig. 9.10 would be illegal in Java. A generic circular queue in Java would instead store the queue's elements in

```
int num = int.Parse(args[0]);
int i = 0x761;
while (i < num) {
  i++;
  if (((i % 4) == 0)
     && (((i % 100) != 0) || ((i % 400) == 0)))
  {
      InOut.PrintI(i);
  }
}
InOut.PrintC(10);
```

Fig. 9.13 The C# code decompiled from the CLI bytecode in the right-hand column of Fig. 9.9

an `ArrayList<T>`, which is invariant in its type parameter and therefore does not need the assignment check; see Sect. 6.6.

- On the positive side, for a language such as Scala [21] that compiles to JVM bytecode but has a different and more powerful type system than Java, it is an advantage that there are no generic types in the JVM bytecode. Since Scala can compile polymorphic types by erasing type parameters, just like Java, interoperability between the two languages becomes much easier. Compiling Scala to CLI is more problematic because the CLI type system does not match Scala's; compilation by erasure would circumvent this mismatch, but then Scala programs cannot conveniently use the generics-based .NET libraries.

9.6 Decompilers for Java and C#

Because of the need to perform load-time checking ("verification", see Sect. 9.3.4) of the bytecode in JVM and .NET CLI, the compiled bytecode files contain much so-called *metadata*, such as the name of classes and interfaces; the name and type of fields; the name, return type and parameter types of methods; and so on. For this reason, and because the Java and C# compilers generate relatively straightforward bytecode, one can usually *decompile* the bytecode files to obtain source programs (in Java or C#) that are very similar to the original programs.

For instance, Fig. 9.13 shows the result of decompiling the .NET CLI bytecode in Fig. 9.9, using the Reflector tool [23] originally developed by Lutz Roeder. The resulting C# is very similar to the original source code shown in Fig. 9.8.

There exist decompilers for JVM and Java also, including Atanas Neshkov's DJ decompiler [20]. Decompilers are controversial because they can be used to reverse engineer Java and C# software that is distributed only in "compiled" bytecode form, so they make it relatively easy to "steal" algorithms and other intellectual property. To fight this problem, people develop obfuscators, which are tools that transform bytecode files to make it harder to decompile them. For instance, an obfuscator may change the names of fields and methods to keywords such as `while` and `if`, which is legal in the bytecode but illegal in the decompiled programs.

9.7 Just-in-Time Compilation

An abstract machine may be implemented as an interpreter of bytecodes. For instance, our simple stack machine from Sect. 8.2 is implemented by an interpreter in Java (Sect. 8.2.4) and by an interpreter in C (Sect. 8.2.5).

However, interpretation may impose considerable run-time overhead, for two reasons. First, the repeated dispatch on the bytecode instruction, as performed by the `switch` statements in the two interpreters, incurs a cost in addition to the code (in the branches of the switch) that performs the real work. Second, the data storage of an interpreter (typically a stack of values) must be general and hence is less efficient than storage (such as registers) that is specialized to the bytecode program that we want to execute.

Therefore a high-performance implementation of an abstract machine typically compiles the bytecode to "real" machine code, for instance for the x86 architecture. This compilation may be done immediately when the abstract machine loads the bytecode program, or it may be done adaptively, so that only bytecode fragments that are executed frequently (for instance, inside a loop) will be compiled to real machine code. In both cases this process is called *just-in-time compilation* or JIT compilation. In particular, most desktop and server versions of the JVM (from Sun/Oracle, IBM and others) and the CLI (from Microsoft and Mono) use just-in-time compilation.

A just-in-time compiler must meet conflicting demands. It should be fast, otherwise it delays the startup of the bytecode program; but it should also generate fast high-quality machine code, otherwise it the program execution itself will be slow. Clearly, in a server application that will be running for weeks, faster code is more important than fast startup; in an interactive application, the opposite holds. For this reason, some abstract machines, such as the Oracle JVM, may be invoked with options `-server` (slower code generation, faster generated code) or `-client` (faster code generation, slower generated code), depending on the application's needs.

Modern just-in-time compilers in general appear to produce good machine code, though not quite as good as a highly optimizing C or Fortran compiler. It is instructive to study the quality of the resulting code. The machine code generated by the Mono implementation of CLI may be inspected by invoking the run-time with `mono -v -v`, which will produce a very verbose trace of the run-time system's actions.

For instance, the x86 machine code generated by Microsoft .NET 4.0 from the CLI bytecode in the right-hand column of Fig. 9.9 is shown in Fig. 9.14. Overall the x86 machine code has the same structure as the bytecode, but it duplicates the loop condition (lines 27–2d and 66–68) for speed. It completely avoids using the machine stack by keeping all intermediate results in machine registers. Local variable 0 (variable n in the C# program in Fig. 9.8) is kept in register `edi`, and local variable 1 (variable y) is kept in register `esi`. The apparently convoluted way of computing

```
22 mov   esi,761h              // y = 1889;
27 cmp   edi,761h
2d jle   0000006A              // if (n <= 1889) skip
2f inc   esi                   // y = y + 1;
30 mov   eax,esi
32 and   eax,80000003h
37 jns   0000003E
39 dec   eax
3a or    eax,0FFFFFFFCh
3d inc   eax
3e test  eax,eax
40 jne   00000066              // y%4!=0
42 mov   eax,esi
44 mov   ecx,64h
49 cdq                         // (sign-extend eax into edx)
4a idiv  eax,ecx               // (int division, remainder in edx)
4c test  edx,edx
4e jne   0000005E              // y%100!=0
50 mov   eax,esi
52 mov   ecx,190h
57 cdq
58 idiv  eax,ecx
5a test  edx,edx
5c jne   00000066              // y%400!=0
5e mov   ecx,esi
60 call  dword ptr ds:[...]    // InOut.PrintI(y)
66 cmp   esi,edi
68 jl    0000002F              // while (y<n) ...
6a ...
```

Fig. 9.14 Machine code (32-bit x86) generated from lines 0009 through 003d of the CLI bytecode in the right-hand column of Fig. 9.9

$y\%4$ in lines 32–3d is probably faster than the general code that uses integer division in lines 44–4a and lines 52–58.

9.8 History and Literature

The book by Smith and Nair [25] gives a comprehensive account of abstract machines and their implementation. It covers the JVM kind of virtual machine as well as virtualization of hardware (not discussed here), as used in IBM mainframes and Intel's recent processors. Diehl, Hartel and Sestoft [9] give an overview of a range of abstract machines.

The authoritative but informal description of the JVM and JVM bytecode is given by Lindholm and Yellin [17]. Bertelsen [4] is one of the many attempts at a more precise formalization of the Java Virtual Machine. A more comprehensive effort that also relates the JVM and Java source code, is by Stärk, Schmid, and Börger [27].

The Microsoft Common Language Infrastructure is described by Gough [13], Lidin [16], and Stutz [26]. Microsoft's CLI specifications and implementations have been standardized by Ecma International since 2003 [10].

Kotzmann et al. describe Sun/Oracle's client JVM [15], and Suganuma et al. have a series of papers [28] describing IBM's JVM; in addition, whitepapers at company websites describe these and other implementations of JVM and CLI. A recent trend in the academic literature on just-in-time compilation is the design of so-called tracing JITs, see for instance Bebenita et al. [3].

One can argue that abstract machines, such as the 1936 Turing machine [30], predate the construction of actual stored-program computers in hardware in the mid-1940es. However, Turing's machine, with its very local control and unbounded sequential storage tapes, is quite far removed from practical computer hardware designs.

A particularly beautiful early theoretical development that is also more "realistic" is found in Corrado Böhm's 1951 PhD dissertation. In just 46 pages the dissertation develops an abstract machine, a small programming language, and a compiler from that language to the abstract machine, with the compiler written in the language itself. The original dissertation is in French but there is a translation into English [7].

9.9   Exercises

The main goal of these exercises is to improve understanding of the mainstream virtual machines such as the Java Virtual Machine and the .NET Common Language Infrastructure, including their intermediate code, metadata, and garbage collectors.

Download and unpack `virtual.zip` which contains the programs needed in the exercises below.

Exercise 9.1 Consider the following C# method from file `Selsort.cs`:

```
public static void SelectionSort(int[] arr) {
  for (int i = 0; i < arr.Length; i++) {
    int least = i;
    for (int j = i+1; j < arr.Length; j++)
      if (arr[j] < arr[least])
        least = j;
    int tmp = arr[i]; arr[i] = arr[least]; arr[least] = tmp;
  }
}
```

(i) From a Visual Studio Command Prompt, compile it using Microsoft's C# compiler with the optimize flag (`/o`), then disassemble it, saving the output to file `Selsort.il`:

```
csc /o Selsort.cs
ildasm /text Selsort.exe > Selsort.il
```

Open Selsort.il in a text editor, find method SelectionSort and its body (bytecode), and delete everything else. Now try to understand the purpose of each bytecode instruction. Write comments to the right of the instructions (or between them) as you discover their purpose. Also describe which local variables in the bytecode (local 0, 1, ...) correspond to which variables in the source code.

To see the precise description of a .NET Common Language Infrastructure byte-code instruction such as ldc.i4.0, consult the Ecma-335 standard [10], find Partition III (PDF pages 324-471 in the December 2010 version) of that document, and search for ldc.

(ii) Now do the same with the corresponding Java method in file Selsort.java. Compile it, then disassemble the Selsort class:

```
javac Selsort.java
javap -verbose -c Selsort > Selsort.jvmbytecode
```

Then investigate and comment Selsort.jvmbytecode as suggested above. For the precise description of JVM bytecode instructions, see [17, Chap. 6].

Hand in the two edited bytecode files with your comments.

Exercise 9.2 This exercise investigates the garbage collection impact in Microsoft .NET of using repeated string concatenation to create a long string. This exercise also requires a Visual Studio Command Prompt.

(i) Compile the C# program StringConcatSpeed.cs and run it with count in the program set to 30,000:

```
csc /o StringConcatSpeed.cs
StringConcatSpeed
(and press enter to see next result)
```

You will probably observe that the first computation (using a StringBuilder) is tremendously fast compared to the second one (repeated string concatenation), although they compute exactly the same result. The reason is that the latter allocates a lot of temporary strings, each one slightly larger than the previous one, and copies all the characters from the old string to the new one.

(ii) In this part, try to use the Windows Performance Monitor to observe the .NET garbage collector's behavior when running StringConcatSpeed.

- In the Visual Studio Command Prompt, start perfmon.
- In the perfmon window, remove the default active performance counters (shown in the list below the display) by clicking the "X" button above the display three times.
- Start StringConcatSpeed and let it run till it says Press return to continue....

- In the `perfmon` window, add a new performance counter, like this:
  - press the "+" button above the display, and the "Add Counters" dialog pops up;
  - select Performance object to be ".NET CLR Memory";
  - select the counter "% Time in GC";
  - select instance to be "StringConcatSpeed" — note (***);
  - press the Add button;
  - close the dialog, and the "% Time in GC" counter should appear in the display.
- Press return in the Visual Studio Command Prompt to let the StringConcatSpeed program continue. You should now observe that a considerable percentage of execution time (maybe 30–50 percent) is spent on garbage collection. For most well-written applications, this should be only 0–10 percent, so the high percentage is a sign that the program is written in a sick way.
- Hand in your quantitative observations together with a description of the platform (version of .NET etc).

(iii) Find another long-running C# program or application (you may well run it from within Visual Studio) and measure the time spent in garbage collection using the `perfmon` as above. Note: It is very important that you attach the performance counter to the particular process ("instance") that you want to measure, in the step marked (***) above, otherwise the results will be meaningless.

References

1. aJile Systems: Homepage. http://www.ajile.com/
2. ASM bytecode Manipulation Framework. http://asm.ow2.org/
3. Bebenita, M., et al.: Spur: a trace-based JIT compiler for CIL. In: Object Oriented Programming, Systems, Languages and Applications (OOPSLA), pp. 708–725. ACM Press, New York (2010)
4. Bertelsen, P.: Semantics of Java bytecode. Technical report, Royal Veterinary and Agricultural University, Denmark (1997). http://citeseerx.ist.psu.edu/viewdoc/summary?doi=10.1.1.48.8315
5. Bruneton, E.: ASM 4.0. A Java Bytecode Engineering Library (2011). http://download.forge.objectweb.org/asm/asm4-guide.pdf
6. Bytecode Engineering Library (BCEL): Home Page. http://commons.apache.org/proper/commons-bcel/
7. Böhm, C.: Digital computers. On encoding logical-mathematical formulas using the machine itself during program conception. Doctoral dissertation, ETH Zürich 1954. http://www.itu.dk/people/sestoft/boehmthesis/ (2016). English translation (from the French original) by Peter Sestoft. p. 50
8. Chiba, S.: Load-time structural reflection in Java. In: ECOOP 2000. Object-oriented Programming. Lecture Notes in Computer Science, vol. 1850, pp. 313–336 (2000)
9. Diehl, S., Hartel, P., Sestoft, P.: Abstract machines for programming language implementation. Fut. Gen. Comput. Syst. **16**(7), 739–751 (2000)
10. ECMA International: Common Language Infrastructure (CLI). Standard ECMA-335, 6th edn. ECMA International (2012). http://www.ecma-international.org/publications/standards/Ecma-335.htm
11. Gnu.Bytecode Bytecode generation Tools: Home Page. http://www.gnu.org/software/kawa/

12. Gosling, J.A.: System and method for pre-verification of stack usage in bytecode program loops. US Patent 5,668,999 (1997)
13. Gough, J.: Compiling for the .Net Common Language Runtime (CLR). Prentice-Hall, Upper Saddle River (2002)
14. Javassist: Home Page. http://jboss-javassist.github.io/javassist/
15. Kotzmann, T., et al.: Design of the Java HotSpot client compiler for Java 6. ACM Trans. Architect. Code Optim. 5(1), 7:1–7:32 (2008)
16. Lidin, S.: Expert .NET 2.0 IL Assembler. Apress (2006)
17. Lindholm, T., Yellin, F., Bracha, G., Buckley, A.: The Java Virtual Machine Specification, Java se 8 edn. Addison-Wesley, Boston (2015). http://docs.oracle.com/javase/specs/jvms/se8/jvms8.pdf
18. Microsoft: .Net documentation. Web Page. https://docs.microsoft.com/en-us/dotnet/
19. Mono Project: http://www.mono-project.com/
20. Neshkov, A.: DJ Java Decompiler. Web Page. http://www.neshkov.com/
21. Odersky, M., Spoon, L., Venners, B.: Programming in Scala. Artima Press (2007)
22. Parallel Virtual Machine (PVM) Project: http://www.csm.ornl.gov/pvm/
23. Roeder, L.: .NET Reflector. Homepage. http://www.red-gate.com/products/dotnet-development/reflector/
24. Sanders, J., Kandrot, E.: CUDA by Example: An Introduction to General-purpose GPU Programming. Addison-Wesley, Boston (2010)
25. Smith, J.E., Nair, R.: Virtual Machines. Versatile Platforms for Systems and Processes. Morgan Kaufmann, Burlington (2005)
26. Stutz, D., Neward, T., Shilling, G.: Shared Source CLI Essentials. O'Reilly (2003)
27. Stärk, R., Schmid, J., Börger, E.: Java and the Java Virtual Machine – Definition, Verification, Validation. Springer, Berlin (2001)
28. Suganuma, T., et al.: Overview of the IBM Java just-in-time compiler. IBM Syst. J. 39(1), 175–193 (2000)
29. The LLVM Compiler Infrastructure. http://llvm.org/
30. Turing, A.M.: On computable numbers, with an application to the Entscheidungsproblem. In: Proceedings of the London Mathematical Society, vol. 2 (Published 1937), vol. 42, s2–42(1), 230–265 (1937)

Chapter 10
Garbage Collection

Heap-allocation and garbage collection are not specific to abstract machines, but has finally become accepted in the mainstream thanks to the Java Virtual Machine and the Common Language Infrastructure/.NET.

10.1 Files for This Chapter

File	Contents
ListC/Absyn.fs	abstract syntax for list-C language
ListC/CLex.fsl	lexer specification for list-C language
ListC/CPar.fsy	parser specification for list-C language
ListC/Machine.fs	definition of list-C abstract machine instructions
ListC/Comp.fs	compiler for list-C language
ListC/ParseAndComp.fs	parser and compiler for list-C language
ListC/listmachine.c	list-C abstract machine in C, w garbage collector

10.2 Predictable Lifetime and Stack Allocation

In the machine models for micro-C studied so far, the main storage data structure was the stack. The stack was used for storing activation records (stack frames) holding the values of parameters and local variables, and for storing intermediate results. An important property of the stack is that if value v2 is pushed on the stack after value v1, then v2 is popped off the stack before v1; last in, first out. Stack allocation is very efficient, just increment the stack pointer to leave space for more data; and

© Springer International Publishing AG 2017
P. Sestoft, *Programming Language Concepts*, Undergraduate Topics
in Computer Science, DOI 10.1007/978-3-319-60789-4_10

deallocation is just as efficient, just decrement the stack pointer so the next allocation overwrites the old data. The possibility of stack allocation follows from the design of micro-C:

• micro-C has static (or lexical) scope rules: the binding of a variable occurrence x can be determined from the program text only, without taking into account the program execution;
• micro-C has nested scopes: blocks { ... } within blocks;
• micro-C does not allow functions to be returned from functions, so there is no need for closures;
• micro-C does not have dynamic data structures such as trees or lists, whose lifetime may be hard to predict.

Thanks to these restrictions, the *lifetime* of a value can be easily determined when the value is created. In fact, a value can live no longer than any value created before it. This makes stack-like allocation possible.

As an aside, note that in micro-C as in real C and C++, one may try to "break the rules" of stack allocation as follows: A function may allocate a variable in its stack frame, use the address operator to obtain a pointer to the newly allocated variable, and return that pointer to the calling function. However, this creates a useless *dangling pointer*, because the stack frame is removed when the function returns, and the pointed-to variable may be overwritten in an unpredictable way by any subsequent function call.

10.3   Unpredictable Lifetime and Heap Allocation

Most modern programming languages do permit the creation of values whose lifetime cannot be determined at their point of creation. In particular, they have functions as values, and hence need closures (Scheme, ML, Scala), they have dynamic data structures such as lists and trees (Scheme, ML, Haskell, Scala), they have thunks or suspensions (representing lazily evaluated values, in Haskell), or they have objects (Simula, Java, C#, Scala).

Values with unpredictable lifetime are stored in another storage data structure, the so-called *heap*. Here "heap" means approximately "disorderly collection of data"; it has nothing to do with heap in the sense "priority queue", as in algorithmics.

Data are explicitly allocated in the heap by the program, but cannot be explicitly deallocated: deallocation is done automatically by a so-called garbage collector. A heap with automatic garbage collection is used in Lisp (1960), Simula (1967), Scheme (1975), ML (1978), Smalltalk (1980), Haskell (1990), Java (1994), C# (1999), and most scripting languages, such as Perl and Python. A major advantage of Java and C# over previous mainstream languages such as Pascal, C and C++ is the use of automatic garbage collection.

In Pascal, C and C++ the user must manually and explicitly manage data whose lifetime is unpredictable. Such data can be allocated outside the stack using `new` (in Pascal or C++) or `malloc` (in C):

```
new(iarray);                                        Pascal
int *iarray = (int*)malloc(len*sizeof(int));        C
int *iarray = new int[len];                         C++
```

but such data must be explicitly deallocated by the program using `dispose` (in Pascal), `free` (in C), or `delete` (in C++):

```
dispose(iarray);                                    Pascal
free(iarray);                                       C
delete[] iarray;                                    C++
```

One would think that the programmer knows best when to deallocate his data, but in practice, this is difficult and the programmer makes grave mistakes. Either data get deallocated too early, creating dangling pointers and causing a program crash, or too late, and the program uses more and more space while running and must be restarted every so often: it has a *space leak*. To permit local deallocation (and also as a defense against unintended updates), C++ programmers often copy or clone their objects before storing or passing them to other functions, causing the program to run slower than strictly necessary. Also, because it is so cumbersome to allocate and deallocate data dynamically in C and C++, there is a tendency to use statically allocated fixed-size buffers. These are prone to buffer overflows and cause server vulnerabilities that are exploited by Internet worms. Also, this approach prevents library functions from being thread-safe.

10.4 Allocation in a Heap

In Java and C#, every new array or object (including strings) is allocated in the heap. Assume we have the following class declarations, where LinkedList is the same as in Fig. 9.4:

```
class Node {
  Node next, prev;
  int item;
}


class LinkedList {
  Node first, last;
  ...
}
```

Then calling a method `m()` will create a new stack frame with room for variables `lst` and `node`:

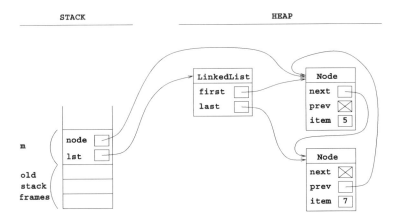

Fig. 10.1   Java allocates all objects in the heap (example `virtual/ex6java.java`)

```
void m() {
  LinkedList lst = new LinkedList();
  lst.addLast(5);
  lst.addLast(7);
  Node node = lst.first;
}
```

Executing m's method body will allocate objects in the heap and make the stack-allocated variables refer to those objects, as shown in Fig. 10.1. The figure also shows that a field of an object may refer to other heap-allocated objects (but never to the stack, in Java and in the safe subset of C#).

Similarly, in F# and ML, closures (`fun x -> y * x`) and constructed data such as pairs (`3, true`), lists `[2; 3; 5; 7; 11]`, strings, arrays, etc. will most likely be allocated in the heap, although ML implementations have a little more freedom to choose how and where to store objects than Java or C# implementations have.

10.5   Garbage Collection Techniques

The purpose of the garbage collector is to make room for new data in the heap by reclaiming space occupied by old data that are no longer used. There are many different garbage collection algorithms to choose from. It is customary to distinguish between the *collector* (which reclaims unused space) and the *mutator* (which allocates new values and possibly updates old values). The collector exists for the sake of the mutator, which does the real useful work. In our case, the mutator is the abstract machine that executes the bytecode.

All garbage collection algorithms have a notion of *root set*. This is typically the variables of all the active (not yet returned-from) function calls or method calls of the program. Thus the root set consists of those references to the heap found in the activation records on the stack and in machine registers (if any).

10.5.1 The Heap and the Freelist

Most garbage collectors organize the heap so that it contains allocated blocks (objects, arrays, strings) of different sizes, mixed with unused blocks of different sizes. Every allocated block contains a header with a size field and other information about the block, and possibly a description of the rest of the block's contents.

Some garbage collectors further make sure that the unused blocks are linked together in a so-called *freelist*: each unused block has a header with a size field, and its first field contains a pointer to the next unused block on the freelist. A pointer to the first block on the freelist is kept in a special freelist register by the garbage collector.

A new value (object, closure, string, array) can be allocated from a freelist by traversing the list until a large enough free block is found. If no such block is found, a garbage collection may be initiated. If there is still no large enough block, the heap must be extended by requesting more memory from the operating system, or the program fails because of insufficient memory.

The main disadvantage of allocation from a freelist is that the search of the freelist for a large enough free block may take a long time, if there are many too-small blocks on the list. Also, the heap may become fragmented. For instance, we may be unable to allocate a block of 36 bytes although there are thousands of unused (but non-adjacent) 32-byte blocks on the freelist. To reduce fragmentation one may try to find the *smallest* block, instead of the first block, on the freelist that is large enough for the requested allocation, but if there are many small free blocks that may be very slow.

The freelist approach to allocation can be improved in a number of ways, such as keeping distinct freelists for distinct sizes of free blocks. This can speed up allocation and reduce fragmentation, but also introduces new complexity in deciding how many distinct freelists to maintain, when to move free blocks from one (little used) freelist to another (highly used) freelist, and so on.

10.5.2 Garbage Collection by Reference Counting

One may implement garbage collection by associating a reference count with each object on the heap, which counts the number of references to the object from other objects and from the stack. Reference counting involves the following operations:

- Each object is created with reference count zero.
- When the mutator performs an assignment x = null, it must decrement the reference count of the object previously referred to by x, if any.
- When the mutator performs an assignment x = o of an object reference to a variable or a field, it must (1) increment the reference count of the object o, and (2) decrement the reference count of the object previously referred to by x, if any.
- Whenever the reference count of an object o gets decremented to zero, the object may be deallocated (by putting it on the freelist), and the reference counts of every object that o's fields refer to must be decremented too.

Some of the advantages and disadvantages of reference counting are:

- Advantages: Reference counting is fairly simple to implement. Once allocated, a value is never moved, which is important if a pointer to the value has been given to external code, such as a input-output routine.
- Disadvantages: Additional memory is required to hold each object's reference count. The incrementing, decrementing and testing of reference counts slow down all assignments of object references. When decrementing an object's reference count to zero, the same must be done recursively to all objects that it refers to, which can take a long time, causing a long pause in the execution of the program. A serious problem with reference counting is that it cannot collect cyclic object structures; after the assignments n = new Node(); n.next = n the reference count of the node object will be two, and setting n = null will only bring it back to one, where it will remain forever. In languages that support cyclic closures, this means that useless data will just accumulate and eventually fill up all available memory.

In addition, reference counting with a freelist suffers the weaknesses of allocation from the freelist; see Sect. 10.5.1.

10.5.3   Mark-Sweep Collection

With mark-sweep garbage collection, the heap contains allocated objects of different sizes, and unused blocks of different sizes. The unallocated blocks are typically managed with a freelist; see Sect. 10.5.1.

Mark-sweep garbage collection is done in two phases; see Fig. 10.2:

1. *The mark phase:* Mark all blocks that are reachable from the root set. This can be done by first marking all those blocks pointed to from the root, and recursively mark the unmarked blocks pointed to from marked blocks. This works even when there are pointer cycles in the heap. The recursive step can use a stack, but can also be done without it, at the cost of some extra complication. After this phase all live blocks are marked.
2. *The sweep phase:* Go through all blocks in the heap, unmark the marked blocks and put the unmarked blocks on the freelist, joining adjacent free blocks into a single larger block.

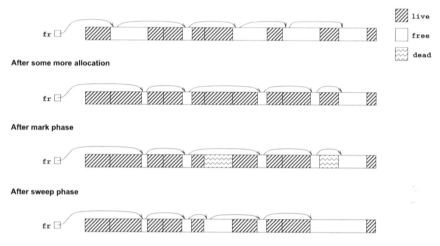

Fig. 10.2 Mark-sweep garbage collection

Some of the advantages and disadvantages of mark-sweep collection are:

- Advantages: Mark-sweep collection is fairly simple to implement. Once allocated, a value is never moved, which is important if a pointer to the value has been given to an external code, such as an input-output routine.
- Disadvantages: Whereas the mark phase will visit only the live objects, the sweep phase must look at the entire heap, also the (potentially very many) dead objects that are about to be collected. A complete cycle of marking and sweeping may take much time, causing a long pause in the execution of the program. This may be mildly irritating in an interactive program, seriously annoying a music-streaming application, and catastrophic in a real-time physical control system.
  In addition, mark-sweep with a freelist suffers the usual weaknesses of allocation from the freelist; see Sect. 10.5.1.

Many variants of mark-sweep garbage collection are possible. It can be made incremental, so that the mark phase consists of many short so-called *slices*, separated by execution of the mutator, and similarly for the sweep phase. This requires a few bits of extra administrative data in each heap block.

10.5.4 Two-Space Stop-and-Copy Collection

With two-space stop-and-copy garbage collection, the heap is divided into two equally large *semispaces*. At any time, one semispace is called the *from-space* and the other is called the *to-space*. After each garbage collection, the two semispaces swap roles. There is no freelist. Instead an *allocation pointer* points into the from-space; all memory from the allocation pointer to the end of the from-space is unused.

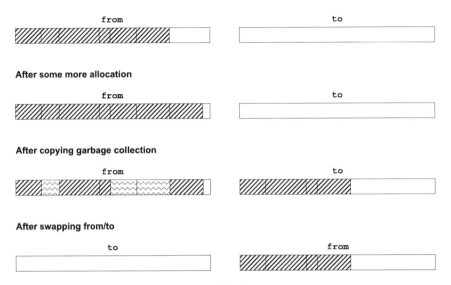

Fig. 10.3 Two-space stop-and-copy garbage collection

Allocation is done in the from-space, at the point indicated by the allocation pointer. The allocation pointer is simply incremented by the size of the block to be allocated. If there is not enough space available, a garbage collection must be made.

Garbage collection moves all live values from the from-space to the to-space (initially empty). Then it sets the allocation pointer to point to the first available memory cell of the to-space, ignores whatever is in the from-space, and swaps from-space and to-space. See Fig. 10.3.

At the end of a garbage collection, the (new) from-space contains all live values and has room for new allocations, and the (new) to-space is empty and remains empty until the next garbage collection.

During the garbage collection, values are copied from the from-space to the to-space as follows. Initially every from-space value reachable from the root set is moved into the to-space (allocating from one end of the initially empty to-space); any root set pointers to the value must be updated to point to the new location. Whenever a value is moved, a forwarding pointer is stored in the old (from-space) copy of the value. Next all values in the to-space are inspected for pointers. If such a pointer points to a value in from-space, then that value is inspected. If the value contains a forwarding pointer, then the pointer (stored in a to-space value) is updated to refer to the (new) to-space address. If the from-space value does not contain a forwarding pointer, then it is moved to the to-space, and a forwarding pointer is stored in the old (from-space) copy of the value.

- Advantages: No stack is needed for garbage collection, only a few pointers. Copying collection automatically performs *compaction*, that is, moves live objects next to each other, leaving no unused holes between them. Compaction avoids *frag-*

mentation of the heap, where the unused memory is scattered over many small holes, all of which are too small to hold the object we want to allocate. Second, compaction improves reference locality, possibly making the memory caches work better.

- Disadvantages: Copying collection (with two spaces) can use at most half of the available memory space for live data. If the heap is nearly full, then every garbage collection will copy almost all live data, but may reclaim only very little unused memory. Thus as the heap gets full, performance may degrade and get arbitrarily bad. A data value may be moved at any time after its allocation, so a pointer to a value cannot be passed to external code without extra safeguards.

10.5.5 Generational Garbage Collection

Generational garbage collection starts from the observation that most allocated values die young. Therefore it is wasteful to copy all the live, mostly old, values in every garbage collection cycle, only to reclaim the space occupied by some young, now dead, values.

Instead, divide the heap into several generations, numbered $1, \ldots, N$. Always allocate in generation 1. When generation 1 is full, do a *minor garbage collection*: promote (move) all live values from generation 1 to generation 2. Then generation 1 is empty and new objects can be allocated into it. When generation 2 is full, promote live values from generation 2 to generation 3, and so on. Generation N, the last generation, may then be managed by a mark-sweep garbage collection algorithm. A *major garbage collection* is a collection that frees all unused spaces in all generations.

When there are only two generations, generation 1 is called the young generation, and generation 2 is called the old generation.

- Advantages: Generational garbage collection reclaims short-lived values very efficiently. If desirable, it can avoid moving old data (which is important if pointers to heap-allocated data need to be passed to external code).
- Disadvantages: Generational garbage collection is more complex to implement. Also, it imposes a certain overhead on the mutator because of the so-called *write barrier* between old and young generations. Whenever a pointer to a young generation data object is stored in an old generation data object, that pointer must be recorded in a separate data structure so that the garbage collector knows all pointers into the young generation. For instance, this may happen in a Java or C# program when executing an assignment such as `o.f = new C(...)`. Thus an extra run-time check must be performed before *every* assignment to a field or element of a heap-allocated object, and extra space is needed to store those pointers. This slows down reference assignments in F# and ML, and assignments to object fields in Java and C#. Since functional programs perform fewer assignments, this overhead hurts functional languages much less than object-oriented ones.

10.5.6   Conservative Garbage Collection

Above we have assumed *precise* garbage collection, that is, that the garbage collector can distinguish exactly between memory bit patterns that represent references to heap objects, and memory patterns that represent other values, such as an integer, a floating-point number, a fragment of a string, or program code.

When one cannot distinguish exactly between heap object references and other bit patterns, one may instead use a *conservative* garbage collector. A conservative garbage collector will assume that if a bit pattern looks like a reference then it *is* a reference, and the pointed-to object will survive the collection. For instance, it may say that if the bit pattern looks like an address inside the allocated heap, and the memory it points at has the proper structure of a heap-allocated object, then it is probably a reference.

But note that some integer, representing maybe a customer number, may look like a reference into the heap. If such an integer is mistakenly assumed to be a reference, then some arbitrary memory data may be assumed to be a live object, which in turn may contain references to other heap data. Hence an innocent integer that looks like a reference may cause a *memory leak*: a large amount of memory may be considered live and this might seriously increase the memory consumption of a program. This is particularly nasty because it is a combination of the (accidental) heap memory addresses and the program's current input data that cause the space leak. Hence a program may run fine a million times, and then suddenly crash for lack of memory when given a particular input parameter.

A conservative garbage collector cannot be compacting. When a compacting garbage collector needs to move a block at heap address p, it must update all references to that block. However, if it cannot distinguish exactly between a reference p and another bit pattern (say, a customer number) that happens to equal p, then there is a risk that the garbage collector will update the customer number, thereby ruining the application's data.

The garbage collectors used in implementations of functional languages and of Java and C# are usually precise, whereas garbage collectors plug-ins for C, C++ and Objective-C (used for programming the Apple iPhone) are usually conservative. A particularly well-known conservative collector is the Boehm-Demers-Weiser collector, which is freely available as a library for C and C++ [4, 5].

10.5.7   Garbage Collectors Used in Existing Systems

The Sun JDK Hotspot Java Virtual Machine version 1.3 through version 6 use a three-generation collector [22]. The three generations are called the *young*, the *old*, and the *permanent* generation. The young generation is further divided into the *eden* and two *survivor spaces*. Most small objects are allocated into the eden, whereas method code and classes, which are likely to be long-lived, are allocated in the permanent generation. A young generation collection (or minor collection) copies from the eden to one of the survivor spaces, and uses stop-and-copy garbage collection between the two survivor spaces. When an object has survived several minor collections, it is moved to the old generation. A major (or full) collection is one that involves the old and the permanent generations; by default it uses non-incremental mark-sweep collection with compaction. Recent versions support several alternative garbage collectors: the parallel collector, the parallel compacting collector, and the concurrent mark-sweep collector [20]. Major collections can be made incremental (resulting in shorter collection pauses) by passing the option -Xincgc to the Java virtual machine. Some information about the garbage collector's activities can be observed by using option java -verbosegc when running a Java program.

Oracle JDK Hotspot JVM version 7 and later contain a new garbage collector, called the *Garbage-First Garbage Collector (G1)* [7, 19]. It is a parallel, generational, compacting collector, designed to exploit the parallelism of multi-core machines better. Both JDK garbage collectors are based on work by David Detlefs and Tony Printezis.

Starting from ca. 2010, IBM's JVM uses an advanced low-latency highly parallel server-oriented garbage collector, based on the Metronome collector [1, 2] developed by David F. Bacon and others at IBM Research. The commercial version is known as Websphere Realtime.

Microsoft's implementation of the .NET Common Language Infrastructure [9] (desktop and server version) uses a garbage collector whose small-object heap has three generations, and whose large-object heap (for arrays and similar greater than e.g. 85 KB) uses a single generation [18]. Small objects are allocated in generation 0 of the small-object heap, and when it is full, live objects are moved to generation 1 by stop-and-copy. When generation 1 is full, live objects are moved to generation 2. Generation 2 is managed by mark-sweep, with occasional compaction to avoid fragmentation. The activity of the garbage collector over time can be observed using Windows performance counters: Start the perfmon tool (from a command prompt), press the (+) button, select ".NET CLR memory" on the "Performance object" dropdown, and then select e.g. "# Gen 0 Collections" and press "Add", to get a graph of the number of generation 0 collections performed over time.

Traditionally, the Mono CLI implementation [16] used the Boehm-Demers-Weiser conservative garbage collector mentioned in Sect. 10.5.6, but now uses SGen, a modern generational and concurrent garbage collector [17].

10.6 Programming with a Garbage Collector

10.6.1 Memory Leaks

Recall the circular queue class in Fig. 9.10. The Dequeue method erases the dequeued item from the queue by performing the assignment items[deqAt] = default(T). But why? The queue would work perfectly also without that extra assignment. However, that seemingly wasteful assignment avoids a *memory leak*. Consider a scenario where an 8 MB array of doubles is enqueued and then immediately dequeued (and never used again), after which a few small objects are put on the queue and dequeued only much later:

```
CircularQueue<double[]> cq = new CircularQueue<double[]>(10);
cq.Enqueue(new double[1000000]);
int n = cq.Dequeue().Length;
... enqueue five more items, and dequeue them much later ...
```

So long as the queue object `cq` is live, the array `items` used to implement it will be live, and therefore everything that `items` refers to will be live. Hence if the `Dequeue` method did not erase the dequeued item from `items`, the garbage collector might be prevented from recycling the useless 8 MB double array for a long time, needlessly increasing the program's memory consumption.

A program that uses more memory than necessary will also be slower than necessary because the garbage collector occasionally has to look at, and perhaps move, the data. There are real-life programs whose running time was reduced from 24 h to 10 min just by eliminating a single memory leak. But as the example shows, the culprit may be difficult to find: the memory leak may hide in an innocent-looking library. For more advice, see Bloch [3, Item 6].

10.6.2   Finalizers

A *finalizer* is a method, associated with an object, that gets called when the garbage collector discovers that the object is dead and collects it. The purpose of a finalizer typically is to release some resource held by the object, such as a file handle or database handle. However, if little garbage is created, a long time may pass from the last use of an object till the garbage collector actually removes it and calls its finalizer. For this and other reasons, finalizers should generally be avoided; see Bloch [3, Item 7].

10.6.3   Calling the Garbage Collector

Most systems include a way to activate the garbage collector; for instance, on the JVM one can call `System.gc()` to request a major garbage collection; in Microsoft .NET the call `System.CG.Collect()` does the same. A programmer may make such requests with the noble intention of "helping" the garbage collector reclaim dead objects, but the garbage collector is usually better informed than the programmer, and such requests therefore have disastrous performance consequences. Don't use those methods.

10.7 Implementing a Garbage Collector in C

In this section we describe in more detail a simple precise non-concurrent non-compacting mark-sweep collector with a freelist, and the abstract machine (mutator) that it cooperates with.

10.7.1 The List-C Language

The language list-C extends micro-C from Sect. 7.6 with a datatype of heap-allocated cons cells, as in the Lisp [14, 15] and Scheme [23] programming languages. A cons cell is a pair of values, where a list-C value either is a micro-C value (such as an integer), or a reference to a cons cell, or nil which denotes the absence of a reference. Using cons cells, one can build lists, trees and other data structures. The purpose of the list-C language is to allow us to generate bytecode for the list-C machine defined in Sect. 10.7.2 below, and thereby exercise the garbage collector of the list-C machine.

The list-C language has an additional type called `dynamic`, whose value may be a micro-C value or a reference to a cons cell or nil. The list-C language moreover has the following additional expressions:

- `nil` evaluates to a null reference, which is neither an integer nor a reference to a heap-allocated cons cell. In a conditional expression this value is interpreted as false.
- `cons(e1, e2)` evaluates to a reference to a new cons cell `(v1 . v2)` on the heap, whose components `v1` and `v2` are the values of `e1` and `e2`. In a conditional expression, this value is interpreted as true.
- `car(e)` evaluates to the first component of the cons cell referred to by `e`.
- `cdr(e)` evaluates to the second component of the cons cell referred by `e`.
- `setcar(p, v)` updates the first component of the cons cell referred to by `p` so that it has value `v`, and then returns `p`.
- `setcdr(p, v)` updates the second component of the cons cell referred to by `p` so that it has value `v`, and then returns `p`.

To illustrate the use of these new expressions, we consider some list-C programs. The program `ex34.lc` allocates a cons cell `(11 . 33)` containing the values 11 and 33 in the heap, and then extracts and prints these values:

```
void main(int n) {
  dynamic c;
  c = cons(11, 15+18);
  print car(c);
  print cdr(c);
}
```

The program ex30.lc, when run with argument n, creates n cons cells of form
(n . 22), (n-1 . 22),..., (1 . 22), and prints the first component of each
such cell:

```
void main(int n) {
  dynamic xs;
  while (n>0) {
    xs = cons(n, 22);
    print car(xs);
    n = n - 1;
  }
}
```

Without a garbage collector, this program will run out of memory for a sufficiently
large n, because each cons cell takes up some space on the heap. However, since the
previous cons cell becomes unreachable (and therefore dead) as soon as the stack-
allocated variable xs is overwritten with a reference to a new cons cell, the program
can run for an arbitrarily long time with a garbage collector (provided the heap has
room for at least two cons cells).

On the other hand, even with a garbage collector, this program (ex31.lc) will
run out of memory for a sufficiently large n:

```
void main(int n) {
  dynamic xs;
  xs = nil;
  while (n>0) {
    xs = cons(n,xs);
    n = n - 1;
  }
}
```

The reason is that this program creates a list of all the cons cells it creates, where
the second field of each cons cell (except the first one) contains a reference to the
previously allocated cons cell. So all the cons cells will remain reachable from the
stack-allocated variable xs and therefore live, so the garbage collector cannot collect
and recycle them.

One can print the contents of such a list of cons cells using this list-C function:

```
void printlist(dynamic xs) {
  while (xs) {
    print car(xs);
    xs = cdr(xs);
  }
}
```

Calling printlist(xs) after the while-loop above would print 1 2 ... n.

A few more functions for manipulating lists of cons cells can be found in file
ex33.lc. Function makelist(n) creates a list like F#'s [1; 2; ...; n]:

```
dynamic makelist(int n) {
  dynamic res;
  res = nil;
  while (n>0) {
    res = cons(n, res);
    n = n - 1;
  }
  return res;
}
```

List-C function `sumlist(xs)` takes such a list and computes the sum of its elements:

```
int sumlist(dynamic xs) {
  int res;
  res = 0;
  while (xs) {
    res = res + car(xs);
    xs = cdr(xs);
  }
  return res;
}
```

List-C function `append(xs,ys)` takes two lists of cons cells and returns a new list that is the concatenation of `xs` and `ys`. Note that it creates as many new cons cells as there are in list `xs`:

```
dynamic append(dynamic xs, dynamic ys) {
  if (xs)
    return cons(car(xs), append(cdr(xs), ys));
  else
    return ys;
}
```

List-C function `reverse(xs)` returns a new list that is the reverse of `xs`. Note that it creates as many new cons cells as there are in list `xs`:

```
dynamic reverse(dynamic xs) {
  dynamic res;
  res = nil;
  while (xs) {
    res = cons(car(xs), res);
    xs = cdr(xs);
  }
  return res;
}
```

The list-C language is implemented by the F# source files in directory `ListC/`, which are basically small variations over those of micro-C. In particular, file

`ListCC.fs` implements a command line compiler for list-C, which can be used as follows:

```
C:\>ListCC ex30.lc
ITU list-C compiler version 1.0.0.0 of 2012-02-08
Compiling ex30.lc to ex30.out
C:\>listmachine ex30.out 334
334 333 332 ...
```

The list-C machine, that can be used to run compiled list-C programs, is described below.

10.7.2   The List-C Machine

The garbage collector must cooperate with the abstract machine (also called the mutator, see the beginning of Sect. 10.5) whose memory it manages. Here we present the list-C machine, a variant of the micro-C abstract machine from Sect. 8.2. In addition to the stack, stack pointer, base pointer, program and program counter of that machine, the extended machine has a heap that may contain *cons cells*, where each cons cell has two fields, which are called "car" and "cdr" for historical reasons.

The extended machine has instructions for loading a null reference, for allocating a new cons cell in the heap, and for reading and writing the two fields of a cons cell, as shown in Fig. 10.4. A partial implementation of the list-C machine, in the real C programming language, is in file `listmachine.c`.

10.7.3   Distinguishing References from Integers

The list-C machine's collector assumes that there is only one primitive datatype, namely 31-bit integers, and that references point only to word-aligned addresses, which are multiples of 4. If we represent a 31-bit abstract machine integer i as the 32-bit C integer `(i<<1) | 1`, the garbage collector can easily distinguish an integer

Instruction	Stack before	Stack after	Effect
26 NIL	s	$\Rightarrow s, nil$	Load *nil* reference
27 CONS	s, v_1, v_2	$\Rightarrow s, p$	Create cons cell $p \mapsto (v_1, v_2)$ in heap
28 CAR	s, p	$\Rightarrow s, v_1$	Component 1 of $p \mapsto (v_1, v_2)$ in heap
29 CDR	s, p	$\Rightarrow s, v_2$	Component 2 of $p \mapsto (v_1, v_2)$ in heap
30 SETCAR	s, p, v	$\Rightarrow s, p$	Set component 1 of $p \mapsto \_$ in heap
31 SETCDR	s, p, v	$\Rightarrow s, p$	Set component 2 of $p \mapsto \_$ in heap

Fig. 10.4   The list-C machine instructions for heap manipulation. These are extensions to the micro-C stack machine shown in Fig. 8.1

(whose least significant bit is 1) from a reference (whose least significant bit is 0). In essence, we *tag* all abstract machine integers with the 1 bit.

The are a few disadvantages to this approach: First, we lose one bit of range from integers so the range becomes roughly minus one billion to plus one billion instead of minus two billion to plus two billion. Second, all operations on abstract machine integers become more complicated because the operands must be untagged before an operation and the result tagged afterwards, which slows down the machine. Third, the abstract machine must have separate arithmetic operations for integers (tagged) and references (untagged), in contrast to the micro-C abstract machine described in Sect. 8.2.4. Nevertheless, this style of garbage collector has been used for many years, in Standard ML of New Jersey, Moscow ML and OCaml. Gudeman [10] discusses various approaches to maintaining such run-time type information in dynamically typed languages.

The tagging is easily performed using a couple of C macros:

```
#define IsInt(v) (((v)&1)==1)
#define Tag(v)   (((v)<<1)|1)
#define Untag(v) ((v)>>1)
```

10.7.4 Memory Structures in the Garbage Collector

The list-C machine's heap is completely covered by blocks, each consisting of one or more 32-bit words. The first word is a header that describes the block; see Fig. 10.5.

A cons cell is a block that consists of three 32-bit words, namely:

- The block header ttttttttnnnnnnnnnnnnnnnnnnnnnngg that contains 8 tag bits (t), 22 length bits (n) and 2 garbage collection bits (g). For a cons cell the tag bits will always be 00000000 and the length bits will be 00...0010, indicating that the cons cell has two words, not counting the header word. The garbage collection bits gg will be interpreted as colors: 00 means white, 01 means grey, 10 means black, and 11 means blue.

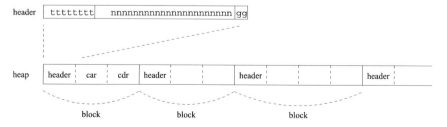

Fig. 10.5 The list-C run-time heap is covered by blocks. Each block consists of a header word and n>=0 other words, each being 32 bits. A header is divided into 8 tag bits, 22 size bits (representing n), and 2 garbage collection bits

- A first field, called the "car" field, which can hold any abstract machine value.
- A second field, called the "cdr" field, which can hold any abstract machine value.

The garbage collector maintains a *freelist* as described in Sect. 10.5.1. A block on the freelist consists of at least two words, namely:

- A block header tttttttttnnnnnnnnnnnnnnnnnnnnnnnnnggg exactly as for a cons cell. In a free cell the tag bits do not matter, whereas the length bits indicate the number N of words in the free block in addition to the header word, and the garbage collection bits must be 11 (blue).
- A field that either is all zeroes, meaning that this is the last block on the freelist, or contains a pointer to the next block on the freelist.
- Further $N - 1$ words that belong to this free block.

Again, it is convenient to define some C macros to access the different parts of a block header:

```
#define BlockTag(hdr)  ((hdr)>>24)
#define Length(hdr)    (((hdr)>>2)&0x003FFFFF)
#define Color(hdr)     ((hdr)&3)
```

Let us further define constants for the colors and a macro Paint(hdr,color) to create a copy of a header word, possibly with a different color:

```
#define White 0
#define Grey  1
#define Black 2
#define Blue  3
#define Paint(hdr, color)  (((hdr)&(~3))|(color))
```

Then we can program parts of the garbage collector quite neatly, like this:

```
if (Color(sweep[0])==Black)          // Make live block white
    sweep[0] = Paint(sweep[0], White);
```

10.7.5   Actions of the Garbage Collector

When the mutator asks the garbage collector for a new object (a block), the garbage collector inspects the freelist register. If it is non-null, the freelist is traversed to find the first free block that is large enough for the new object. If that free block is of exactly the right size, the freelist register is updated to point to the free block's successor; otherwise the allocated object is cut out of the free block. In case the free block is one word larger than the new object, this may produce an orphan word that is neither in use as an object nor on the freelist. An orphan must be blue to prevent the sweep phase from putting it on the freelist.

If no sufficiently large object is found, then a garbage collection is performed; see below. If, after the garbage collection, the freelist still contains no large enough block, then the abstract machine has run out of memory and stops with an error message.

A garbage collection is performed in two phases, as described in Sect. 10.5.3. Before a garbage collection, all blocks in the heap must be white or blue.

- The *mark phase* traverses the mutator's stack to find all references into the heap. A value in the stack is either (1) a tagged integer (perhaps representing a return address, an old base pointer value, or an array address in the stack), or (2) a heap reference.

  In case (2), when we encounter a heap reference to a white block, we mark it black, and recursively process all the block's words in the same way.

  After the mark phase, every block in the heap is either black because it is reachable from the stack by a sequence of references, white because it is not reachable from the mutator stack, or blue because it is on the freelist (but was too small to satisfy the most recent allocation request).

- The *sweep phase* visits all blocks in the heap. If a block is white, it is painted blue and added to the freelist. If the block is black, then its color is reset to white.

  Hence after the sweep phase, the freelist contains all (and only) blocks that are not reachable from the stack. Moreover, all blocks in the heap are white, except those on the freelist, which are blue.

The mark phase as described above may be implemented by a recursive C function that traverses the block graph depth-first. However, if the heap contains a deep data structure, say, a list with 10,000 elements, then the mark phase performs recursive calls to a depth of 10,000 which uses a lot of C stack space. This is unacceptable in practice, so the following may be used instead:

- The *mark phase* traverses the mutator's stack to find all references into the heap. When it encounters a heap reference to a white block, its paints the block grey. When the stack has been traversed, all blocks directly reachable from the stack are grey. Then we traverse the heap, and whenever we find a grey block, we mark the block itself black, and then look at the words in the block. If a field contains a reference to a white block, we make that block grey (but do not process it recursively). We traverse the heap repeatedly this way until no grey blocks remain.

  At this point, every block in the heap is either black because it is reachable from the stack by a sequence of references, or white because it is not reachable from the mutator stack, or blue because it is on the freelist.

The sweep phase is the same as before.

This version of the mark phase requires no recursive calls and hence no C stack, but it may require many traversals of the heap. The extra traversals can be reduced by maintaining a "grey set" of references to grey blocks, and a "mark" pointer into the heap, with the invariant that all grey blocks below the "mark" pointer are also in the grey set. Then we first process the references in the grey set, and only if that set becomes empty we process the blocks after the "mark" pointer. The grey set can be represented in a (small) fixed size array of references, but then we run the risk of not being able to maintain the invariant because the array overflows. In that case we must reset the "mark" pointer to the beginning of the heap and perform at least one more traversal of the heap to look for grey blocks. When the grey set array is big enough, and the heap does not contain deeply nested data structures, a single traversal of the heap will suffice.

10.8   History and Literature

Mark-sweep collection was invented for Lisp by John McCarthy in 1960. Two-space copying garbage collection was proposed by C.J. Cheney in 1970 [6]. Generational garbage collection was proposed by Henry Lieberman and Carl Hewitt at MIT [13]. The terms *collector* and *mutator* are due to Dijkstra [8]. The list-C garbage collector outlined in Sects. 10.7.3 through 10.7.5 owes much to the generational and incremental mark-sweep garbage collector [21] for Caml Light developed by Damien Doligez at INRIA, France.

Even though garbage collectors have been used for five decades, it remains a very active research area, for at least three reasons: First, new hardware (multicore processors, shared memory, cache strategies) offer new technological opportunities. Second, new programming languages (functional, object-oriented and mixtures of these) put different demands on garbage collectors. Third, new kinds of applications expect lower latency and less run-time overhead from the garbage collector. Twenty years ago, nobody could dream of managing 5000 MB of mixed-size data by a garbage collector in a server application, such as video on demand, that must offer guaranteed fast response times and run without interruption for months.

Two comprehensive but somewhat dated surveys of garbage collection techniques are given by Paul Wilson [24], and by Richard Jones and Rafael Lins [12]. Jones also maintains the most comprehensive bibliography on garbage collection [11].

10.9   Exercises

The goal of these exercises is to get hands-on experience with a low-level C implementation of some simple garbage collectors.

Unpack archive listc.zip, whose file listmachine.c contains the abstract machine implementation described in Sect. 10.7, complete with instruction execution, initialization of the heap, and allocation of cons cell in the heap. However, garbage collection is not implemented:

```
void collect(int s[], int sp) {
  // Garbage collection not implemented
}
```

Therefore running `listmachine ex30.out 1000` will fail with the message `Out of memory` because everything the program (`ex30.out` from Sect. 10.7.1) allocates in the heap will remain there forever.

Exercise 10.1 To understand how the abstract machine and the garbage collector work and how they collaborate, answer these questions:

(i) Write 3–10 line descriptions of how the abstract machine executes each of the following instructions:

- ADD, which adds two integers.
- CSTI i, which pushes integer constant i.
- NIL, which pushes a `nil` reference. What is the difference between NIL and CSTI 0?
- IFZERO, which tests whether an integer is zero, or a reference is `nil`.
- CONS
- CAR
- SETCAR

(ii) Describe the result of applying each C macro `Length`, `Color` and `Paint` from Sect. 10.7.4 to a block header tttttttttnnnnnnnnnnnnnnnnnnnnnnnngg, that is, a 32-bit word, as described in the source code comments.
(iii) When does the abstract machine, or more precisely, its instruction interpretation loop, call the `allocate(...)` function? Is there any other interaction between the abstract machine (also called the mutator) and the garbage collector?
(iv) In what situation will the garbage collector's `collect(...)` function be called?

Exercise 10.2 Add a simple mark-sweep garbage collector to listmachine.c, like this:

```
void collect(int s[], int sp) {
  markPhase(s, sp);
  sweepPhase();
}
```

Your `markPhase` function should scan the abstract machine stack `s[0..sp]` and call an auxiliary function `mark(word* block)` on each non-nil heap reference in the stack, to mark live blocks in the heap. Function `mark(word* block)` should recursively mark everything reachable from the block.

The `sweepPhase` function should scan the entire heap, put white blocks on the freelist, and paint black blocks white. It should ignore blue blocks; they are either already on the freelist or they are orphan blocks which are neither used for data nor on the freelist, because they consist only of a block header, so there is no way to link them into the freelist.

This may sound complicated, but the complete solution takes less than 30 lines of C code.

Running `listmachine ex30.out 1000` should now work, also for arguments that are much larger than 1000.

Remember that the listmachine has a tracing mode `listmachine -trace ex30.out 4` so you can see the stack state just before your garbage collector crashes.

Also, calling the `heapStatistics()` function in `listmachine.c` performs some checking of the heap's consistency and reports some statistics on the number of used and free blocks and so on. It may be informative to call it before and after garbage collection, and between the mark and sweep phases.

When your garbage collector works, use it to run the list-C programs `ex35.lc` and `ex36.lc` and check that they produce the expected output (described in their source files). These programs build shared and cyclic data structures in the heap, and this may reveal flaws in your garbage collector.

Exercise 10.3 Improve the sweep phase so that it joins adjacent dead blocks into a single dead block. More precisely, when sweep finds a white (dead) block of length n at address p, it checks whether there is also a white block at address $p + 1 + n$, and if so join them into one block.

Don't forget to run the list-C programs `ex35.lc` and `ex36.lc` as in Exercise 10.2.

Exercise 10.4 Further improve the sweep phase so that it can join any number of adjacent dead blocks in to a single dead block. This is important to avoid fragmentation when allocated blocks may be of different sizes.

Exercise 10.5 Change the mark phase function so that it does not use recursion. Namely, the `mark` function may overflow the C stack when it attempts to mark a deep data structure in the heap, such as a long list created from cons cells.

Instead the mark phase must (A) paint grey all blocks that are directly reachable from the stack. Then (B) it should traverse the heap and whenever it finds a grey block b, paint it black, and then paint grey all white blocks that are reachable from b. The heap traversal must be repeated until there are no more grey blocks in the heap.

So color grey means "this block is live, but the blocks it directly refers to may not have been painted yet", and color black means "this block is live, and all the blocks it directly refers to have been painted grey (or even black)".

Don't forget to run the list-C programs `ex35.lc` and `ex36.lc` as in Exercise 10.2.

Exercise 10.6 Replace the freelist and the mark-sweep garbage collector with a two-space stop-and-copy garbage collector.

The `initheap(...)` function must allocate two heap-spaces (that is, twice as much memory as before), and there must be must be two heap pointers, `heapFrom` and `heapTo`, corresponding to the two heap spaces, and two after-heap pointers `afterFrom` and `afterTo`.

That is, the `freelist` pointer no longer points to a list of unused blocks, but to the first unused word in from-space. All words from that one until (but not including) `afterFrom` are unused. The `allocate(...)` function can therefore be much simpler: it just allocates the requested block in from-space, starting at `freelist` and ending at `freelist+length`, like this:

```
word* allocate(unsigned int tag, unsigned int length,
               int s[], int sp)
{
  int attempt = 1;
  do {
    word* newBlock = freelist;
    freelist += length + 1;
    if (freelist <= afterFrom) {
      newBlock[0] = mkheader(tag, length, White);
      return newBlock;
    }
    // No free space, do a garbage collection and try again
    if (attempt==1)
      collect(s, sp);
  } while (attempt++ == 1);
  printf("Out of memory\n");
  exit(1);
}
```

When there is no longer enough available space between the `freelist` allocation pointer and the end of from-space, a garbage collection will be performed.

The `markPhase` and `sweepPhase` functions are no longer needed. Instead the garbage collector calls a new function `copyFromTo(int[] s, int sp)` that must copy all live blocks from from-space to to-space. After all live blocks have been copied, we must swap the `heapFrom` and `heapTo` pointers (and the `afterFrom` and `afterTo` pointers) so that the next allocations happen in the new from-space. Right after the garbage collection, the `freelist` pointer must point to the first unused word in the new from-space.

Your `copyFromTo(int[] s, int sp)` function must take the following problems into account:

- Function `copyFromTo` must not only copy a live block at address from from-space to to-space, it must also update all references that point to that block.
- Function `copyFromTo` must copy each live block exactly once, otherwise it might duplicate some data structures and lose sharing, as in this case:

```
xs = cons(11, 22);
ys = cons(xs, xs);
```

where the heap should contain a single copy of the cons cell (11 . 22) referred to by `xs`, both before and after the garbage collection.

This will also handle the case where the heap contains a cyclic data structure; the `copyFromTo` function should not attempt to unfold that cyclic structure to an infinite one.

Hence function `copyFromTo` must be able to recognize when it has already copied a block from from-space to to-space.

The following simple approach should work: When all parts of a block has been copied from address `oldB` in from-space to address `newB` in to-space, the first non-header word `oldB[1]` in from-space is overwritten by the new address `newB`; this is called a forwarding pointer. Since from-space and to-space do not overlap, we know that a given block `oldB` in from-space has been copied to to-space precisely when its first field `oldB[1]` contains a pointer into to-space; that is, when this condition holds:

```
oldB[1] != 0 && !IsInt(oldB[1]) && inToHeap(oldB[1])
```

An implementation of `copyFromTo` could use a recursive auxiliary function

```
word* copy(word* block)
```

that copies the indicated block from from-space to to-space, and in any case returns the new to-space address of that block. If the block has already been copied, it just returns the forwarding address obtained from `block[1]`, without copying anything. If the block has not yet been copied, function `copy` claims space for it in to-space, copies all `length+1` words (including header) from from-space to to-space, sets `block[1]` to the new address, and recursively processes and updates the block's fields in to-space.

Function `copyFromTo(s, sp)` makes the initial calls to `copy` by scanning the abstract machine stack `s[0..sp]`, updating each stack entry that refers to a heap block so that it will refer to the copy of the block in to-space.

Don't forget to run the list-C programs `ex30.lc` and `ex35.lc` and `ex36.lc` as in Exercise 10.2.

Exercise 10.7 Improve your stop-and-copy collector from the previous exercise, to avoid recursion in the `copy` function (which may overflow the C stack, just like the recursive `mark` function). One can simply remove the recursive calls from the `copy` function, and introduce an iterative scan of the to-space.

Maintain an extra scan-pointer in to-space, with the following invariant: every block field `toHeap[i]` below the scan-pointer refers into to-space; that is, (1) the block in from-space that `toHeap[i]` originally referred to has been copied to to-space, and (2) the reference at `toHeap[i]` has been updated to refer to the new location of that block. The scan-pointer can make one pass through the to-space; when it catches up with the allocation pointer, the copying from from-space to to-space is complete. No recursion is needed, and no extra memory.

Don't forget to run the list-C programs `ex30.lc` and `ex35.lc` and `ex36.lc` as in Exercise 10.2.

References

1. Bacon, D.F.: Realtime garbage collection. ACM Queue **5**(1), 40–49 (2007)
2. Bacon, D.F., Cheng, P., Rajan, V.: A real-time garbage collector with low overhead and consistent utilization. In: Thirtieth ACM Symposium on Principles of Programming Languages, pp. 285–298. ACM (2003)
3. Bloch, J.: Effective Java Programming Language Guide, 2nd edn. Addison-Wesley, Boston (2008)
4. Boehm, H.: A garbage collector for C and C++. http://www.hpl.hp.com/personal/Hans_Boehm/gc/
5. Boehm, H., Weiser, M.: Garbage collection in an uncooperative environment. Softw. Pract. Exp. **18**, 807–820 (1988)
6. Cheney, C.: A nonrecursive list compacting algorithm. Commun. ACM **13**(11), 677–678 (1970)
7. Detlefs, D., Flood, C., Heller, S., Printezis, T.: Garbage-first garbage collection. In: Fourth international Symposium on Memory Management, pp. 37–48. ACM Press (2004)
8. Dijkstra, E.W.: On-the-fly garbage collection: an exercise in multiprocessing. Technical Report EWD492, Burroughs Corporation (1975). http://www.cs.utexas.edu/users/EWD/ewd04xx/EWD492.PDF
9. Ecma International: Common Language Infrastructure (CLI). Standard ECMA-335, 6th edn. Ecma International (2012). http://www.ecma-international.org/publications/standards/Ecma-335.htm
10. Gudeman, D.: Representing type information in dynamically typed languages. Technical Report TR 93-27, Department of Computer Science, University of Arizona (1993)
11. Jones, R.: The garbage collection bibliography. Web site (2009). http://www.cs.kent.ac.uk/people/staff/rej/gcbib/gcbib.html
12. Jones, R., Lins, R.: Garbage Collection: Algorithms for Automatic Dynamic Memory Management. Wiley, New York (1996)
13. Lieberman, H., Hewitt, C.: A real-time garbage collector based on the lifetimes of objects. Commun. ACM **26**(6), 419–429 (1983)
14. McCarthy, J.: Recursive functions of symbolic expressions. Commun. ACM **3**(4), 184–195 (1960)
15. McCarthy, J., et al.: Lisp 1.5 Programmer's Manual. MIT Press, Cambridge (1962)
16. Mono project. http://www.mono-project.com/
17. Mono Project: Generational GC. http://www.mono-project.com/docs/advanced/garbage-collector/sgen/
18. MSDN: Fundamentals of garbage collection. Documentation page. https://msdn.microsoft.com/en-us/library/ee787088(v=vs.110).aspx
19. Oracle: What is the garbage-first garbage collector? Web page (2009). http://docs.oracle.com/javase/7/docs/technotes/guides/vm/G1.html
20. Printezis, T., Detlefs, D.: A generational mostly-concurrent garbage collector. In: Second international Symposium on Memory Management, pp. 143–154. ACM Press (2000). http://dl.acm.org/citation.cfm?id=362422.362480
21. Sestoft, P.: The garbage collector used in Caml Light (1994). http://para.inria.fr/~doligez/caml-guts/Sestoft94.txt
22. Sperber, M., Dybvig, R.K., Flatt, M., van Straaten, A. (eds.): Revised [6] Report on the Algorithmic Language Scheme. Cambridge University Press, Cambridge (2010)
23. Sun Microsystems: Memory management in the Java Hotspot virtual machine. Whitepaper (2006)
24. Wilson, P.: Uniprocessor garbage collection techniques. Technical report, University of Texas (1994). ftp://ftp.cs.utexas.edu/pub/garbage/bigsurv.ps

Chapter 11
Continuations

This chapter introduces the concept of *continuation*, which helps understand such notions as tail call, exceptions and exception handling, execution stack, and backtracking.

Basically, a continuation is an explicit representation of "the rest of the computation", what will happen next. Usually this is implicit in a program: after executing one statement, the computation will continue with the next statement; when returning from a method, the computation will continue where the method was called. Making the continuation explicit has the advantage that we can ignore it (and so model abnormal termination), and that we can have more than one (and so model exception handling and backtracking).

11.1 Files for This Chapter

File	Contents
Cont/Contfun.fs	a first-order functional language with exceptions
Cont/Contimp.fs	a naive imperative language with exceptions
Cont/Icon.fs	micro-Icon, a language with backtracking
Cont/Factorial.java	factorial in continuation-style, in Java
Cont/testlongjmp.c	demonstrating `setjmp` and `longjmp` in C

© Springer International Publishing AG 2017
P. Sestoft, *Programming Language Concepts*, Undergraduate Topics
in Computer Science, DOI 10.1007/978-3-319-60789-4_11

11.2   Tail-Calls and Tail-Recursive Functions

11.2.1   A Recursive but Not Tail-Recursive Function

A recursive function is one that may call itself. For instance, the factorial function
$n! = 1 \cdot 2 \cdots n$ may be implemented by a recursive function `facr` as follows:

```
let rec facr n =
    if n=0 then 1 else n * facr(n-1)
```

A function call is a *tail call* if it is the last action of the calling function. For instance,
the call from `f` to itself here is a tail call:

```
let rec f n = if n=0 then 17 else f(n-1)
```

and the call from `f` to `g` here is a tail call:

```
let rec f n = if n=0 then g 8 else f(n-1)
```

The recursive call from `facr` to itself (above) is not a tail call. When evaluating the
else-branch

```
n * facr(n-1)
```

we must first compute `facr(n-1)`, and when we are finished with that and have
obtained a result v, then we must compute n * v and return to the caller. Thus the
call `facr(n-1)` is not the last action of `facr`; after the call there is still some work
to be done (namely the multiplication by n).

The evaluation of `facr 3` requires a certain amount of stack space to remember
then outstanding multiplications by n:

$$
\begin{aligned}
& \texttt{facr 3} \\
\Rightarrow\ & \texttt{3 * facr 2} \\
\Rightarrow\ & \texttt{3 * (2 * facr 1)} \\
\Rightarrow\ & \texttt{3 * (2 * (1 * facr 0))} \\
\Rightarrow\ & \texttt{3 * (2 * (1 * 1))} \\
\Rightarrow\ & \texttt{3 * (2 * 1)} \\
\Rightarrow\ & \texttt{3 * 2} \\
\Rightarrow\ & \texttt{6}
\end{aligned}
$$

Remembering the "work still to be done" after the call requires some space, and
therefore a computation of `facr(N)` requires space proportional to N. This could
be seen clearly already in Fig. 8.3.

11.2.2   A Tail-Recursive Function

On the other hand, consider this alternative definition of factorial:

```
let rec faci n r =
    if n=0 then r else faci (n-1) (r * n)
```

An additional parameter `r` has been introduced to hold the result of the computation, with the intention that `faci n 1` equals `facr n` for all non-negative n. The parameter `r` is called an *accumulating parameter* because the parameter gradually builds up the result of the function.

The recursive call `faci (n-1) (r * n)` to `faci` is a *tail-call*, and the function is said to be *tail-recursive* or *iterative*. There is no "work still to be done" after the recursive call, as shown by this computation of `faci 3 1`:

$$
\begin{aligned}
&\texttt{faci 3 1} \\
\Rightarrow\ &\texttt{faci 2 3} \\
\Rightarrow\ &\texttt{faci 1 6} \\
\Rightarrow\ &\texttt{faci 0 6} \\
\Rightarrow\ &\texttt{6}
\end{aligned}
$$

Indeed, most implementations of functional languages, including F#, execute tail-calls in constant space.

Most implementations of imperative and object-oriented languages (C, C++, Java, C#, ...) do not care to implement tail calls in constant space. Thus the equivalent C or Java or C# method declaration:

```
static int faci(int n, int r) {
  if (n == 0)
    return r;
  else
    return faci(n-1, r * n);
}
```

would most likely not execute in constant space. This could be seen clearly in Fig. 8.3, which shows the stack for execution of recursive factorial in micro-C.

Imperative languages do not have to care as much about performing tail calls in constant space because they provide for- and while-loops to express iterative computations in a natural way. Thus the function `faci` would be expressed more naturally like this:

```
static int faci(int n) {
  int r = 1;
  while (n != 0) {
    r = n * r; n = n - 1;
  }
  return r;
}
```

Expression e	Status of subexpressions
let $x = e_r$ in e_b end	e_b is in tail position, e_r is not
$e_1 + e_2$	neither e_1 nor e_2 is in tail position
if e_1 then e_2 else e_3	e_2 and e_3 are in tail position, e_1 is not
let f $x = e_r$ in e_b end	e_b is in tail position, e_r is not
f e	e is not in tail position

Fig. 11.1   Which subexpressions of e are in tail position

11.2.3 Which Calls Are Tail Calls?

A call is a tail call if it is the last action of the containing function. But what does "last action" mean? Let us consider the small eager (call-by-value) functional language from Chap. 4, and let us define systematically the notion of *tail position*. The idea is that a call in tail position is a tail call.

The function body as a whole is in tail position. If we assume that an expression e is in tail position, then some of e's subexpressions will be in tail position too, as shown in Fig. 11.1.

If an expression is not in tail position, then no subexpression is in tail position. A *tail call* is a call in tail position. Thus all the calls to g below are tail calls, whereas those to h are not:

```
g 1
g(h 1)
h 1 + h 2
if 1=2 then g 3 else g(h 4)
let x = h 1 in g x end
let x = h 1 in if x=2 then g x else g 3 end
let x = h 1 in g(if x=2 then h x else h 3) end
let x = h 1 in let y = h 2 in g(x + y) end end
```

11.3 Continuations and Continuation-Passing Style

A *continuation* k is an explicit representation of "the rest of the computation", typically in the form of a function *from* the value of the current expression *to* the result of the entire computation.

A function in *continuation-passing style* (CPS) takes an extra argument, the continuation k, which "decides what will happen to the result of the function".

11.3.1   Writing a Function in Continuation-Passing Style

To see a concrete function in continuation-passing style, consider again the recursive factorial function `facr`:

```
let rec facr n =
    if n=0 then 1 else n * facr(n-1)
```

To write this function in continuation-passing style, we give it a continuation parameter `k`:

```
let rec facc n k =
    if n=0 then ?? else ??
```

Usually the then-branch would just return 1. In continuation-passing style, it should not return but instead give the result 1 to the continuation `k`, so it should be:

```
let rec facc n k =
    if n=0 then k 1 else ??
```

Now consider the else-branch of `facr`:

```
n * facr(n-1)
```

The continuation for the else-branch `n * facr(n-1)` is the same as that for the call `facc n k` to `facc`, that is, `k`. But what is the continuation for the subexpression `facr(n-1)`? That continuation must be a function that accepts the result `v` of `facr(n-1)`, computes `n * v`, and then passes the result to `k`. Thus the continuation of the recursive call can be expressed like this:

```
fun v -> k(n * v)
```

so this is the factorial function in continuation-passing style:

```
let rec facc n k =
    if n=0 then k 1 else facc (n-1) (fun v -> k(n * v))
```

If we define the identity function `id: 'a -> 'a` by

```
let id = fun v -> v
```

then it holds that `facr n` equals `facc n id` for all non-negative n.

Note that the resulting function `facc` is tail-recursive; in fact this will always be the case. This does not mean that the function now magically will run in constant space where previously it did not: the continuations will have to be created and stored until they are applied.

11.3.2   *Continuations and Accumulating Parameters*

Sometimes one can represent the action of the continuation very compactly, by a non-function, to obtain a constant-space tail-recursive function where the continuation has been replaced by an accumulating parameter.

For instance, in the case of `facc`, all a continuation ever does is to multiply its argument `v` by some number `m`. Too see this, observe that the initial identity continuation `fun v -> v` is equivalent to `fun v -> 1 * v`, which multiplies its argument `v` by 1. Inductively, if we assume that continuation `k` can be written as `fun u -> m * u` for some `m`, then the new continuation `fun v -> k(n * v)` can be written as `fun v -> m * (n * v)` which is the same as `fun v -> (m * n) * v`.

Thereby we have proven that any continuation `k` of `facc` can be written as `fun u -> r * u`. So why not simply represent the continuation by the number `r`? Then, instead of calling `k`, we should just multiply its argument by `r`. If we rewrite `facc n k` systematically in this way, we obtain, perhaps to our surprise, the iterative `faci` function shown in Sect. 11.2.2:

```
let rec faci n r =
    if n=0 then r else faci (n-1) (r * n)
```

Also, `faci` should be called initially with `r=1`, since 1 represents the identity continuation `fun v -> v`. Things do not always work out as neatly, though. Although every recursive function can be transformed into a tail-recursive one (and hence into a loop), the continuation may not be representable as a simple value such as a number.

11.3.3   *The CPS Transformation*

There is a systematic transformation which can transform any expression or function into continuation-passing style (CPS). The transformation (for eager or call-by-value languages) is easily expressed for the pure untyped lambda calculus (Sect. 5.6) because it has only three different syntactic constructs: variable x, function $\lambda x.e$, and function application $e_1\,e_2$. Let $[e]$ denote the CPS-transformation of the expression e. Then:

$$
\begin{array}{l}
[x] \ is \ \lambda k.k\,x \\
[\lambda x.e] \ is \ \lambda k.k\,(\lambda x.[e]) \\
[e_1\,e_2] \ is \ \lambda k.[e_1]\,(\lambda m.[e_2]\,(\lambda n.m\,n\,k))
\end{array}
$$

It is somewhat more cumbersome to express the CPS transformation for F# or even for our higher-order functional example language from Chap. 5.

11.4 Interpreters in Continuation-Passing Style

The interpreters we have considered in this book have been written as F# functions, and therefore they too can be rewritten in continuation-passing style.

When an interpreter for a functional language is written in continuation-passing style, a continuation is a function from the value of an expression to the "answer" or "final result" of the entire computation of the interpreted program.

When an interpreter for an imperative language is written in continuation-passing style, a continuation is a function from a store (created by the execution of a statement) to the "answer" (the "final store") produced by the entire computation.

In itself, rewriting the interpreter (`eval` or `exec` function) in continuation-passing style achieves nothing. The big advantage is that by making "the rest of the computation" explicit as a continuation parameter, the interpreter is free to ignore the continuation and return a different kind of "answer". This is useful for modeling the throwing of exceptions and similar abnormal termination.

11.4.1 A Continuation-Based Functional Interpreter

We now consider our simple functional language from Chap. 4 and extend it with exceptions. The language now also has an expression of the form:

```
Raise exn
```

that raises exception `exn`, and an expression

```
TryWith (e1, exn, e2)
```

that evaluates `e1` and returns its value if `e1` does not raise any exception; if `e1` raises exception `exn`, then it evaluates `e2`; and if `e1` raises another exception `exn1`, then the entire expression raises that exception.

The expression `Raise exn` corresponds to the F# expression `raise exn`, see Sect. A.8, which is similar to the Java or C# statement

```
throw exn;
```

The expression `TryWith(e1, exn, e2)` corresponds to the F# expression `try e1 with exn -> e2` which is similar to the Java or C# statement

```
try { e1 }
catch (exn) { e2 }
```

The abstract syntax of our small functional language is extended as follows:

```
type exn =
  | Exn of string

type expr =
  | ...
```

```
| Raise of exn
| TryWith of expr * exn * expr
```

For now we consider only the raising of exceptions. In an interpreter for this language, a continuation may be a function `cont : int -> answer` where type `answer` is defined as follows:

```
type answer =
  | Result of int
  | Abort of string
```

The continuation `cont` is called the normal (or success) continuation. It is passed to the evaluation function `coEval1`, which must apply the continuation to any normal result it produces. But when `coEval1` evaluates `Raise exn` it may just ignore the continuation, and return `Abort s` where s is some message derived from `exn`. This way we can model abnormal termination of the interpreted object language program:

```
let rec coEval1 (e : expr) (env : value env)
                (cont : int -> answer) : answer =
    match e with
    | CstI i -> cont i
    | CstB b -> cont (if b then 1 else 0)
    | Var x  ->
      match lookup env x with
      | Int i -> cont i
      | _        -> Abort"coEval1 Var"
    | ...
    | Raise (Exn s) -> Abort s
```

This allows the interpreted object language program to raise exceptions without using exceptions in the interpreter (the meta language).

To allow object language programs to also catch exceptions, not only raise them, we add yet another continuation argument `econt` to the interpreter, called the error (or failure) continuation. The error continuation expects to receive an exception value, and will look at the value to decide what action to take: catch the exception, or pass it to an older failure continuation.

More precisely, to evaluate `TryWith(e1, exn, e2)` the interpreter will create a new error continuation `econt1`. If the evaluation of `e1` does not throw an exception, then the normal continuation will be called as usual and the error continuation will be ignored. However, if evaluation of `e1` throws an exception `exn1`, then the new error continuation will be called and will look at `exn1`, and if it matches `exn`, then it will evaluate `e2`; otherwise it will pass `exn1` to the outer error continuation `econt`, thus propagating the exception:

```
let rec coEval2 (e : expr) (env : value env)
                (cont : int -> answer)
                (econt : exn -> answer) : answer =
```

```
match e with
  | CstI i -> cont i
  | CstB b -> cont (if b then 1 else 0)
  | ...
  | Raise exn -> econt exn
  | TryWith (e1, exn, e2) ->
    let econt1 exn1 =
        if exn1 = exn then coEval2 e2 env cont econt
                      else econt exn1
    coEval2 e1 env cont econt1
```

File `Contfun.fs` gives all details of the two continuation-passing interpreters `coEval1` and `coEval2` for a functional language. The former implements a language where exceptions can be thrown but not caught, and the latter implements a language where exceptions can be thrown as well as caught.

11.4.2 Tail Position and Continuation-Based Interpreters

Expressions in tail positions are exactly those that are interpreted with the same continuations as the enclosing expression. Consider for instance the evaluation of a let-binding:

```
let rec coEval1 (e : expr) (env : value env)
                (cont : int -> answer) : answer =
    match e with
    | ...
    | Let(x, eRhs, letBody) ->
      coEval1 eRhs env (fun xVal ->
                  let bodyEnv = (x, Int xVal) :: env
                  coEval1 letBody bodyEnv cont)
    | ...
```

Here the let-body `letBody` is in tail position and is evaluated with the same continuation `cont` as the entire let-expression. By contrast, the right-hand side `eRhs` is not in tail position and is evaluated with a different continuation, namely (`fun xVal -> ...`).

This is no coincidence: a subexpression has the same continuation as the enclosing expression exactly when evaluation of the subexpression is the last action of the enclosing expression.

11.4.3 A Continuation-Based Imperative Interpreter

An imperative language with exceptions, a throw statement and a try-catch statement (as in C++, Java, and C#) can be modelled using continuations in much the same way

as the functional language in Sect. 11.4.1. Let the abstract syntax be an extension of
the naive imperative language from Sect. 7.2:

```
type stmt =
    | ...
    | Throw of exn
    | TryCatch of stmt * exn * stmt
```

An interpreter that implements throw and try-catch must take a normal continuation
cont as well as an error continuation econt. The error continuation must take two
arguments: an exception and the store that exists when the exception is thrown.

Usually the interpreter applies cont to the store resulting from some command,
but when executing a throw statement it applies econt to the exception and the store.
When executing a try-catch block the interpreter creates a new error continuation
econt1; if called, that error continuation decides whether it will handle the exception exn1 given to it and execute the handler body stmt2, or pass the exception to
the outer error continuation, thus propagating the exception:

```
let rec coExec2 stmt (store : naivestore)
        (cont : naivestore -> answer)
        (econt : exn * naivestore -> answer) : answer =
    match stmt with
    | Asgn(x, e) ->
      cont (setSto store (x, eval e store))
    | If(e1, stmt1, stmt2) ->
      if eval e1 store <> 0 then
        coExec2 stmt1 store cont econt
      else
        coExec2 stmt2 store cont econt
    | ...
    | Throw exn ->
      econt(exn, store)
    | TryCatch(stmt1, exn, stmt2) ->
      let econt1 (exn1, sto1) =
          if exn1 = exn then coExec2 stmt2 sto1 cont econt
                        else econt (exn1, sto1)
      coExec2 stmt1 store cont econt1
```

In summary, the execution of a statement stmt by coExec2

```
coExec2 stmt store cont econt
```

can terminate in two ways:

- If the statement stmt terminates normally, without throwing an exception, then its
  execution ends with calling the normal continuation cont on a new store sto1;
  it evaluates cont sto1.
- Otherwise, if the execution of stmt throws an exception exn1, then its execution
  ends with calling the error continuation econt on exn1 and a new store sto1;

it evaluates `econt (exn1, sto1)`. Any handling of the exception is left to `econt`.

File `Contimp.fs` contains two continuation-passing interpreters for an imperative language, `coExec1` and `coExec2`. The former implements exceptions using a single normal continuation (but no means for catching exceptions), and the latter implements exceptions (that may be caught) using two continuations: one for computations that terminate normally, and one for computations that throw an exception.

Note that only statements, not expressions, can throw an exception in the imperative language modelled here. If expressions could throw exceptions, then the expression evaluator `eval` would have to be written in continuation-passing style too, and would have to take two continuation arguments: a normal continuation of type `value -> answer` and an error continuation of type `exn -> answer`. Provided that an expression can have no side effects on the store, we can omit the store parameter to these expression continuations, because we can build the store into the continuation of the expression. The statement interpreter would have to pass suitable continuations to the expression interpreter; for instance when executing an assignment statement:

```
let rec coExec2 stmt (store : naivestore)
        (cont : naivestore -> answer)
        (econt : exn * naivestore -> answer) : answer =
    match stmt with
    | Asgn(x, e) ->
      eval e store (fun xval -> cont (setSto store (x, xval)))
                   (fun exn  -> econt (exn, store))
    | ...
```

11.5 The Frame Stack and Continuations

As shown in Chap. 8, a micro-C program can be compiled to instructions that are subsequently executed by an abstract stack machine. In the abstract machine, the frame stack represents the (normal) continuation for the function call currently being executed.

The program counter `pc` and the top-most stack frame represent the local continuation inside the currently executing function: they say what instruction must be executed next. The return address and the old base pointer, both stored in the top-most stack frame, together with all the older stack frames, represent the "global" continuation: the code to be executed once the current function returns.

11.6 Exception Handling in a Stack Machine

How could we represent an error continuation for exception handling in the stack machine? One approach is to store exception handler descriptions in the evaluation stack and introduce an additional exception handler register hr. The exception handler register hr is the index (in the stack) of the most recent exception handler description, or −1 if there is no exception handler. For this discussion, let us assume that an exception is represented simply by an integer (rather than an object as in Java or C#, or a value of the special type exn as in F#).

An exception handler description (in the stack) has three parts:

- the identity exn of the exception that this handler handles;
- the address a of the associated handler, that is, the code of the catch block;
- a pointer to the previous exception handler description (further down in the stack), or −1 if there is no previous exception handler.

Thus the exception handler descriptions in the stack form a list with the most recent exception handler first, pointed to by hr. Older exception handler descriptions are found by following the pointer to the previous exception handler. This list can be thought of as a stack representing the error continuation; this stack is simply merged into the usual evaluation stack.

A try-catch block

```
try stmt1
catch (exc) stmt2
```

is compiled to the following code

```
    push exception handler (exn, code address for stmt2, hr)
    code for stmt1
    pop exception handler
L:  ...
```

The code for stmt2 must end with GOTO L where L is a label just after the code that pops the exception handler description.

The execution of

```
throw exn
```

must look through the chain of exception handlers in the stack until it finds one that will handle the thrown exception exn. If it does find such a handler (exn, a, h) it will pop the evaluation stack down to the point just below that handler, set hr to h and set pc to a, thus executing the code for the associated exception handler (catch clause) at address a. The popping of the evaluation stack may mean that many stack frames for unfinished function calls (above the exception handler) will be thrown away, and execution will continue in the function that declared the exception handler (the try-catch block), as desired. The base pointer bp must be restored as stack frames are thrown away.

Instruction	Stack before	After	Effect
PUSHHDLR *exn a*	*s*	$\Rightarrow s, exn, a, hr$	Push handler
POPHDLR	*s, exn, a, h*	$\Rightarrow s$	Pop handler
THROW *exn*	s_1, exn, a, h, s_2	$\Rightarrow s_1$	Handler found; go to *a*
THROW *exn*	*s*	$\Rightarrow \_$	No handler found; abort

Fig. 11.2 Exception handling in the micro-C stack machine (see text)

Thus we could implement exceptions in the micro-C stack machine (Fig. 8.1) by adding instructions PUSHHDLR, POPHDLR, and THROW for pushing a handler, popping a handler, and throwing an exception, respectively. These additional instructions for pushing, popping and invoking handlers are shown in Fig. 11.2.

The instructions should work as follows:

- Instruction PUSHHDLR *exn a* pushes the handled exception name *exn*, the handler address *a* and the old handler register *hr*, and also sets the handler register *hr* to the address of *exn* in the stack.
- Instruction POPHDLR pops all three components (*exn*, *a*, and *h*) of the exception handler description from the stack, and resets the handler register *hr* to *h*.
- Instruction THROW *exn*, which corresponds to executing the statement throw exn, searches for an appropriate exception handler on the stack, starting from the handler that *hr* points to:

```
while (hr != -1 && s[hr] != exn)
    hr = s[hr+2];           // Try next exception handler
if (hr != -1) {             // Found a handler for exn
    pc = s[hr+1];           //   execute the handler code (a)
    hr = s[hr+2];           //   with current handler being hr
    sp = hr-1;              //   after popping frames above hr
    while (bp > sp)         // Restore bp to stack frame
        bp = s[bp-1]        // for continuation function.
} else {
    print"uncaught exception";
    stop machine;
}
```

Either it finds a handler for the thrown exception (hr!=-1) and executes that handler, or the exception propagates to the bottom of the stack and the program aborts.

11.7 Continuations and Tail Calls

If a function call is in tail position, then the continuation cont of the call is the same as the continuation of the entire enclosing function body. Moreover, the called function's body is evaluated in the same continuation as the function call. Hence the continuation of a tail-called function's body is the same as that of the calling function's body:

```
let rec coEval1 (e : expr) (env : value env)
                (cont : int -> answer) : answer =
    match e with
    | ...
    | Call(f, eArg) ->
      let fClosure = lookup env f
      match fClosure with
      | Closure (f, x, fBody, fDeclEnv) ->
        coEval1 eArg env
                (fun xVal ->
                    let fBodyEnv = (x, Int xVal)
                                        :: (f, fClosure) :: fDeclEnv
                    coEval1 fBody fBodyEnv cont)
      | _ -> Abort "eval Call: not a function"
```

In Chap. 12 we shall see how one can compile micro-C tail calls so that a function can make an arbitrary number of tail-recursive calls in constant space (example ex12.c):

```
int f(int n) {
  if (n)
    return f(n-1);
  else
    return 17;
}
```

The trick is to discard f's old stack frame, which contains the values of its local variables and parameters, such as n, and replace it by the called function's new stack frame. Only the return address and the old base pointer must be retained from f's old stack frame. It is admissible to throw away f's local variables and parameters because there is no way they could be used after the recursive call has returned (the call is the last action of f).

This works also when one function f calls another function g by a tail call: then f's old stack frame is discarded (except for the return address and the old base pointer), and is replaced by g's new stack frame. Our stack machine has a special instruction for tail calls:

```
TCALL m n a
```

that discards n old variables from the stack frame, pushes m new arguments, and executes the code at address a. It does not push a return address or adjust the base pointer, so basically a TCALL is a specialized kind of jump (GOTO).

11.8   Callcc: Call with Current Continuation

In some languages, notably Scheme and the New Jersey implementation of Standard
ML (SML/NJ), one can capture the current evaluation's continuation k. In SML/NJ,
the continuation is captured using `callcc`, and reactivated using `throw`:

```
callcc (fn k => ... throw k e ...)
```

In Scheme, use `call-with-current-continuation` instead of `callcc`,
and simply apply the captured continuation k as any other function:

```
(call-with-current-continuation (lambda (k) ... (k e) ...))
```

This can be exploited in powerful but often rather mysterious programming tricks.
For example, in SML/NJ:

```
open SMLofNJ.Cont;
1 + callcc (fn k => 2 + 5)            evaluates to 1 + (2 + 5)
1 + callcc (fn k => 2 + throw k 5)    evaluates to 1 + 5
```

In both of the two latter lines, the continuation captured as k is the continuation
that says "add 1 to my argument". The corresponding examples in Scheme work
precisely the same way:

```
(+ 1 (call-with-current-continuation (lambda (k) (+ 2 5))))
(+ 1 (call-with-current-continuation (lambda (k) (+ 2 (k 5)))))
```

In a sense, the classic `setjmp` function in C captures the current continuation (like
`callcc`) and the corresponding function `longjmp` reactivates it (like `throw`).
This is useful for implementing a kind of exception handling in C programs, but C's
notion of continuation is much weaker than that of Scheme or SML/NJ. In fact, the
C implementation of `setjmp` just stores the current machine registers, including
the stack pointer, in a structure. Applying `longjmp` to that structure will restore the
machine registers, including the stack pointer. The effect is that program execution
continues at the point where `setjmp` was called — exactly as in the SML/NJ and
Scheme examples above.

   However, when the function that called `setjmp` returns, the stack will be trun-
cated below the point at which the stored stack pointer points. Calling `longjmp`
after this has happened may have strange effects (most likely the program crashes),
since the restored stack pointer now points into a part of memory where there is no
longer any stack, or where possibly a completely unrelated stack frame has been
stored.

11.9   Continuations and Backtracking

Some programming languages support *backtracking*: When a subexpression produces a result *v* that later turns out to be inadequate, the computation may backtrack
to that subexpression to ask for a new result *v′* that may be more adequate.

Continuations can be used to implement backtracking. To see this, we shall study a
small subset of the Icon language, a language for so-called goal-directed computation
[5]. The logic programming language Prolog also computes using backtracking.

11.9.1   Expressions in Icon

In the language Icon, the evaluation of an expression may fail, producing no result, or
succeed, producing a result. Because of backtracking, it may succeed multiple times.
The *result sequence* of an expression is the sequence of results it may produce. This
sequence is empty if the expression fails.

Figure 11.3 shows some typical expressions in Icon, their result sequence, and
their side effect. A simple constant i succeeds once, producing the integer i. As
in most other languages, an expression may have a side effect. In particular, the
expression write(e) succeeds with the result of e every time e succeeds, and as
a side effect prints the result of e.

The operator every(e) forces e to produce it complete result sequence, and
then every(e) fails. This is useful only if e has a side effect.

An expression such as (1 to 3) is called a *generator* because it produces a
sequence of results. An ordinary arithmetic operator, such as e1 + e2, succeeds
once for every combination $v_1 + v_2$ of the results v_1 of e1 and the results v_2 of e2. A

Expression	Result seq.	Output	Comment
5	5		Integer constant
write 5	5	5	Integer constant
(1 to 3)	1 2 3		Range
write (1 to 3)	1 2 3	1	Print as side effect
every(write (1 to 3))	⟨empty⟩	1 2 3	Force all results
(1 to 0)	⟨empty⟩		Empty range
&fail	⟨empty⟩		Fails
(1 to 3) + (4 to 5)	5 6 6 7 7 8		All combinations
3 < 4	4		Comparison succeeds
4 < 3	⟨empty⟩		Comparison fails
3 < (1 to 5)	4 5		Succeeds twice
(1 to 3) | (4 to 5)	1 2 3 4 5		Left, then right
(1 to 3) & (4 to 5)	4 5 4 5 4 5		Right for every left
(1 to 3) ; (4 to 5)	4 5		Don't backtrack
(1 to 0) ; (4 to 5)	4 5		Don't backtrack

Fig. 11.3   Example expressions in the Icon language

comparison operator e1 < e2 does not return a boolean result. Instead it succeeds once for every combination, of the results v_1 of e1 and the results v_2 of e2, for which $v_1 < v_2$. When it succeeds, its value is v_2.

The operator (e1 | e2) produces the result sequence of e1, then that of e2. It therefore behaves like sequential logical "or" (| |) in C/C++/Java/C#.

The operator (e1 & e2) produces the result sequence of e2, for every result of e1. It therefore behaves like sequential logical "and" (&&) in C/C++/Java/C#.

The operator (e1 ; e2) evaluates e1 once, and regardless whether it succeeds or fails, then produces the result sequence of e2. Once it has started evaluating e2 it never backtracks to e1 again.

The conditional expression if e1 then e2 else e3 evaluates e1, and if that succeeds, it evaluates e2; otherwise e3. Once it has started evaluating e2 or e3, it never backtracks to e1 again.

11.9.2 Using Continuations to Implement Backtracking

Backtracking as in Icon can be implemented using two continuations [6]:

- A failure continuation fcont : unit -> answer
- A success continuation cont : int -> fcont -> answer

The success continuation's failure continuation argument is used for backtracking: go back and ask for more results.

The failure continuation may also be called a *backtracking continuation* or a *resumption*. It is used by an expression to "ask for more results" from a subexpression, by backtracking into the subexpression, resuming the subexpression's evaluation.

Figure 11.4 shows an interpreter (from file Icon.fs) for variable-free Icon expressions. The interpreter uses two continuations, cont for success and econt for failure, or backtracking.

The evaluation of an integer constant i succeeds once only, and therefore simply calls the success continuation on i and the given failure continuation.

The evaluation of FromTo(i1, i2) succeeds once for each value i between i1 and i2, both included. If i1>i2, it fails immediately.

The evaluation of write(e) evaluates e with a success continuation that grabs the value v of e, prints it, and calls the success continuation on v and on e's failure continuation econt1. Thus backtracking into write(e) will backtrack into e, printing also the subsequent results of e.

An ordinary arithmetic operator such as e1 + e2 will evaluate e1 with a success continuation that evaluates e2 with a success continuation that adds the results v1 and v2 and calls the original success continuation on the sum, and on the failure continuation econt2 of e2. Thus backtracking into e1 + e2 will backtrack into e2. Since e2 was evaluated with e1's econt1 as failure continuation, failure of e2 will further backtrack into e1, thus producing all combinations of their results.

```
let rec eval (e : expr) (cont : cont) (econt : econt) =
    match e with
    | CstI i -> cont (Int i) econt
    | CstS s  -> cont (Str s) econt
    | FromTo(i1, i2) ->
      let rec loop i =
          if i <= i2 then
              cont (Int i) (fun () -> loop (i+1))
          else
              econt ()
      loop i1
    | Write e ->
      eval e (fun v -> fun econt1 -> (write v; cont v econt1))
            econt
    | Prim(ope, e1, e2) ->
      eval e1 (fun v1 -> fun econt1 ->
          eval e2 (fun v2 -> fun econt2 ->
              match (ope, v1, v2) with
              | ("+", Int i1, Int i2) ->
                  cont (Int(i1+i2)) econt2
              | ("*", Int i1, Int i2) ->
                  cont (Int(i1*i2)) econt2
              | ("<", Int i1, Int i2) ->
                  if i1<i2 then
                      cont (Int i2) econt2
                  else
                      econt2 ()
              | _ -> Str "unknown prim2")
              econt1)
          econt
    | And(e1, e2) ->
      eval e1 (fun _ -> fun econt1 -> eval e2 cont econt1)
            econt
    | Or(e1, e2) ->
      eval e1 cont (fun () -> eval e2 cont econt)
    | Seq(e1, e2) ->
      eval e1 (fun _ -> fun econt1 -> eval e2 cont econt)
            (fun () -> eval e2 cont econt)
    | If(e1, e2, e3) ->
      eval e1 (fun _ -> fun _ -> eval e2 cont econt)
            (fun () -> eval e3 cont econt)
    | Every e ->
      eval e (fun _ -> fun econt1 -> econt1 ())
            (fun () -> cont (Int 0) econt)
    | Fail -> econt ()
```

Fig. 11.4 Micro-Icon expression evaluation with backtracking

The less-than operator e1 < e2 evaluates e1 and e2 as above, and succeeds (calls the success continuation) if v1 is less than v2, else fails (calls the failure continuation of e2).

The (e1 | e2) expression evaluates e1 with the original success continuation and with a failure continuation that evaluates e2 with the original continuations. Hence if e1 succeeds (is true) we pass its result to the context; if e1 fails (is false) we evaluate e2. Subsequent backtracking into (e1 | e2) will backtrack into e1, and if e1 fails, then into e2, producing first the result sequence of e1, then that of e2.

The expression (e1 & e2) is the dual. It evaluates e1 with a success continuation that ignores e1's result and then evaluates e2 with the original success continuation and e1's failure continuation. Subsequent backtracking into (e1 & e2) will backtrack into e2, and when that fails, into e1, producing the result sequence of e2 for every result of e1.

Note the difference to (e1 ; e2) which evaluates e1 with success and failure continuations that behave the same. Both ignore e1's result (if any) and then evaluate e2 with the original continuations. Subsequent backtracking into (e1 ; e2) will backtrack into e2, but not into e1, because the failure continuation (possibly) produced by e1 gets ignored; we say that expression e1 is *bounded* when it appears to the left of the sequential composition ";" [5, p. 90].

The conditional expression if (e1) then e2 else e3 is similar but evaluates e2 in the success continuation and e3 in the failure continuation. Again the failure continuation (possibly) produced by e1 gets ignored, so there is no backtracking into e1; that is, e1 is bounded when it appears as the condition of if.

The expression &fail simply fails, by calling the failure continuation.

11.10 History and Literature

Continuations were invented (or discovered?) independently by a number of people around 1970 [8]. The name is due to Christopher Wadsworth, a student of Christopher Strachey, whose 1967 *Fundamental Concepts* we discussed in Sect. 7.7. Strachey and Wadsworth [12] present the use of continuations in the description ("mathematical semantics") of programming language constructs that disrupt the normal flow of computation, such as jumps (goto) and return from subroutines.

Reynolds [9] shows how to use continuation-passing style in interpreters to make the object language evaluation order independent of the meta-language evaluation order (eager, lazy, left-to-right, or right-to-left).

The original CPS transformations (Sect. 11.3.3) were discovered independently by Fischer [4] and Plotkin [7]. Danvy and Filinski [2] gave a lucid analysis and improved the transformation.

Danvy [3] also demonstrates that Gudeman's [6] somewhat magic continuation implementation of Icon (Sect. 11.9.2) can be obtained by CPS transformation (and

additional tools) from a more straightforward implementation that works with lists
of results.

Wand describes several program transformations, including the introduction of
an accumulating parameter shown in Sect. 11.3.2, in terms of continuations [13].

In 1993, Reynolds [8] looks back on the many times continuations were discovered
(or invented).

Guy Steele [10] shows that if functions (lambda abstractions) and function calls are
implemented properly, via continuation-passing style, then all other constructs can
be implemented efficiently in terms of these. This idea was realized by Steele in the
1978 Rabbit compiler for Scheme [11], the first compiler to use continuation-passing
style, giving a breakthrough in efficiency of functional language implementations.

Andrew Appel [1] describes the design of the Standard ML of New Jersey
(SML/NJ) compiler which initially transforms the entire program into continuation-passing style, as suggested by Steele.

The complete text of Griswold and Griswold's 1996 book on the Icon programming language is available for free [5].

11.11   Exercises

The main goal of these exercises is to master the somewhat mind-bending notion
of continuation. But remember that a continuation is just something — usually a
function — that represents the rest of a computation.

Exercise 11.1 (i) Write a continuation-passing (CPS) version `lenc` :
`'a list ->(int ->'b) ->'b` of the list length function `len`:

```
let rec len xs =
    match xs with
    | []     -> 0
    | x::xr -> 1 + len xr;;
```

Try calling the resulting function with `lenc [2; 5; 7] id`, where the initial
continuation `let id = fun v -> v` is the identity function, and with `lenc
[2; 5; 7] (printf "The answer is '% d' \n")`, where the initial
continuation consumes the result and prints it.

(ii) What happens if you call it as `lenc xs (fun v -> 2*v)` instead?

(iii) Write also a tail-recursive version `leni : int list -> int -> int`
of the length function, whose second parameter is an accumulating parameter. The
function should be called as `leni xs 0`. What is the relation between `lenc` and
`leni`?

Exercise 11.2 (i) Write a continuation-passing version `revc` of the list reversal function `rev`:

```
let rec rev xs =
    match xs with
    | []     -> []
    | x::xr -> rev xr @ [x];;
```

The resulting function `revc` should have type `'a list -> ('a list -> 'a list) -> 'a list` or a more general type such as `'a list -> ('a list -> 'b) -> 'b`. The function may be called as `revc xs id`, where `let id = fun v -> v` is the identity function.

(ii) What happens if you call it as `revc xs (fun v -> v @ v)` instead?

(iii) Write a tail-recursive reversal function `revi : 'a list -> 'a list-> 'a list`, whose second parameter is an accumulating parameter, and which should be called as `revi xs []`.

Exercise 11.3 Write a continuation-passing version `prodc : int list -> (int -> int) -> int` of the list product function `prod`:

```
let rec prod xs =
    match xs with
    | []     -> 1
    | x::xr -> x * prod xr;;
```

Exercise 11.4 Optimize the CPS version of the `prod` function above. It could terminate as soon as it encounters a zero in the list (because any list containing a zero will have product zero), assuming that its continuation simply multiplies the result by some factor. Try calling it in the same two ways as the `lenc` function in Exercise 11.1. Note that even if the non-tail-recursive `prod` were improved to return 0 when encountering a 0, the returned 0 would still be multiplied by all the x values previously encountered.

Write a tail-recursive version `prodi` of the `prod` function that also terminates as soon as it encounters a zero in the list.

Exercise 11.5 Write more examples using exceptions and exception handling in the small functional and imperative languages implemented in `Contfun.fs` and `Contimp.fs`, and run them using the given interpreters.

Exercise 11.6 What statements are in tail position in the simple imperative language implemented by `coExec1` in file `Contimp.fs`? Intuitively, the last statement in a statement block { ... } is in tail position provided the entire block is. Can you argue that this is actually the case, looking at the interpreter `coExec1`?

Exercise 11.7 The `coExec1` version of the imperative language interpreter in file `Contimp.fs` supports a *statement* Throw to throw an exception. This Throw statement is similar to `throw` in Java. Add an *expression* `EThrow` to the expression abstract syntax to permit throwing exceptions also inside an expression, as in F#'s `fail` expression. You will need to rewrite the expression interpreter `eval` in continuation-passing style; for instance, it must take a continuation as an additional argument. Consequently, you must also modify `coExec1` so that every call to `eval` has a continuation argument.

The return type of your new expression interpreter should be `answer` as for `coExec1`, and it should take a normal continuation of type `(int -> answer)` as argument, where `answer` is the exact same type used in the `coExec1` statement interpreter. (Like `coExec1`, your new expression interpreter need not take an error continuation, because we do not intend to implement exception handling.)

Your interpreter should be able to execute `run1 ex4` and `run1 ex5` where

```
let ex4 =
    Block[If(EThrow (Exn "Foo"), Block[], Block[])];;

let ex5 =
    While(EThrow (Exn "Foo"), Block[]);;
```

Exercise 11.8 The micro-Icon expression `2 * (1 to 4)` succeeds four times, with the values 2 4 6 8. This can be shown by evaluating

```
open Icon;;
run (Every(Write(Prim("*", CstI 2, FromTo(1, 4)))));;
```

using the interpreter in `Icon.fs` and using abstract syntax instead of the concrete syntax `(2 * (1 to 4))`. We must use abstract syntax because we have not written lexer and parser specification for micro-Icon. A number of examples in abstract syntax are given at the end of the `Icon.fs` source file.

(i) Write an expression that produces and prints the values 3 5 7 9. Write an expression that produces and prints the values 21 22 31 32 41 42.

(ii) The micro-Icon language (like real Icon) has no boolean values. Instead, failure is used to mean `false`, and success means `true`. For instance, the less-than comparison operator (<) behaves as follows: 3 < 2 fails, and 3 < 4 succeeds (once) with the value 4. Similarly, thanks to backtracking, 3 < (1 to 5) succeeds twice, giving the values 4 and 5. Use this to write an expression that prints the least multiple of 7 that is greater than 50.

(iii) Extend the abstract syntax with unary (one-argument) primitive functions, like this:

```
type expr =
  | ...
  | Prim1 of string * expr
```

Extend the interpreter `eval` to handle such unary primitives, and define two such primitives: (a) define a primitive `sqr` that computes the square $x \cdot x$ of its argument x; (b) define a primitive `even` that fails if its argument is odd, and succeeds if it is even (producing the argument as result). For instance, `square(3 to 6)` should succeed four times, with the results 9, 16, 25, 36, and `even(1 to 7)` should succeed three times with the results 2, 4, 6.

(iv) Define a unary primitive `multiples` that succeeds infinitely many times, producing all multiples of its argument. For instance, `multiples(3)` should produce 3, 6, 9, ... Note that `multiples(3 to 4)` would produce multiples of 3 forever, and would never backtrack to the subexpression (3 to 4) to begin producing multiples of 4.

Exercise 11.9 Write lexer and parser specifications for micro-Icon so Exercise 11.8 above could be solved using concrete syntax.

Exercise 11.10 (*For adventurous Java or C# hackers*): Implement a class-based abstract syntax and an interpreter for a backtracking Icon-style language subset, in the spirit of `Icon.fs`, but do it in C# or Java. If you use Java, you can draw some inspiration from method `facc` in `Factorial.java`. With C#, you should use lambda expressions (`v => v * 2`) or possibly the older-style anonymous delegates(`delegate(int v) { return v * 2; }`).

In any case, the result will probably appear rather incomprehensible, and could be used to impress people in the Friday bar. Nevertheless, it should not be too hard to write if you take a systematic approach.

Exercise 11.11 (*Project*) Implement a larger subset of the language Icon. This involves deciding on the subset, writing lexer and parser specifications, and writing an extended interpreter in the style of `Icon.fs`. The interpreter must at least handle assignable variables.

Exercise 11.12 (*Project*) Write a program to transform programs into continuation-passing style, using the Danvy and Filinski presentation [2] which distinguishes between administrative redexes and other redexes.

Exercise 11.13 (*Somewhat hairy project*) Extend a higher order functional language with the ability to capture the current (success) continuation, and to apply it. See papers by Danvy, Malmkjær, and Filinski. It would be a good idea to experiment with `call-with-current-continuation` in Scheme first.

References

1. Appel, A.W.: Compiling with Continuations. Cambridge University Press, Cambridge (1992)
2. Danvy, O., Filinski, A.: Representing control. A study of the CPS transformation. Math. Struct. Comput. Sci. **2**, 361–391 (1992)

3. Danvy, O., Grobauer, B., Rhiger, M.: A unifying approach to goal-directed evaluation. New Gener. Comput. **20**(1), 53–73 (2002)
4. Fischer, M.J.: Lambda calculus schemata. ACM Conf. Proving Assert. About Prog. SIGPLAN Not. **7**, 104–109 (1972)
5. Griswold, R.E., Griswold, M.T.: The Icon Programming Language, 3rd edn. Peer-to-Peer Communications (1996). http://www.cs.arizona.edu/icon/lb3.htm
6. Gudeman, D.A.: Denotational semantics of a goal-directed language. ACM Trans. Program. Lang. Syst. **14**(1), 107–125 (1992)
7. Plotkin, G.: Call-by-name, call-by-value and the lambda calculus. Theor. Comput. Sci. **1**, 125–159 (1975)
8. Reynolds, J.: The discoveries of continuations. Lisp Symb. Comput. **6**(3/4), 233–247 (1993)
9. Reynolds, J.: Definitional interpreters for higher-order languages. Higher-order Symb. Comput. **11**(4), 363–397 (1998). Originally published 1972
10. Steele, G.L.: LAMBDA: The ultimate declarative. MIT AI Lab memo AIM-379, MIT (1976). ftp://publications.ai.mit.edu/ai-publications/0-499/AIM-379.ps
11. Steele, G.L.: A compiler for Scheme (a study in compiler optimization). MIT AI Lab technical report AITR-474, MIT (1978). ftp://publications.ai.mit.edu/ai-publications/0-499/AITR-474.ps
12. Strachey, C., Wadsworth, C.: Continuations, a mathematical semantics for handling full jumps. Higher-order Symb. Comput. **13**, 135–152 (2000). Written 1974
13. Wand, M.: Continuation-based program transformation strategies. J. ACM **27**(1), 164–180 (1980)

Chapter 12
A Locally Optimizing Compiler

In this chapter we shall see that thinking in continuations is beneficial also when compiling micro-C to stack machine code. Generating stack machine code backwards may seem silly, but it enables the compiler to inspect the code that will consume the result of the code being generated. This permits the compiler to perform many optimizations (code improvement) easily.

12.1 Files for This Chapter

In addition to the micro-C files mentioned in Sect. 7.1, the following file is provided:

File	Contents
MicroC/Contcomp.fs	compile micro-C backwards

12.2 Generating Optimized Code Backwards

In Chap. 8 we compiled micro-C programs to abstract machine code for a stack machine, but the code quality was poor, with many jumps to jumps, addition of zero, tests of constants, and so on.

Here we present a simple optimizing compiler that optimizes the code on the fly, while generating it. The compiler does not rely on advanced program analysis or program transformation. Instead it combines local optimizations (so-called peephole optimizations) with backwards code generation.

© Springer International Publishing AG 2017
P. Sestoft, *Programming Language Concepts*, Undergraduate Topics
in Computer Science, DOI 10.1007/978-3-319-60789-4_12

In backwards code generation, one uses a "compile-time continuation" to represent the instructions following the code currently being generated. The compile-time continuation is simply a list of the instructions that will follow the current one. At run-time, those instructions represent the continuation of the code currently being generated: that continuation will consume any result produced (on the stack) by the current code.

Using this approach, a one-pass compiler:

- can optimize the compilation of logical connectives (such as !, && and ||) into efficient control flow code;
- can generate code for a logical expression e1 && e2 that is adapted to its context of use:

  - will the logical expression's value be bound to a variable:

        b = e1 && e2

  - or will be used as the condition in an if- or while-statement:

        if (e1 && e2) ...;

- can avoid generating jumps to jumps in most cases;
- can eliminate some dead code (instructions that cannot be executed);
- can recognize tail calls and compile them as jumps (instruction TCALL) instead of proper function calls (instruction CALL), so that a tail-recursive function will execute in constant space.

Such optimizations might be called backwards optimizations: they exploit information about the "future" of an expression: the use of its value. Forwards optimizations, on the other hand, would exploit information about the "past" of an expression: its value. A forwards optimization may for instance exploit that a variable has a particular constant value, and use that value to simplify expressions in which the variable is used (constant propagation). This is possible only to a very limited extent in backwards code generation.

12.3   Backwards Compilation Functions

In the old forwards compiler from Chap. 8, the compilation function cExpr for micro-C expressions had the type

    cExpr : expr -> varEnv -> funEnv -> instr list

In the backwards compiler, it has this type instead:

    cExpr : expr -> varEnv -> funEnv -> instr list -> instr list

The only change is that an additional argument of type instr list, that is, list of instructions, has been added; this is the code continuation C. All other compilation functions (cStmt, cAccess, cExprs, and so on, listed in Fig. 8.4) are modified similarly.

To see how the code continuation is used, consider the compilation of simple expressions such as constants CstI i and unary (one-argument) primitives Prim1("!", e1).

In the old forwards compiler, code fragments are generated as instruction lists and are concatenated together using the append operator (@):

```
and cExpr (e : expr) (varEnv : varEnv)                        // OLD
        (funEnv : funEnv) : instr list =
    match e with
    | ...
    | CstI i            -> [CSTI i]
    | Prim1(ope, e1) ->
      cExpr e1 varEnv funEnv
      @ (match ope with
         | "!"      -> [NOT]
         | "printi" -> [PRINTI]
         | "printc" -> [PRINTC]
         | _        -> failwith "unknown primitive 1")
    | ...
```

For instance, the expression !false, which is Prim1("!", CstI 0) in abstract syntax, is compiled to [CSTI 0] @ [NOT], that is, [CSTI 0; NOT].

In a backwards (continuation-based) compiler, the corresponding compiler fragment would look like this:

```
and cExpr (e : expr) varEnv funEnv                           // NEW
        (C : instr list) : instr list =
    match e with
    | ...
    | CstI i            -> CSTI i :: C
    | Prim1(ope, e1) ->
      cExpr e1 varEnv funEnv
        (match ope with
         | "!"      -> NOT :: C
         | "printi" -> PRINTI :: C
         | "printc" -> PRINTC :: C
         | _        -> failwith "unknown primitive 1")
    | ...
```

So the new instructions generated are simply stuck onto the front of the code C already generated. This in itself achieves nothing, except that it avoids using the append function @ on the generated instruction lists, which could be costly. The code generated for !false is CSTI 0 :: [NOT] with is [CSTI 0; NOT], as before.

12.3.1   Optimizing Expression Code While Generating It

Now that the code continuation C is available, we can use it to optimize (improve) the generated code. For instance, when the first instruction in C (which is the next instruction to be executed at run-time) is NOT, then there is no point in generating the instruction CSTI 0; the NOT will immediately turn the zero into a one. Instead we should generate the constant CSTI 1, and throw away the NOT instruction. We can easily modify the expression compiler cExpr to recognize such special situations, and generate optimized code:

```
and cExpr (e : expr) varEnv funEnv
          (C : instr list) : instr list =
    match e with
    | ...
    | CstI i -> match (i, C) with
                  | (0, NOT :: C1) -> CSTI 1 :: C1
                  | (_, NOT :: C1) -> CSTI 0 :: C1
                  | _              -> CSTI i :: C)
    | ...
```

With this scheme, the code generated for !false will be [CSTI 1], which is shorter and faster.

In practice, we introduce an auxiliary function addCST to take care of these optimizations, both to avoid cluttering up the main functions, and because constants (CSTI) are generated in several places in the compiler:

```
and cExpr (e : expr) varEnv funEnv
          (C : instr list) : instr list =
    match e with
    | ...
    | CstI i -> addCST i C
    | ...
```

The addCST function is defined by straightforward pattern matching:

```
let rec addCST i C =
    match (i, C) with
    | (0, ADD       :: C1) -> C1
    | (0, SUB       :: C1) -> C1
    | (0, NOT       :: C1) -> addCST 1 C1
    | (_, NOT       :: C1) -> addCST 0 C1
    | (1, MUL       :: C1) -> C1
    | (1, DIV       :: C1) -> C1
    | (0, EQ        :: C1) -> addNOT C1
    | (_, INCSP m   :: C1) -> if m < 0 then addINCSP (m+1) C1
                              else CSTI i :: C
    | (0, IFZERO lab :: C1) -> addGOTO lab C1
```

```
| (_, IFZERO lab :: C1) -> C1
| (0, IFNZRO lab :: C1) -> C1
| (_, IFNZRO lab :: C1) -> addGOTO lab C1
| _                     -> CSTI i :: C
```

Note in particular that instead of generating [CSTI 0; IFZERO lab] this would generate an unconditional jump [GOTO lab]. This optimization turns out to be very useful in conjunction with other optimizations.

The auxiliary functions addNOT, addINCSP, and addGOTO generate NOT, INCSP, and GOTO instructions, inspecting the code continuation C to optimize the code if possible.

An attractive property of these local optimizations is that one can easily see that they are correct. Their correctness depends only on some simple code equivalences for the abstract stack machine, which are quite easily proven by considering the state transitions of the abstract machine shown in Fig. 8.1.

Concretely, the function addCST above embodies these instruction sequence equivalences:

0, EQ	has the same meaning as NOT	
0, ADD	has the same meaning as ⟨empty⟩	
0, SUB	has the same meaning as ⟨empty⟩	
0, NOT	has the same meaning as 1	
n, NOT	has the same meaning as 0	when $n \neq 0$
1, MUL	has the same meaning as ⟨empty⟩	
1, DIV	has the same meaning as ⟨empty⟩	
n, INCSP m	has the same meaning as INCSP $(m + 1)$	when $m < 0$
0, IFZERO a	has the same meaning as GOTO a	
n, IFZERO a	has the same meaning as ⟨empty⟩	when $n \neq 0$
0, IFNZRO a	has the same meaning as ⟨empty⟩	
n, IFNZRO a	has the same meaning as GOTO a	when $n \neq 0$

Additional equivalences are used in other optimizing code-generating functions (addNOT, makeINCSP, addINCSP, addGOTO):

NOT, NOT has the same meaning as ⟨empty⟩	(see Note)
NOT, IFZERO a has the same meaning as IFNZRO a	
NOT, IFNZRO a has the same meaning as IFZERO a	
INCSP 0 has the same meaning as ⟨empty⟩	
INCSP m_1, INCSP m_2 has the same meaning as INCSP $(m_1 + m_2)$	
INCSP m_1, RET m_2 has the same meaning as RET $(m_2 - m_1)$	

Note: The NOT, NOT equivalence holds when the resulting value is used as a boolean value: that is, when no distinction is made between 1 and other non-zero values. The code generated by our compiler satisfies this requirement, so it is safe to use the optimization.

12.3.2   The Old Compilation of Jumps

To see how the code continuation is used when optimizing jumps (instructions GOTO, IFZERO, IFNZRO), consider the compilation of a conditional statement:

```
if (e) stmt1 else stmt2
```

The old forwards compiler (file Comp.fs) used this compilation scheme:

```
let labelse = newLabel()
let labend  = newLabel()
cExpr e varEnv funEnv @ [IFZERO labelse]
@ cStmt stmt1 varEnv funEnv @ [GOTO labend]
@ [Label labelse] @ cStmt stmt2 varEnv funEnv
@ [Label labend]
```

That compiler fragment generates various code pieces (instruction lists) and concatenates them to form code such as this:

```
    <e> IFZERO L1
    <stmt1> GOTO L2
L1: <stmt2>
L2:
```

where <e> denotes the code generated for expression e, and similarly for the statements.

A plain backwards compiler would generate exactly the same code, but do it backwards, by sticking new instructions in front of the instruction list C, that is, the compile-time continuation:

```
let labelse = newLabel()
let labend  = newLabel()
cExpr e varEnv funEnv (IFZERO labelse
  :: cStmt stmt1 varEnv funEnv
     (GOTO labend :: Label labelse
      :: cStmt stmt2 varEnv funEnv (Label labend :: C)))
```

12.3.3   Optimizing a Jump While Generating It

The backwards compiler fragment above unconditionally generates new labels and jumps. But if the instruction after the if-statement were GOTO L3, then it would wastefully generate a jump to a jump:

```
    <e> IFZERO L1
    <stmt1> GOTO L2
L1: <stmt2>
L2: GOTO L3
```

One should much rather generate GOTO L3 than the GOTO L2 that takes a detour around another jump. (Such jumps slow down pipelined processors because they cause instruction pipeline stalls. So-called branch prediction logic in modern processors mitigates this effect to some degree, but still it is better to avoid excess jumps.) Thus instead of mindlessly generating a new label labend and a GOTO, we call an auxiliary function makeJump that checks whether the first instruction of the code continuation C is a GOTO (or a return RET or a label) and generates a suitable jump instruction jumpend, adding a label to C if necessary, giving C1:

```
let (jumpend, C1) = makeJump C
```

The makeJump function is easily written using pattern matching. If C begins with a return instruction RET (possibly below a label), then jumpend is RET; if C begins with label lab or GOTO lab, then jumpend is GOTO lab; otherwise, we invent a new label lab to stick onto C, and then jumpend is GOTO lab:

```
let makeJump C : instr * instr list =
    match C with
    | RET m              :: _ -> (RET m, C)
    | Label lab :: RET m :: _ -> (RET m, C)
    | Label lab          :: _ -> (GOTO lab, C)
    | GOTO lab           :: _ -> (GOTO lab, C)
    | _                       -> let lab = newLabel()
                                 (GOTO lab, Label lab :: C)
```

Similarly, we need to stick a label in front of <stmt2> above only if there is no label (or GOTO) already, so we use a function addLabel to return a label labelse, possibly sticking it in front of <stmt2>:

```
let (labelse, C2) = addLabel (cStmt stmt2 varEnv funEnv C1)
```

Note that C1 (that is, C possibly preceded by a label) is the code continuation of stmt2.

The function addLabel uses pattern matching on the code continuation C to decide whether a label needs to be added. If C begins with a GOTO lab or label lab, we can just reuse lab; otherwise we must invent a new label for C:

```
let addLabel C : label * instr list =
    match C with
    | Label lab :: _ -> (lab, C)
    | GOTO lab :: _  -> (lab, C)
    | _              -> let lab = newLabel()
                        (lab, Label lab :: C)
```

Finally, when compiling an if-statement with no else-branch:

```
if (e)
    stmt
```

we do not want to get code like this, with a jump to the next instruction:

```
    <e> IFZERO L1
    <stmt1> GOTO L2
L1:
L2:
```

to avoid this, we introduce a function addJump which recognizes this situation and avoids generating the GOTO.

Putting everything together, we have this optimizing compilation scheme for an if-statement If(e, stmt1, stmt2):

```
let (jumpend, C1) = makeJump C
let (labelse, C2) = addLabel (cStmt stmt2 varEnv funEnv C1)
cExpr e varEnv funEnv (IFZERO labelse
   :: cStmt stmt1 varEnv funEnv (addJump jumpend C2))
```

This gives a flavor of the optimizations performed for if-statements. Below we show how additional optimizations for constants improve the compilation of logical expressions.

12.3.4   Optimizing Logical Expression Code

As in the old forwards compiler (file Comp.fs) logical non-strict connectives such as && and || are compiled to conditional jumps, not to special instructions that manipulate boolean values.

Consider the example program in file ex13.c. It prints the leap years between 1890 and the year n entered on the command line:

```
void main(int n) {
  int y;
  y = 1889;
  while (y < n) {
    y = y + 1;
    if (y % 4 == 0 && (y % 100 != 0 || y % 400 == 0))
      print y;
  }
}
```

The non-optimizing forwards compiler generates this code for the while-loop:

```
    GOTO L3;
L2: GETBP; 1; ADD; GETBP; 1; ADD; LDI; 1; ADD; STI; INCSP -1;
    GETBP; 1; ADD; LDI; 4; MOD; 0; EQ; IFZERO L7;
    GETBP; 1; ADD; LDI; 100; MOD; 0; EQ; NOT; IFNZRO L9;
    GETBP; 1; ADD; LDI; 400; MOD; 0; EQ; GOTO L8;
L9: 1;
L8: GOTO L6;
```

```
L7: 0;
L6: IFZERO L4; GETBP; 1; ADD; LDI; PRINTI; INCSP -1; GOTO L5;
L4: INCSP 0;
L5: INCSP 0;
L3: GETBP; 1; ADD; LDI; GETBP; 0; ADD; LDI; LT; IFNZRO L2;
```

The above code has many deficiencies:

- an occurrence of 0; ADD could be deleted, because $x + 0$ equals x
- INCSP 0 could be deleted (twice)
- two occurrences of 0; EQ could be replaced by NOT, or the subsequent test could be inverted
- instead of jumping to L8, which immediately jumps to L6, one could jump straight to L6
- if L9 is reached, a 1 will be pushed and execution will continue at L6, but the jump to L4 there will not be taken; so instead of going to L9 one could go straight to the code following IFZERO L4
- similarly, if L7 is reached, the jump to L4 at L6 definitely will be taken; so instead of going to L7 one could go straight to L4
- instead of executing GOTO L6 followed by IFNZRO L4 one could execute IFNZRO L4 right away.

The optimizing backwards compiler solves all those problems, and generates this code:

```
    GOTO L3;
L2: GETBP; 1; ADD; GETBP; 1; ADD; LDI; 1; ADD; STI; INCSP -1;
    GETBP; 1; ADD; LDI; 4; MOD; IFNZRO L3;
    GETBP; 1; ADD; LDI; 100; MOD; IFNZRO L4;
    GETBP; 1; ADD; LDI; 400; MOD; IFNZRO L3;
L4: GETBP; 1; ADD; LDI; PRINTI; INCSP -1;
L3: GETBP; 1; ADD; LDI; GETBP; LDI; LT; IFNZRO L2;
```

To see that the compilation of a logical expression adapts itself to the context of use, contrast this with the compilation of the function leap year (file ex22.c):

```
int leapyear(int y) {
  return y % 4 == 0 && (y % 100 != 0 || y % 400 == 0);
}
```

which returns the value of the logical expression instead of using it in a conditional:

```
L2: GETBP; LDI; 4; MOD; IFNZRO L5;            y%4==0
    GETBP; LDI; 100; MOD; IFNZRO L6;          y%100!=0
    GETBP; LDI; 400; MOD; NOT; RET 1;         y%400==0
L6: 1; RET 1;                                 true
L5: 0; RET 1;                                 false
```

The code between L2 and L6 is essentially the same as before, but the code following L6 is different: it leaves a (boolean) value on the stack top and returns from the function.

12.3.5   Eliminating Dead Code

Instructions that cannot be executed are called dead code. For instance, the instructions immediately after an unconditional jump (GOTO or RET) cannot be executed, unless they are preceded by a label. We can eliminate dead code by throwing away all instructions after an unconditional jump, up to the first label after that instruction (function deadcode). This means that instructions following an infinite loop are thrown away (file ex7.c):

```
while (1) {
  i = i + 1;
}
print 999999;
```

The following code is generated for the loop:

```
L2: GETBP; GETBP; LDI; 1; ADD; STI; INCSP -1; GOTO L2
```

where the statement print 999999 has been thrown away, and the loop conditional has been turned into an unconditional GOTO.

12.3.6   Optimizing Tail Calls

As we have seen before, a tail call f (...) occurring in function g is a call that is the last action of the calling function g. When the called function f returns to g, function g will do nothing more before it too returns.

In code for the abstract stack machine from Sect. 8.2, a tail call can be recognized as a call to f that is immediately followed by a return from g: a CALL instruction followed by a RET instruction. For example, consider this program with a tail call from main to main (file ex12.c):

```
int main(int n) {
  if (n)
    return main(n-1);
  else
    return 17;
}
```

The code generated by the old forwards compiler is

```
L1: GETBP; 0; ADD; LDI; IFZERO L2;
```

Ordinary call and two returns

	ret addr	old bp1	g's vars etc

CALL f

	ret addr	old bp1	g's vars etc	ret addr	old bp2	f's vars etc

RET (from f)

	ret addr	old bp1	g's vars etc

RET (from g)

Tail call and one return

	ret addr	old bp1	g's vars etc

TCALL f

	ret addr	old bp1	f's vars etc

RET (from f)

Fig. 12.1 Example replacement of a call and a return by a tail call. On the *left*, g calls f by the CALL instruction, f returns to g, and g returns to its caller. On the *right*, g calls f by the TCALL instruction, discarding g's stack frame but keeping its return address and old base pointer, so that f returns straight to g's caller

```
    GETBP; 0; ADD; LDI; 1; SUB; CALL (1,L1); RET 1; GOTO L3;
L2: 17; RET 1;
L3: INCSP 0; RET 0
```

The tail call is apparent as CALL (1, L1); RET. Moreover, the GOTO L3 and the code following label L3 are *unreachable*: those code fragments cannot be executed, but that's less important.

When function f is called by a tail call in g:

```
void g(...) {
    ... f(...) ...
}
```

then if the call to f ever returns to g, it is necessarily because of a RET instruction in f, so two RET instructions will be executed in sequence:

```
CALL m f; ... RET k; RET n
```

The tail call instruction TCALL of our stack machine has been designed so that the above sequence of executed instructions is equivalent to this sequence of instructions:

```
TCALL m n f; ... RET k
```

This equivalence is illustrated by an example in Fig. 12.1. More formally, Fig. 12.2 uses the stack machine rules to show that the equivalence holds between two sequences of executed instructions:

```
CALL m f; ...RET k; RET n  equals  TCALL m n f; ...; RET k
```

provided function f at address a transforms the stack $s, r_2, b_2, v_1, \ldots, v_m$ before the call into the stack $s, r_2, b_2, w_1, \ldots, w_k, v$ after the call, without using the lower part s of the stack at all.

Stack	Action
Ordinary call and two returns	
$s, r_1, bp_1, u_1, .., u_n, v_1, .., v_m$	CALL m f (at address r_2)
$\Rightarrow s, r_1, bp_1, u_1, .., u_n, r_2, bp_2, v_1, .., v_m$	code in the body of f
$\Rightarrow s, r_1, bp_1, u_1, .., u_n, r_2, bp_2, w_1, .., w_k, v$ RET k	
$\Rightarrow s, r_1, bp_1, u_1, .., u_n, v$	RET n (at address r_2)
$\Rightarrow s, v$	
Tail call and one return	
$s, r_1, bp_1, u_1, .., u_n, v_1, .., v_m$	TCALL m n f (at address r_2)
$\Rightarrow s, r_1, bp_1, v_1, .., v_m$	code in the body of f
$\Rightarrow s, r_1, bp_1, w_1, .., w_k, v$	RET k
$\Rightarrow s, v$	

Fig. 12.2 A tail call is equivalent to a call followed by return

The new continuation-based compiler uses an auxiliary function `makeCall` to recognize tail calls:

```
let makeCall m lab C : instr list =
    match C with
    | RET n            :: C1 -> TCALL(m, n, lab) :: C1
    | Label _ :: RET n :: _  -> TCALL(m, n, lab) :: C
    | _                      -> CALL(m, lab) :: C
```

It will compile the above example function `main` to the following abstract machine code, in which the recursive call to `main` has been recognized as a tail call and has been compiled as a TCALL:

```
L1: GETBP; LDI; IFZERO L2;                    if (n)
    GETBP; LDI; 1; SUB; TCALL (1,1,"L1");     main(n-1)
L2: 17; RET 1                                 17
```

Note that the compiler will recognize a tail call only if it is immediately followed by a RET. Thus a tail call inside an if-statement (file `ex15.c`), like this one:

```
void main(int n) {
    if (n!=0) {
        print n;
        main(n-1);
    } else
        print 999999;
}
```

is optimized to use the TCALL instruction only if the compiler never generates a GOTO to a RET, but directly generates a RET. Therefore the `makeJump` optimizations made by our continuation-based compiler are important also for efficient implementation of tail calls.

In general, it is unsound to do what we do here: implement tail calls in C and micro-C by removing the calling function's stack frame and replacing it by the called function's stack frame. In C, an array allocated in a function g can be used also in a function f called by g, as in this program:

```
void g() {
  int a[10];
  a[1] = 117;
  f(1, a);
}

void f(int i, int a[]) {
  print a[i];
}
```

However, that would not work if g's stack frame, which contains the a array, were removed and replaced by f's stack frame. Most likely, the contents of array cell a[1] would be overwritten, and f would print some nonsense. The same problem appears if the calling function passes a pointer that point inside its stack frame to a called function. Note that in Java, in which no array is ever allocated on the stack, and pointers into the stack cannot be created, this problem does not appear. On the other hand, C# has similar problems as C in this respect.

To be on the safe side, a compiler should make the tail call optimization only if the calling function does not pass any pointers or array addresses to the function called by a tail call. The continuation-based compiler in Contcomp.fs performs this unsound optimization anyway, to show what impact it has. See micro-C example ex21.c.

12.3.7 Remaining Deficiencies of the Generated Code

There are still some problems with the code generated for conditional statements. For instance, compilation of this statement (file ex16.c):

```
if (n)
  { }
else
  print 1111;
print 2222;
```

generates this machine code:

```
L1: GETBP; LDI; IFZERO L3;
    GOTO L2;
L3: CSTI 1111; PRINTI; INCSP -1;
L2: CSTI 2222; PRINTI; RET 1
```

which could be optimized by inverting IFZERO L3 to IFNZRO L2 and deleting the GOTO L2. Similarly, the code generated for certain trivial while-loops is unsatisfactory. We might like the code generated for

```
void main(int n) {
  print 1111;
  while (false) {
    print 2222;
  }
  print 3333;
}
```

to consist only of the print 1111 and print 3333 statements, leaving out the while-loop completely, since its body will never be executed anyway. Currently, this is not ensured by the compiler. This is not a serious problem: some unreachable code is generated, but it does not slow down the program execution.

12.4   Other Optimizations

There are many other kinds of optimizations that an optimizing compiler might perform, but that are not performed by our simple compiler:

- *Constant propagation*: if a variable x is set to a constant value, such as 17, and never modified, then every use of x can be replaced by the use of the constant 17. This may enable further optimizations if the variable is used in expressions such as

  ```
  x * 3 + 1
  ```

- *Common subexpression elimination*: if the same (complex) expression is computed twice with the same values of all variables, then one could instead compute it once, store the result (in a variable or on the stack top), and reuse it. Common subexpressions frequently occur behind the scenes. For instance, the assignment

  ```
  a[i] = a[i] + 1;
  ```

  is compiled to

  ```
  GETBP; aoff; ADD; LDI; GETBP; ioffset; ADD; LDI; ADD;
  GETBP; aoff; ADD; LDI; GETBP; ioffset; ADD; LDI; ADD; LDI;
  1; ADD; STI
  ```

  where aoff is the offset of array a, and the address (lvalue) of the array element a[i] is computed twice. It might be better to compute it once, and store it in the stack. However, the address to be reused is typically buried under some other stack elements, and our simple stack machine has no instruction to duplicate an element some way down the stack (like the JVM's dup_x1 instruction).

- *Loop invariant computations*: If an expression inside a loop (`for`, `while`) does not depend on any variables modified by execution of the loop body, then the expression may be computed outside the loop (unless evaluation of the expression has a side effect, in which case it must be evaluated inside the loop). For instance, in

```
while (...) {
  a[i] = ...
}
```

part of the array indexing `a[i]` is loop invariant, namely the computation of the array base address:

```
GETBP; aoffset; ADD; LDI
```

so this could be computed once and for all before the loop.
- *Dead code elimination*: if the value of a variable or expression is never used, then the variable or expression may be removed (unless evaluation of the expression has side effects, in which case the expression must be preserved).

12.5   A Command Line Compiler for Micro-C

So far we have run the micro-C compiler inside an F# interactive session. Here we shall wrap it as an `.exe` file that can be invoked from the command line. The compiler gets the name of the micro-C source file (say, `ex11.c`) from the command line, reads, parses and compiles the contents of that file, and writes the output to file `ex11.out`:

```
let args = System.Environment.GetCommandLineArgs();;
let _ = printf "Micro-C backwards compiler v 1.0.0.0\n";;
let _ =
    if args.Length > 1 then
        let source = args.[1]
        let stem = if source.EndsWith(".c")
                     then source.Substring(0,source.Length-2)
                     else source
        let target = stem + ".out"
        printf "Compiling %s to %s\n" source target;
        try ignore (Contcomp.contCompileToFile
                          (Parse.fromFile source) target)
        with Failure msg -> printf "ERROR: %s\n" msg
    else
        printf "Usage: microcc <source file>\n";;
```

We build the micro-C compiler using the F# compiler `fsc`, like this:

```
fsc -r FSharp.PowerPack.dll Absyn.fs CPar.fs CLex.fs Parse.fs \
```

```
Machine.fs Contcomp.fs MicroCC.fs -o microcc.exe
```

The micro-C compiler is called `microcc` in analogy with `gcc` (Gnu C), `javac` (Java), `csc` (C#) and other command line compilers. To compile micro-C file `ex11.c`, we use it as follows:

```
C:\>microcc.exe ex11.c
Micro-C backwards compiler v 1.0.0.0
Compiling ex11.c to ex11.out
```

12.6   History and Literature

The influential programming language textbook by Abelson, Sussman and Sussman [1] hints at the possibility of optimization on the fly in a continuation-based compiler. Xavier Leroy's 1990 report [2] describes optimizing backwards code generation for an abstract machine. This is essentially the machine and code generation technique used in Caml Light, OCaml, and Moscow ML. The same idea is used in Mads Tofte's 1990 Nsukka lecture notes [3], but the representation of the code continuation given there is more complicated and provides fewer opportunities for optimization.

The idea of generating code backwards is probably much older than any of these references.

12.7   Exercises

The main goal of these exercises is to realize that the bytecode generated by micro-C compilers can be improved, and to see how the backwards (continuation-based) micro-C compiler can be modified to achieve further improvements in the bytecode.

Exercise 12.1 The continuation-based micro-C compiler (file `Contcomp.fs`) still generates clumsy code in some cases. For instance, the statement (file `ex16.c`):

```
if (n)
  { }
else
  print 1111;
print 2222;
```

is compiled to this machine code:

```
    GETBP; LDI; IFZERO L3;
    GOTO L2;
L3: CSTI 1111; PRINTI; INCSP -1;
L2: CSTI 2222; PRINTI; RET 1
```

which could be optimized to this by inverting the conditional jump and deleting the GOTO L2 instruction:

```
    GETBP; LDI; IFNZRO L2;
L3: CSTI 1111; PRINTI; INCSP -1;
L2: CSTI 2222; PRINTI; RET 1
```

Improve the compiler to recognize this situation. It must recognize that it is about to generate code of this form:

```
IFZERO L3; GOTO L2; Label L3; ....
```

where the conditional jump jumps over an unconditional jump. Instead it should generate code such as this:

```
IFNZRO L2; Label L3; ....
```

Define a new auxiliary function addIFZERO lab3 C which tests whether C has the structure shown above. In the code generation for If(e,s1,s2) in cStmt, instead of doing IFZERO labelse:: code you must call the auxiliary to do the consing, as in addIFZERO labelse code.

In fact, everywhere in the compiler where you would previously just cons IFZERO lab onto something, you should call addIFZERO instead to make sure the code gets optimized.

A similar optimization can be made for IFNZRO L3; GOTO L2; Label L3. This is done in much the same way.

Exercise 12.2 Improve code generation in the continuation-based micro-C compiler so that a less-than comparison with *constant* arguments is compiled to its truth value. For instance, 11 < 22 should compile to the same code as true, and 22 < 11 should compile to the same code as false. This can be done by a small extension of the addCST function in Contcomp.fs.

Further improve the code generation so that all comparisons with constant arguments are compiled to the same code as true (e.g. 11 <= 22 and 11 != 22 and 22 > 11 and 22 >= 11) or false.

Check that if (11<=22) print 33; compiles to code that unconditionally executes print 33 without performing any test or jump.

Exercise 12.3 Extend the micro-C abstract syntax (file Absyn.fs) with conditional expressions Cond(e1, e2, e3), corresponding to this concrete syntax (known from C, C++, Java and C#):

```
e1 ? e2 : e3
```

The expression Cond(e1, e2, e3) must evaluate e1, and if the result is non-zero, must evaluate e2, otherwise e3. (If you want to extend also the lexer and parser to accept this new syntax, then note that ? and : are right associative; but implementing them in the lexer and parser is not strictly necessary for this exercise).

Schematically, the conditional expression should be compiled to the code shown below:

```
      <e1>
      IFZERO L1
      <e2>
      GOTO L2
  L1: <e3>
  L2:
```

Extend the continuation-based micro-C compiler (file Contcomp.fs) to compile conditional expressions to stack machine code. Your compiler should optimize code while generating it. Check that your compiler compiles the following two examples to code that works properly:

```
   true ? 1111 : 2222              false ? 1111 : 2222
```

The first one has abstract syntax Cond(CstI 1, CstI 1111, CstI 2222). Unless you have implemented conditional expressions (e1 ? e2 : e3) in the lexer and parser, the simplest way to experiment with this is to invoke the cExpr expression compilation function directly, like this, where the two first [] represent empty environments, and the last one is an empty list of instructions:

```
   cExpr (Cond(CstI 1, CstI 1111, CstI 2222))
         ([], 0) [] [];
```

Do not waste too much effort trying to get your compiler to optimize away everything that is not needed. This seems impossible without traversing and modifying already generated code.

Exercise 12.4 The compilation of the short-cut logical operators (&&) and (||) in Contcomp.fs is rather complicated. After Exercise 12.3 one can implement them in a somewhat simpler way, using these equivalences:

$$\begin{array}{lll} \text{e1 \&\& e2} & \text{is equivalent to} & \text{(e1 ? e2 : 0)} \\ \text{e1 || e2} & \text{is equivalent to} & \text{(e1 ? 1 : e2)} \end{array}$$

Implement the sequential logical operators (&& and ||) this way in your extended compiler from Exercise 12.3. You should change the parser specification in CPar.fsy to build Cond(...) expressions instead of Andalso(...) or Orelse(...). Test this approach on file ex13.c and possibly other examples. How does the code quality compare to the existing complicated compilation of && and ||?

Exercise 12.5 Improve the compilation of assignment expressions that are really just increment operations, such as these

```
   i = i + 1
   a[i] = a[i] + 1
```

It is easiest to recognize such cases in the abstract syntax, not by looking at the code continuation.

Exercise 12.6 Try to make sense of the code generated by the continuation-based compiler for the n-queens program in file `ex11.c`. Draw a flowchart of the compiled program, connecting each jump to its target label.

Exercise 12.7 Implement a post-optimizer for stack machine symbolic code as generated by the micro-C compilers. This should be a function:

```
optimize : instr list -> instr list
```

where `instr` is defined in `Machine.fs`. The idea is that `optimize` should improve the code using the local bytecode equivalences shown in Sect. 12.3.1. Also, it may delete code that is unreachable (code that cannot be executed). Function `optimize` should be *correct*: the code it produces must behave the same as the original code when executed on the stack machine in `Machine.java`.

The function would have to make two passes over the code. In the *first pass* it computes a set of all reachable labels. A label, and the instructions following it, is reachable if (1) it can be reached from the beginning of the code, or (2) there is a jump or call (`GOTO`, `IFZERO`, `IFNZRO`, `CALL`, `TCALL`) to it from a reachable instruction.

In the *second pass* it can go through the instruction sequences at reachable labels only, and simplify them using the bytecode equivalences.

Note that simplification of [`CSTI 1; IFZERO L1`] may cause label `L1` to be recognized as unreachable. Also, deletion of the code labeled `L1` in [`CST 0`; `GOTO L2`; `Label L1`; `...`; `Label L2`; `ADD`] would enable further local simplifications. Hence the computation of reachable labels and simplification of code may have to be repeated until no more simplifications can be made.

References

1. Abelson, H., Sussman, G.J., Sussman, J.: Structure and Interpretation of Computer Programs. MIT Press (1985)
2. Leroy, X.: The Zinc experiment: An economical implementation of the ML language. Rapport Technique 117, INRIA Rocquencourt, France (1990)
3. Tofte, M.: The PL/0 machine. University of Nigeria, Nsukka, Lecture notes (1990)

Chapter 13
Compiling Micro-SML

By Niels Hallenberg

In Chaps. 4 and 5 we presented a small functional language, micro-ML, and implemented an interpreter for its dynamic semantics as defined in Fig. 4.3. The static semantics for the first-order language was defined in Fig. 4.7 and the higher-order static semantics in Fig. 6.1. Based on this a type checker and a type inference algorithm were implemented in Sect. 6.4. Here we round out the topic of functional languages by presenting an extended version of micro-ML called micro-SML. The language micro-SML is inspired by Core Standard ML [1]. In addition to a compiler for micro-SML we also include an interpreter and an implementation of type inference. The implementations make use of topics introduced as part of working with micro-C: free variables (Chap. 2), the virtual byte code machine (Chap. 9), garbage collection (Chap. 10), continuations (Chap. 11), and the local optimization techniques applied to micro-C (Chap. 12).

13.1 Files for This Chapter

The files follow the same structure as the micro-ML files listed in Sect. 4.1.

File	Contents
Sml/Absyn.fs	the abstract syntax (see Fig. 13.3)
Sml/FunLex.fsl	lexer specification
Sml/FunPar.fsy	parser specification
Sml/TypeInference.fs	type inference algorithm
Sml/HigherFun.fs	interpreter
Sml/Contcomp.fs	backward compiler with local optimizations
Sml/ParseTypeAndRun.fs	combining lexer, parser, interpreter and compiler
Sml/Machine.fs	micro-SML stack machine instruction definitions
Sml/MicroSMLC.fs	read arguments from command line
Sml/msmlmachine.c	micro-SML stack machine in C
Sml/*.sml	example programs for micro-SML

© Springer International Publishing AG 2017
P. Sestoft, *Programming Language Concepts*, Undergraduate Topics
in Computer Science, DOI 10.1007/978-3-319-60789-4_13

13.2   Grammar for Micro-SML

The grammar for micro-SML is shown in Fig. 13.1. It is closely based on Core
Standard ML but is missing pattern matching, data type declarations, records and
tuples.

A program consists of a number of global value declarations *vds* followed by
a main expression *e*. Values, exceptions and mutually recursive functions can be
declared globally or inside local `let` expressions. Mutually recursive function
declarations use the keywords `fun` and `and`. Anonymous function expressions use
the keyword `fn`. For simplicity, all micro-SML functions take exactly one argument.

Grammar		Comment
Prog:	*vds* begin *e* end	A program has global declarations and an expression
Valdecs:	fun *f* *x* = *e*	Mutually recursive functions; the first one
	and *g* *x* = *e*	Additional functions
	val *x* = *e*	Value declaration, global or `let`-bound local
	exception *exn*	Exception declaration, global or `let`-bound local
Expr:	*i*	Integer constant
	x	Variable access
	true	Boolean constant true
	false	Boolean constant false
	nil	Empty list constant
	if *e* then *e* else *e*	Conditional expression
	fn *x* -> *e*	Anonymous function
	let *vds* in *e* end	Local declarations and an expression
	e *e*	Function application
	raise *e*	Exceptions can be raised
	try *e* with *exn* -> *e* end	Exceptions can be handled
	print *e*	A built-in print primitive
	e + *e*	Binary operators such as +, −, *
	e && *e*	Logical operators such as && and ||
	e :: *e*	List construction
	isnil *e*	Test for empty list
	hd *e*	Head of list
	tl *e*	Tail of list
	e ; *e*	Sequence of two expressions

Fig. 13.1 Grammar for micro-SML. The symbols *f*, *g* and *x* range over function names and
variables. The symbol *exn* ranges over exception names and *e* ranges over expressions *Expr*. A
constant is an integer, boolean, or empty list. The symbol *vds* represents a sequence of zero or more
value declarations *Valdecs*; declarations are allowed both globally and inside a local `let` expression

Functions taking more than one argument have been covered in the exercises in Chap. 4.

Lists are supported using the empty list `nil`, the cons operator (`::`), and the unary operators `isnil`, `hd` and `tl`. Integer and boolean constants are also supported. Exceptions are declared using an *exception name* which is introduced by the `exception` keyword. Exceptions in micro-SML are generative, see Sect. 13.4, just like exceptions in Standard ML [1].

The lexer and parser specifications for the grammar, as defined in Fig. 13.1, are found in files `FunLex.fsl` and `FunPar.fsy`.

13.2.1 Example Programs

Micro-SML file names end with `.sml`. The program `ex01.sml` below declares two global mutually recursive functions:

```
fun f x = x + g 4
and g x = x

begin
  print (f 1)
end
```

The program `ex02.sml` below generates a list and applies a mapping function on the list. The program also shows that `print` will automatically adapt to the type of value to print. Note the use of the sequence operator (`;`) between the two print expressions.

```
fun genList n =
  let
    fun loop n = fn acc ->
      if n < 0 then acc else loop (n-1) (n::acc)
  in
    loop n nil
  end

fun map f = fn xs ->
  if isnil xs then nil else f (hd xs) :: map f (tl xs)

begin
  let
    val xs = genList 10
  in
```

```
      print xs;
      print (map (fn x -> x + 1) xs)
   end
end
```

Figure 13.2 gives an overview of the example programs provided.

13.2.2   Abstract Syntax

The abstract syntax for micro-SML (Fig. 13.3) is similar to the abstract syntax for micro-ML (Fig. 4.1) except that we use separate abstract syntax types for value declarations, exception names and expressions. We also add a field of polymorphic type 'a option to hold additional information created and used by the compilation phases. Thus expr<t> is an expression tree whose nodes may hold additional information of type t. For instance, a value of type expr<int> may have a source line number attached to each subexpression.

The constant CstN represents value nil as in the list-C machine (Sect. 10.7.2). The list operations nil, hd and tl are represented by the Prim1 constructor, and cons (::) is represented by the Prim2 constructor. The Let and Prog constructors take a list of value declarations, valdec<'a>, corresponding to the grammar in Fig. 13.1. Exceptions are raised with the Raise constructor and handled with the TryWith constructor. The Fundecs constructor represents a group of mutually recursive function declarations.

A program, Prog, is a list of global value declarations and then an expression between the begin and end keywords.

13.2.3   Prettyprinting

The function ppProg in file Absyn.fs can be used to prettyprint the abstract syntax including the additional information represented by type variable 'a. This is

File	Contents
Sml/exXY.sml	simple programs illustrating features of micro-SML
Sml/exnXY.sml	programs using exceptions
Sml/list.sml	program using common list operations
Sml/queens.sml	program solving the n-queens puzzle
Sml/test.sml	tests covering parts of the grammar, see Fig. 13.1
Sml/testgc.sml	tests allocating intensively on the heap for garbage collection

Fig. 13.2 Example micro-SML programs

```
type expr<'a> =
  | CstI of int * 'a option
  | CstB of bool * 'a option
  | CstN of 'a option
  | Var of string * 'a option
  | AndAlso of expr<'a> * expr<'a> * 'a option
  | OrElse of expr<'a> * expr<'a> * 'a option
  | Seq of expr<'a> * expr<'a> * 'a option
  | Prim2 of string * expr<'a> * expr<'a> * 'a option
  | Prim1 of string * expr<'a> * 'a option
  | If of expr<'a> * expr<'a> * expr<'a>
  | Fun of string * expr<'a> * 'a option
  | Call of expr<'a> * expr<'a> * bool option * 'a option
  | Let of valdec<'a> list * expr<'a>
  | Raise of expr<'a> * 'a option
  | TryWith of expr<'a> * exnvar * expr<'a>
and valdec<'a> =
  | Fundecs of (string * string * expr<'a>) list
  | Valdec of string * expr<'a>
  | Exn of exnvar * 'a option
and exnvar =
  | ExnVar of string
and program<'a> =
  | Prog of valdec<'a> list * expr<'a>
```

Fig. 13.3 Abstract syntax for micro-SML. The fields of polymorphic type `'a` `option` allow different compilation phases to attach different types of information to the abstract syntax tree

especially useful for debugging. We will add type information to the abstract syntax in Sect. 13.3.

13.2.4 Tail Calls

Figure 11.1 shows how tail calls can be identified in a simple expression language. Function `tailcalls` in file `Absyn.fs` implements tail call detection for micro-SML, see Fig. 13.4. Expressions representing the body of a function (constructors `Fun` and `Fundecs`) or the body of a program (constructor `Prog`) are in tail position and hence the function `tc'` is called with `true`. Expressions not in tail position call `tc'` with `false`, e.g., e1 of `AndAlso`, e1 of `Seq` etc. Subexpressions of operations `Prim1` and `Prim2` are not in tail position because the operation must be evaluated after the operands. The expression e1 of the `TryWith` construct is not in tail position because the exception handler must be popped, see Sect. 13.5.6.

The `Call` constructor has an optional boolean value representing whether the call has been identified as a tail call or not. This is annotated by the code `Some` `tPos` in function `tc'`. The compiler uses this information to generate tail call byte code instructions in Sect. 13.5.5.

```
let tailcalls p : program<'a> =
  let rec tc' tPos e =
    match e with
    | CstI _ -> e
    | AndAlso(e1,e2,aOpt) ->
        AndAlso(tc' false e1,tc' tPos e2,aOpt)
    | Seq(e1,e2,aOpt) -> Seq(tc' false e1,tc' tPos e2,aOpt)
    | Prim2(ope,e1,e2,aOpt) ->
        Prim2(ope,tc' false e1,tc' false e2,aOpt)
    | Prim1(ope,e,aOpt) -> Prim1(ope,tc' false e,aOpt)
    | Fun(x,e,aOpt) -> Fun(x,tc' true e,aOpt)
    | Call(e1,e2,_,aOpt) ->
        Call(tc' false e1,tc' false e2,Some tPos,aOpt)
    | Let(valdecs,letBody) ->
        Let(List.map (tcValdec' false) valdecs,tc' tPos letBody)
    | Raise(e1,aOpt) -> e
    | TryWith(e1,exn,e2) ->
        TryWith(tc' false e1, exn, tc' tPos e2)
    | ...
  and tcValdec' tPos = function
    | Valdec(x,eRhs) -> Valdec(x,tc' tPos eRhs)
    | Fundecs(fs) ->
        Fundecs(List.map (fun (f,x,e) -> (f,x,tc' true e)) fs)
    | Exn(x,aOpt) -> Exn(x,aOpt)
  and tcProg' = function
    | Prog (valdecs,body) ->
        Prog(List.map (tcValdec' false) valdecs,tc' true body)
  tcProg' p
```

Fig. 13.4 The function `tailcalls` identifies tail call positions for micro-SML. Some constructors are left out. The boolean argument `tPos` in a call `tc' tPos e` says whether expression e is in tail position, and propagates this information to the subexpressions of e

13.2.5 Free Variables

The concept of free variable was discussed in Sect. 2.3.3. The compiler needs information about free variables of a function to create a closure; see Sect. 13.5.4. The function `freevars` in file `Absyn.fs` calculates the set of free variables of a micro-SML expression; see Fig. 13.5.

As explained in Sect. 2.3.3, the set of free variables in `let x=erhs in ebody end` is the union of the set of free variables in `erhs` with the set of free variables of `ebody` except the bound variable `x`. A sequence *vds* (Fig. 13.1) of micro-SML bindings can bind any number of variables, so we use a set `bvs` of bound variables to keep track of the variables to subtract. This works in both local (`let`) and global (program) contexts.

The exception name `exn` in a `TryWith` construct is free because it is used to match against a raised exception. The bound variables, `bvs`, are accumulated when calculating free variables of value declarations in function `freevarsValdec`.

```
let rec freevars e : string Set =
  match e with
  | Let(valdecs,letBody) ->
    let (fvs,bvs) =
      List.fold freevarsValdec (Set.empty, Set.empty) valdecs
      (freevars letBody) + fvs - bvs
  | Fun(x,fBody,_) -> freevars fBody - (set [x])
  | Call(eFun, eArg,_,_) -> freevars eFun + (freevars eArg)
  | Raise(e1,_) -> freevars e1
  | TryWith(e1,ExnVar exn,e2) ->
      (freevars e1) + (set [exn]) + (freevars e2)
  | ...
and freevarsValdec (fvs, bvs) = function
    Valdec(x,eRhs) ->
      (fvs + ((freevars eRhs) - set [x]),bvs + set [x])
  | Exn (ExnVar exn,aOpt) -> (fvs,bvs + set [exn])
  | Fundecs(fs) ->
    let fEnv = Set.ofList (List.map (fun (f,_,_) -> f) fs)
    let funFree =
      List.foldBack
        (fun (_,x,fBody) acc ->
          (acc + (freevars fBody - fEnv - set [x]))) fs fvs
      (funFree, bvs + fEnv)
```

Fig. 13.5 The function `freevars` calculates the set of free variables of a micro-SML expression. Some constructors are left out. The operators (+) and (−) from F#'s Set module compute set union and set difference

13.3 Type Inference for Micro-SML

The Fig. 6.1 shows type rules for micro-ML. Figure 13.6 shows additional type rules $g1$ to $g12$ for micro-SML. We have added a type `exn` to represent exceptions, and a polymorphic type α `list` to represent lists. As in Fig. 6.1, the environment ρ maps variable names to type schemes and the notation $[t_1/\alpha_1, \ldots, t_n/\alpha_n]t$ is used for substitution. In Fig. 6.1 the rules for `let` bindings were simplified to allow only one value, exception or group of mutually recursive function declarations. By contrast, micro-SML allows an arbitrary number of declarations in a `let` construct.

- Rules $g1$ to $g5$: The type for `nil` is polymorphic to fit in any type of list. The types for the operations `hd`, `tl` and `::` make sure that all elements of a list expression have the same type. The `isnil` operator works on any list type.
- Rules $g6$ and $g7$: In expression `raise e`, the argument e must have type `exn`. The expression as a whole can have any type t since it must match the type of the expression it appears in.
- Rules $g7$: Both expressions e_1 and e_2 in the `try-with` construct must have the same type since both can be the construct's final result.
- Rule $g8$: The result of e_1 is thrown away when evaluated as part of the sequence operator (;) so it does not matter what type t_1 expression e_1 has.

$$\frac{}{\rho \vdash \texttt{nil} \ : \ t \ \texttt{list}} \ (g1)$$

$$\frac{\rho \vdash e : t \ \texttt{list}}{\rho \vdash \texttt{hd} \ e \ : \ t} \ (g2)$$

$$\frac{\rho \vdash e : t \ \texttt{list}}{\rho \vdash \texttt{tl} \ e \ : \ t \ \texttt{list}} \ (g3)$$

$$\frac{\rho \vdash e : t \ \texttt{list}}{\rho \vdash \texttt{isnil} \ e \ : \ \texttt{bool}} \ (g4)$$

$$\frac{\rho \vdash e_1 : t \qquad \rho \vdash e_2 : t \ \texttt{list}}{\rho \vdash e_1 :: e_2 \ : \ t \ \texttt{list}} \ (g5)$$

$$\frac{\rho \vdash e : \texttt{exn}}{\rho \vdash \texttt{raise} \ e \ : \ t} \ (g6)$$

$$\frac{\rho \vdash e_1 : t \qquad \rho \vdash e_2 : t \qquad \rho(exn) = \texttt{exn}}{\rho \vdash \texttt{try} \ e_1 \ \texttt{with} \ exn \ \texttt{->} \ e_2 \ : \ t} \ (g7)$$

$$\frac{\rho \vdash e_1 : t_1 \qquad \rho \vdash e_2 : t_2}{\rho \vdash e_1 \ ; e_2 \ : \ t_2} \ (g8)$$

$$\frac{\rho[x \mapsto t_x] \vdash e : t_r}{\rho \vdash \texttt{fn} \ x \ \texttt{->} \ e \ : \ t_x \to t_r} \ (g9)$$

$$\frac{\rho \vdash e_r : t_r \qquad \rho[x \mapsto \forall \alpha_1 \ldots \alpha_n.t_r] \vdash e_b : t \qquad \alpha_1 \ldots \alpha_n \ \text{not free in} \ \rho}{\rho \vdash \texttt{let val} \ x = e_r \ \texttt{in} \ e_b \ \texttt{end} \ : \ t} \ (g10)$$

$$\frac{\rho[exn \mapsto \texttt{exn}] \vdash e_b : t}{\rho \vdash \texttt{let exception} \ exn \ \texttt{in} \ e_b \ \texttt{end} \ : \ t} \ (g11)$$

$$\frac{\begin{array}{c} \rho' = \rho[f_1 \mapsto t_{x1} \to t_{r1}, \ldots, f_n \mapsto t_{xn} \to t_{rn}] \\ \rho'[x_i \mapsto t_{xi}] \vdash e_i : t_{ri} \qquad i \in [1, \ldots, n] \\ \rho[f_1 \mapsto \forall \alpha_{11} \ldots \alpha_{1m}.t_{x1} \to t_{r1}, \ldots, f_n \mapsto \forall \alpha_{n1} \ldots \alpha_{no}.t_{xn} \to t_{rn}] \vdash e_b : t \\ \alpha_{11} \ldots \alpha_{no} \ \text{not free in} \ \rho \end{array}}{\begin{array}{l} \texttt{let fun} \ f_1 \ x_1 = e_1 \\ \rho \vdash \qquad\qquad \vdots \\ \texttt{and} f_n \ x_n = e_n \ \texttt{in} \ e_b \ \texttt{end} \ : \ t \end{array}} \ (g12)$$

Fig. 13.6 The type rules $g1$ to $g12$ together with type rules in Figs. 4.7 and 6.1 cover all of micro-SML

- Rule $g11$: The bound variable exn has type $\texttt{exn}$ in ρ so it can be used in a $\texttt{raise}$ or $\texttt{try-with}$ construct in e_b, or be bound to some variable x — the latter explains why $\texttt{raise}$ in rule $g6$ takes an expression argument e of type $\texttt{exn}$ and not just an exception name exn.
- Rule $g12$: The rule is similar to rule $p8$ in Fig. 6.1 extended to work on mutually recursive functions. As the functions $f_1, \ldots, f_n$ are mutually recursive the environment ρ' contains all function types. For a function body e_i, we use the

environment ρ' extended with the parameter x_i. The environment does not include parameter types for all functions when typing the body e_i of some function f_i. For instance, consider two functions having the same parameter name x, see example ex05.sml:

```
fun h x = x + g (23::nil)   (* x has type int *)
and g x = hd x              (* x has type int list *)
```

The types for x in the two functions g and h differ and the type rule would not work if all type parameters were extended to ρ' when typing f_i. Typing e_b is done in the environment with proper type schemes for all functions f_i.

13.3.1 Type Inference Implementation

The type inference algorithm presented in Chap. 6 has been extended to cover rules $g1$ to $g12$ in Fig. 13.6, see file TypeInference.fs. The extensions are as follows:

- The type typ is extended with a polymorphic list type and an exception type:

```
type typ =
   ...
   | TypL of typ  (* list types    *)
   | TypE         (* exception type *)
```

  Helper functions like resolveType, freeTypevars, copyType, showType and typeToString have been extended accordingly.
- Unification needs to accommodate the new (list and exception) types:

```
let rec unify t1 t2 : unit =
   let t1' = normType t1
   let t2' = normType t2
   match (t1', t2') with
   ...
   | (TypL t1, TypL t2) -> unify t1 t2
   | (TypE, TypE) -> ()
   ...
```

  Unifying two lists requires the element types of the two lists to be the same, ensured by unify t1 t2.

The two main type inference functions are typExpr and typValdec. The result type of typExpr is typ * expr<typ> where the abstract syntax expr has been annotated with type information. For instance, the type 'a list of a nil constant is annotated on the CstN node of the abstract syntax.

```
let rec typExpr (lvl : int) (env : tenv)
                (e : expr<'a>) : typ * expr<typ> =
   match e with
```

```
...
| CstN _        ->
  let lTyp = TypL(TypV(newTypeVar lvl))
  (lTyp, CstN (Some lTyp))
...
```

This makes it possible to prettyprint the type information, and to make use of this information in the compiling phase.

The function `typValdec` is used to type declarations, i.e., mutually recursive function groups, value declarations and exception names. The result is a new type environment containing the types of the functions, values and exceptions together with type annotated abstract syntax. The result type is `tenv * valdec<typ>`. For instance, to type a `let`-construct we combine rules $g10$, $g11$ and $g12$ as follows:

```
let rec typExpr (lvl : int) (env : tenv)
                (e : expr<'a>) : typ * expr<typ> =
  match e with
  ...
  | Let(valdecs,letBody) ->
    let (valdecs',letEnv) = typValdecs lvl env valdecs
    let (tLetBody,letBody') = typExpr lvl letEnv letBody
    (tLetBody, Let(List.rev valdecs',letBody'))
  ...
```

We find the type of the value declarations `valdecs` and use the enriched environment `letEnv` to find the type of the `let` expression's body. The function `typValdecs` is folding over the list of value declarations and accumulates the new environment.

```
and typValdecs (lvl:int) (env:tenv) (valdecs:valdec<'a> list)
               : valdec<typ> list * tenv =
  List.fold (fun (valdecs,env) valdec ->
             let (env',valdec') = typValdec lvl env valdec
             (valdec'::valdecs,env')) ([],env) valdecs
```

The hard work is done in `typValdec`. For instance, rule $g12$ is as follows:

```
and typValdec (lvl:int) (env:tenv)
              (t:valdec<'a>) : tenv * valdec<typ> =
  match t with
  | Fundecs fs ->
    let lvl1 = lvl + 1
    let genFunTypes (f, x, fBody) =
      let fTyp = TypV(newTypeVar lvl1)
      let xTyp = TypV(newTypeVar lvl1)
      let xTypeScheme = (x, TypeScheme([], xTyp))
      let fTypeScheme = (f, TypeScheme([], fTyp))
      (xTyp, fTyp, xTypeScheme, fTypeScheme,f,x,fBody)
    let funTypes = List.map genFunTypes fs
    let funBodyEnv = List.foldBack
```

```
                              (fun (_,_,_,fTypeScheme,_,_,_) env ->
                                   fTypeScheme :: env) funTypes env
     let fs' =
       List.map
         (fun (xTyp,fTyp,xTypeScheme,_,f,x,fBody) ->
           let (rTyp,fBody') = typExpr lvl1
                                   (xTypeScheme :: funBodyEnv) fBody
           unify fTyp (TypF(xTyp,rTyp));
           (f,x,fBody')) funTypes
     let bodyEnv =
       List.foldBack
         (fun (_,fTyp,_,_,f,_,_) env ->
           (f,generalize lvl fTyp) :: env) funTypes env
     (bodyEnv,Fundecs fs')
   | ...
```

The environment ρ' is found in `funBodyEnv` where only the `fTypeScheme` is added for each function. Typing each function (`fs'`) is done with environment `xTypeScheme :: funBodyEnv` where the type for the argument is added. The result environment `bodyEnv` contains the generalized type schemes for the functions being used in the body of the `let` or `begin-end` construct, depending on whether the declarations are local or global (when called from `typProg`).

13.3.2 Annotated Type Information

Giving the command line argument `-verbose` to the micro-SML compiler causes it to print the annotated type information along with the compiled program. For instance, compiling `ex05.sml` (from the explanation of rule $g12$ on p. 254), shows the following type information for the two global functions:

```
Program with types:
fun h x = (x:int + g:((int list) -> int)
          (23:int :: nil:(int list)):(int list):int):int
and g x = hd(x:(int list)):int
```

13.4 Interpreting Micro-SML

The Fig. 4.3 shows the evaluation rules for the first-order version of micro-ML, and Fig. 13.7 shows additional rules for micro-SML. We reuse micro-ML's representation of the environment ρ and values, i for integers, b for booleans. The symbols x and f represent variables and e expressions. List values are represented as in F#, that is, $[]$ is the empty list and $v_1 :: v_2$ has first element v_1 and tail v_2. We use `true` and `false` for the two boolean values. We use *exn* to represent an exception value. The value `Abort` is used to signal an error condition and evaluation stops.

$$\frac{}{\rho \vdash \mathtt{nil} \Rightarrow []} \ (h1)$$

$$\frac{\rho \vdash e \Rightarrow []}{\rho \vdash \mathtt{hd}\ e \Rightarrow \mathtt{Abort}} \ (h2)$$

$$\frac{\rho \vdash e \Rightarrow v_1 \mathtt{::} v_2}{\rho \vdash \mathtt{hd}\ e \Rightarrow v_1} \ (h2')$$

$$\frac{\rho \vdash e \Rightarrow []}{\rho \vdash \mathtt{tl}\ e \Rightarrow \mathtt{Abort}} \ (h3)$$

$$\frac{\rho \vdash e \Rightarrow v_1 \mathtt{::} v_2}{\rho \vdash \mathtt{tl}\ e \Rightarrow v_2} \ (h3')$$

$$\frac{\rho \vdash e \Rightarrow []}{\rho \vdash \mathtt{isnil}\ e \Rightarrow \mathtt{true}} \ (h4)$$

$$\frac{\rho \vdash e \Rightarrow v_1 :: v_2}{\rho \vdash \mathtt{isnil}\ e \Rightarrow \mathtt{false}} \ (h4')$$

$$\frac{\rho \vdash e_1 \Rightarrow v_1 \quad \rho \vdash e_2 \Rightarrow v_2 \quad v = v_1{::}v_2}{\rho \vdash e_1 :: e_2 \Rightarrow v} \ (h5)$$

$$\frac{\rho \vdash e_1 \Rightarrow v_1 \quad \rho \vdash e_2 \Rightarrow v_2}{\rho \vdash e_1 \ ; e_2 \Rightarrow v_2} \ (h6)$$

$$\frac{\rho \vdash e \Rightarrow exn}{\rho \vdash \mathtt{raise}\ e \Rightarrow exn} \ (h7)$$

$$\frac{\rho \vdash e_1 \Rightarrow v_1 \quad v_1 \text{ is not an exception value } exn}{\rho \vdash \mathtt{try}\ e_1 \mathtt{\ with}\ exn \mathtt{\ ->}\ e_2 \Rightarrow v_1} \ (h8)$$

$$\frac{\rho \vdash e_1 \Rightarrow v_1 \quad v_1 \text{ is an exception value } exn', \text{ and } exn = exn' \quad \rho \vdash e_2 \Rightarrow v_2}{\rho \vdash \mathtt{try}\ e_1 \mathtt{\ with}\ exn \mathtt{\ ->}\ e_2 \Rightarrow v_2} \ (h8')$$

$$\frac{\rho \vdash e_1 \Rightarrow v_1 \quad v_1 \text{ is an exception value } exn', \text{ and } exn <> exn' \quad \rho \vdash \mathtt{raise}\ exn' \Rightarrow v_2}{\rho \vdash \mathtt{try}\ e_1 \mathtt{\ with}\ exn \mathtt{\ ->}\ e_2 \Rightarrow v_2} \ (h8'')$$

$$\frac{f = \text{newName}()}{\rho \vdash \mathtt{fn}\ x \mathtt{\ ->}\ e \Rightarrow (f,x,e,\rho)} \ (h9)$$

$$\frac{\rho \vdash e_r \Rightarrow v_r \quad \rho[x \to v_r] \vdash e_b \Rightarrow v_b}{\rho \vdash \mathtt{let\ val}\ x = e_r \mathtt{\ in}\ e_b \mathtt{\ end} \Rightarrow v_b} \ (h10)$$

$$\frac{exn = \text{freshExnName}() \quad \rho[x \mapsto exn] \vdash e_b \Rightarrow v_b}{\rho \vdash \mathtt{let\ exception}\ x \mathtt{\ in}\ e_b \mathtt{\ end} \Rightarrow v_b} \ (h11)$$

$$\rho' = \rho[f_1 \mapsto (f_1,x_1,e_1,\rho'),\dots,f_n \mapsto (f_n,x_n,e_n,\rho')]$$

$$\frac{\rho' \vdash e_b \Rightarrow v_b}{\begin{array}{l} \mathtt{let\ fun}\ f_1\ x_1 = e_1 \\ \rho \vdash \qquad\qquad \vdots \qquad\qquad \Rightarrow v_b \\ \mathtt{and}\, f_n\ x_n = e_n \mathtt{\ in}\ e_b \mathtt{\ end} \end{array}} \ (h12)$$

Fig. 13.7 Additional evaluation rules for micro-SML based on the rules in Fig. 4.3

The rules in Fig. 13.7 are explained as follows:

- Rules $h1$, $h2$, $h2'$, $h3$, $h3'$, $h4$, $h4'$ and $h5$ work on lists. The constant `nil` is the empty list. The `hd` and `tl` operations check whether the list is non-empty and return the head or tail. If the list is empty, the `Abort` value is returned, that is, program stops execution. The cons operator ($::$) evaluates the two expressions and inserts the value v_1 in the list value v_2.
- Rule $h6$ is the sequence operator. First e_1 is evaluated, and then e_2. The value v_1 is discarded and v_2 is returned.
- Rules $h7$, $h8$, $h8'$ and $h8''$ represent exceptions. The `raise` operation evaluates e to an exception value exn which is returned. The `try-with` expression evaluates e_1. If no exception is raised, then v_1 is returned ($h8$). If an exception is raised and the exception matches the one in the `try-with` construct, then e_2 is evaluated and v_2 returned ($h8'$). In case the raised exception does not match, then the exception is raised again ($h8''$).
- Rule $h9$ evaluates an anonymous function. A unique name is generated (by function `newName()` in the interpreter), which is used to identify the function. An ordinary closure for the function is returned.
- Rule $h10$ declares a variable x.
- Rule $h11$ generates a fresh exception name, exn. Exceptions are generative just like exceptions in Standard ML, [1, Sect. 6.2]. This means that each declared exception is unique. In practice the function `freshExnName()` provides a new unique number which is the exception value, exn. The example `exn04.sml` illustrates the generative behaviour:

```
fun genExn x = let exception E in E end
fun genRaise E = fn x -> raise E
fun genTryWith E = fn g -> try g 1 with E -> 1
begin
  let
    val E1 = genExn 1
    val r1 = genRaise E1
    val h1 = genTryWith E1
    val E2 = genExn 2
    val r2 = genRaise E2
  in
    h1 r2
  end
end
```

The function `genExn` generates the same exception E but two different exception values are returned, hence E1 and E2 do not match. For this reason, the call to h1 with r2 as argument will not match E in the `try-with` expression and an unhandled exception is the result of the evaluation.
- Rule $h12$ declares n functions and evaluates the body e_b in an environment where the functions f_i are accessible. Notice the recursive definition of ρ'. In the inter-

preter implementation, a closure uses an assignable reference to create a cyclic representation.

Type inference makes sure the evaluation rules can be used. For instance, if we have the construct e_1 :: e_2, then we know e_1 will evaluate to a value of the same type as the elements in the list that e_2 evaluates to.

13.4.1   Continuations

The main evaluation functions are

```
let rec evalExpr (env : value env) (e : expr<typ>)
                 (cont: value -> answer)
                 (econt: value -> answer) : answer = ...
```

and

```
and evalValdecs (env:value env) (ts:valdec<typ> list)
                (body: expr<typ>) (cont: value -> answer)
                (econt: value -> answer) : answer = ...
```

where `answer` is defined to be either a result with a value, or an indication of failure with a message:

```
type answer =
  | Result of value
  | Abort of string
```

The implementation uses continuations as explained in Sect. 11.4.1. The `cont` continuation is used for normal flow and `econt` for abnormal flow. The answer `Abort` is used when the program has to stop immediately. For instance, micro-SML has no built-in exceptions, so if a program applies `hd` on an empty list (last case) then the interpreter just stops (by returning `Abort`) instead of throwing an exception (by calling `econt`):

```
let rec evalExpr (env : value env) (e : expr<typ>)
                 (cont: value -> answer)
                 (econt: value -> answer) : answer =
  match e with
  ...
  | Prim1(ope,e1,_) ->
    evalExpr env e1
      (fun v1 ->
        match (ope,getTypExpr e1) with
        | ("print",TypI) ->
            printf "%s " (ppValue v1); cont v1
        | ("print",TypB) ->
            printf "%s " (if v1=Int 0 then "false"
```

```
                                          else "true"); cont v1
      | ("hd",_) -> match v1 with
                      | List [] -> Abort "Prim1: Can't do hd ..."
                      | List (x::_) -> cont x
   ...
```

Notice also how we use type information to guide the evaluation of `print`.

13.4.2 Sequence

The sequence operator (;) is implemented by evaluating the first expression and throwing away its result, as indicated by the wildcard parameter (_) of the continuation function for the evaluation of e_1:

```
| Seq(e1,e2,_) ->
    evalExpr env e1 (* Disregard result of e1 and return e2 *)
      (fun _ -> evalExpr env e2 cont econt) econt
```

13.4.3 Functions

An anonymous function implements rule $h9$ (Fig. 13.7); evaluation creates a closure and passes it to the success continuation:

```
| Fun(x,fBody,_) ->
  let freeVars = Set.toList (freevars fBody - (set [x]))
  let freeVarsEnv = List.filter (fun (f,_) ->
                     List.exists ((=)f) freeVars) env
  cont (ClosureRef (ref (Closure(newFuncName(),
                     x, fBody, freeVarsEnv))))
```

The list of free variables is used to limit the size of the environment `freeVarsEnv` to include in the closure.

Mutually recursive functions make use of recursive closures to implement rule $h12$ in Fig. 13.7.

```
| Fundecs fs :: ts' ->
  let closureRefs = List.map (fun (f,x,fBody) ->
    (f, ref (Closure(f,x,fBody,env)))) fs
  let updClosRef (f,closRef) =
    (match !closRef with
     | Closure(f,x,fBody,_) ->
       let freeVars = Set.toList (freevars fBody - (set [x;f]))
       let freeVarsEnv = List.filter (fun (f,_) ->
                          List.exists ((=)f) freeVars) env
```

```
      let freeClosureRefs =
        List.filter (fun (f,_) ->
          List.exists ((=)f) freeVars) closureRefs
      let fBodyEnv =
        (List.map
          (fun (f,closRef) -> (f, ClosureRef closRef))
            freeClosureRefs) @ freeVarsEnv
        (closRef := Closure(f,x,fBody,fBodyEnv)))
    let _ = List.iter updClosRef closureRefs
    let env' =
      (List.map
        (fun (f, closRef) ->
          (f, ClosureRef closRef)) closureRefs) @ env
    evalValdecs env' ts' body cont econt
```

Initially closures for all functions are built with an arbitrary fake environment
(closureRefs). The set freeVars of free variables for each function f is calcu-
lated and the environment is filtered to only contain these, giving freeVarsEnv.
Even though each function is allowed to call all other functions, this is not necessarily happening. The list freeClosureRefs are those functions called from within
f. The environment for f (fBodyEnv) are the free variables (freeVarsEnv)
plus the closures of the functions called (freeClosureRefs). The environment
fBodyEnv is then inserted in the closure for f. The result environment env' is
the environment env extended with all function closures in the group of mutually
recursive functions (closureRefs).

13.4.4 Exceptions

The run-time value of an exception is an integer, i.e., the unique number identify-
ing the exception. A new number is generated each time an exception is declared
(freshExnName()), see rule $h11$ (Fig. 13.7):

```
and evalValdecs (env:value env) ... =
  ...
  | Exn(ExnVar x,_)::ts' ->
      evalValdecs ((x,Int (freshExnName()))) :: env)
        ts' body cont econt
```

The raise e construct is evaluated simply by evaluating e, since type inference
guarantees that e evaluates to an exception value, and then passing e's value to the
error continuation:

```
  | Raise(e,aOpt) -> evalExpr env e econt econt
```

The `try-with` construct uses the error continuation to propagate the exception, as described in Sect. 11.4.1. The success continuation of `e1` in `try-with` is the same as the `try-with` expression's. The error continuation of `e1` looks at the raised expression to see whether it wants to handle it, and if not passes it on to the `try-with` expression's error continuation:

```
| TryWith(e1,ExnVar exn,e2) ->
  evalExpr env e1 cont
    (fun vExn1 ->
      match lookupOpt env exn with
      | None -> Abort ("HigherFun.TryWith: Can't ... )
      | Some vExn2 ->
          if vExn1 = vExn2 then evalExpr env e2 cont econt
                          else econt vExn1)
```

Rule $h8$ (Fig. 13.7) is the case where `cont` is used as the continuation of evaluating e_1. Rule $h8'$ is the case where `vExn1` is equal to `vExn2`, i.e., when e_2 is evaluated. Rule $h8''$ is the case where `vExn1` is given as argument to `econt`, i.e., we raise the exception again.

13.5 Compiling Micro-SML

The compilation of micro-SML has many similarities to the compilation of micro-C as described in Chaps. 8 and 12. The main differences are micro-SML's absence of statements, the run-time generative exceptions, and micro-SML's functions being first class values. With functions as first class values, a separate compile-time environment for (first-order only) functions is not needed. Similarly to the optimizing compiler for micro-C introduced in Chap. 12, we here present an optimizing compiler for micro-SML.

The main functions of this micro-SML compiler (file `Sml/Contcomp.fs`) are listed in Fig. 13.8.

13.5.1 Extensions to Abstract Machine Instruction Set

The instruction set for the abstract machine, shown in Fig. 8.1, has additional instructions to handle closures, cons cells, closure based function calls and print instructions for booleans and lists (Fig. 13.9).

The `NIL` instruction pushes the value 0, the run-time representation of the constant `nil` on the stack. The `CONS` instruction allocates a cons cell on the heap at address p containing the value v and pointer to the next cons cell or nil, i.e., the tail t. A tag (`CONSTAG`) is used to distinguish cons cells from other heap allocated objects, see Sect. 10.7.4 and file `msmlmachine.c`.

`cProgram : program<typ> -> instr list`
Compile an entire micro-SML program into an instruction sequence. The abstract syntax has type `program<typ>` where type information of type `typ` has been annotated. Tail calls are annotated directly on the abstract syntax. As for micro-C, the compiler produces instructions for globals and functions, and compiles the program body into a main function. The main function is called after the initialization of globals.

`cExpr : (kind: int -> var) -> varEnv -> expr<typ> ->`
`         instr list -> instr list`
Compile a micro-SML expression into a sequence of instructions. The compilation takes place in a compile-time environment (`varEnv`) mapping global variables to absolute addresses (`Glovar`), local variables to relative addresses within a stack frame (`Locvar`) and free variables of a function to relative addresses within a closure (`Closvar`). The `kind` function represents the current context of the compilation. For instance, if x is a globally declared variable with absolute address 42, then the call `kind 42` will return a value `Glovar 42` used when the variable `"x"` is added to the compile-time environment `varEnv`.

`genValdecEnv : (kind: int -> var) -> varEnv -> valdec<typ>`
`                -> varEnv * varEnv`
The function builds the compile-time environments necessary to generate code for the value declarations. A value declaration of type `valdec<typ>` can be a let-bound value, an exception value or a group of mutually recursive functions, see Sect. 13.5.4. The `kind` function represents the context in which the value declarations are compiled, i.e., locally or globally.

`cValdec : (kind: int -> var) -> (valdec<typ> * varEnv) ->`
`           instr list -> instr list`
The compile-time environment `varEnv` is the environment in which the value declaration must be compiled. The `kind` is the context in which the compilation happens, i.e., either locally or globally. The compilation is described in Sect. 13.5.4.

`loadVar : varEnv -> string -> instr list -> instr list`
Generate code for variable access, see Sect. 13.5.3.

`nextExnNumCode : varEnv -> instr list -> instr list`
Exception values are generated using a global counter. The function increments the global counter and puts the fresh exception value on the stack.

Fig. 13.8 Main compilation functions of the micro-SML compiler in file `Sml/Contcomp.fs`. A `varEnv` is a pair of a compile-time variable environment and the next available stack frame offset. A `kind` represents the compilation context, e.g., global or local. The compiler is backwards and use code continuations

The instructions PUSHLAB, HEAPSTI and ACLOS are used to allocate and create closures. The PUSHLAB instruction pushes a code address (label) on the stack. The HEAPSTI instruction copies n elements, $v_1, \ldots, v_n$, from the stack to a heap allocated object at address p. The ACLOS instruction allocates an empty closure with tag CLOSTAG and size n on the heap. The closure's address p is left on the stack.

The instruction HEAPLDI pushes a value stored in a closure at address p and offset n onto the stack. The offset n is always known at compile time.

Using type information annotated on the abstract syntax the compiler can generate print instructions matching the type of the value printed by the built-in `print` expression in micro-SML; see Fig. 13.1. The instructions PRINTB and PRINTL can

Instruction	Stack before	Stack after	Effect
26 NIL	s	$\Rightarrow s,\text{nil}$	Push nil on stack
27 CONS	s,v,t	$\Rightarrow s,p$	Create cons cell on heap
32 PUSHLAB l	s	$\Rightarrow s,l$	Push label l
33 HEAPSTI n	$s,v_1,...,v_n,p$	$\Rightarrow s,p$	Copy from stack to heap
34 ACLOS n	s	$\Rightarrow s,p$	Allocate closure on heap
35 CLOSCALL m	$s,cp,v_1,...,v_m$	$\Rightarrow s,r,bp,cp,v_1,...,v_m$	Call function closure cp
36 HEAPLDI n	s,p	$\Rightarrow s,v$	Push n'th value of closure p
37 PRINTB	s,v	$\Rightarrow s,v$	Print boolean v
38 TCLOSCALL m	$s,r,bp,cp_1,u_1,...,u_n,$		Tail call to closure cp_2
	$cp_2,v_1,...,v_m$	$\Rightarrow s,r,bp,cp_2,v_1,...,v_m$	
39 PRINTL	s,v	$\Rightarrow s,v$	Print list v

Fig. 13.9 The additional byte code instructions used to compile micro-SML. The first column gives the numeric instruction codes and the second column gives the symbolic instruction names. See files Sml/Machine.fs and Sml/msmlmachine.c for their implementation

print booleans and lists. Integers are already covered by the PRINTI instruction; see Fig. 8.1.

A function value is always stored as a closure. If a function has no free variables the closure only contains the code pointer for the function code. The instructions CLOSCALL and TCLOSCALL are used to call a function using the code pointer stored in a closure. Section 8.3 explains the run-time stack for micro-C. For micro-SML the stack frame is extended with a closure pointer cp right after the old base pointer; see Fig. 13.10. The CLOSCALL and TCLOSCALL work like CALL and TCALL, except for the extra closure pointer, and the code pointer is fetched from the closure. The TCALL instruction has an extra parameter n for how many arguments to remove from the stack when performing a recursive tail call, see instruction TCALL in Fig. 8.1. This extra parameter has been avoided for TCLOSCALL as one can use the base pointer bp to calculate the number of arguments to remove.

Instructions for exceptions, PUSHHDLR, POPHDLR and THROW are defined in Fig. 11.2.

Instructions for lists, i.e., NIL, CAR and CDR are defined in Fig. 10.4. We do not use the SETCAR and SETCDR instructions. Lists are built with the CONS and NIL instructions defined above.

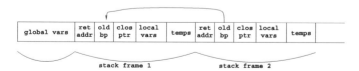

Fig. 13.10 Stack layout at run-time. The base pointer bp points at the cell right after the old base pointer, which is the cell containing the closure pointer cp

$E[\![i]\!] =$
         CSTI i

$E[\![true]\!] =$
         CSTI 1

$E[\![false]\!] =$
         CSTI 0

$E[\![nil]\!] =$
         NIL

$E[\![print\ e]\!] =$ where e has type integer, boolean or list
         $E[\![e]\!]$
         PRINTX PRINTI, PRINTB or PRINTL depending on type of e

$E[\![hd\ e]\!] =$
         $E[\![e]\!]$
         CAR

$E[\![tl\ e]\!] =$
         $E[\![e]\!]$
         CDR

$E[\![isnil\ e]\!] =$
         $E[\![e]\!]$
         NIL
         EQ

$E[\![!e]\!] =$ Similar to unary primitive Micro-C operations
         $E[\![e]\!]$
         NOT

$E[\![e1\ *\ e2]\!] =$ Similar to two-argument primitive Micro-C expressions
         $E[\![e1]\!]$
         $E[\![e2]\!]$
         MUL   Use ADD, SUB, EQ, CONS, etc. for other binary operations

$E[\![e1\ ;\ e2]\!] =$
         $E[\![e1]\!]$
         INCSP -1 Remove result of e1
         $E[\![e2]\!]$

Fig. 13.11 Compilation schemes for primitive micro-SML expressions. The net effect of the code for an expression is to leave the expression's value (rvalue) on the stack top

13.5.2 Compilation of Primitive Micro-SML Expressions

The Fig. 13.11 shows the compilation schemes for the primitive micro-SML expressions. To compare with micro-C, see Figs. 8.5 and 8.6. For instance, conditionals follow the same structure except a value is left on the stack in micro-SML.

The constants true and false are encoded as 1 and 0 at run-time. The nil constant (empty list) uses the NIL instruction.

The print primitive uses dedicated print instructions depending on the type of e annotated on the abstract syntax. Alternatively one could have implemented a general PRINT instruction in the abstract machine which could use the tagging information

```
A[[Glovar addr]] =              addr is an absolute address
         CSTI addr
         LDI
A[[Locvar offset]] =            offset is relative to current bp
         GETBP
         CSTI offset
         ADD
         LDI
A[[Closvar offset]] =           offset is relative to current cp
         GETBP
         LDI                    Put cp on stack
         HEAPLDI offset         Load value relative to cp
```

Fig. 13.12 Compilation schemes for accessing a variable. The closure pointer cp is always at offset 0 from the base pointer, see Fig. 13.10

to distinguish scalar values like integers and booleans from heap allocated objects like lists. But such an instruction would not be able to distinguish between integers and booleans as they use the same encoding.

A lists is represented as a linked chain of pairs. For each pair the first component, CAR, is the value, and the second component, CDR, is a pointer to the next pair, i.e., the tail of the list. The compilation of isnil compares the result of e with the nil constant.

The compilation of unary and two-argument primitives is similar to micro-C, see Fig. 8.6 and Fig. 13.12. The compilation schemes for logical expressions, && and ||, are also similar to micro-C, see Chap. 12. The compilation scheme for the if e_1 then e_2 else e_3 expression is not shown but similar to micro-C except that e_2 and e_3 are expressions that leave a result value on the stack.

13.5.3 Compilation of Variable Access

The function loadVar (Fig. 13.8) generates code for accessing a variable. A variable can be globally declared with an absolute address on the stack, locally declared with a relative address in a stack frame, or a free variable stored in a closure. Figure 13.12 shows the compilation schemes. Two instructions, CSTI and LDI, are saved by having the closure pointer cp being at offset 0 to the base pointer bp when accessing free variables.

```
VD⟦fun f x = e⟧ =
            ACLOS sizeClos      Allocate closure (iaClos)
            PUSHLAB lab1
            A⟦fv₁⟧               Fetch free variables
            ...                 to go in the
            A⟦fvₙ⟧               closure (iFillClos)
            A⟦f⟧                 Fetch closure pointer (iFillClos)
            HEAPSTI sizeClos    Move data to closure (iFillClos)
            addINCSP -1         Pop closure pointer (iFillClos)

F⟦fun f x = e⟧ =
            E⟦e⟧                 Compile body (codefBody)
            RET 2               Two arguments: closure and argument (codefBody)

VD⟦val x = e⟧ =
            E⟦e⟧

VD⟦exception exn⟧ =              nextExnNumCode
            CSTI addr           Address of global exception counter
            CSTI addr           Address of global exception counter
            LDI                 Load exception number
            CSTI 1
            ADD                 Increase number by one
            STI                 Store new number and leave on stack
```

Fig. 13.13 Simplified compilation schemes for value declarations VD⟦ · ⟧ where we only consider one value declaration at the time. Code for a function body is generated by F⟦ · ⟧. Annotations refer back to the F# code

13.5.4   Compilation of Value Declarations

A value declaration can either be a simple bound value (val), a group of mutually recursive functions (fun/and) or an exception value (exception). Consider the following example from ex07.sml:

```
val c = 42
fun f x = x + g (x-1)
and g x = if x < 1 then c else x + f (x-1)

begin
  f 5
end
```

The calculation of free variables is explained in Sect. 13.2.5. Notice the functions f and g are both accessible from within the function bodies of f and g. The variable c, however, is not accessible in c's right-hand side 42.

Compiling value declarations is a tight combination of maintaining compile-time environments and generating code. Figure 13.13 shows simplified compilation schemes focusing on code structure only. The schemes refer to the F# code below, combining both code generation and the maintenance of compile-time environments.

- The function genValdecEnv calculates two compile-time environments for each value declaration vd. The first environment is for compiling later value dec-

larations or the body a `begin` or `let`. The second environment is for compiling
the body of the value declaration itself, e.g., `42` or `x + g (x-1)`.

```
and genValdecEnv (kind: int->var) ((env,fdepth) as curEnv) vd =
  match vd with
  | Fundecs fs ->
    let newEnv =
      List.fold
        (fun (env,fdepth) (f,x,fBody) ->
          ((f,kind fdepth) :: env, fdepth+1)) curEnv fs
    (newEnv,newEnv)
  | Valdec (x,eRhs) ->




    (((x,kind fdepth)::env,fdepth+1),curEnv)
  | Exn(ExnVar exn,_) ->
    (((exn,kind fdepth)::env,fdepth+1),curEnv)
```

For mutually recursive function bindings the two environments are the same:
`newEnv`. For `val` and `exception` bindings the introduced variable is not accessible from within the binding's own, i.e., the second environment `curEnv` is
"smaller" than the first environment `newEnv`.

The following steps are all implemented in function `cValdec`, see Fig. 13.8.

- For each function calculate the set of free variables to copy into the closure. This
  is a subset of the compile-time environment, e.g., there is no need to copy global
  variables into the closure. This is safe because values are immutable. The variable
  `fs` holds the list of mutually recursive functions in the group. A tuple is returned
  for each function holding information necessary for code generation, including
  closure allocated free variables (`fvsClos`), size of the closure, and a function
  label.

```
and cValdec (kind: int->var) (vd:valdec<typ>, varEnv: varEnv)
            (C: instr list) : instr list =
  match vd with
  | Fundecs fs ->
    let fsfvs = (* Calculate fvs for each function in fs. *)
      List.map
        (fun (f,x,fBody) ->
          (* To minimize closures, do not copy globals. *)
          let fvsAll = freevars fBody - (set [x;f])
          let fvsGlobalInScope =
            filterGlobalsInScope varEnv fvsAll
          let fvsClos = Set.toList (fvsAll - fvsGlobalInScope)
          let labFunc = newLabelWName ("LabFunc_" + f)
          (f,x,fBody,fvsGlobalInScope,fvsClos,
           List.length fvsClos + 1,labFunc)) fs
```

• Create code to heap allocate a closure for each function. All closures must be allocated before free variables are copied as the closures themselves are potentially free.

```
(* Code to allocate closures *)
let iaClos C =
  List.foldBack
    (fun (_,_,_,_,_,sizeClos,_) C -> ACLOS sizeClos::C) fsfvs C
```

• For each function, create code to copy code pointer and free variables into the closure.

```
(* Code to copy free variables and code label to each closure *)
let iFillClos C =
  List.foldBack
    (fun (f,_,_,_,fvsClos,sizeClos,funcLab) C ->
      let codefvsClos C = List.foldBack (loadVar varEnv) fvsClos C
      let codeClosPtr C = loadVar varEnv f C
      PUSHLAB funcLab ::
      codefvsClos (codeClosPtr
                    (HEAPSTI sizeClos::addINCSP -1 C))) fsfvs C
```

The HEAPSTI instruction expects all free variables plus the code pointer (funcLab) and the pointer to the closure to be on the stack, see Fig. 13.9.

• For each function declaration, we generate code for its body. The compile-time environment used will have closure allocated variables bound with context Closvar, i.e., they are accessible within the closure; not within a stack frame or in the global address space.

```
(* Generate code for each function body *)
let codefBody (f,x,fBody,fvsGlobalInScope,fvsClos,_,funcLab) =
  (* Stack Frame: Closure at index 0, argument at index 1 *)
  (* Closure: Code pointer at index 0, fvl at index 1, etc. *)
  let varEnvBody =
    (f, Locvar 0) :: (x, Locvar 1) ::
    (List.mapi (fun i x -> (x,Closvar (i+1))) fvsClos) @
    (List.map
      (fun x -> (x,lookup (fst varEnv) x))
      (Set.toList fvsGlobalInScope))
  addFunc funcLab (cExpr Locvar (varEnvBody,2) fBody [RET 2])
let _ = List.iter codefBody fsfvs
let insts = iaClos (iFillClos C)
insts
```

The function addFunc makes sure the code for the function is emitted later in the compilation process. The return instruction RET 2 is used because a function call always pushes a closure pointer and one argument value on the stack, see Fig. 13.10. This also explains why the first local value has offset 2 when compiling the body of the function: cExpr Locvar (varEnvBody,2) fBody [RET 2].

• The body of a simple val bound value declaration is compiled by the function cExpr. For an exception declaration, call compiler function nextExnNumCode to generate code to create a fresh exception number at run-time.

E⟦let vds in e end⟧ =   where vds are value declarations
  VD⟦vds⟧   Code for the vds
  GETSP
  CST *numVals* - 1
  SUB   Address of first vds on stack
  E⟦e⟧   Compile e
  STI   Store result of e at first vds on stack
  INCSP -*numVals*   Pop vds from stack

E⟦e1 e2⟧ =
  E⟦e1⟧
  E⟦e2⟧   Always one argument.
  CLOSCALL 1   Use TCLOSCALL 1 in case of tail call.

Fig. 13.14 Compilation schemes for let expressions and applications. The net effect of the code for an expression is to leave the expression's value (rvalue) on the stack top

```
| Valdec (x,eRhs) -> cExpr kind varEnv eRhs C
| Exn(ExnVar exn,_) ->
  (* Code to push next exn number on stack *)
  nextExnNumCode varEnv C
```

Many optimizations are possible for handling closures. For instance, one could separate the code pointer from the closure and thereby share the same object with free variables for all mutually recursive functions in the group.

13.5.5 Compilation of Let Expressions and Functions

The Fig. 13.14 shows the compilation scheme for let expressions and function application.

The let construct let vds in e end has zero, one or more value declarations vds and a body e. Section 13.5.4 explained the compilation of value declarations vds. The vds must be popped after evaluating the body e and still keep the result of e. The following works for an arbitrary number of value declarations:

1. Calculate the address of the first value declaration: GETSP, CST *numVals* - 1 and SUB.
2. After evaluating e, use STI to move its result into the stack position occupied by the first value declaration.
3. Pop the remaining values (INCSP -*numVals*).

This also works if there are no value declarations. For instance, try example ex08.sml with -trace enabled. Optimizing the code for special cases with zero or one value declaration is left as an exercise.

Compiling anonymous functions fn x − > e is similar to mutually recursive functions, see Sect. 13.5.4.

$$E[\![\, \texttt{raise e} \,]\!] =$$
$$\quad E[\![\, \texttt{e} \,]\!]$$
$$\quad \texttt{THROW}$$

$$E[\![\, \texttt{try e1 with exn -> e2 end} \,]\!] =$$
$$\quad A[\![\, \texttt{exn} \,]\!]$$
$$\quad \texttt{PUSHHDLR lab1}$$
$$\quad E[\![\, \texttt{e1} \,]\!]$$
$$\quad \texttt{POPHDLR}$$
$$\quad \texttt{GOTO lab2}$$
$$\quad \texttt{lab1: } E[\![\, \texttt{e2} \,]\!]$$
$$\quad \texttt{lab2:}$$

Fig. 13.15 Compilation schemes for the `raise` and `try-with` expressions. The net effect of the code for an expression is to leave the expression's value (rvalue) on the stack top

Instruction	Stack before	After	Effect
40 THROW	s, exn_1, a, h, exn_2	$\Rightarrow s$	Handler found $exn_1 = exn_2$; go to a
40 THROW	s, exn_2	$\Rightarrow\ \_$	No handler found; abort
41 PUSHHDLR a	s, exn	$\Rightarrow s, exn, a, hr$	Push handler
42 POPHDLR	s, exn, a, h, v	$\Rightarrow s, v$	Pop handler; preserve v

Fig. 13.16 Instructions for exception handling in the micro-SML stack machine

Compiling a function call `e1 e2` is simply compiling `e1`, then `e2`, then adding the instruction `CLOSCALL 1` in the general case and `TCLOSCALL 1` if the call is in tail position. A micro-SML function always expects exactly one argument.

13.5.6 Compilation of Exceptions

The Fig. 13.15 shows the compilation schemes for `raise` and `try-with` expressions. The compilation is similar to exceptions in micro-C (Sect. 11.6), except that exceptions are generative and there are no statements, only expressions. An expression e must be evaluated to an exception value before it can be thrown. For `try-with`, the exception value `exn` is put on the stack before the exception handler is pushed by `PUSHHDLR`. The expression `e1` is evaluated and in case no exceptions are raised out of `e1`, then the handler is popped and execution continues at lab2.

The `PUSHHDLR` and `THROW` instructions (Fig. 13.16) do not have the exception value exn in the byte code as with the versions used for micro-C, see Fig. 11.2. The exception value must be evaluated on the stack before it can be pushed or thrown. The `POPHDLR` instruction for micro-SML must preserve the value v just above the exception handler, in contrast to the version used for micro-C, see Fig. 11.2.

13.6 Exercises

The goal is to understand how compiling for a functional language is both similar to and different from compiling for an imperative language like micro-C. Many optimizations are the same, and some can utilize specific properties such as immutable data, e.g., for closures.

More exercises can be found on the book's homepage.

Exercise 13.1 Download `microsml.zip` from the book homepage, unpack it to a folder `Sml`, and build the micro-SML compiler as explained in `README.TXT` step A to C.

Compile the micro-SML example `ex09.sml` with all options, `-opt`, `-verbose` and `-eval`, enabled. This provides the following result:

- A file `ex09.out` being the byte code for file `ex09.sml`.
- A lot of output on the console, including abstract syntax with tail call and type information, the result of evaluating the program and the assembly byte code.

Now execute `ex09.out` with the bytecode machine, by running `msmlmachine ex09.out`. The result will be written to the console.

Using the information above, answer the following:

1. What is the result value of running `ex09.out`?
2. What type does the result value have? (Look at the result produced by the interpreter).
3. What application calls have been annotated as tail calls? Explain how this matches the intuition behind a tail call.
4. What type has been annotated for the call sites to the functions f and g? Function f is called in two places, and g in one place.
5. What is the running time for executing the example using the evaluator, and what is the running time using the byte code `ex09.out` using `msmlmachine`?
6. Now compile the example `ex09.sml` without optimizations. How many byte code instructions did the optimization save for this small example?

Exercise 13.2 In this exercise we extend micro-SML with a pair expression (e_1, e_2). We can create a pair, and we can access the first and second components of a pair p by `fst(p)` and `snd(p)`.

The example program `pair.sml` shows a use of pairs where the pair's first and second components are accessed.

```
val p = (1,43)
fun f p = if fst(p) < 0 then g p else f (fst(p)-1,snd(p))
and g p = (fst(p),snd(p)-1)

begin
  print (f p)
end
```

The goal of this exercise is to implement lexing, parsing, type inference, interpretation and compilation of pairs, and then to run the program. For instance, the type annotated abstract syntax should be as follows:

```
Program with types:
val p = (1:int,43:int):(int * int)
fun f p =
  if (fst(p:(int * int)):int < 0:int):bool
    then g:((int * int) -> (int * int))_tail p:(int * int):(int * int)
    else f:((int * int) -> (int * int))_tail
           ((fst(p:(int * int)):int - 1:int):int,
             snd(p:(int * int)):int):(int * int):(int * int)
and g p = (fst(p:(int * int)):int,
           (snd(p:(int * int)):int - 1:int):int):(int * int)
begin
  print(f:((int * int) -> (int * int)) p:(int * int):(int * int)):(int * int)
end
Result type: (int * int)
```

The type of p is int * int. The type of f is int * int − > int * int. The final result type is also a pair int * int.

Interpreting the program you get

```
Result value: Result (PairV (Int -1,Int 42))
```

You can use the following steps to implement support for pairs:

1. Write type rules for the primitives fst and snd, see Fig. 13.6.
2. Write evaluation rules for the primitives fst and snd, see Fig. 13.7.
3. **FunLex.fsl**: Extend with token COMMA and unary primitives snd and fst.
4. **FunPar.fsy**: Extend with token COMMA and a rule for creating a pair. The concrete syntax is (e_1, e_2).
5. **Absyn.fs**: Extend the abstract syntax with a pair expression:

   ```
   type expr<'a> =
       . . .
       | Pair of expr<'a> * expr<'a> * 'a option
       . . .
   ```

   Some compiler functions must also be extended to handle pair expressions: ppProg, getOptExpr, tailcalls and freevars.
6. **TypeInference.fs**: Extend the typ type with the new pair type:

   ```
   type typ =
       . . .
       | TypP of typ * typ
   ```

Some compiler functions must be extended: resolveType, freeTypeVars, typeToString, unify, copyType, showType, typExpr. Type function typExpr must be extended with type inference for unary primitives fst, snd and then the pair construction $Pair(e_1, e_2, \_)$ expression.

7. **HigherFun.fs**: The interpreter must be able to handle pair values:

```
type value =

    . . .
    | PairV of value * value
```

Thus the following interpreter functions must be extended: `ppValue`, `evalExpr` and `check`.

8. **msmlmachine.c**: Two new byte code instructions are needed. One for creating a pair, `PAIR` and one for printing a pair, `PRINTP`. To simplify matters you can implement `PRINTP` assuming that pairs will always contain scalar values. This is of course not always the case.

Instruction	Stack before	Stack after	Effect
42 PAIR	s, v_1, v_2	$\Rightarrow s, p$	Create pair cell (v_1, v_2) on heap
44 PRINTP	s, p	$\Rightarrow s, p$	Print pair value pointed at by p

9. **ContComp.fs**: The compiler must be extended to generate code for creating a pair in the heap and for accessing the first and second component with `fst` and `snd` respectively.

   The primitives `fst` and `snd` are easily done using `CAR` and `CDR` in the bytecode. A pair is created using the new byte code instruction `PAIR`.
   The compiler function `cExpr` must be extended.

10. **Machine.fs**: The byte code instructions `PRINTP` and `PAIR` must be added. You have to assign unique instruction codes to `PRINTP` and `PAIR` that match with same instructions in `msmlmachine.c`.

Reference

1. Milner, R., Tofte, M., Harper, R., MacQueen, D.: The Definition of Standard ML (Revised). MIT Press, Cambridge (1997)

Chapter 14
Real Machine Code

In Chap. 8 we presented a compiler from micro-C to code for an abstract stack machine. In this chapter we describe real machine code in the form of assembly code for the x86 architecture, and show how to compile micro-C programs to such code. Executing micro-C programs translated into real machine code will be much faster, both because it avoids the interpretive overhead incurred by the abstract machine, and because it uses machine registers instead of the stack for expression evaluation.

14.1 Files for This Chapter

The following files are provided for this chapter:

File	Contents
Assembly/macsimple.asm	a small assembly program, Sect. 14.2.5
Assembly/macbetter.asm	a more complete assembly program
Assembly/macfac.asm	a factorial function in assembly
Assembly/X86.fs	definition of symbolic x86 instructions
Assembly/X86Comp.fs	compile micro-C to x86 instructions
Assembly/driver.c	a C program to call the generated machine code
Assembly/ex*.c	example micro-C programs as in Fig. 7.8
Assembly/Makefile	makefile for compilation, assembly and linking

We modify the micro-C compiler to generate a list of x86 instructions using a simple intermediate representation, and output this list of x86 instructions as symbolic assembly code in a text file. We then deploy the Nasm assembler [8] to convert this text file into a binary x86 code file, and use the C linker to link the binary x86 code together with a small driver program (`main` function) and the C library. The result is

© Springer International Publishing AG 2017
P. Sestoft, *Programming Language Concepts*, Undergraduate Topics
in Computer Science, DOI 10.1007/978-3-319-60789-4_14

an executable file that can be run directly on the operating system without additional
run-time support.

Thus compilation and execution of a micro-C program, for instance a file ex1.c,
comprises the following phases:

lexing	from the characters of file ex1.c to tokens
parsing	from tokens to abstract syntax tree
static checks	check that variables are declared, ...
code generation	from abstract syntax to x86 instruction list
code emission	from x86 instruction list to textual assembly code ex1.asm
assembly	from textual assembly code to binary machine code ex1.o
linking	of binary code and driver into executable ex1 file
execution	of the binary executable ex1 by a real x86 machine

14.2 The x86 Processor Family

In this section we describe the target machine for this chapter's micro-C compiler:
the x86 processor family. We first describe the history of this processor, then its
register structure, and finally the small subset of its sprawling instruction set that we
shall use when generating code from micro-C programs.

14.2.1 Evolution of the x86 Processor Family

The first x86 processor was the Intel 8086 from 1978, which was used in the original
IBM PC, but its roots can be traced back to 1972. The x86 architecture has been
implemented and extended by several companies besides Intel, most notably AMD
which contributed much of the 64-bit instruction set, often called x86-64. Today the
x86 processor family dominates desktop and server (but not mobile or embedded)
computing, having outcompeted cleaner and more elegant alternatives such as MIPS,
HP/PA, PowerPC and Sun Sparc, which are so-called Reduced Instruction Set (RISC)
architectures.

We shall compile micro-C as if for the 80386, which was the first "serious computer" version of the x86 architecture. Its 32-bit registers and facilities for memory
management made it suitable for running modern multitasking operating systems
of the Unix family. Thus Linux Torvalds initially developed Linux for the 80386 in
1991, finding earlier x86 processors inadequate.

Figure 14.1 describes select members of the x86 family and its predecessors,
giving the register size in bits, the year of introduction, the clock speed in MHz and
the typical transistor count [4, 6]. Observe that the clock speed has increased by
30,000 times, and the transistor count by 360,000 times, over 40 years: the more

Model	Bits	Year	Clock/MHz	Transistors	Remark
Intel 4004	4	1971	0.1	2,300	First Intel microprocessor
Intel 8008	8	1972	0.8	3,500	
Intel 8080	8	1974	2	4,500	
Intel 8086	16	1978	5	29,000	In original IBM PC; first x86 CPU
Intel 80286	16	1978	6	134,000	
Intel 80386	32	1985	16	275,000	Memory management; Linux
Intel 80486	32	1989	25	1,200,000	Integrated floating-point
Intel Pentium	32	1993	66	3,100,000	
Intel Pentium II	32	1997	300	7,500,000	
Intel Pentium III	32	1999	500	9,500,000	SSE floating-point vector instructions
Intel Xeon	32	2001	1700	55,000,000	
AMD Athlon 64	64	2003	2000	106,000,000	AMD64, x86-64 instructions
Intel Core 2 Duo	64	2006	2930	291,000,000	Intel 64, x86-64 instructions
Intel i3, i5, i7	64	2008	3000	820,000,000	

Fig. 14.1 Some members of the x86 processor family and its predecessors, showing register size in bits, year of introduction, clock speed in MHz, and transistor count. Data from [4, 6]

recent processor models are much faster and vastly more complex than the early ones; also, their internal structure is very different. Nevertheless, the x86 architecture has remained backwards compatible for four decades and some traits of the early processors are still visible in today's instruction set. For instance, in x86 terminology, a "word" is 16 bits, a "doubleword" is 32 bits, and a "quadword" is 64 bits, although for an Intel i7 in 2017 it would be more natural to let "word" denote a 64-bit quantity.

For the purpose of compiling micro-C to x86 assembly language we treat the x86 as a 32-bit machine à la 80386, although the x86-64 architecture has provided 64-bit registers and operations since 2003.

Regardless of the register size (8, 16, 32 or 64 bits) all x86 machines use byte addressing of memory, including the stack. Hence when pushing a 32-bit register's contents onto the stack, the stack pointer must be adjusted by 4, not 1.

14.2.2 Registers of the x86 Architecture

The 32-bit x86 has only a modest number of general-purpose 32-bit registers, shown in Fig. 14.2.

In addition, for backwards compatibility, AX is a 16-bit register containing EAX's 16 least significant bits. In turn, AX has two halves AH : AL where AH is an 8-bit register containing AX's 8 most significant bits and AL contains AX's 8 least significant bits; consequently it also contains EAX's 8 least significant bits. The registers EBX, ECX and EDX have similarly named 16-bit and 8-bit subregisters. This remnant of previous generations of x86 processors will be ignored here except that we shall use `setl al` and related instructions to set the AL register and hence set the least significant 8 bits of EAX after comparisons.

Name	r	Use
EAX	0	General register, accumulator for `imul` and `idiv` instructions
EBX	3	General register
ECX	1	General register
EDX	2	General register, set by `imul` and read by `idiv`
ESP	4	Stack pointer, points at the stack top
EBP	5	Base pointer, points at the base of the current stack frame
ESI	6	General register, source index register
EDI	7	General register, destination index register
EIP		Instruction pointer: address of next instruction to execute
EFLAGS		Status register

Fig. 14.2 The 32-bit registers of the x86 processor family since the 80386 processor

Flag	b	Meaning	
CF	0	Carry	Set if arithmetic operation carried (add) or borrowed (sub)
ZF	6	Zero	Set if result is zero (comparison gave "equal to")
SF	7	Sign	Set if the result is negative (comparison gave "less than")
OF	11	Overflow	Set if the result of a signed arithmetic operation is too large

Fig. 14.3 Some x86 status flags. Bit number b of register EFLAGS contains the status flag

Modern x86-64 machines also have 64-bit registers named RAX, RBX, ..., RDI where naturally EAX contains the least significant 32 bits of RAX and similarly for the seven other 32-bit registers, which can furthermore be referred to as RrD where r is the register number shown in the table. In addition there are eight new 64-bit registers named R8 through R15, whose lower 32 bits can be referred to as R8D through R15D. All the registers mentioned so far are integer registers; these are supplemented by floating-point registers (since the 80486) and floating-point vector registers (since AMD K6-2 and Intel Pentium III) with a large number of associated instruction variants.

As mentioned previously, for simplicity we shall generate code as if for an 80386 processor and hence shall stick to the "classic" 32 bit integer registers EAX through EDI shown in Fig. 14.2.

The instruction pointer register EIP contains the address of the next x86 instruction to execute. The EIP register is not manipulated explicitly, only implicitly by unconditional and conditional jump instructions `jmp`, `jnz` and `jz`, and the `call` and `ret` instructions. These work simply by updating EIP, thereby affecting which instruction is executed next.

The EFLAGS status register contains so-called status bits, typically reflecting the outcome of the most recent arithmetic operation or comparison. The relevant status bits for our purposes are shown in Fig. 14.3.

x86 Instruction	Effect
add [reg1], reg2	Add reg2 to memory at address reg1
add reg1, cst	Add integer cst to register reg1
add reg1, reg2	Add reg2 to reg1
and reg1, cst	Compute in reg1 the bitwise "and" of reg1 and cst
call addr	Push EIP on stack, then jump to addr
cdq	Convert doubleword EAX to quadword EDX:EAX before division
cmp reg1, reg2	Compare: subtract reg2 from reg1 but set flags only
idiv reg1	Divide EDX:EAX by reg1; quotient in EAX, remainder in EDX
imul reg1	Multiply EAX by reg1, put result in EDX:EAX
jmp near addr	Jump to address addr
jnz near addr	Jump to address addr if flag ZF=0, or comparison not equal
jz near addr	Jump to address addr if flag ZF=1, or comparison equal
lea reg1, [ebp+cst]	Load ebp plus integer cst into reg1
mov [reg1], reg2	Copy reg2 to memory at address reg1
mov reg1, [reg2]	Copy contents of memory at address reg2 to reg1
mov reg1, reg2	Copy reg2 to reg1
pop reg1	Copy memory at address ESP to reg1 and increment ESP by 4
popad	Pop EDI, ESI, EBP, EBX, EDX, ECX, EAX from stack
push reg1	Copy reg1 to memory at address ESP and decrement ESP by 4
pushad	Push EAX, ECX, EDX, EBX, ESP, EBP, ESI, EDI onto stack
ret	Pop return address off stack and jump to that address
sal reg1, cst	Shift reg1 left by cst bits
sete r8	Equal to: set r8 to 1 if flag ZF=1, else 0
setg r8	Greater than: set r8 to 1 if flag ZF=0 and SF=OF, else 0
setge r8	Greater than or equal to: set r8 to 1 if flag SF=OF, else 0
setl r8	Less than: set r8 to 1 if flag SF$\neq$OF, else 0
setle r8	Less than or equal to: set r8 to 1 if flag ZF=1 or SF$\neq$OF, else 0
setne r8	Not equal to: set r8 to 1 if flag ZF=0, else 0
sub [reg1], reg2	Subtract reg2 from memory at address reg1
sub reg1, cst	Subtract integer cst from reg1
sub reg1, reg2	Subtract reg2 from reg1
xor reg1, reg2	Compute in reg1 the bitwise "exclusive or" of reg1 and reg2

Fig. 14.4 The x86 instructions used in this chapter. The reg1 and reg2 are 32-bit registers; r8 is an 8-bit register such as AL; addr is an assembly label; and cst is a signed integer constant

14.2.3 The x86 Instruction Set

For historical reasons and backwards compatibility, the instruction set of the x86 is large and irregular. Figure 14.4 shows the small subset that we use in this book.

We use the instruction syntax from the Nasm assembler [8] and from Intel's reference materials [3, 5]. Some assemblers, notably GNU's gas and inline assembly in the GNU C compiler, have the instruction operands in the opposite order [11].

An x86 symbolic assembly program, or machine code program, is written one instruction per line, where the instruction may be preceded by a label lab: and followed by a semicolon and a comment. The instruction itself typically consists of an instruction name ins followed by a destination operand dst and a source operand dst:

```
lab:          ins dst, src          ; comment
```

For instance, the x86 instruction

```
sub eax, ebx
```

will subtract the contents of the EBX register from the EAX register and leave the result in EAX, and set the CF, ZF and SF flags (Fig. 14.3). Likewise,

```
mov eax, ebx
```

will copy the contents of the EBX register to the EAX register (and set no flags).

In the assembler syntax, putting square brackets [. . .] around a register means that the register's contents will be interpreted as a memory address. Thus

```
mov eax, [ebx]
```

means to consider the contents of register EBX as a memory address and copy the value at that address into register EAX. Likewise,

```
mov [eax], ebx
```

means to copy the value of EBX to the memory address contained in register EAX (without changing EAX). The instruction lea, meaning "load effective address", is useful for variable access relative to the base pointer EBP. For instance,

```
lea eax, [ebp - 48]
```

will compute the address of [ebp - 48] in EAX, that is, EBP minus 48.

There are literally thousands of other x86 instructions and instruction variants, and hundreds of additional variants of the instructions already mentioned; see Intel's manuals [5] or online sources [3].

14.2.4   The x86 Stack Layout

The native x86 stack is simply some part of memory, and the stack top is the memory location pointed to by the ESP register. Unlike the abstract machine presented in Chap. 8, the stack grows towards lower addresses. Hence pushing onto the stack will decrement the stack pointer ESP (before pushing), and popping from the stack will increment the stack pointer ESP (after popping). Since we work with 32-bit numbers, each using 4 bytes of memory, and the x86 memory is byte addressed, the stack looks like this with the top to the right:

```
... : [ESP+16] : [ESP+12] : [ESP+8] : [ESP+4] : [ESP]
```

14.2.5   An Assembly Code Example

An assembler is a program that inputs a text file (such as ex1.asm) containing symbolic machine code and outputs a file (such as ex1.o) that contains the corresponding "assembled" binary machine code. An assembler is a simple kind of compiler. It translates the symbolic machine instructions into binary instructions line by line, but also replaces symbolic program labels and address names by numeric ones, expands macros into machine code sequences, and so on.

Here we shall use the portable Netwide Assembler (Nasm) [8] for x86, which works on the MacOS, Linux and Windows operating systems. An input file to Nasm consists of some declarations, a "text" section containing symbolic x86 instructions, and a "data" section containing data declarations, and may be as simple as this file `macsimple.asm`:

```
global _main            ; Define entry point for this code
extern _printf          ; Refer to C library function

section .text

_main:
        push ebp             ; Save old base pointer
        mov ebp, esp         ; Set new base pointer
        mov eax, [myint]     ; Load constant 3456 into EAX
        add eax, 120000      ; Add 120000 to EAX
        push eax             ; Push EAX value to print
        push dword mystring  ; Push format string reference
        call _printf         ; Call C library printf function
        add esp, 8           ; Discard arguments, 8 bytes
        mov eax, 0           ; Set return value, success
        mov esp, ebp         ; Reset stack to base pointer
        pop ebp              ; Restore old base pointer
        ret                  ; Return to caller

section .data
        myint        dd 3456
        mystring     db      'The result is ->%d<-', 10, 0
```

The global declaration defines label _main as entry point for this code, and the extern declaration says that the code may refer to the _printf function, which will be defined later, when linking with the C library. The .text section header say that what follows is code, and the .data section describes data. The assembler will turn both sections into binary data, putting them in different parts of the object file. The name myint is the address of the decimal (dd) constant 3456, and the name mystring is the address of the first byte of the string constant that begins with "T" and ends with the null-termination byte (0), as required for C strings. The second-last character (10) is the decimal ASCII code for newline (\ n). In total the string starting at address mystring has 22 bytes.

The _main label in the .text section marks a point in the code, here the address of the push ebp instruction. The 12 instructions of the _main function do the following:

- First the old base pointer is saved to the stack by push ebp (so it can later be restored by pop ebp just before the return), and the base pointer register EBP is set to point to the stack top (this is not actually needed in this function).

- Next we perform a simple computation: Load the constant 3456 from the memory address indicated by myint into register EAX, then add decimal 120000 to EAX, push the result on the stack, and push the address mystring of the string in the data section. These two 4-byte values on the stack are the arguments of the C library function _printf, which is called next. By the C (not micro-C) *calling convention*, the function's arguments are pushed from right to left, so that the first (leftmost) argument is on the top of the stack [8, Sect. 9.1.2].

- After _printf returns, we "remove" _printf's arguments from the stack by incrementing the stack pointer by 8 bytes; remember that the stack grows from larger to smaller addresses. Then we put the function's result 0, which indicate success, in the EAX register (as required by C calling convention), restore the stack pointer to the value in EBP, retrieve the old base pointer from the stack, and return to the address pushed on the stack by the call to _main.

You can assemble the macsimple.asm file to a binary machine code object file try.o like this, where -f macho specifies the MacOS format for the object file:

```
nasm -f macho macsimple.asm -o try.o
```

Then you can link the binary object file with the C library like this, where -arch i386 specifies 32-bit x86 and the mysterious -Wl,-no_pie option tells the linker (l) not to generate position-independent (PIE) code:

```
gcc -arch i386 -Wl,-no_pie try.o -o try
```

Finally, you can run the assembled and linked binary executable:

```
./try
```

This should produce the following output on the console:

```
The result is ->123456<-
```

Here the number 123456 was computed by the assembly code and the rest is from the format string defined in the data segment above. While the above simple code works, there are more subtleties to writing correct assembler code on MacOS; see example file macbetter.asm for more details.

See file Assembly/README.TXT for how to assemble, link and run x86 machine code programs on Linux and Windows.

14.3 Compiling Micro-C to x86 Code

The micro-C compiler (in file X86Comp.fs) compiles micro-C programs into sequences of x86 instructions. The generated instruction sequence consists of initialization code followed by code representing the bodies of compiled micro-C functions. The initialization code checks the number of command line arguments, allocates global variables (those declared outside micro-C functions), loads the program's command line arguments (if any) onto the stack, and then calls the micro-C program's main function.

The overall structure of the compiler is very similar to that in Sect. 8.4, except that it generates code for a real machine implemented in hardware, not an abstract machine implemented in software.

14.3.1 Compilation Strategy

Compilation of a high-level language to a low-level one requires some major decisions:

- How to organize the compiled program's state (variables, arrays, call stack) at run-time.
- How to pass arguments to functions and return results from them.
- How to generate low-level code to use and maintain the program state.

Concerning the first point, we shall store all program variables and arrays on the x86 stack, with global variables at the stack bottom (high addresses). On top of these we keep stack frames corresponding to function calls. Each stack frame contains a function invocation's arguments and local variables, including arrays, exactly as in the Chap. 8 abstract machine.

However, in contrast to the abstract stack machine, we keep intermediate values of subexpressions in x86 machine registers, not on the stack. To see how we envision this to work in the generated code, consider the assignment expression x = y + 42 and assume that local variable x has (byte) offset 8 relative to the base pointer EBP, and y has offset 12. Then the code for the assignment must load the memory address of x into a register such as ECX; load the memory address of y into a register such as EBX; load the memory contents [EBX] into EBX itself; load the constant 42 into a register such as EDX; add EDX into EBX; and finally write EBX to memory address [ECX], or concretely:

```
lea ecx, [ebp - 8]      ; load x's address into ECX
lea ebx, [ebp - 12]     ; load y's address into EBX
mov ebx, [ebx]          ; load y's value into EBX
mov edx, 42             ; store 42 in EDX
add ebx, edx            ; add EDX into EBX
mov [ecx], ebx          ; store EBX into x's address
```

Note that we use the x86 instruction mov ebx, [ebx] to the same effect as the LDI abstract machine instruction, and mov [ecx], ebx to the same effect as the STI instruction, both from Fig. 8.1.

As an alternative to using x86 registers, we could put all intermediate results on the x86 stack, in the manner of the Chap. 8 abstract machine. That would work fine, but the execution would be slower due to the additional memory traffic.

Concerning the second point, in micro-C we pass all function arguments on the stack, from left to right (unlike real C). We expect a function to return its result, if any, in the EBX register (unlike real C). This is the *micro-C x86 calling convention*.

Concerning the third point, we describe the compiler's representation of x86 code in Sect. 14.3.2, how to generate code for the creation and disposal of stack frames in Sect. 14.3.3, and the compilation of statements and expressions in Sects. 14.6–14.8.

14.3.2   Representing x86 Machine Code in the Compiler

For use in the compiler, we define an intermediate representation of x86 instructions as an F# datatype (in file `X86.fs`), and also provide F# functions to emit a list of x86 instructions in text form. Thus the code emitter, implemented by function `code2x86asm`, transforms an `instr list` into a `string list`.

The 32-bit x86 registers from Fig. 14.2 are represented by the `reg32` data type:

```
type reg32 =
  | Eax | Ecx | Edx | Ebx | Esi | Edi | Esp | Ebp
```

Operands of x86 instructions are described by the `rand` type, but note that in reality there are many other variants of x86 operands:

```
type rand =
  | Cst of int          (* immediate integer constant n  *)
  | Reg of reg32        (* register, eg. ebx             *)
  | Ind of reg32        (* register indirect, eg. [ebx]  *)
  | EbpOff of int       (* ebp offset indirect [ebp - n] *)
  | Glovars             (* stackbase [glovars]           *)
```

Instructions are represented by the `x86` type, where `Ins`, `Ins1` and `Ins2` are used to represent 0-, 1- and 2-operand x86 instructions, as in `Ins2("sub", Reg Eax, Reg Ebx)` or `Ins1("imul", Reg Ebx)`, which represent `sub eax, ebx` and `imul ebx`, respectively.

Unconditional and conditional jumps, and function calls, are represented using `Jump`, as in `Jump("je", "lab1")`, and `PRINTI` and `PRINTC` represent calls to C functions (defined in file `driver.c`) for printing integers and characters. The pseudo-instructions `Label` and `FLabel` represent plain assembly code labels and function entry labels. We distinguish them because the function entry code must set up the function's stack frame; see Sect. 14.3.3.

```
type x86 =
  | Label of label              (* code label; pseudo-instr *)
  | FLabel of flabel * int      (* function label; pseudo   *)
  | Ins of string               (* eg. sub esp, 4           *)
  | Ins1 of string * rand       (* eg. push eax             *)
  | Ins2 of string * rand * rand (* eg. add eax, [ebp - 32] *)
  | Jump of string * label      (* eg. jz near lab          *)
  | PRINTI                      (* print [esp] as integer   *)
  | PRINTC                      (* print [esp] as character *)
```

14.3.3   Stack Layout for Micro-C x86 Code

When compiling micro-C to x86 code, the run-time stack layout will be exactly as shown in Fig. 8.2 for the abstract machine in Sect. 8.3, but of course using the "real" x86 stack pointer register ESP and base pointer register EBP instead of the abstract machine's SP and BP.

Function arguments and local variables (integers, pointers and arrays) are all stored in the function's stack frame, and are accessed relative to the bottom of the stack frame, using the base pointer register EBP.

Global variables are allocated at the bottom of the entire stack (high addresses) and are accessed using an offset relative to the address of the first global variable, which is held in global location glovars. The glovars assembly code variable is in the .data section of the generated assembly file, and its value is set by initialization code generated by X86.fs.

The pseudo-instruction FLabel(f,m) represents the entry point of an m-argument micro-C function f. Thus the x86 code generated for FLabel(f,m) must set up the stack frame of the newly called function, which chiefly requires sliding the m arguments 8 bytes up the stack to make room for the return address and the base pointer at the bottom of the stack frame. In the Sect. 8.3 abstract machine, this is done by the CALL(m, a) instruction in Fig. 8.1, but here we want to use the native x86 call instruction which does not do this work.

The x86 code generated for FLabel(lab,m) will look as follows:

```
_f:
            pop eax              ; Pop return address into EAX
            pop ebx              ; Pop old base pointer into EBX
            sub esp, 8           ; Add two stack positions
            mov esi, esp
            mov ebp, esp         ; Put EBP := ESP+4*m to point
            add ebp, 4*m         ;   below future first arguments
_f_pro_1:                        ; Loop to slide m arguments
            cmp ebp, esi
            jz _f_pro_2          ; If ESI=EBP, exit loop
            mov ecx, [esi+8]     ; Move one argument
            mov [esi], ecx       ;   up by 2 positions
            add esi, 4           ; Next argument
            jmp _f_pro_1
_f_pro_2:
            sub ebp, 4           ; Make EBP point to first arg
            mov [ebp+8], eax     ; Write return address and
            mov [ebp+4], ebx     ;   old base pointer below args
```

First the return address and the old base pointer are popped from stack into registers. Now the m arguments are on the stack top, and ESP points to the topmost argument. Then ESI is set to point to the topmost argument also, and EBP to point below the future first argument position. Then the loop between the two labels performs m iterations, each iteration moving an argument two positions (8 bytes) up the stack, from address esi+8 to address esi. The loop terminates when ESI equals EBP,

Fig. 14.5 Compilation
schemes for micro-C
statements to x86 code. The
lab1 and lab2 represent
fresh labels

$S[\![\texttt{if (e) stmt1 else stmt2}]\!] =$
    $E[\![\texttt{e}]\!]$ `Ebx`
    `cmp ebx, 0`
    `jz lab1`
    $S[\![\texttt{stmt1}]\!]$
    `jmp lab2`
   `lab1:` $S[\![\texttt{stmt2}]\!]$
   `lab2:`   ...

$S[\![\texttt{while (e) body}]\!] =$
    `jmp lab2`
   `lab1:` $S[\![\texttt{body}]\!]$
   `lab2:` $E[\![\texttt{e}]\!]$ `Ebx`
    `cmp ebx, 0`
    `jnz lab1`

$S[\![\texttt{e; }]\!] =$

    $E[\![\texttt{e}]\!]$ `Ebx`

$S[\![\texttt{\{stmtordec1, ..., stmtordecn\}}]\!] =$
    $D[\![\texttt{stmtordec1}]\!]$
    ...
    $D[\![\texttt{stmtordecn}]\!]$
    `add esp, 4*locals`

$S[\![\texttt{return; }]\!] =$

    `add esp, 4*locals`
    `pop ebp`
    `ret`

$S[\![\texttt{return e; }]\!] =$
    $E[\![\texttt{e}]\!]$ `Ebx`
    `add esp, 4*locals`
    `pop ebp`
    `ret`

after which EBP is adjusted to point to the first argument. Finally the return address and the old base pointer are written to the stack, below the arguments.

At this point the stack frame for the called function f has been set up as in Fig. 8.2, and the code generated for the function's body can be executed.

When function f returns, it must remove the stack frame created by the code above by resetting ESP and EBP to point to the caller's stack frame. This is done by incrementing ESP so that it points at the address containing the old EBP, popping (old) EBP from there, and executing a `ret` instruction which will pop the return address and jump to it. Code to do so is generated for `return` and `return e` statements (see Fig. 14.5), and also attached to the end of the function body in case the function returns by "dropping off the end". Typically it looks like this:

```
add esp, 8              ; 4*number of local variables
pop ebp
ret
```

Moreover, the code for the function's body must leave the function's result value, if any, in register EBX. This is accomplished simply by making the compilation of a

---

cProgram : program -> x86 list * int * x86 list * x86 list
Compile an entire micro-C program into a tuple (globalinit, argc, maincall, functions) of x86 code to allocate global variables, the main function's arity, x86 code to call the main function, and x86 code for all the program's functions, including main.

cStmt : stmt -> varEnv -> funEnv -> x86 list
Compile a micro-C statement into a sequence of x86 instructions.

cStmtOrDec: stmtordec -> varEnv -> funEnv -> varEnv * x86 list
Compile a statement or declaration (as found in a statement block { int x; ... }) to a sequence of x86 instructions, either for the statement or for allocation of the declared variable (of type int or array or pointer). Return a possibly extended environment as well as the instruction sequence.

cExpr : expr->varEnv->funEnv->reg32->reg32 list->x86 list
Compile a micro-C expression into a sequence of x86 instructions. The compilation takes place in a compile-time variable environment and a compile-time function environment. The code satisfies the net effect principle for compilation of expressions: If the compilation (cExpr e env fenv tr pres) of expression e returns the instruction sequence instrs, then the execution of instrs will leave the rvalue of expression e in x86 register tr and will preserve the values of x86 registers in the pres list.

cAccess : access->varEnv->funEnv->reg32->reg32 list->x86 list
Compile an access (variable x, pointer dereferencing *e, or array indexing a[i]) into a sequence of instructions, again relative to a compile-time environment. The net effect of executing the generated instructions is to leave a stack address, representing the lvalue of the access expression, in x86 register tr and leave the registers in pres unchanged.

cExprs : expr list -> varEnv -> funEnv -> reg32 -> x86 list
Compile a list of expressions into a sequence of instructions, using and possibly modifying x86 register tr.

allocate: varkind -> typ*string -> varEnv -> varEnv * x86 list
Given a micro-C type (int, pointer, or array) and a variable name, bind the variable in the compile-time environment. Return the extended environment together with x86 code for allocating store for the variable at run-time. The varkind indicates whether the variable is local (to a function), or global (to the program).

Fig. 14.6 Main x86 compilation functions of the micro-C compiler. A varEnv is a pair of a compile-time variable environment and the next available offset for local variables. A funEnv is a compile-time function environment. The use of the pres : reg32 list argument is described in Sect. 14.9

return e statement compile expression e with target register EBX, as shown at the end of Fig. 14.5.

14.4 The micro-C x86 Compiler

The compiler (in file X86Comp.fs) compiles a micro-C program into a sequence of x86 instructions. The code has entry label _asm_main which is called from the main function of the driver.c file (shown below). The generated x86 code has these parts:

- a call to function `checkargc` defined in file `driver.c` to check that the number of command line arguments matches the arity of the micro-C `main` function;
- initialization code for global variables;
- pushing the integer command line arguments to the stack;
- calling the micro-C program's `main` function;
- cleaning up the stack after that function returns, and returning to the C `main` function in `driver.c`;
- compiled code for each of the micro-C functions in the source file.

This overall code structure is produced by function `compileToFile` in file `X86Comp.fs`. The file `driver.c` contains these C function definitions:

```
extern void asm_main(int,int*);
int printc(int c) { printf("%c", c); return c; }
int printi(int i) { printf("%d ", i); return i; }
void checkargc(int a, int b) { ... }
int main(int argc, char **argv) {
  int i, args[argc-1];
  for (i=1; i<argc; i++)
    args[i-1] = atoi(argv[i]);
  asm_main(argc-1,args);
  printf("\nRan %.3f s\n",(clock())*1.0/CLOCKS_PER_SEC);
  exit(0);
}
```

The C extern declaration describes the generated x86 code's entry point `asm_main`. The C functions `printc` and `printi` are called from the generated x86 code to print characters and integers; the `checkargc` function is called from generated x86 code to check that a compiled micro-C program is called with the correct number of command line arguments. The C `main` function starts the entire execution by converting textual command line arguments to integers, calling the `asm_main` entry point and thereby the compiled micro-C `main` function with these integer arguments, and finally printing the processor time spent.

In the sections below we will focus on the code generation for a single micro-C function.

14.5 Compilation Schemes for Micro-C

The compilation of micro-C constructs can be summarized using compilation schemes, corresponding to the main micro-C compiler functions listed in Fig. 14.6:

- S⟦ stmt ⟧ is the result of compiling statement `stmt` as shown in Fig. 14.5 and corresponds to compilation function `cStmt`.
- E⟦ e ⟧ tr is the result of compiling expression e with target register `tr` as shown in Figs. 14.7 and 14.8 and corresponds to compilation function `cExpr`.
- A⟦ acc ⟧ tr is the result of compiling access expression `acc` as shown in Fig. 14.9 and corresponds to compilation function `cAccess`.

The lab1 and lab2 that appear in the compilation schemes are labels, assumed to be fresh in each of the compilation scheme cases.

14.6 Compilation of Statements

To understand the compilation schemes, consider the compilation of the statement if (e) stmt1 else stmt2 in Fig. 14.5. The generated x86 code will first evaluate e and leave its value in register EBX, then compare it to zero using cmp ebx, 0. The instruction jz lab1 will jump to label lab1 if the value was zero (which represents false). In that case, the compiled code for stmt2 will be executed, as expected. In the opposite case, when the value of e is not zero, the compiled code for stmt1 will be executed, and then the instruction jmp lab2 will jump to lab2, thus avoiding the execution of stmt2.

The compiled x86 code for while (e) body begins with a jump to label lab2. The code at lab2 computes the condition e, leaving its value in register EBX, and then compares that to zero. The instruction jnz lab1 jumps to label lab1 if the value was non-zero (true). The code at label lab1 is the compiled body of the while-loop. After executing that code, the code compiled for expression e is executed again, and so on.

The compiled x86 code for an expression statement e; consists of the compiled code for e, whose execution will leave the value in register EBX, where it is ignored.

The compilation of a return statement is shown in Fig. 14.5 also. When the return statement has an argument expression as in return e we generate code to evaluate e, leaving the result in register EBX as required by the micro-C x86 calling convention in Sect. 14.3.1. Whether or not the return statement has an argument expression, it will additionally remove all local variables and parameters from the stack by incrementing ESP. At this point only the old base pointer and the return address are left in the stack frame, so the code will pop EBP and execute an x86 ret which will pop the return address and return to the caller.

14.7 Compilation of Expressions

The compilation of an expression e to x86 code is similar to the compilation to stack machine code described in Sect. 8.7. However, here the *net effect* of the code for an expression must be to leave the expression's value (rvalue) in the compilation target register tr, not on the stack. We use the notation E⟦ acc ⟧ tr to describe code generated for expression e that leaves e's value in target register tr.

Figure 14.7 shows the compilation schemes for variables, assignments, constants, arithmetic operations and function calls.

A variable access x or pointer dereferencing *e or array indexing a[i] is compiled by generating code to compute an address in the store and leave it in register

$E[\![acc]\!]\,tr =$ where acc is an access expression

```
            A[[acc]] tr
            mov tr, [tr]
```

$E[\![acc=e]\!]\,tr =$

```
            A[[acc]] tr'
            E[[e]] tr
            mov [tr'], tr
```

$E[\![i]\!]\,tr =$

```
            mov tr, i
```

$E[\![null]\!]\,tr =$

```
            mov tr, 0
```

$E[\![\&acc]\!]\,tr =$

```
            A[[acc]] tr
```

$E[\![e1 + e2]\!]\,tr =$

```
                E[[e1]] tr
                E[[e2]] tr'
                add tr, tr'
```

$E[\![e1 * e2]\!]\,tr =$

```
                E[[e1]] tr
                E[[e2]] tr'
                mov eax, tr
                imul tr'
                mov tr, eax
```

$E[\![e1 / e2]\!]\,tr =$ remainder (%) is similar, with result in EDX not EAX

```
                E[[e1]] tr
                E[[e2]] tr'
                mov eax, tr
                cdq
                idiv tr'
                mov tr, eax
```

$E[\![f(e1, \ldots, en)]\!]\,tr =$

```
                E[[e1]] tr
                push tr
                ...
                E[[en]] tr
                push tr
                push ebp
                call labf
                mov tr, ebx
```

Fig. 14.7 Compilation schemes for some micro-C expressions to x86 code. The `tr'` represents a fresh target register; see Sect. 14.9

`tr`, and then appending the x86 instruction `mov tr, [tr]` to load the value at that address into register `tr`.

An assignment `x = e` is compiled by generating code for the access expression `x` to leave its lvalue (which is `x`'s address) in a register `tr'`, generating code for the right-hand side `e` to leave its value in register `tr`, and appending the x86 instruction mov [tr'], tr that copies e's value to x's store address. Note that this still leaves in e's value in tr, as required by the C semantics of the expression x = e.

An integer constant i and the null pointer constant are compiled to x86 code like mov tr, i.

An address-of expression &acc is compiled to code that evaluates acc to an address and simply leaves that address in the desired target register (instead of dereferencing it as in a variable access).

A two-argument primitive operation such as addition e1 + e2 is compiled to code that first evaluates e1 with result in tr, then evaluates e2 with result in tr', and then executes x86 instruction add tr, tr' to add the two numbers, leaving the sum in tr as desired. Subtraction is similar, but multiplication is more cumbersome: the multiplicand must be copied from tr to EAX, and after the x86 imul instruction the result will be in EAX (32 least significant bits) and EDX (32 most significant bits), so the result must be copied from EAX to tr. Division (/) and remainder (%) are also complicated: the divisor must be in EAX and must be sign-extended into EDX using a cdq instruction, and after the x86 idiv instruction the quotient is in EAX and the remainder in EDX and must be copied from there to the target register tr.

A function call f(e1, ..., en) is compiled to code that first evaluates e1, ..., en in that order, pushing each one of them onto the stack, pushes (old) EBP onto the stack, calls f using the x86 instruction call f, and, after f returns, copies its result from EBX into the target register tr.

Figure 14.8 shows the compilation schemes for comparisons and logical expressions.

A comparison e1 < e2 is compiled to code that first evaluates e1 with result in tr, evaluates e2 with result in tr', compares them using cmp, sets the lower byte AL of EAX to true (1) or false (0) from the comparison using setl al, and finally copies EAX to the target register tr.

Logical negation !e is compiled to code that first evaluates e, leaving its value in register tr, sets EAX to zero by xor eax, eax, compares tr to zero (in EAX), uses sete al to set EAX to true (1) or false (0) according as e was 0 or not, and finally copies EAX to register tr.

The short-cut conditional e1 && e2 is compiled to code that first evaluates e1, leaves its value in tr and compares it to zero. Then if it is zero (meaning false), it jumps to label lab1 at the end of the code; the result is in tr. Otherwise, if the value of e1 is non-zero (true), then e2 is evaluated with result in tr, and that value is the value of the entire expression.

The short-cut conditional e1 || e2 is dual to e1 && e2 and is compiled in the same way, but zero has been replaced with non-zero and vice versa.

E[[e1 < e2]] tr =   other comparisons are similar, using sete, setg, ...
                E[[e1]] tr
                E[[e2]] tr'
                xor eax, eax
                cmp tr, tr'
                setl al
                mov tr, eax
E[[!e1]] tr =
                E[[e1]] tr
                xor eax, eax
                cmp tr, eax
                sete al
                mov tr, eax
E[[e1 && e2]] tr =
                E[[e1]] tr
                cmp tr, 0
                jz lab1
                E[[e2]] tr
        lab1:   ...
E[[e1 || e2]] tr =
                E[[e1]]
                cmp tr, 0
                jnz lab1
                E[[e2]]
        lab1:   ...

Fig. 14.8 Compilation schemes for micro-C comparisons and logical expressions to x86 code. Above, lab1 represents a fresh label, and tr' represents a fresh target register; see Sect. 14.9

14.8   Compilation of Access Expressions

Figure 14.9 shows the compilation schemes for access expressions. The *net effect* of the code for an access expression must be to leave an address (lvalue) in the compilation's target register tr.

If acc is a global variable x, the compiled code puts the global store address of x in tr; this is computed as the base address of global variables minus the global offset of x. If acc is a local variable or parameter x, then the compiled code must compute the base pointer register ebp minus the variable's offset in the local stack frame.

If the access expression acc is a pointer dereferencing *e then the compiled code simply evaluates e and leaves that value in tr as a store address.

If the access expression is an array indexing a[i], then the compiled code evaluates access expression a to obtain in tr an address where the base address of the array is stored, executes instruction mov tr, [tr] to load that base address into tr, then evaluates expression i to obtain an array index in register tr', shifts it left by 2 bits, thus multiplying it by 4, and finally subtracts the result from the tr register. (Recall that the x86 stack grows toward lower addresses).

$A[\![\,x\,]\!]\ tr =$ when x is global at offset a

        `mov tr, [glovars]`

        `sub tr, 4*a`

$A[\![\,x\,]\!]\ tr =$ when x is local at offset a

        `lea tr, [ebp - 4*a]`

$A[\![\,*e\,]\!]\ tr =$

        $[\![\,e\,]\!]\ tr$

$A[\![\,a[i]\,]\!]\ tr =$

        $A[\![\,a\,]\!]\ tr$

        `mov tr, [tr]`

        $E[\![\,i\,]\!]\ tr'$

        `sub tr, tr'`

Fig. 14.9 Compilation schemes for micro-C access expressions: variable x, pointer dereferencing *e or array indexing a[i]

14.9 Choosing Target Registers

The expression compilation schemes in Figs. 14.7, 14.8 and 14.9 must choose fresh labels as well as fresh target registers `tr'`. Choosing a fresh label is easy since there are infinitely many distinct labels `lab1`, `lab2`, ..., but choosing a fresh register is more difficult since there are only few 32-bit x86 registers. To choose a fresh target register `tr'` we need to know which registers are already in use and should be preserved by the expression evaluation.

The actual compilation functions `cExpr` and `cAccess` for expressions and accesses therefore have an additional parameter `pres` which is a list of registers to preserve, and it uses an auxiliary function `getTempFor pres` that attempts to return a fresh target register not already in the list `pres`.

For instance, the compilation of an addition operation `e1 + e2` looks like this:

```
and cExpr e varEnv funEnv tr (pres : reg32 list) : x86 list =
    match e with
    ...
    | Prim2("+", e1, e2) ->
        cExpr e1 varEnv funEnv tr pres
        @ let tr' = getTempFor (tr @ pres)
          in cExpr e2 varEnv funEnv tr' (tr :: pres)
             @ [Ins2("add", Reg tr, Reg tr')]
    | ...
```

To generate code for `e1 + e2` with target register `tr`, we generate code for `e1` with target register `tr`, choose a fresh target register `tr'` that is not in (`tr :: pres`), generate code for `e2` with target register `tr'`, and generate code to add the contents of `tr'` into `tr`. The code generated for `e1` must preserve the registers in `pres`, and the code generated for `e2` must additionally preserve `tr`, which is used by the instruction after `e2`.

The `getTempFor` function chooses one of the five 32-bit registers ECX, EDX, EBX, ESI, and EDI, out of those shown in Fig. 14.2. One cannot easily use EAX for temporary results because it is the only register that can hold the multiplier in integer multiplication (`imul`) and hold the divisor in integer division and remainder (`idiv`). Also, we use EAX in comparisons such as (<) and so on where we set the AL 8-bit subregister from status flags using `setl` and related instructions. These restrictions follow from the x86's somewhat irregular design, and the historical role of the EAX register. Also, we obviously cannot use EBP and ESP for temporary results because they hold the base pointer and stack pointer.

When `pres` list contains all the available registers, `getTempFor pres` cannot return an unused one, and raises an exception instead, causing compilation to fail. This happens when the expression to compile is too complex; for instance, when compiling the assignment

```
dummy = n + (n + (n + (n + n))); // Too complex
```

where `dummy` and `n` are local variables. Namely, evaluating this would require six registers, one for `dummy`'s address and five for each of the copies of `n`, and we have only five registers available. This is a serious limitation of our micro-C to x86 compiler; see Sect. 14.10 for how to lift it. Nevertheless, the compiler can handle all the example programs listed in Fig. 7.8. Moreover, when an expression is too complex, one can introduce an extra micro-C variable to hold part of it while evaluating the rest.

14.10   Improving the Compiler

Our micro-C to x86 compiler generates real machine code that is much faster than that of the abstract machine in Chap. 8. Yet the compiler has a number of limitations:

One deficiency was noted in Sect. 14.9: it cannot compile complicated micro-C expressions because of the simplistic allocation of registers for temporary values. This problem can be solved by proper register allocation; see Sect. 8.9 and Exercise 14.8.

Another deficiency of this chapter's micro-C to x86 compiler is that the compilation of pointer arithmetics expressions such as (`p` + `i`), where `p` is an `int` pointer and `i` an `int`, is wrong, whereas it was correct in the Chap. 8 micro-C compiler. That is because the x86 machine is byte-addressed so an `int` takes four memory locations, whereas Chap. 8's abstract machine is (32-bit) word-addressed so an `int` takes one memory location. Moreover, the x86 stack grows toward lower addresses. Real C semantics therefore requires `i` in (`p` + `i`) to be multiplied by four in the x86 code, and subtracted from rather than added to `p`; see Exercise 14.7. To make this chapter's micro-C compiler do this, it needs to know the types of `p` and `i`, which requires a type analysis; see Exercise 14.6.

14.11 History and Literature

The historical development of the x86 architecture is evident from its register names as described in Sect. 14.2.2: 8-bit registers (AH, AL, BH, BL, ...), 16-bit registers (AX, BX, ...), 32-bit registers (EAX, EBX, ...), and 64-bit registers (RAX, RBX, ...). Moreover, the EAX register has a special status; for instance, it is the only register that can be involved in integer multiplication imul and integer division idiv. This shows the influence from the very earliest digital stored-program computer, the 1946 Princeton IAS machine design [2]. The IAS machine design had a single accumulator register AR that was the target of most operations, and a multiplier register MR used mostly to hold the other operand of a multiplication. The IAS machine design influenced almost all early computers, both in the USA and internationally, such as the 1949 Cambridge EDSAC [10], the 1949 Manchester Mark I, the 1952 IBM 701, the 1953 Swedish BESK, and the 1957 Danish DASK.

As shown in Sect. 14.2.1, the backwards compatible x86 architecture developed over a long time and hence is rather irregular, with a complicated instruction set. Intel itself (along with Hewlett-Packard) tried to introduce the Itanium processor around year 2000 as a possible replacement for the x86, with a more regular design and more (compiler-determined) instruction-level parallelism. The Itanium never gained the popularity of the x86, and in May 2017 Intel announced that it would stop further development of Itanium.

In the early days of electronic computers, they were programmed directly in binary code, because machine time was vastly more costly than programmer time, and optimal use of the hardware more important than ease of programming. Some people even considered the use of the computer itself for mundane tasks such as translating one text (symbolic assembly) into another text (binary machine code) to be abuse of an expensive scientific instrument.

The first practically significant assembler program was the "initial orders" program suite developed for the Cambridge EDSAC in 1950 [10, 12]. It allowed programs to be written in a somewhat symbolic form, for instance using the letter A instead of the binary digits 11100 to indicate the EDSAC's addition instruction. The EDSAC initial orders would read the symbolic code from a paper tape and convert it into binary instructions, stored into the machine's memory. This useful tool suite influenced many others, including that developed in 1957 for the Danish DASK computer [9]. For the international history of early assemblers (then usually called autocodes) and early compilers, see Bauer [1] and Knuth [7]; for early developments in the Nordic countries, see Sestoft [9].

14.12 Exercises

The main goal of these exercises is to familiarize yourself with the compilation of micro-C to machine code, and explore how the micro-C compiler could be improved.

Exercise 14.1 Modify the `macsimple.asm` assembly program from Sect. 14.2.5 to add the numbers 7, 9 and 13 and print the result. Assemble, link, and run the program.

Exercise 14.2 Write an x86 assembly program to compute the sum $1+2+\cdots+1000$. It must really do the summation, not use the closed-form expression $\frac{n(n+1)}{2}$ with $n = 1000$.

Exercise 14.3 Investigate the code generated by the micro-C x86 compiler for the `ex1.c` example program; this code is in file `ex1.asm`.

Describe the various parts of the code, relate them to the outline of the compiler given in Sect. 14.4 and to the source code in `ex1.c`, and describe which parts of the micro-C compiler in `X86Comp.fs` and `X86.fs` have generated which parts of the `ex1.asm` file.

Exercise 14.4 Write an x86 assembly program that defines a function `fib` that computes the (naive, exponential-time) Fibonacci function

```
let rec fib n = if n<2 then n else fib(n-1) + fib(n-2)
```

Your `fib` function should take its argument from the stack top and leave its result in the EAX register. Use the x86 stack and the `call` and `ret` instructions. Make it compute and print `fib(35)`. Then make it compute `fib(n)` for all n in the range 0, 1, ..., 35. Compare the speed of this with micro-C example `ex23.c`. Compare your hand-written assembly code with that generated by the micro-C compiler in `ex23.asm`.

You may draw inspiration from the `macfac.asm` example.

Exercise 14.5 Write a peephole optimizer for x86 assembly code, as a function `simplify : x86 list -> x86 list`. The function should identify instructions that can be deleted and instruction sequences that can be shortened. For instance, it could transform instruction sequences like this:

Replace	By
add reg, 0	(nothing)
sub reg, 0	(nothing)
add reg, i1; add reg, i2	add reg, (i1+i2)
sub reg, i1; sub reg, i2	sub reg, (i1+i2)
lea reg, [ebp - 0]; mov reg, [reg]	mov reg, [ebp]
lea reg, [ebp - i]; mov reg, [reg]	mov reg, [ebp - i]

Exercise 14.6 Implement type analysis for micro-C expressions, via functions `tExpr` and `tAssign` with the following signatures:

```
tExpr : expr -> varEnv -> funEnv -> typ
tAccess : access -> varEnv -> funEnv -> typ
```

Exercise 14.7 Use the type analysis from Exercise 14.6 to make the compilation of pointer arithmetics correct (see Sect. 14.10). For instance, when p is an int pointer and i an int, the expression (p+i) should be compiled as p-4*i because the size of an int is 4 bytes and the stack grows toward lower addresses.

Exercise 14.8 Make the micro-C compiler handle much more complicated expression by using as many registers as needed, spilling excess ones to the stack.

References

1. Bauer, F.L.: Historical remarks on compiler construction. In: Bauer, F.L., et al. (eds.) Compiler Construction, An Advanced Course. Lecture Notes in Computer Science, pp. 603–621. Springer, x (1974)
2. Burks, A., Goldstine, H., von Neumann, J.: Preliminary discussion of the logical design of an electronic computing instrument. Technical report, Institute of Advanced Studies, Princeton, USA (1946). http://library.ias.edu/files/Prelim_Disc_Logical_Design.pdf
3. Cloutier, F.: x86 instruction set reference. http://www.felixcloutier.com/x86/
4. Intel: The evolution of a revolution. Poster. http://download.intel.com/pressroom/kits/IntelProcessorHistory.pdf
5. Intel 64 and IA-32 Architectures Software Developer's Manual, volumes 2A and 2B (2016)
6. Intel: Intel chips. Poster (2012). http://www.intel.com/content/www/us/en/history/history-intel-chips-timeline-poster.html
7. Knuth, D.E., Pardo, L.T.: The early development of programming languages. In: Belzer, J., Holzman, A.G., Kent, A. (eds.) Encyclopedia of Computer Science and Technology, vol. 7, pp. 419–493. Marcel Dekker (1977). Reprinted in Selected Papers on Computer Languages, CSLI 2003, pp. 1–93
8. Nasm Development Team: Nasm. The Netwide Assembler. Version 2.12.02 (2016). http://www.nasm.us/xdoc/2.12.02/nasmdoc.pdf
9. Sestoft, P.: Early Nordic compilers and autocodes. In: Gram, C., Rasmussen, P., Østergaard, S.D. (eds.) History of Nordic computing 4, 4th IFIP WG 9.7 Conference, HiNC4, Copenhagen, Denmark, pp. 350–366. Springer (2015)
10. Wheeler, D.J.: Automatic computing with the EDSAC. Ph.D. thesis, University of Cambridge (1951). http://www.markpriestley.net/wheeler.pdf
11. Wikibooks: X86 assembly/gas syntax. Wiki book (2016). https://en.wikibooks.org/wiki/X86_Assembly/GAS_Syntax
12. Wilkes, M.V., Wheeler, D.J., Gill, S.: The preparation of programs for an electronic digital computer, with special reference to the EDSAC and the use of a library of subroutines. Addison-Wesley (1951)

Appendix A
Crash Course in F#

This chapter introduces parts of the F# programming language as used in this book; Hansen and Rischel [1] give a proper introduction to functional programming with F#. The F# programming language belongs to the ML family, which includes classical ML from 1978, Standard ML [3] from 1986, CAML from 1985, Caml Light [2] from 1990, and OCaml [5] from 1996, where F# resembles the latter most. All of these languages are strict, mostly functional, and statically typed with parametric polymorphic type inference.

Originally developed on Windows, F# is available also on MacOS and Linux, for instance using the Mono implementation [4] of CLI/.NET.

A.1 Files for This Chapter

File	Contents
Intro/Appendix.fs	All examples shown in this chapter

A.2 Getting Started

To get the F# interactive prompt, start `fsharpi` from the command line. It allows you to enter declarations and evaluate expressions:

```
F# Interactive for F# 4.1
For help type #help;;
> let rec fac n = if n=0 then 1 else n * fac(n-1);;
val fac : n:int -> int
> fac 10;;
```

© Springer International Publishing AG 2017
P. Sestoft, *Programming Language Concepts*, Undergraduate Topics
in Computer Science, DOI 10.1007/978-3-319-60789-4

```
val it : int = 3628800
> #q;;
```

Text starting with an angle symbol (>) is entered by the user; the other lines show the F# system's response. One can also run F# Interactive inside Microsoft Visual Studio, but that may cause challenges when we start using the F# lexer and parser tools.

A.3   Expressions, Declarations and Types

F# is a mostly-functional language: a computation is performed by evaluating an *expression* such as $3 + 4$. If you enter an expression in the interactive system, followed by a double semicolon (;;) and a newline, it will be evaluated:

```
> 3+4;;
val it : int = 7
```

The system responds with the value (7) as well as the type (int) of the expression.

A *declaration* let v = e introduces a variable v whose value is the result of evaluating e. For instance, this declaration introduces variable res:

```
> let res = 3+4;;
val res : int = 7
```

After the declaration one may use res in expressions:

```
> res * 2;;
val it : int = 14
```

A.3.1   Arithmetic and Logical Expressions

Expressions are built from constants such as 2 and 2.0, variables such as res, and operators such as multiplication (*). Figure A.1 summarizes predefined F# operators.

Expressions may involve functions, such as the predefined function sqrt. Function sqrt computes the square root of a floating-point number, which has type float, a 64-bit floating-point number. We can compute the square root of 2.0 like this:

```
> let y = sqrt 2.0;;
val y : float = 1.414213562
```

Floating-point constants must be written with a decimal point (2.0) or in scientific notation (2E0) to distinguish them from integer constants.

To get help on F#, consult http://msdn.microsoft.com/fsharp/ where you may find the library documentation and the language specification [7].

Operator	Type	Meaning
f e		Function application
!	'a ref -> 'a	Dereference
-	num -> num	Arithmetic negation
**	float * float -> float	Power
/	float * float -> float	Quotient
/	int * int -> int	Quotient, round toward 0
%	int * int -> int	Remainder of int quotient
*	num * num -> num	Product
+	string * string -> string	String concatenation
+	num * num -> num	Sum
-	num * num -> num	Difference
::	'a * 'a list -> 'a list	Cons onto list (right-assoc.)
+	string * string -> string	Concatenate
@	'a list * 'a list -> 'a list	List append (right-assoc.)
=	'a * 'a -> bool	Equal
<>	'a * 'a -> bool	Not equal
<	'a * 'a -> bool	Less than
>	'a * 'a -> bool	Greater than
<=	'a * 'a -> bool	Less than or equal
>=	'a * 'a -> bool	Greater than or equal
&&	bool * bool -> bool	Logical "and" (short-cut)
||	bool * bool -> bool	Logical "or" (short-cut)
,	'a * 'b -> 'a * 'b	Tuple element separator
:=	'a ref * 'a -> unit	Reference assignment

Fig. A.1 Some F# operators grouped according to precedence. Operators at the top have high precedence (bind strongly). For overloaded operators, num means int, float or another numeric type. All operators are left-associative, except (::) and (@)

You can also use (static) methods from the .NET class libraries, after opening the relevant namespaces:

```
> open System;;
> let y = Math.Sqrt 2.0;;
val y : float = 1.414213562
```

Logical expressions have type bool:

```
> let large = 10 < res;;
val large : bool = false
```

Logical expressions can be combined using logical "and" (conjunction), written &&, and logical "or" (disjunction), written | |. Like the similar operators of C, C++, Java and C#, these use short-cut evaluation, so that && will evaluate its right operand only if the left operand is true (and dually for | |):

```
> y > 0.0 && 1.0/y > 7.0;;
val it : bool = false
```

Logical negation is written not e:

```
> not false ;;
val it : bool = true
```

The (!) operator is used for another purpose, as described in Sect. A.12.

Logical expressions are typically used in *conditional expressions*, written if e1
then e2 else e3, which correspond to (e1 ? e2 : e3) in C or C++ or
Java or C#:

```
> if 3 < 4 then 117 else 118;;
val it : int = 117
```

A.3.2 String Values and Operators

A text string has type string. A string constant is written within double quotes
("). The string concatenation operator (+) constructs a new string by concatenating
two strings:

```
> let title = "Prof.";;
val title : string = "Prof."
> let name = "Lauesen";;
val name : string = "Lauesen"
> let junk =  "Dear " + title + " " + name + ", You won $$$!";;
val junk : string = "Dear Prof. Lauesen, You won $$$!"
```

The instance property Length on a string returns its length (number of characters):

```
> junk.Length;;
val it : int = 32
```

and the string index operation s.[i] gets the i'th character of string s, counting
from 0.

A.3.3 Types and Type Errors

Every expression has a type, and the compiler checks that operators and functions are
applied only to expressions of the correct type. There are no implicit type conversions.
For instance, sqrt expects an argument of type float and thus cannot be applied
to the argument expression 2, which has type int. Some F# types are summarized
in Fig. A.2; see also Sect. A.10. The compiler complains in case of type errors, and
refuses to compile the expression:

```
> sqrt 2;;
  sqrt 2;;
  -----^
```

```
stdin(51,6): error FS0001: The type 'int' does not support
                           any operators named 'Sqrt'
```

The error message points to the argument expression 2 as the culprit and explains that it has type `int` which does not support any function `Sqrt`. It is up to the reader to infer that the solution is to write `2.0` to get a constant of type `float`.

Some arithmetic operators and comparison operators are *overloaded*, as indicated in Fig. A.1. For instance, the plus operator (+) can be used to add two expressions of type `int` or two expressions of type `float`, but not to add an `int` and a `float`. Overloaded operators default to `int` when there are no `float` or `string` or `char` arguments.

Type	Meaning	Examples
Primitive types		
`int`	Integer number (32 bit)	`0, 12, ~12`
`float`	Floating-point number (64 bit)	`0.0, 12.0, ~12.1, 3E~6`
`bool`	Logical	`true, false`
`string`	String	`"A", "", "den Haag"`
`char`	Character	`'A', ' '`
`Exception`	Exception	`Overflow, Fail "index"`
Functions (Sects. A.3.4–A.3.6, A.9.3, A.11)		
`float -> float`	Function from `float` to `float`	`sqrt`
`float -> bool`	Function from `float` to `bool`	`isLarge`
`int * int -> int`	Function taking `int` pair	`addp`
`int -> int -> int`	Function taking two `int`s	`addc`
Pairs and tuples (Sect. A.5)		
`unit`	Empty tuple	`()`
`int * int`	Pair of integers	`(2, 3)`
`int * bool`	Pair of `int` and `bool`	`(2100, false)`
`int * bool * float`	Three-tuple	`(2, true, 2.1)`
Lists (Sect. A.6)		
`int list`	List of integers	`[7; 9; 13]`
`bool list`	List of booleans	`[false; true; true]`
`string list`	List of strings	`["foo"; "bar"]`
Records (Sect. A.7)		
`{x : int; y : int}`	Record of two `int`s	`{x=2; y=3}`
`{y:int; leap:bool}`	Record of `int` and `bool`	`{y=2100; leap=false}`
References (Sect. A.12)		
`int ref`	Reference to an integer	`ref 42`
`int list ref`	Reference to a list of integers	`ref [7; 9; 13]`

Fig. A.2 Some monomorphic F# types

A.3.4   Function Declarations

A *function declaration* begins with the keyword `let`. The example below defines
a function `circleArea` that takes one argument `r` and returns the value of
`System.Math.PI * r * r`. The function can be applied (called) simply by
writing the function name before an argument expression:

```
> let circleArea r = System.Math.PI * r * r;;
val circleArea : float -> float
> let a = circleArea 10.0;;
val a : float = 314.1592654
```

The system infers that the type of the function is `float -> float`. That is,
the function takes a floating-point number as argument and returns a floating-point
number as result. This is because the .NET library constant `PI` is a floating-point
number.

Similarly, this declaration defines a function `mul2` from `float` to `float`:

```
> let mul2 x = 2.0 * x;;
val mul2 : float -> float
> mul2 3.5;;
val it : float = 7.0
```

A function may take any type of argument and produce any type of result. The
function `makejunk` below takes two arguments of type `string` and produces a
result of type `string`:

```
> let makejunk title name =
    "Dear " + title + " " + name + ", You won $$$!";;
val makejunk : string -> string -> string
> makejunk "Vice Chancellor" "Tofte";;
val it : string = "Dear Vice Chancellor Tofte, You won $$$!"
```

Note that F# is layout-sensitive (like a few other programming languages, such as
Haskell and Python). If the second line of the `makejunk` function declaration had
had no indentation at all, then we would get an error message (but strangely, in this
particular case the declaration would still be accepted):

```
> let makejunk title name =
"Dear " + title + " " + name + ", You won $$$!";;

  "Dear " + title + " " + name + ", You won $$$!";;
  ^^^^^^^^
stdin(16,1): warning FS0058: Possible incorrect indentation:
val makejunk : string -> string -> string
```

A.3.5 Recursive Function Declarations

A function may call any function, including itself; but then its declaration must start with `let rec` instead of `let`, where `rec` stands for *recursive*:

```
> let rec fac n = if n=0 then 1 else n * fac(n-1);;
val fac : int -> int
> fac 7;;
val it : int = 5040
```

If two functions need to call each other by so-called *mutual recursion*, they must be declared in one declaration beginning with `let rec` and connecting the two declarations by `and`:

```
> let rec even n = if n=0 then true else odd (n-1)
  and odd n = if n=0 then false else even (n-1);;
val even : int -> bool
val odd : int -> bool
```

A.3.6 Type Constraints

As you can see from the examples, the compiler automatically infers the type of a declared variable or function. Sometimes it is good to use an explicit *type constraint* for documentation. For instance, we may explicitly require that the function's argument x has type `float`, and that the function's result has type `bool`:

```
> let isLarge (x : float) : bool = 10.0 < x;;
val isLarge : float -> bool
> isLarge 89.0;;
val it : bool = true
```

If the type constraint is wrong, the compiler refuses to compile the declaration. A type constraint cannot be used to convert a value from one type to another as in C. Thus to convert an `int` to a `float`, you must use function `float : int -> float`. Similarly, to convert a `float` to an `int`, use a function such as `floor`, `round` or `ceil`, all of which have type `float -> int`.

A.3.7 The Scope of a Binding

The *scope* of a variable binding is that part of the program in which it is visible. In a local `let`-expression such as `let x = ...` below, the scope of variable x is the *body* expression x * x. The indentation shows that expression x * x belongs to the inner `let`-expression:

```
let r = let x = 9 + 16
        x * x
```

The value of the inner `let`-expression is $(9 + 16) \cdot (9 + 16) = 625$ but the sum is computed only once. The introduction of local variable x does not disturb any existing variables, not even variables with the same name. For instance:

```
> let x = 42;;
val x : int = 42                      (* outer x is 42      *)
> let r = let x = 9 + 16
-           x * x;;                   (* inner x is 25      *)
val r : int = 625
> x;;
val it : int = 42                     (* outer x unchanged *)
```

A.4   Pattern Matching

Like all languages in the ML family, but unlike most other programming languages, F# supports *pattern matching*. Pattern matching is performed by an expression of the form `match e with ...`, which consists of the expression e whose value must be matched, and a list (...) of match branches. For instance, the factorial function can be defined by pattern matching on the argument n, like this:

```
> let rec facm n =
      match n with
      | 0 -> 1
      | _ -> n * facm(n-1);;
val facm : int -> int
```

The patterns in a match are tried in order from top to bottom, and the right-hand side corresponding to the first matching pattern is evaluated. For instance, calling facm 7 will find that 7 does not match the pattern 0, but it does match the *wildcard pattern* (_) which matches any value, so the right-hand side n * facm(n-1) gets evaluated.

A slightly more compact notation for one-argument function definitions uses the `function` keyword, which combines parameter binding with pattern matching:

```
> let rec faca =
      function
      | 0 -> 1
      | n -> n * faca(n-1);;
val faca : int -> int
```

Pattern matching in the ML languages is similar to, but much more powerful, than switch-statements in C/C++/Java/C#, because matches can involve also tuple patterns (Sect. A.5) and algebraic datatype constructor patterns (Sect. A.9) and any combination of these. This makes the ML-style languages particularly useful for writing programs that process other programs, such as interpreters, compilers, program analysers, and program transformers.

Moreover, ML-style languages, including F#, usually require the compiler to detect both *incomplete* matches and *redundant* matches; that is, matches that either leave some cases uncovered, or that have some branches that are not usable:

```
> let bad1 n =
     match n with
     | 0 -> 1
     | 1 -> 2;;
warning FS0025: Incomplete pattern matches on this expression.
For example, the value '2' may not be covered by the patterns.
> let bad2 n =
     match n with
     | _ -> 1
     | 1 -> 2;;

     | 1 -> 2;;
     --------^
warning FS0026: This rule will never be matched
```

A.5   Pairs and Tuples

A *tuple* has a fixed number of components, which may be of different types. A *pair* is a tuple with two components. For instance, a pair of integers is written simply (2, 3), and its type is int * int:

```
> let p = (2, 3);;
val p : int * int = (2, 3)
> let w = (2, true, 3.4, "blah");;
val w : int * bool * float * string = (2, true, 3.4, "blah")
```

A function may take a pair as an argument, by performing pattern matching on the pair pattern (x, y):

```
> let add (x, y) = x + y;;
val add : int * int -> int
> add (2, 3);;
val it : int = 5
```

In principle, function add takes only one argument, but that argument is a pair of type int * int. Pairs are useful for representing values that belong together; for instance, the time of day can be represented as a pair of hours and minutes:

```
> let noon = (12, 0);;
```

```
val noon : int * int = (12, 0)
> let talk = (15, 15);;
val talk : int * int = (15, 15)
```

Pairs can be nested to any depth. For instance, a function can take a pair of pairs of values as argument:

```
> let earlier ((h1, m1),(h2, m2)) = h1<h2 || (h1=h2 && m1<m2);;
```

The empty tuple is written () and has type unit. This seemingly useless value is returned by functions that are called for their side effect only, such as WriteLine from the .NET class library:

```
> System.Console.WriteLine "Hello!";;
Hello!
val it : unit = ()
```

Thus the unit type serves much the same purpose as the void return type in C/C++/Java/C#.

A.6   Lists

A *list* contains zero or more elements, all of the same type. For instance, a list may hold three integers; then it has type int list:

```
> let x1 = [7; 9; 13];;
val x1 : int list = [7; 9; 13]
```

The empty list is written [], and the operator (::) called "cons" prepends an element to an existing list. Hence this is equivalent to the above declaration:

```
> let x2 = 7 :: 9 :: 13 :: [];;
val x2 : int list = [7; 9; 13]
> let equal = (x1 = x2);;
val equal : bool = true
```

The cons operator (::) is right associative, so 7 :: 9 :: 13 :: [] reads 7 :: (9 :: (13 :: [])), which is the same as [7; 9; 13].

A list ss of strings can be created just as easily as a list of integers; note that the type of ss is string list:

```
> let ss = ["Dear"; title; name; "you won $$$!"];;
val ss : string list = ["Dear"; "Prof."; "Lauesen";
                        "you won $$$!"]
```

The elements of a list of strings can be concatenated to a single string using the String.concat function:

```
> let junk2 = String.concat " " ss;;
val junk2 : string = "Dear Prof. Lauesen you won $$$!"
```

Functions on lists are conveniently defined using pattern matching and recursion. The sum function computes the sum of an integer list:

```
> let rec sum xs =
      match xs with
      | []     -> 0
      | x::xr -> x + sum xr;;
val sum : int list -> int
> let x2sum = sum x2;;
val x2sum : int = 29
```

The sum function definition says: The sum of an empty list is zero. The sum of a list whose first element is x and whose tail is xr, is x plus the sum of xr.

Many other functions on lists follow the same paradigm:

```
> let rec prod xs =
      match xs with
      | []     -> 1
      | x::xr -> x * prod xr;;
val prod : int list -> int
> let x2prod = prod x2;;
val x2prod : int = 819
> let rec len xs =
      match xs with
      | []     -> 0
      | x::xr -> 1 + len xr;;
val len : 'a list -> int
> let x2len = len x2;;
val x2len : int = 3
> let sslen = len ss;;
val sslen : int = 4
```

Note the type of len. Since the len function does not use the list elements, it works on all lists regardless of the element type; see Sect. A.10.

The append operator (@) creates a new list by concatenating two given lists:

```
> let x3 = [47; 11];;
val x3 : int list = [47; 11]
> let x1x3 = x1 @ x3;;
val x1x3 : int list = [7; 9; 13; 47; 11]
```

The append operator does not copy the list elements, only the "spine" of the left-hand operand x1, and it does not copy its right-hand operand at all. In the computer's memory, the tail of x1x3 is shared with the list x3. This works as expected because lists are *immutable*: One cannot destructively change an element in list x3 and thereby inadvertently change something in x1x3, or vice versa.

Some commonly used F# list functions are shown in Fig. A.3.

Appendix A: Crash Course in F#

Function	Type	Meaning
append	`'a list -> 'a list -> 'a list`	Append lists
exists	`('a -> bool) -> 'a list -> bool`	Does any satisfy...
filter	`('a -> bool) -> 'a list -> 'a list`	Those that satisfy...
fold	`('r -> 'a -> 'r) -> 'r -> 'a list -> 'r`	Fold (left) over list
foldBack	`('a -> 'r -> 'r) -> 'r -> 'a list -> 'r`	Fold (right) over list
forall	`('a -> bool) -> 'a list -> bool`	Do all satisfy...
iter	`('a -> unit) -> 'a list -> unit`	Apply to all
length	`'a list -> int`	Number of elements
map	`('a -> 'b) -> 'a list -> 'b list`	Transform elements
nth	`'a list -> int -> 'a`	Get n'th element
rev	`'a list -> 'a list`	Reverse list

Fig. A.3 Some F# list functions, from the `List` module. The function name must be qualified by `List`, as in `List.append [1; 2] [3; 4]`. Some of the functions are polymorphic (Sect. A.10) or higher-order (Sect. A.11.2). For the list operators cons (: :) and append (@), see Fig. A.1

A.7 Records and Labels

A *record* is basically a tuple whose components are labelled. Instead of writing a pair (`"Kasper"`, 5170) of a name and the associated phone number, one can use a record. This is particularly useful when there are many components. Before one can create a record value, one must create a record type, like this:

```
> type phonerec = { name : string; phone : int };;
type phonerec =
  {name: string;
   phone: int;}
> let x = { name = "Kasper"; phone = 5170 };;
val x : phonerec = {name = "Kasper";
                    phone = 5170;}
```

Note how the type of a record is written, with colon (:) instead of equals (=) as used in record expressions and values. One can extract the components of a record using a *record component selector*, very similar to field access in Java and C#:

```
> x.name;;
val it : string = "Kasper"
> x.phone;;
val it : int = 5170
```

A.8   Raising and Catching Exceptions

Exceptions can be declared, raised and caught as in C++/Java/C#. In fact, the exception concept of those languages is inspired by Standard ML. An `exception` declaration declares an exception constructor, of type `Exception`. A `raise` expression throws an exception:

```
> exception IllegalHour;;
exception IllegalHour
> let mins h =
      if h < 0 || h > 23 then raise IllegalHour
      else h * 60;;
val mins : int -> int
> mins 25;;
> [...] Exception of type 'IllegalHourException' was thrown.
   at FSI_0152.mins(Int32 h)
   at <StartupCode$FSI_0153>.$FSI_0153.main@()
stopped due to error
```

A `try`-with-expression (`try e1 with exn -> e2`) evaluates `e1` and returns its value, but if `e1` throws exception `exn`, it evaluates `e2` instead. This serves the same purpose as `try`-`catch` in C++/Java/C#:

```
> try (mins 25) with IllegalHour -> -1;;
val it : int = -1
```

As a convenient shorthand, one can use the function `failwith` to throw the standard `Failure` exception, which takes a string message as argument. The variant `failwithf` takes as argument a `printf`-like format string and a sequence of arguments, to construct a string argument for the `Failure` exception:

```
> let mins h =
      if h < 0 || h > 23 then failwith "Illegal hour"
      else h * 60;;
val mins : int -> int
> mins 25;;
Microsoft.FSharp.Core.FailureException: Illegal hour
> let mins h =
      if h < 0 || h > 23 then failwithf "Illegal hour, h=%d" h
      else h * 60;;
val mins : int -> int
> mins 25;;
Microsoft.FSharp.Core.FailureException: Illegal hour, h=25
```

A.9   Datatypes

A *datatype*, sometimes called an *algebraic datatype* or *discriminated union*, is useful
when data of the same type may have different numbers and types of components. For
instance, a person may either be a Student who has only a name, or a Teacher
who has both a name and a phone number. Defining a person datatype means that
we can have a list of person values, regardless of whether they are Students or
Teachers. Recall that all elements of a list must have the same type, so without the
common person type, we could not mix students and teachers in the same list.

```
> type person =
        | Student of string            (* name              *)
        | Teacher of string * int;;    (* name and phone no *)
type person =
   | Student of string
   | Teacher of string * int
> let people = [Student "Niels"; Teacher("Peter", 5083)];;
val people : person list = [Student "Niels";
                                Teacher ("Peter",5083)]
> let getphone1 person =
     match person with
     | Teacher(name, phone) -> phone
     | Student name          -> failwith "no phone";;
val getphone1 : person -> int
> getphone1 (Student "Niels");;
Microsoft.FSharp.Core.FailureException: no phone
```

Multiple type declarations that depend on each other can be connected with the
keyword and.

A.9.1   The option Datatype

A frequently used datatype is the option datatype, used to represent the presence
or absence of a value.

```
> type intopt =
        | Some of int
        | None;;
type intopt =
   | Some of int
   | None
> let getphone2 person =
     match person with
        | Teacher(name, phone) -> Some phone
```

```
        | Student name              -> None;;
   val getphone2 : person -> intopt
   > ge\texttt{}tphone2 (Student "Niels");;
   val it : intopt = None
```

In Java and C#, some methods return `null` to indicate the absence of a result, but that is a poor substitute for an `option` type, both in the case where the method should never return `null`, and in the case where `null` is a legitimate result from the method. The type inferred for function `getphone2` clearly says that we cannot expect it to always return an integer, only an `intopt`, which may or may not hold an integer.

In F#, there is a predefined polymorphic datatype `'a option` with constructors `Some` and `None`; using those instead of `intopt` above, function `getphone2` would have type `person -> int option`.

A.9.2 Binary Trees Represented by Recursive Datatypes

A datatype declaration may be recursive, which means that a value of the datatype `t` can have a component of type `t`. This can be used to represent trees and other data structures. For instance, a binary integer tree `inttree` may be defined to be either a leaf `Lf`, or a branching node `Br` that holds an integer and a left subtree and a right subtree:

```
   > type inttree =
          | Lf
          | Br of int * inttree * inttree;;
   type inttree =
     | Lf
     | Br of int * inttree * inttree
   > let t1 = Br(34, Br(23,Lf,Lf), Br(54,Lf,Br(78,Lf,Lf)));;
   val t1 : inttree = Br(34,Br(23,Lf,Lf),Br(54,Lf,Br(78,Lf,Lf)))
```

The tree represented by `t1` has 34 at the root node, 23 at the root of the left subtree, and so on, like this, where a solid dot represents an `Lf` value:

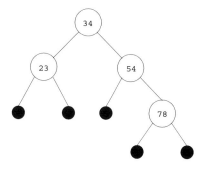

Functions on trees and other datatypes are conveniently defined using pattern matching and recursion. This function computes the sum of the nodes of an integer tree:

```
> let rec sumtree t =
      match t with
      | Lf -> 0
      | Br(v, t1, t2) -> v + sumtree t1 + sumtree t2;;
val sumtree : inttree -> int
> let t1sum = sumtree t1;;
val t1sum : int = 189
```

The definition of `sumtree` reads: The sum of a leaf node `Lf` is zero. The sum of a branch node `Br(v, t1, t2)` is `v` plus the sum of `t1` plus the sum of `t2`.

A.9.3   Curried Functions

A function of type `int * int -> int` that takes a pair of arguments is closely related to a function of type `int -> int -> int` that takes two arguments. The latter is called a *curried* version of the former; this is a pun on the name of logician Haskell B. Curry, who proposed this idea. For instance, function `addc` below is a curried version of function `addp`. Note the types of `addp` and `addc` and how the functions are applied to arguments:

```
> let addp (x, y) = x + y;;
val addp : int * int -> int
> let addc x y = x + y;;
val addc : int -> int -> int
> let res1 = addp(17, 25);;
val res1 : int = 42
> let res2 = addc 17 25;;
val res2 : int = 42
```

A major advantage of curried functions is that they can be partially applied. Applying `addc` to only one argument, 17, we obtain a new function of type `int -> int`. This new function adds 17 to its argument and can be used on as many different arguments as we like:

```
> let addSeventeen = addc 17;;
val addSeventeen : (int -> int)
> let res3 = addSeventeen 25;;
val res3 : int = 42
> let res4 = addSeventeen 100;;
val res4 : int = 117
```

A.10   Type Variables and Polymorphic Functions

We saw in Sect. A.6 that the type of the `len` function was `'a list -> int`:

```
> let rec len xs =
      match xs with
      | []     -> 0
      | x::xr -> 1 + len xr;;
  val len : 'a list -> int
```

The `'a` is a *type variable*. Note that the prefixed prime (`'`) is part of the type variable name `'a`. In a call to the `len` function, the type variable `'a` may be instantiated to any type whatsoever, and it may be instantiated to different types at different uses. Here `'a` gets instantiated first to `int` and then to `string`, in two different applications of `len`:

```
> len [7; 9; 13];;
val it : int = 3
> len ["Oslo"; "Aarhus"; "Gothenburg"; "Copenhagen"];;
val it : int = 4
```

A.10.1   Polymorphic Datatypes

Some data structures, such as a binary trees, have the same shape regardless of the element type. Fortunately, we can define polymorphic datatypes to represent such data structures. For instance, we can define the type of binary trees whose leaves can hold a value of type `'a` like this:

```
> type 'a tree =
        | Lf
        | Br of 'a * 'a tree * 'a tree;;
  type 'a tree =
    | Lf
    | Br of 'a * 'a tree * 'a tree
```

Compare this with the monomorphic integer tree type in Sect. A.9.2. Values of this type can be defined exactly as before, but the type is slightly different:

```
> let t1 = Br(34, Br(23,Lf,Lf), Br(54,Lf,Br(78,Lf,Lf)));;
  val t1 = Br(34,Br(23,Lf,Lf),Br(54,Lf,Br(78,Lf,Lf))) : int tree
```

The type of `t1` is `int tree`, where the type variable `'a` has been instantiated to `int`.

Likewise, functions on such trees can be defined as before:

```
> let rec sumtree t =
```

```
      match t with
      | Lf -> 0
      | Br(v, t1, t2) -> v + sumtree t1 + sumtree t2;;
  val sumtree : int tree -> int
> let rec count t =
      match t with
      | Lf -> 0
      | Br(v, t1, t2) -> 1 + count t1 + count t2;;
  val count : 'a tree -> int
```

The argument type of sumtree is int tree because the function adds the node values, which must be of type int.

The argument type of count is 'a tree because the function ignores the node values v, and therefore works on an 'a tree regardless of the node type 'a.

Function preorder1 : 'a tree -> 'a list returns a list of the node values in a tree, in *preorder*, that is, the root node comes before the left subtree which comes before the right subtree:

```
> let rec preorder1 t =
      match t with
      | Lf               -> []
      | Br(v, t1, t2) -> v :: preorder1 t1 @ preorder1 t2;;
  val preorder1 : 'a tree -> 'a list
> preorder1 t1;;
  val it : int list = [34; 23; 54; 78]
```

A side remark on efficiency: When the left subtree t1 is large, then the call preorder1 t1 will produce a long list of node values, and the list append operator (@) will be slow. Moreover, this happens recursively for all left subtrees.

Function preorder2 does the same job in a more efficient, but slightly more obscure way. It uses an auxiliary function preo that has an *accumulating parameter* acc that gradually collects the result without ever performing an append (@) operation:

```
> let rec preo t acc =
      match t with
      | Lf               -> acc
      | Br(v, t1, t2) -> v :: preo t1 (preo t2 acc);;
  val preo : 'a tree -> 'a list -> 'a list
> let preorder2 t = preo t [];;
  val preorder2 : 'a tree -> 'a list
> preorder2 t1;;
  val it : int list = [34; 23; 54; 78]
```

The following relation holds for all t and xs:

```
preo t xs = preorder1 t @ xs
```

It follows that

```
preorder2 t = preo t [] = preorder1 t @ [] = preorder1 t
```

A.10.2   Type Abbreviations

When a type, such as (string * int) list, is used frequently, it is convenient
to abbreviate it using a name such as intenv:

```
> type intenv = (string * int) list;;
type intenv = (string * int) list
> let bind1 (env : intenv) (x : string, v : int) : intenv =
-        (x, v) :: env;;
val bind1 : intenv -> string * int -> intenv
```

The type declaration defines a *type abbreviation*, not a new type, as can be seen
from the compiler's response. This also means that the function can be applied to a
perfectly ordinary list of string * int pairs:

```
> bind1 [("age", 47)] ("phone", 5083);;
val it : intenv = [("phone", 5083); ("age", 47)]
```

A.11   Higher-Order Functions

A *higher-order function* is one that takes another function as an argument. For
instance, function map below takes as argument a function f and a list, and applies
f to all elements of the list:

```
> let rec map f xs =
      match xs with
      | []     -> []
      | x::xr -> f x :: map f xr;;
val map : ('a -> 'b) -> 'a list -> 'b list
```

The type of map says that it takes as arguments a function from type 'a to type 'b,
and a list whose elements have type 'a, and produces a list whose elements have
type 'b. The type variables 'a and 'b may be independently instantiated to any
types. For instance, we can define a function mul2 of type float -> float and
use map to apply that function to all elements of a list:

```
> let mul2 x = 2.0 * x;;
val mul2 : float -> float
> map mul2 [4.0; 5.0; 89.0];;
val it : float list = [8.0; 10.0; 178.0]
```

Or we may apply a function isLarge of type float -> bool (defined on p. 308) to all elements of a float list:

```
> map isLarge [4.0; 5.0; 89.0];;
val it : bool list = [false; false; true]
```

Function map is so useful that it is predefined in F#'s List module; see Fig. A.3.

A.11.1 Anonymous Functions

Sometimes it is inconvenient to introduce named auxiliary functions. In this case, one can write an anonymous *function expression* using fun instead of a named *function declaration* using let:

```
> fun x -> 2.0 * x;;
val it : float -> float = <fun:clo@0-1>
```

The expression (fun x -> ...) evaluates to a closure, or function value, which can be passed around exactly like any other F# value. This is particularly useful in connection with higher-order functions such as map:

```
> map (fun x -> 2.0 * x) [4.0; 5.0; 89.0];;
val it : float list = [8.0; 10.0; 178.0]
> map (fun x -> 10.0 < x) [4.0; 5.0; 89.0];;
val it : bool list = [false; false; true]
```

The function tw defined below takes a function closure g and an argument x and applies g twice; that is, it computes g (g x). Using tw one can define a function quad that applies mul2 twice, thus multiplying its argument by 4.0:

```
> let tw g x = g (g x);;
val tw : ('a -> 'a) -> 'a -> 'a
> let quad = tw mul2;;
val quad : (float -> float)
> quad 7.0;;
val it : float = 28.0
```

An anonymous function created with fun may take any number of arguments. A function that takes two arguments is similar to one that takes the first argument and then returns a new anonymous function that takes the second argument:

```
> fun x y -> x+y;;
val it : int -> int -> int = <fun:clo@0-2>
> fun x -> fun y -> x+y;;
val it : int -> int -> int = <fun:clo@0-3>
```

The difference between fun and function is that a fun can take more than one parameter but can have only one match case, whereas a function can take only one parameter but can have multiple match cases. For instance, two-argument `increaseBoth` is most conveniently defined using `fun` and one-argument `isZeroFirst` is most conveniently defined using `function`:

```
> let increaseBoth = fun i (x, y) -> (x+i, y+i);;
val increaseBoth : int -> int * int -> int * int
> let isZeroFirst = function | (0::_) -> true | _ -> false;;
val isZeroFirst : int list -> bool
```

A.11.2   Higher-Order Functions on Lists

Higher-order functions are particularly useful in connection with polymorphic datatypes. For instance, one can define a function `filter` that takes as argument a predicate (a function of type `'a -> bool`) and a list, and returns a list containing only those elements for which the predicate is `true`. This may be used to extract the even elements (those divisible by 2) in a list:

```
> let rec filter p xs =
      match xs with
      | []     -> []
      | x::xr -> if p x then x :: filter p xr
                 else filter p xr;;
val filter : ('a -> bool) -> 'a list -> 'a list
> let onlyEven =
      filter (fun i -> i%2 = 0) [4; 6; 5; 2; 54; 89];;
val onlyEven : int list = [4; 6; 2; 54]
```

Note that the filter function is polymorphic in the argument list type. The `filter` function is predefined in F#'s `List` module; see Fig. A.3. Another very general predefined polymorphic higher-order list function is `foldr`, for *fold right*, which exists in F# under the name `List.foldBack`:

```
> let rec foldr f xs e =
      match xs with
      | []     -> e
      | x::xr -> f x (foldr f xr e);;
val foldr : ('a -> 'b -> 'b) -> 'a list -> 'b -> 'b
```

One way to understand `foldr f xs e` is to realize that it systematically and recursively replaces the list constructors by other operators as follows:

$$\text{replace } [] \qquad \text{by } e$$
$$\text{replace } (x :: xr) \text{ by } f\ x\ xr$$

The `foldr` function presents a general procedure for processing a list, and is closely related to the visitor pattern in object-oriented programming, although this may not appear very obvious.

Many other functions on lists can be defined in terms of `foldr`:

```
> let len xs    = foldr (fun _ res -> 1+res) xs 0;;
val len : 'a list -> int
> let sum xs    = foldr (fun x res -> x+res) xs 0;;
val sum : int list -> int
> let prod xs   = foldr (fun x res -> x*res) xs 1;;
val prod : int list -> int
> let map g xs = foldr (fun x res -> g x :: res) xs [];;
val map : ('a -> 'b) -> 'a list -> 'b list
> let listconcat xss = foldr (fun xs res -> xs @ res) xss [];;
val listconcat : 'a list list -> 'a list
> let stringconcat xss = foldr (fun xs res -> xs+res) xss "";;
val stringconcat : string list -> string
> let filter p xs =
      foldr (fun x r -> if p x then r else x :: r) xs [];;
val filter : ('a -> bool) -> 'a list -> 'a list
```

The functions `map`, `filter`, `fold`, `foldBack` and many others are predefined in the F# `List` module; see Fig. A.3.

A.12   F# Mutable References

A *reference* is a handle to a *memory cell*. A reference in F# is similar to a reference in Java/C# or a pointer in C/C++, but the reference cannot be `null` or uninitialized. Moreover, the memory cell cannot be uninitialized and cannot be accidentally changed by other memory write operations, only through the reference.

A new unique memory cell and a reference to it is created by applying the `ref` constructor to a value. Applying the dereferencing operator (`!`) to a reference returns the value in the corresponding memory cell. The value in the memory cell can be changed by applying the assignment (`:=`) operator to the reference and a new value:

```
> let r = ref 177;;
val r : int ref = {contents = 177;}
> let v = !r;;
val v : int = 177
> r := 288;;
val it : unit = ()
> !r;;
val it : int = 288
```

A typical use of references and memory cells is to create a sequence of distinct names or labels:

```
> let nextlab = ref -1;;
val nextlab : int ref = {contents = -1;}
> let newLabel () =
-       (nextlab := 1 + !nextlab; "L" + string (!nextlab));;
val newLabel : unit -> string
> newLabel();;
val it : string = "L0"
> newLabel();;
val it : string = "L1"
> newLabel();;
val it : string = "L2"
```

References are used also to implement efficient algorithms with destructive update, such as graph algorithms.

A.13   F# Arrays

An F# array is a zero-based indexable fixed-size collection of mutable elements of a particular type, just like a .NET array, but it uses a different syntax for array creation, indexing and update. The F# array type is generic in its element type:

```
> let arr = [| 2; 5; 7 |];;
val arr : int array = [|2; 5; 7|]
> arr.[1];;
val it : int = 5
> arr.[1] <- 11;;
val it : unit = ()
> arr;;
val it : int array = [|2; 11; 7|]
> arr.Length;;
val it : int = 3
```

The .NET method `System.Environment.GetCommandLineArgs()` has type `string array` and holds the command line arguments of an F# when invoked from a command prompt. The element at index 0 is the name of the running executable, the element at index 1 is the first command line argument, and so on (as in C).

A.14   Other F# Features

The F# language has a lot more features than described in this appendix, including facilities for object-oriented programming and convenient use of the .NET libraries and programs written in other .NET languages, and many advanced functional programming features. For a more comprehensive description of F# and its libraries, see [6, 7] and the F# resources linked from the book homepage.

For instance, F# can use .NET's exact high-range `decimal` type for accounting and other calculations with money, which should never be done using floating-point numbers. Constants of type `decimal` must be written with an upper-case M suffix, as in C#:

```
> let tomorrow =
      let nationalDebt = 14349539503882.02M
      let perSecond = 45138.89M
      nationalDebt + 86400M * perSecond;;
  val tomorrow : decimal = 14353439503978.02M
```

For another example, F#'s type `bigint` is System.Numerics.BigInteger from .NET and supports arbitrary-range integers. Constants of type `bigint` must be written with an upper-case I suffix, as in `42I`, but are otherwise used just like any other numbers:

```
> let rec fac (n:bigint) = if n=0I then 1I else n * fac(n-1I);;
val fac : bigint -> bigint
> fac 104I;;
val it : System.Numerics.BigInteger =
   10299016745145627623848583864765044283053772454999907218232549
   17768878717324752871745427098716838880032359657041416383776955
   1797419791755887247360000000000000000000000000I
```

A.15   Exercises

The goal of these exercises is to make sure that you understand functional programming with algebraic datatypes, pattern matching and recursive functions. This is a necessary basis for using this book.

Do This First
Make sure you have F# installed. It can be downloaded from http://fsharp.org, for Linux, MacOS and Windows.

Exercise A.1 Define the following functions in F#:

• A function `max2 : int * int -> int` that returns the largest of its two integer arguments. For instance, `max(99, 3)` should give 99.

- A function max3 : int * int * int -> int that returns the largest of its three integer arguments.
- A function isPositive : int list -> bool so that isPositive xs returns true if all elements of xs are greater than 0, and false otherwise.
- A function isSorted : int list -> bool so that isSorted xs returns true if the elements of xs appear sorted in non-decreasing order, and false otherwise. For instance, the list [11; 12; 12] is sorted, but [12; 11; 12] is not. Note that the empty list [] and all one-element lists such as [23] are sorted.
- A function count : inttree -> int that counts the number of internal nodes (Br constructors) in an inttree, where the type inttree is defined in Sect. A.9.2. That is, count (Br(37, Br(117, Lf, Lf), Br(42, Lf, Lf))) should give 3, and count Lf should give 0.
- A function depth : inttree -> int that measures the depth of a tree, that is, the maximal number of internal nodes (Br constructors) on a path from the root to a leaf. For instance, depth (Br(37, Br(117, Lf, Lf), Br(42, Lf, Lf))) should give 2, and depth Lf should give 0.

Exercise A.2 Define an F# function linear : int -> int tree so that linear *n* produces a right-linear tree with *n* nodes. For instance, linear 0 should produce Lf, and linear 2 should produce Br(2, Lf, Br(1, Lf, Lf)).

Exercise A.3 Section A.10.1 presents an F# function preorder1 : 'a tree -> 'a list that returns a list of the node values in a tree, in *preorder* (root before left subtree before right subtree).

Now define a function inorder that returns the node values in *inorder* (left subtree before root before right subtree) and a function postorder that returns the node values in *postorder* (left subtree before right subtree before root):

```
inorder   : 'a tree -> 'a list
postorder : 'a tree -> 'a list
```

Thus if t is Br(1, Br(2, Lf, Lf), Br(3, Lf, Lf)), then inorder t is [2; 1; 3] and postorder t is [2; 3; 1].

It should hold that inorder (linear n) is [n; n-1; ...; 2; 1] and postorder (linear n) is [1; 2; ...; n-1; n], where linear n produces a right-linear tree as in Exercise A.2.

Note that the postfix (or reverse Polish) representation of an expression is just a *postorder list of the nodes in the expression's abstract syntax tree.*

Finally, define a more efficient version of inorder that uses an auxiliary function ino : 'a tree -> 'a list -> 'a list with an accumulating parameter; and similarly for postorder.

References

1. Hansen, M.R., Rischel, H.: Functional Programming Using F#. Cambridge University Press, Cambridge (2013)
2. Leroy, X.: The Zinc experiment: an economical implementation of the ML language. Rapport Technique 117, INRIA Rocquencourt, France (1990)
3. Milner, R., Tofte, M., Harper, R., MacQueen, D.: The Definition of Standard ML (Revised). MIT Press, Cambridge (1997)
4. Mono project. http://www.mono-project.com/
5. OCaml: Home page. http://ocaml.org/
6. Syme, D., Granicz, A., Cisternino, A.: Expert F#. Apress (2007)
7. Syme, D., et al.: The F# 4.0 language specification. Technical report, Microsoft (2016). http://fsharp.org/specs/language-spec/

Index

© Springer International Publishing AG 2017
P. Sestoft, *Programming Language Concepts*, Undergraduate Topics
in Computer Science, DOI 10.1007/978-3-319-60789-4

Printed in the United States
By Bookmasters